W0193366

Vulnerable Earth

Vulnerable Earth is a study of the literature of climate crisis. Building on the assumption that the crisis is planetary in scope even if differential and unequal in effects, it examines literary fiction, graphic novels, memoirs about toxic wastes and neo-slavery narratives, mostly from the contemporary decades, but touching upon select antecedents as well, and from all over the world. The study covers texts that fictionalize a 'hydrocrisis', those that are concerned with species extinction and experimental solutions such as rewilding, fiction and memoirs that are interested in exploring the conversations between and across species in multispecies encounters and, finally, texts that show the linkage between social justice and environmental justice.

Focusing on aesthetics, narrative modes and constructions of damaged, wasted and at-risk worlds, this book shows how the literature of climate crisis foregrounds a feature that humans and nonhumans, the living and the non-living share, differentially, with the planet: vulnerability.

Pramod K. Nayar teaches at the University of Hyderabad, India, where he holds the UNESCO Chair in Vulnerability Studies. He is an elected Fellow of the English Association and the Royal Historical Society, and a recipient of the Visitor's Award for the Best Research in Arts, Humanities and Social Sciences from the President of India. He is the author, most recently, of *Nuclear Cultures* (2023), *The Raj* (2023), *Alzheimer's Disease Memoirs* (2022), *The Human Rights Graphic Novel* (2021), *Ecoprecarity* (2019), *Bhopal's Ecological Gothic* (2017), *Human Rights and Literature* (2016) and other books.

Vulnerable Earth

The Literature of Climate Crisis

Pramod K. Nayar

CAMBRIDGE
UNIVERSITY PRESS

Shaftesbury Road, Cambridge CB2 8EA, United Kingdom

One Liberty Plaza, 20th Floor, New York, NY 10006, USA

477 Williamstown Road, Port Melbourne, VIC 3207, Australia

314–321, 3rd Floor, Plot 3, Splendor Forum, Jasola District Centre, New Delhi – 110025, India

103 Penang Road, #05–06/07, Visioncrest Commercial, Singapore 238467

Cambridge University Press is part of Cambridge University Press & Assessment, a department of the University of Cambridge.

We share the University's mission to contribute to society through the pursuit of education, learning and research at the highest international levels of excellence.

www.cambridge.org
Information on this title: www.cambridge.org/9781009496919

First published 2024

Printed in India by Avantika Printers Pvt. Ltd.

A catalogue record for this publication is available from the British Library

ISBN 978-1-009-49691-9 Hardback

Contents

Foreword

Benno Böer

The Anthropocene is a time of human activity causing massive environmental degradation. This phase has begun. It is characterized by biodiversity loss, climate change and pollution, with huge ramifications on food, water and energy security. In order for our species to survive this critical chapter, we need to mobilize everybody. Every person has to participate and understand that there are science-and-technology-based solutions available, waiting to be applied. Urgently. Decision makers need to support an action-based approach towards human survivability. Our resilience does not depend only on overcoming pandemics, armed conflicts and wars, but also on functioning ecosystems providing clean air, food and water, and ensuring climate justice for all species.

The importance of science, the social sciences and the arts, and education must no longer be undervalued. It is with this in mind that I am happy for this scholarly book *Vulnerable Earth* being produced, with the aim of examining multiple vulnerabilities, as documented in numerous literary texts across the world.

I congratulate Professor Pramod K. Nayar, UNESCO Chair in Vulnerability Studies at the University of Hyderabad, for the timely production of this important educational tool.

Vulnerable Earth is a study of the literature of climate crisis. But the climate crisis cannot be looked at in isolation. We need to look at the whole picture at large. We must look at the cumulative effect of the *triple planetary crisis*. This book brings to the reading public a vast corpus of literary material that foregrounds species loss, habitat destruction, climate injustice and its antecedents, and other themes. It covers a range of themes that enable a bringing-to-consciousness the nature of our present crisis, at this critical juncture in our planetary history.

Vulnerable Earth, I hope, will function to enhance the knowledge of and as an encouragement for the reader to actively recognize this triple planetary crisis, and engage in the search for and application of solutions in support of the UN Decade on Ecosystem Restoration.

Benno Böer is the Natural Sciences Specialist of the UNESCO New Delhi Office, which covers Bangladesh, Bhutan, India, Nepal, the Maldives and Sri Lanka.

Preface

This book examines the proverbial tip of the (now-vanishing, climatologically speaking) iceberg, the literature of climate crisis, in terms of four discrete but interrelated themes. It employs for this purpose a considerable body of textual material, from fiction to memoirs, from the late twentieth to the early twenty-first century, weighted more towards the latter. It cites from this material extensively, often even as block quotes, in order to demonstrate rather than illustrate the textual archive and imagination of climate crisis. I have picked texts from all over the world, mainly to see overlaps and intersections, and this has, admittedly, elided historical specificities of, say, the tradition of African ecological literature or Native American texts on the theme. Admitting to a certain kind of universalization of the discourse of environmentalism, the book stays within the ambit of such a risky stance in order to speak planet rather than region or country. Thus, while the employment of texts from everywhere evidences a global concern with planetary precarity, individual cultures and bioregionalisms have different priorities and problems that need to be acknowledged – but this book does not attempt that. Also, domains such as animal trafficking, organ trade and biocapitalism that have informed the genre of ecological literature and ecocriticism as well as genres like petrofiction do not come in for any sustained attention in this book, which already grew to be more voluminous than was expected. Debates around the idea of the wilderness or 'ecotopia' that are current and exemplified in novels like Diane Cook's *The New Wilderness* (2020) or the fiction of Becky Chambers (*Psalm for the Wild-Built*, 2021) are also excluded. It also does not examine the pedagogic imperatives when teaching cli-fi – Stephen Siperstein, Shane Hall and Stephanie LeMenager's *Teaching Climate Change in the Humanities* (2017) does the job brilliantly – or debates around stewardship and care, which Rachel Carnell and Chris Mounsey's (eds.) *Stewardship and the Future of the Planet: Promise and Paradox* (2022) examines so effectively.

But 'tis enough, 'twill serve.

Acknowledgements

I am delighted to acknowledge the many contributors – multispecies, as befits the subject – who enabled and energized this work:

Qudsiya Ahmed and Anwesha Rana of Cambridge University Press and Assessment for the efficiency with which they overcame the initial hurdles of finding a reviewer and enabling this project to reach this stage.

My parents, who have stood by me, indulged me and trained me in more ways than they know and I can even begin to inventory.

My parents-in-law, whom I do not meet as often as I ought to, for their breadth of understanding of my workaholism.

Nandini and Pranav, each busy with their chosen fields, inured to my strange working hours and quantum of work – Pranav may have different definitions of 'quantum' now – but offer the necessary loving and loyal support.

Ajeet, Panikkar, Bhalla, Kulsoom, Om, Vaishali, Haneef, Neelu, Sai Jawahar, Ashish, Premlata, Archana, Krishna Ram, Zahid, Ibrahim, Naveed, Soma, for observing due diligence in checking on me.

Shubha, for magically conjuring up essential materials within minutes of an email request, for her enthusiasm for my work and her friendship.

Molly 'Chechu' for the constant prayers on behalf of and for her 'little one'.

Sharmistha, Kailash and Debashis, for their remote support and friendship (when, in any case, *are* we meeting for coffee?).

K. Narayana Chandran, whose formidable scholarship inspires in ways he cannot imagine.

Nandana Dutta, for unfailingly zeroing in on terms and concepts I invoke – 'tell me, how *exactly* does this term further the argument?' – and the unstinted love and affection she has offered now for over a quarter of a century.

Those in the neighbourhood who greet me with yowls while simultaneously trying to trip me up for not delivering the appropriate belly-rubs, and thus help start the day; then the dozen-plus friends, from the Peaceable Pebbles to the Lovely Luna, who welcome us at the School of Humanities every morning, petitioning that the building be called the *Humanimalities* at the very least, and, of course, Ramesh, redoubtable and resilient. Theirs are the footprints I sometimes take to class on my clothes or come home with, and who energize the everyday – all for a good *paws*.

The mandate of the UNESCO Chair in Vulnerability Studies demands and enables me to think through more aspects of precarity than I was aware of, and this is something I am grateful for, just as I am to the Chair team: Anna and Zahid; Meenakshi and Atul.

And Anna, with whom conversations are always enthusing because of the ways in which she pushes me to transform my half-formed ideas into nearly full-formed ones, her corrections to my language that sometimes skitters and chitters instead of speaking clearly and marching steadily, and for her love and loyalty.

To the anonymous reviewers of the proposal and the manuscript, much gratitude for pointing to certain lacunae in the work.

Sections of the chapter on the hydronovel were delivered in the form of talks: the valedictory address titled 'Disaster Flows: Historical Legacies and Continuing Vulnerability in the Contemporary Hydronovel' at the 'Revisiting History through Literature: Religion, Politics, and Propaganda' organized by the Department of English, University of Allahabad, 25 March 2023, 'Fluid Precarity and the Planet: The Global Hydronovel' at the Faculty Enrichment Program of the University of Kerala on 14 May 2023, and as a keynote at the Sri Lanka Association for Commonwealth Literature and Language Studies' conference, 'Continuing Postcolonialism', 22 July 2023. Sections of the chapter on ecojustice were delivered as the First Annual Alexander D'Souza Memorial Endowment Lecture, Department of English, St Aloysius College, Mangalore, 9 September 2023. The chapter on 'hydropoetics' will appear as 'Writ on Water: Aesthetics and the Contemporary Catachronistic Novel' in Praseeda Gopinath and Laura Bruecke (eds.), *The Routledge Companion to Postcolonial and Decolonial Literature*, and the section on the hydrogothic novel will appear in Sharae Deckard and Claire Westall (eds.), the *Routledge Companion to Literature and the Environment*. Sections of the ecojustice chapter will appear as 'Human Rights and Literature' in Felisa Tibbitts, Cher Weixia Chen, Petro du Preez and Jonathan Liljeblad (eds.), *New Frontiers: Critical Human Rights Education and the Disciplines*, to be published by University of Pennsylvania Press. Parts of the analysis of Nick Hayes' *The Rime of the Modern Mariner* appeared in my *Ecoprecarity* (2019: 57–58). The chapter on extinction took shape as a plenary talk, 'Retrieving Planetary Memory: De-extinction and the Afterlives of (Some) Animals', for the conference on 'Mediations on Memory:

Aesthetics and Poetics of Forgetting' at the Mohanlal Sukhadia University, Udaipur, 26–27 July 2023, and a plenary, 'Extinction Memories', at the International Memory Studies Conference on 'Memory, Ecology, Sustainability', IIT Madras, 20–22 September 2023. Some of its arguments were also rehearsed at a workshop at GITAM University, Hyderabad. The chapter on multispecies found its first articulation as a keynote address, 'Creaturely Texts in the Posthuman Era', at the 'Posthuman Southeast Asia', the ASLE/ASEAN Ecocritical Conference, Mae Fah Luang University, Chiang Rai (Thailand), 23–25 November 2023. The broad themes around 'vulnerable earth' were presented as a keynote address titled 'Planetary Ecoprecarity: Texts and Themes in the End-times' at the conference 'Revamping Indian Tradition and Culture through NEP 2020: Multilingual, Multicultural and Multidisciplinary Modes of Education', IIT Roorkee, 18–19 August 2023. I am grateful to Avishek Parui and Merin Simi Raj, W. S. Perera, D. R. P. Chandra Sekhar, Ignasi Ribo, P. P. Ajaya Kumar, Pradeep Trikha, Vivek Dwivedi and Binod Mishra, and the Department of English, St Aloysius College, Mangalore, for extending me their generous invites to speak at their conferences and their hospitality.

I gratefully acknowledge the Professional Development Fund of the Institution of Eminence project of the University of Hyderabad.

This book was written with one specific memory running through much of the writing: of Sudhakar Marathe, planter-of-trees, objector-to-strewn-garbage, birdwatcher, insect-photographer and indefatigable Teacher, who taught us ways of looking at birds, flowers, caterpillars and poetry, in class, but also out of it.

1

Introduction

The Literature of Climate Crisis

Alexis Wright in *The Swan Book* (2013), a speculative novel set in the future, speaks of the 'Mother catastrophe of flood, fire, drought and Blizzard', thus replacing 'Mother Nature' with 'Mother catastrophe' (unpaginated). She thereby captures the urgency of climate *crisis* – well past the point of climate *change* – so that Nature now is catastrophic in nature.

In *Homegoing* (2016), Yaa Gyasi shows the transformation of an African community:

> Ohene Nyarko came back a week later with the new seeds. The plant was called cocoa, and he said it would change everything. He said the Akuapem people in the Eastern Region were already reaping the benefits of the new plant, selling it to the white men overseas at a rate that was reminiscent of the old trade. (147–148)

Diane Ackerman writes in her *The Rarest of the Rare* (1997):

> [T]he last recorded Caribbean monk seal was spotted in 1952. I was four years old, growing up in a small town in Illinois, playing in the plum orchard across from my house, and learning to count. I didn't know that an animal that had survived for fourteen million years was at that moment becoming extinct, nor that I would one day lament its passing. (Unpaginated)

Wright adopts an apocalyptic tone to speak of the climate-change-driven crisis. Yaa Gyasi describes the bioinvasion by an alien plant species of the African land, which will eventually alter its texture, social fabric and economy forever. Diane Ackerman's is an elegy for the disappeared species.

These excerpts represent three modes – the apocalyptic, the social realist and the elegiac, respectively – of speaking about climate crisis and its attendant losses, dangers and anxieties to address 'the cultural challenge of climate change'.

The 'cultural challenge of climate change', write David Buckland et al., is 'to craft a different language with which to understand the science of climate change, one that is more human and palatable for public consumption' (Buckland et al. 2017: 97).[1] Art, Buckland et al. propose, is 'a possible means – it has the ability to reach into peoples' psyches, where reasoned argument can often fail' (98). Literature – as form, practice and institution – serves the same purpose, enabling a visualization of the human as a geological force that has irrevocably altered the planet, to adapt Dipesh Chakrabarty's influential characterization (2009).

The production of this literature, often termed 'cli-fi' (climate-change fiction or climate-fiction), is co-extensive with not only the burgeoning scholarship in environmental humanities (EH) but also the scientific data on global warming, the popularization of the Intergovernmental Panel for Climate Change (IPCC) reports, the activities of ecowarriors and activists and the coverage of species death and related effects, including desertification and drought. The science of climate change and the Anthropocene in particular – which, Eileen Crist (2013) has noted, is inflected heavily by questionable (western-centric) value systems (also see Ulloa 2017) – finds its way into the ecological unconscious of the literary texts of the contemporary age. Therefore, literature's role – and more broadly, narrative's – has been central to not only the documentation of disasters but also the *imagining* of future disasters, alternative worlds and an environmental ethics that promises justice to human and the more-than-human.

The literary imagination not only constitutes the cultural response to climate crisis but also determines the constructions of Nature, natural disaster, human adaptability and nonhuman encounters, among other themes. This literature is influenced by developments in evolutionary biology, ecological sciences and allied disciplines, and its texts resonate so closely with, say, the International Union for Conservation of Nature (IUCN) Red List or the science of de-extinction. Relatedly, material sciences, object-oriented ontology and posthumanism have influenced climate change discourses and ecocriticism even as the human and social sciences are shaping the production and dissemination of climate change knowledge (Baucom and Omelsky 2017: 2).

Documenting and imagining climate crisis, speculating on forms of multispecies justice and the possibilities of restoring a measure of balance in the planetary ecosystem require that literature also experiment with genres and modes, although the ecological unconscious is integral to all literary-cultural expressions. These literary-cultural expressions over the ages documented the destruction of forests, idealized the pastoral and the arcadian, and argued that human consciousness is formed in the crucible of Nature, with other lifeforms and even the non-living (Buell 1998, 2001, 2005; Heise 2008, 2016; Bate 1991, 2000; Garrard 2011, 2014; deLoughrey 2011, 2015, 2018, 2019; among others). Traditionally, at least in Anglo-American literary studies, the English Romantics and later the Americans Romantics are credited with the rise of ecological thought in poetry (Bate 1991, 2000; Garrard 2011; Newman 2019).

The twentieth century, reiterating the traditions of the previous eras, has also produced a large corpus of poetry informed by and infused with an ecological consciousness, but one more attuned to the crisis facing the planet. A. R. Ammons, for example, in his celebrated *Garbage* (1993) identifies garbage and waste as the motifs of everyday (American) life:

> garbage has to be the poem of our time because
> garbage is spiritual, believable enough
> to get our attention, getting in the way, piling
> up, stinking, turning brooks brownish and
> creamy white: what else deflects us from the
> errors of our illusionary ways, not a temptation
> to trashlessness, that is too far off, and,
> anyway, unimaginable, unrealistic. (8)

Here the very environment, says Ammons, is made up of waste. But it is also significant that Ammons sees garbage as a form of language – 'the poem of our time' – as an enunciation. That is, for Ammons, garbage is both natural and cultural, between human-produced waste and human-crafted language in and through which to describe the waste.

Themes such as species loss and the erosion of the natural world are central to Mary Oliver and Gary Snyder, both widely acknowledged as the 'nature poets' for our age. Oliver writes in 'Watching a Documentary about Polar Bears Trying to Survive on the Melting Ice Floes', in a tone both elegiac and programmatic (with the latter urging humanity to reconsider its stewardship and responsibilities):

> That God had a plan, I do not doubt.
> But what if His plan was, that we would do better? (2008: 56)

Oliver, like Ammons, is sharply critical of human greed that causes us as a species to accumulate and therefore to waste without a thought as to what our accumulation does to other lifeforms. In 'Of the Empire', she writes:

> We will be known as a culture that
> taught
> and rewarded the amassing of things, that
> spoke
> little if at all about the quality of life for people
> people (other people), for dogs, for rivers. (2008: 57)

In 'The Shark', Oliver spectacularizes the violence humanity perpetuates on other lifeforms. She describes the hooked shark, injured, followed by a hundred gulls,

> picking at the red streams,
> as it sang its death song of vomit and bubbles,
> as the blood ran from its mouth. (1986: 85)

Still alive, the shark is

> winched into the air; men
> lifting the last bloody hammers. (86)

Gary Snyder sees, Wordsworth-like, human consciousness shaped by the world around, especially in the poems of the volume *Mountains and Rivers without End* (1996):

> Clearing the mind and sliding in to that created space
> A web of waters streaming over rocks. (5)

Snyder, Oliver, W. S. Merwin, A. R. Ammons and the 'nature poetry' tradition are marked by an 'ecopoetics'. Ecopoetics, 'the incorporation of an ecological or environmental perspective into the study of poetics, and into the reading and writing of (mainly) literary works', has documented the semiotics of nature, culture, the consciousness of the intersection of nature and culture, as well as the multispecies and environmental awareness in literary texts (Rigby 2016: 79). But the tone, genre and mood of the literary text that could best communicate this ecological or environmental perspective remain up for discussion among ecocritics and fiction writers.

Thus, in James Bradley's *Clade* (2017), Adam is frustrated because people do not *see* the crisis bearing down on them:

> There was a time when people talked about boiling the frog, arguing that the warming of the planet was too gradual to galvanise effective action ... at some level people do not understand the scale of transformation that is overtaking them. (Unpaginated)

So, the question Bradley implicitly asks is: would the apocalyptic tone be more appropriate to communicate the sense of crisis? The tone of environmental writing, Bradley suggests, is central to communicating the urgency of the situation. The ecological unconscious – or perhaps, in these texts, one should call it the 'conscious', given the careful attention to one or more aspects of the climate crisis – generates its own narrative demands and responses, as critics have observed.

'Attention to narrative is a vital aspect of the environmental humanities in determining how to articulate our planetary futures,' writes Elizabeth deLoughrey (2015: 352). Martin Puchner in *Literature for a Changing Planet* (2022), having categorized the human as an 'information-hoarding settler ... wreaking havoc on a meteoritic scale', wonders if there is a narrative form equal to the task. He wonders whether such stories of the marauding human should take the form of morality tales apportioning blame, stories of 'unintended consequences and devastating effects' or 'dire warnings' (unpaginated). James Bradley, also meditating on the form, believes that 'social realist novels ... are hopelessly inadequate when it comes to something like climate change' (2010). For Adeline Johns-Putra, climate change novels 'query the adequacy of the parental response to a climate-changed world' but also offer 'radical versions of posterity that might be fitter for purpose in such a world' (2019: 7). Adam Trexler in *Anthropocene Fictions* makes a strong case for literary studies where 'interpreting [cultural and literary] texts can be understood as a way of describing the patterning of enormous cultural transformations' (2015: 5).[2] Further, literary studies resist any 'monovocal account, a set of bare "interests," an immovable orthodoxy, or a predetermined certainty' (5–6). Robert Macfarlane believes that 'climate change is not – not yet – apocalyptic in its consequences', and the problem for literature is 'how to dramatise aggregating detail, how to plot slow change'. Macfarlane offers the following prescription:

Any literary response to the present situation would need to be measured and prudent, and would need to find ways of imagining which remained honest to the scientific evidence.... [I]t might require literary languages which are attentive to the creep of change; which practise a vigilance of attention and a precision of utterance. (2005, unpaginated)

Swerving in a different direction from Trexler, Macfarlane and Puchner, who are emphatic about the crucial role of the literary, Amitav Ghosh in his now-celebrated text *The Great Derangement* (2016), demonstrating considerable impatience with modern and contemporary literature when it comes to the subject of climate change, argues that because the modern novel chooses to focus on the everyday, it precludes contemplations of global corporeal and other vulnerabilities. (Admittedly, Ghosh is not making a charge about the inadequacy of literature in toto, but about the lacunae of the modern forms of the novel.) As he puts it,

> the Anthropocene [resists] the techniques that are most closely identified with the novel: its essence consists of phenomena that were long ago expelled from the territory of the novel – forces of unthinkable magnitude that create unbearably intimate connections over vast gaps in time and space ... [so] that the literary imagination became radically centered on the human. (63)

We need, Ghosh argues, a more heightened, nuanced imaginative response – fiction – that alerts us to the crisis at hand. He points to the centrality of imaginative constructions of crisis but the question whether such constructions should be of other or alternative worlds (Trexler 2015) – terraforming novels such as Frank Herbert's *Dune* (1965) or Kim Stanley Robinson's *Mars* trilogy (1992–1996) would be a case in point (Pak 2016) – or the apocalyptical remains unanswered. Ursula Heise takes issue with Ghosh's view of genres such as sci-fi and writes that 'science fiction ... always addresses its audience's here and now through the detour of imagined futures' (2018, unpaginated). For Heise, then, sci-fi as a genre does give us a sense of unthinkable magnitude, although, as Adeline Johns-Putra has argued about sci-fi and cli-fi such as Kim Stanley Robinson's and Barbara Kingsolver's, the 'potential gulf between naïve technological determinism and a just utopian society has continued to be a topic of concern and scrutiny' for many novelists (John-Putra 2019: 143).

The debate, then, is about the genre and form of literature best suited to the cultural challenge of climate crisis and for addressing subjects and concerns as diverse as the disappearance of species, colonization of other planets, the dying of humanity as a species or bringing back extinct lifeforms.

Take the fiction that I shall term the catachronistic novel, in which the novelist brings the future into the present. I adapt the genre name from the work of Srinivas Aravamudan. A catachronism, which Aravamudan posits as the opposite of the anachronism, 're-characterizes the past and the present in terms of a future proclaimed as determinate but that is of course not yet fully realized' (2013: 8). In this, 'anticipation, belief, and application on the present are integrated as inexorably leading to a known and inevitable outcome' (8). Aravamudan's arguments resonate with Frank Kermode's. Kermode speaks of 'the anxiety reflected by the *fin de siècle* is perpetual, and people don't wait for centuries to end before they express it. Any date can be justified on some calculation or other' (2000: 98). Climate crisis and the concomitant extinction is a crisis-in-waiting, or a crisis-in-process, and much literature looks forward to the crisis appearing over time, scene by scene, species death by species death. The anxiety which Kermode says is 'perpetual' is about a certain – 'certain' in more ways than one – future. This anxiety is akin to 'the prognosis of apocalypse [that] encode[s] a "Pretraumatic Stress Syndrome"' (Kaplan 2016: 1).

The catachronistic novel, then, addresses and re-characterizes the past, brings it into a dialogue with the present, illuminating aspects that are reminders of how we got *here* from *there*. It also alerts us to patterns of human behaviour that would, if it continues in the same mode as we see today, and if unchecked and unaddressed, produce a certain kind of crisis in the future. Such a novel faces the *coming* and *imminence* of precarious lives (human and nonhuman), the building of vulnerable nature(s) and the potential loss of the planet. Ecoprecarity – a shorthand term to describe multiple forms, scales and victims of climate crisis (Nayar 2019a) – as embodied in the catachronistic novel, therefore, is not reducible to the apocalyptic alone even if the 'sense of an ending', in Frank Kermode's evocative phrase (2000), permeates the literature of climate crisis. The state of precarity is the consequence not just of a one-off event but of the many incremental mini-disasters over centuries, as several texts underscore.

Other contemporary forms of assessing, imagining and anticipating climate crisis and its attendant terrors include the eco-thriller, the terraforming novel, disaster fiction, de-extinction and rewilding fiction, and the neo-slave novel examining the rise and role of the Plantationocene – the 'New World' plantation era that inaugurated a racialized capitalism that hinged upon the cultivation of specific crops and slave labour – with a particular emphasis on environmental justice. Within cli-fi, the apocalyptic novel, judging by the sheer quantum of novels about ecoapocalypse, ecocollapse, extinction and ecodisaster in the last few decades, seems to have trumped as a genre, leading Sarah McFarland to characterize climate change fiction as principally 'a genre of apocalyptic and post-apocalyptic writing' (2021: 2). Mary Shelley pioneered the last-human novel in *The Last Man* (1826). In more contemporary times, we have Nevil Shute's nuclear apocalypse, *On the Beach* (1957), and the disaster fiction of J. G. Ballard (*The Drowned World*, 1962; *The Crystal World*, 1966), leading up to the now-cult Cormac McCarthy's *The Road* (2006) along with Alan Weisman's thought experiment, *The World Without Us* (2007). In texts like Bradley's *Clade*, we see an alignment of different forms of disaster: 'The floods in England followed by the deluges in northern Europe and Burma, the escalation of war in the Middle East and the horrors in Chicago' (2017, unpaginated). And later, as the crisis escalates: 'the islands of the Pacific are disappearing, Bangladesh is gone, as is much of Burma and coastal India', alongside social crises embodied in 'the camps, the random harassment by police, the detention and forced expulsion of anyone the government deemed undesirable' (unpaginated). Bradley, like those authors revisiting the plantation era, sees the intersections of state policy, human behaviour, social attitudes and environmental collapse.

Post-apocalyptic texts include survivor tales set on a devastated earth, like Octavia Butler's *Xenogenesis* trilogy (1987–1989), Margaret Atwood's *MaddAddam* trilogy (2003–2013) and N. K. Jemisin's *Broken Earth* trilogy (2015–2017). In many of these imaginings of a post-apocalyptic earth, the structures of the family, childhood, reproduction and society are called into question. In addition to the literary fiction around climate crisis, the last decades of the twentieth century saw the rise of the graphic novel as an important medium to speak of such vast changes as global warming and pollution. A wide variety exists, from the science-heavy Phillipe Squarzoni's *Climate Changed* (2014) to Nick Hayes' reprising of Samuel Taylor Coleridge's classic poem in *The Rime of the Modern Mariner* (2011), animal rights comics (Gerry Alanguilan's *Elmer*, 2010) and adaptations of plantation and environmental justice texts that return us to antebellum USA (Octavia Butler's *Kindred*, 1979, with a graphic adaptation in 2017). Post-apocalyptic themes of the last human(s) and survivorhood also serve the graphic novel well in Jeff Lemire's *Sweet Tooth* (compendium version, 2021) and Brian Vaughan and Pia Guerra's *Y: The Last Man* (2020). The hydronovel finds its graphic expression in Orijit

Sen's *River of Stories* (1994), Sarnath Banerjee's *All Quiet in Vikaspuri* (2015) and Subhash Vyam's *Water* (2018).

Numerous frames, overlapping and intersecting in their attempt to trace the ecological unconscious and crisis subjectivity in this wide variety of texts, have evolved over the last two decades to account for and address various forms of cli-fi.

Contemporary EH and criticism have moved beyond considerations of only humanity – its fragility, vulnerability and possibilities.[3] With the rise of critical plant studies and critical animal studies (McHugh 2011; Laist 2013; Marder 2013; Nealon 2015) and informed by anthropological work on the more-than and other-than human (Kohn 2015; Tsing 2017; Miller 2019), the writings of Karen Barad (2003), Jane Bennett (2010), Cary Wolfe (2003, 2009) and Donna Haraway (2007, 2016), the intersections of human with the nonhuman, the living and the non-living have also found their academic niches. Relatedly, the animal and the nonhuman Other as depicted in literature has come in for sustained attention (Castricano 2008; Huggan and Tiffin 2010; Pick 2011; Singh 2018; Sinha and Bhaishya 2020; Sinha 2023; Walther 2021). Questions of ethics and justice, as well as the politics of care and rescue, have turned to the more-than-human in the work of Sophie Chao (2022), Chao et al. (2022), Ebin Kirksey (2017), Kate Rigby (2015), van Dooren et al. (2016), Elan Abrell (2021) and others, with debates about the legal subjectivity of the nonhuman also receiving attention (Norman 2022). Specific cultural studies of events like extinction have also appeared: Claire Colebrooke (2014), Thom van Dooren (2014), Deborah Bird Rose (2011), Heise (2016), Rose et al. (2017). Eugenic and other dystopias such as Octavia Butler's, Margaret Atwood's or Kazuo Ishiguro's propose a human stewardship theme, directed at the future of the human race in terms of its very continuity and existence, although, as I have argued elsewhere, 'the stewardship for "continuing" humanity is founded on structures of power and knowledge that remain scarred by the political and social pasts of humanity and does not ensure a redemptive future' (Nayar 2023: 87).

The environmental consequences and politics of colonial extraction, exploitation and domination, with their attendant violence and postcolonial legacies, are the subject of work by Rob Nixon (2011) and deLoughrey et al. (2015). Specific studies on colonialism and its history of extraction and exploitation include Amitav Ghosh's *The Great Derangement* (2016) and *The Nutmeg's Curse* (2021) and Laurie Parson's *Carbon Colonialism: How Rich Countries Export Climate Change Breakdown* (2023), among others. Postcolonial studies' intersections with ecocriticism have enabled critics to scrutinize these histories, especially in terms of processes and sites such as the plantation (Singh 2018; Ferdinand 2022; Barua 2023). Holding slavery and the plantation responsible for economic, social and environmental exploitation and spoilage, Katherine McKittrick (2013) and Françoise Vergès (2017), among others, call for greater attention to be paid to the racial aspect of both capital and environmental exploitation and thereby have theorized, with environmental historians like Jason Moore (2017), the Capitalocene and the Plantationocene. In related developments within EH, the impact of climate change on indigenous societies, the role of indigenous knowledges and the global geopolitics of climate change discourse, sustainability initiatives and carbon politics vis-à-vis aboriginal lives have also come in for considerable attention (Ulloa 2005; Suliman et al. 2015). Climate refugees and human rights and their forms of mobilities and displacements figure in contemporary critical work as well (see *Mobilities* 19, no. 3, special issue). In adjacent disciplines such as environmental history, recent work has called attention to the nonhuman histories of the planet. While Anna Tsing and others have examined the entangled histories of plant, fungi and other species and humans, yet others have attempted histories of waves and dunes (Helmreich 2014; Freitas 2020). Writing about dunes, for instance, Joana Gaspar de Freitas argues:

> [Dunes] constitute ecological niches for species adapted to extreme conditions, offering refuge and nesting sites … provide services such as sequestering carbon, filtering pollutants and purifying water. Plus, they support a variety of socio-economic activities, recreational uses, aesthetic, psychological and therapeutic opportunities…. Dunes are materialised environments that offer goods and services, but they are also shaped by how they are perceived, studied, used, explored and managed. And for all that, they are complex social objects. (2020: 2)

Animal care and sanctuaries and the shifting meanings of individual species, such as the much-derided and feared pit bulls, in countries of the Global North have also come in for attention for their construction of species boundaries and the layered cultural politics of rescue, welfare and instrumentality (Abrell 2021; Weaver 2021).

   Recent developments in EH also seek to particularize zones of conflict and crisis, or explore historical legacies and processes that redefined the ecosystems for the human and the nonhuman: to take just three instances, the rise of blue or oceanic humanities (Rajbhandari 2022; Nuttall 2020, 2022;

Hofmeyr 2019), the energy humanities (Szeman and Boyer 2017; Mišík and Kujundžić 2021) and Deborah Rose Bird and Thom van Dooren's work on the *ethos* of particular species (2017), drawing upon the natural and cognitive sciences, are attempts to foreground the necessity of paying attention to the nonhuman. Others have sought to examine the tensions within ecocriticism itself. Most notably, Timothy Clark's *Ecocriticism on the Edge* (2015) argues that what the ecocritics perceive and endorse as environmentally advantageous at one end of the spatiotemporal scale could always have deleterious consequences at the other. Sybil P. Seitzinger at al. call for a shift in thinking towards 'planetary stewardship', defined as 'the active shaping of trajectories of change on the planet, that integrates across scales from the local to the global in order to enhance the combined sustainability of human well-being and the planet's ecosystems and non-living resources' (Seitzinger et al. 2012: 787). Postcolonial literatures of climate crisis have come in for attention too, given the politics of environmentalisms, the uneven nature of science, research and cultural productions but also the inequities of the economy across the Global North or South (McDougall et al. 2021).

Environmental humanities also pays due attention to the *politics* of environmentalism, particularly to questions of national and international negotiations over climate deals, norms imposed on nations and the link between corporate and state power when it comes to political ecology, among others. The actors involved in climate debates and deals are embedded in multiple systems – from science to government – as Richard Peet et al. note:

> IPCC itself as a sort of transnational scientific network operating too as an advocacy group on a public landscape populated by a significant corporate (and Republican Party in the US) presence of climate change deniers. (2011: 3)[4]

In addition to global political ecologies and their consequences for environmental policies, there are other forms of politics that disciplines such as EH have accounted for. Take, for instance, the politics of environmental knowledge itself. Definitions, descriptions and particular ways of talking about the environment mean that these rhetorical strategies (whether in science or policy documents, public discourse or literature) determine how *we perceive the environment and therefore how we enact policy to protect, conserve or destroy it.* In, for example, the pioneering collection *Nature in the Global South* (Greenough and Tsing 2003), we see how different cultures across the Asian continent, including tribal and indigenous, construct 'Nature' and therefore have different modes of valuing the 'natural'. It is in these interstices of hegemonic, counter-hegemonic and resistant cultures of Nature, so to speak, that political movements, campaigns, petitions and politics emerge and accrue. In contemporary environmental movements and policy-making, the rise of discourses and practices such as ecosystem services, notes Esther Turnhout, deploys a 'measurementality logic' that 'combines three powerful discourses that are characteristic of environmental governance … technocratic discourse … managerial discourse … policy discourse' (2018: 366). What Turnhout is pointing to is that the discourse of environmentalism itself relies on multiple discourses which in turn have their own politics, whether of the market or of governance. Environmental movements and attitudes towards the environment, as Ramachandra Guha and Juan Martinez-Alier (1997) and others have shown, work differentially between the Global North and South, whether in terms of sustainability or 'livelihood' debates (see Thaker 2021).

There are novels that foreground environmental policy-making and the politics of environmentalism (although this genre of political ecology novels is not the subject of this present book). In recent times, works such as Paolo Bacigalupi's *The Windup Girl* (2009) and Matthew Glass's *Ultimatum* (2009) address the problem of global cooperation, corporate and state struggles, or greed or incapacity to arrive at a conclusion vis-á-vis climate-change-driven norms and measures (see Trexler 2015: ch. 4 for a detailed examination of what he terms 'eco-nomics', the 'Domesticity, Ecology, and Political Economy'). In Bacigalupi's posthuman work set in a post-apocalyptic world, Thailand is the only country to have survived global agricultural disaster because of its strict national laws on importing of seeds and agro-products and its closely guarded seed-bank projects. In fact, Thailand has been so efficient and so secretive that fruits and vegetables thought to be extinct have been recreated due to the seed-bank. Bacigalupi writes about the intersection of national identity, corporate power and ecology:

> AgriGen and its ilk were threatening embargo over intellectual property infringement, but the Thai Kingdom was still alive. Against all odds, they were alive. As others were crushed under the calorie companies' heels, the Kingdom stood strong.
> *Embargo!* Chaiyanuchit had laughed. *Embargo is precisely what we want! We do not wish to interact with their outside world at all.* And so the walls had gone up – those that the oil collapse had not already created, those that

had not been raised against civil war and starving refugees – a final set of barriers to protect the Kingdom from the onslaughts of the outside world. (Unpaginated, emphasis in original)

Thailand thus becomes, in effect, the saviour of the planet. When the American Lake Anderson demands access to the Thai seed-bank, Akkarat replies: 'The seedbank has kept us independent of your kind. When blister rust and genehack weevil swept the globe, it was only the seedbank that allowed us to stave off the worst of the plagues....' (unpaginated). Akkarat reminds Anderson: 'You're saying that you yoked the world to your patented grains and seeds, happily enslaved us all, and now you finally realize that you are dragging us all to hell' (unpaginated). As I have argued elsewhere,

> Bacigalupi suggests that Thailand's attempt to secure its environment – the ecosystems for its essential crops – through intellectual property regimes is in fact a securitizing of national identity. (Nayar 2019a: 136)

It is interesting to note that Bacigalupi invests the Ministry of Environment with far-reaching powers in the context of Thailand's post-apocalyptic survival:

> At every turn the ministry's purview was expanding. The plagues were but the latest insult to the Kingdom's survival. First came the rising sea levels, and the need to construct the dikes and levees. And then came the oversight in power contracts and trading in pollution credits and climate infractions. The white shirts took over the licensing of methane capture and production. Then there was the monitoring of fishery health and toxin accumulations in the Kingdom's final bastion of calorie support.... And there was the tracking of human health and viruses and bacteria.... There was no end to the duties of the Ministry. (Unpaginated).

Just as the American seeks access to the seed-bank, negotiating with the Thai officers in order to gain favours, in *Ultimatum*, we are shown the nitty-gritty of the climate change negotiations – this time between the USA and China. The climate deal is not easy to push through as the USA's President Joe Benton discovers, nor are the recommendations and norms easy to implement among signatory nations:

> Spend two years negotiating, another five years verifying and finding out no one's in compliance, then start negotiating again. (Glass 2009, unpaginated)

When the debate over emission cuts emerges – Benton offers 18 per cent cuts to China – everyone recognizes how difficult it would be to implement:

> Eighteen percent over such a short time frame was a massive reduction. And all the painless steps to cut emissions had been taken long ago. The economic impact of this would be ... considerable. (Unpaginated)

The tensions between economics and ecology emerge throughout Glass's work. The Chinese Wu points out that these deals about environmental protection norms – the parleys and diplomatic negotiations – are in fact about people staying in power (unpaginated). As the modelling of disaster scenarios proceed, the deal-makers discover that 'even with the most extreme reduction schedule, the U.S. population requiring relocation would range from twenty to twenty-five million. And even in that scenario, Miami went under' (unpaginated). Trexler summarizes the novel neatly when he writes: 'a few powerful men must resolve climate change for the world; there are almost insurmountable economic and political obstacles preventing them from acting' (2015: 128).

Yet another angle in the writing of climate disaster and efforts at its mitigation or prevention has emerged from questions raised about and around the constantly future-directed efforts of disaster management. Commentators have noted that in politics, data collection and humanitarian efforts 'the [climate] emergency is treated as a sudden, unpredictable event that unfolds against a background of perceived normality, which causes widespread suffering or danger and demands an urgent response' (Compton 2020: 2). Such an approach 'presupposes there is a normal order to be reset, and humanitarian reason does not demand a transformation of this order itself ... only an alleviation of their worst effects' (Compton 2020: 2). Caroline Compton notes that increasingly disaster and humanitarian relief projects and thinking focus on 'building back better' because of the recognition that the disaster emerges from a certain past. The emergency is not a break or a radical interruption from the past as much as a continuity with it. It is in this context that, as Compton shows, data from present disaster is used to 'build back better', and thus constitutes a new view of emergency and disaster itself.

Other discourses – of ecodisasters – have their own rhetoric and politics. Ecodystopias and ecodisasters in literature have been studied for their generic conventions, thematic focus and politics. For instance, women in ecodystopias, critics of feminist speculative fiction have argued (see Vint and Buran 2022), are projected as continuing to live under the burden of a certain 'reproductive futurism' (Sheldon 2016), and 'child-figures [in literature and art] are asked to secure not only the reproduction of the human in a generational landscape but also the reproduction of the species in an evolutionary one' (Ashton 2023: 4). The nightmarish scenarios of climate disaster are sketched, both in literary history and in the current era, through Gothic fictions too. As the editors state in the introduction to the volume *The Gothic Anthropocene*, 'the realities of planetary destruction are disseminated in gothic fictions … wherein we can imagine a future world based on what we have done in the past, whether it be excessive consumption, exploitation of resources, murder, or other kinds of transgression' (Edwards et al. 2022: ix). The Anthropocene has produced a massive corpus of work in the last decade, ranging in interest from literary representations (Menely and Taylor 2017) to ethics and conservation (Cielemęcka 2019; Lorimer 2015; Propen 2018; Grusin 2017). Literary and other texts that foreground – imagine – the nonhuman Other are now the subject of studies of the nonhuman (in) narrative (Herman 2018). Very specific accounts, such as Christopher Spicer's study of cyclones in Australian literature (2020), have also appeared. Op-ed pieces have played an influential role in popularizing the literature of climate crisis even as they sought more cultural texts on the crisis. Thus, Bill McKibben (2005) called for more art, poetry, fiction and plays about climate change, and Kathryn Schulz in 'The Ten Best Weather Events in Fiction' (2015) documents weather patterns in literary representations by Joseph Conrad, Zora Neale Hurston, Herman Melville and Emily Brontë, among others.

*

The choice of texts in this book is intentionally global although perhaps slightly tilted towards works from the Global South. While conscious of the problematics of a universalizing discourse of 'vulnerable earth' when different portions of the planet are differentially affected by climate change and climate change policies, this book stays with the global perspective, choosing to draw parallels and links between, say, a novel set in drought-hit Nevada, another about flooding in Namibia and a third about New York deluged. Thus, even when dealing with literatures that demonstrate 'an emphasis on the importance of a "sense of place," the attachment to or "reinhabitation" of the local through prolonged residence, intimate familiarity, affective ties, and ethical commitment', as Ursula Heise (2008: 50) puts it, this book opts for the risk of thinking through echoes, resonances and anxieties that align and animate markedly different literatures. This book therefore moves across texts that demonstrate both bioregionalisms and cosmopolitanisms of various shades – vernacular, cosmetic – in their attitudes towards 'their' environment and that of the planet.

This book focuses on four aspects of the literature of climate crisis through readings of genres such as the memoir and fiction. The themes are discrete but not unrelated, and so are the chapters, dealing with the hydronovel, extinction and rewilding, multispecies worlds and ecojustice.

The chapter 'Hydropoetics: Fluid Fictions' examines the contemporary hydronovel. Histories of colonialism and the nexus between the postcolonial state and the mineral-seeking corporations from America figure as prominent themes in numerous African novels. From America, this same nexus of the state with the corporations and the consequent (mis)management and control over resources such as water, the serious crisis of water in urban as well as rural or suburban regions of Euro-America, Asia and Africa, floods and droughts are the subjects of a genre we can identify as the hydronovel: Helon Habila's *Oil on Water* (2011), Paolo Bacigalupi's *The Water Knife* (2015), Namwali Serpell's *The Old Drift* (2019), Amitav Ghosh's *The Hungry Tide* (2004), Stephen Baxter's *Flood* (2008), Maggie Gee's *The Flood* (2004), Nathaniel Rich's *Odds Against Tomorrow* (2013), and others. These novels locate the water crisis in a specific historical past while projecting such a crisis as the imminent future too. As I shall argue, they speak of the hydrocrisis as the cumulative effect of human interventions in terms of industrialization, techno-urbanisms, regulation of resources, specific historical forces and practices and 'imperial formations' (Stoler 2008). I also study the genre's aesthetics of catastrophic realism and irrealism before turning my attention to a specific subgenre, the hydrogothic graphic texts, from India.

Many texts in the literature of climate crisis refuse to privilege human loss and disaster over that of other life forms and of the non-living. The chapter 'Extinction: After/Lives' examines the literature of extinction. Memoirs and melancholic accounts of species disappearance and rewilding possibilities contribute in a huge measure to the corpus of cultural texts on climate crisis *and* a history of species loss. Besides Ackerman's text cited earlier, we have accounts of individual species loss by Christopher Cokinos' *Hope Is the Thing with Feathers* (2009), Joel Greenberg's *A Feathered River Across the Sky: The Passenger Pigeon's Flight into Extinction* (2014), David Owen's *Thylacine: The Tragic Tale of the Tasmanian Tiger* (2003) and David Quammen's *The Song of the Dodo: Island Biogeography in an Age of Extinctions* (2004), among others.

Fiction such as Charlotte McConaghy's *Migrations* (2021), James Bradley's *Clade* (2017) and Barbara Kingsolver's *Flight Behavior* (2012) are elegies for disappearing species but with the possibilities of some surviving. The chapter concludes with texts speculating on the possibilities of rewilding. Rewilding and the resurrection of extinct species becomes the fantasy theme in *Once There Were Wolves* (2021), James Clade's *Ghost Species* (2020), the ever-popular Michael Crichton's *Jurassic Park* (1990) and prospective biographies based on the science of de-extinction, such as Ben Mezrich's *Woolly: The True Story of the Quest to Revive One of History's Most Iconic Extinct Creatures* (2017) and Richard Stone's *Mammoth: The Resurrection of an Ice Age Giant* (2002). This chapter argues that extinction discourse relies on a rhetoric of plenitude and presence before evoking what I call an anticipatory nostalgia for the species under scrutiny. In the last section of the chapter, I work with fictional and non-fictional texts dealing with the ambitious project of rewilding.

Attention to multispecies and interspecies interactions also finds considerable appeal in the contemporary novel, and makes up the chapter 'Creaturely Texts: Multispecies Encounters'. Plants take centrestage in works like Richard Powers' *The Overstory*. Tania James' *The Tusk That Did the Damage* (2015) focuses on elephants and poaching, while in Marie Darrieussecq's *Pig Tales* (1996) a woman finds herself being transformed into a pig. Mayra Montero's *In the Palm of Darkness* (1997) shows how animal species and humans are both at the mercy of human politics in Haiti. In novels like Louis Nowra's *Into That Jungle* (2012), Neil Abramson's *Unsaid* (2011) and Charles Foster's memoir, *Being a Beast* (2016), we find attempts to imagine the human living as, or becoming, animal. In many of these texts there is the self-conscious attempt to see the world from the animal's point of view. This chapter looks at a multispecies relationality in contemporary creaturely texts. It examines themes and texts in which the human–nonhuman boundary is breached in significant and mutually constitutive ways, especially in terms of shared vulnerabilities and communication across species. In the final section, I examine the biomutation narrative and themes of zoomorphism and the humanimal.

The last chapter, 'Justice Matters: Human and Nonhuman Toxiconomies', examines writings around the broad theme of ecojustice, attentive to iniquities towards the human, the nonhuman and the non-living. As historians have come to recognize the historical form of slavery, plantation cultures and their attendant dehumanization have had deleterious effects in the form of ecological erosion and bioinvasion – processes that damaged land, life and the life chances of humans and nonhumans. The chapter's focus is toxiconomies, the alignment of the toxicity of materials such as land, water, material (human and nonhuman) bodies and economies of colonialism, and modern-day global capitalism. This entails studying the environmental justice perspective in different texts from multiple genres: the neo-slave narrative that revisits the history of plantations, novels about waste – the industry, the waste subjectivity of specific peoples – and memoirs about toxic environments. Isabel Allende's *Island Beneath the Sea* (2010), Edward P. Jones' *The Known World* (2003), Yaa Gyasi's *The Homegoing* (2016), Jesmyn Ward's *Sing, Unburied, Sing* (2017) and Cynthia McLeod's *The Cost of Sugar* (2010) are neo-slavery novels or have components of slave and plantation history as the backdrop and horrific legacy – the subjects of studies by Rushdy (1999) and Ryan (2008) – that foreground larger questions of environmental justice when they speak of historical injustices towards people and places. Under this last category or theme, we see the rise of the novel of waste in Chen Qiufan's *Waste Tide* (2019) and China Miévelle's *Un Lun Dun* (2007). In another set of texts, environmental injustice takes the form of toxified everyday life for people in specific communities and regions. The toxic body memoir, which demonstrates shared corporeal vulnerabilities identified as 'trans-corporeality' by Stacy Alaimo (2010), moves outward from individuals to entire communities to produce prosopographies and toxichorographies of regions. Sandra Steingraber's *Living Downstream: An Ecologist's Personal Investigation of Cancer and the Environment* (1997), Marie Therese Martin's *And Poison Fell from the Sky: A Memoir of Life, Death, and Survival in Maine's Cancer Valley* (2022), Marla Cone's *Silent Snow* (2005), Susanne Antonetta's *Body Toxic* (2001), Dan Fagin's *Toms River* (2013) and Catherine Coleman Flowers' *Waste* (2020) are examples of this genre devoted to the crisis of toxic dumping – which, as Lawrence Buell noted in his early essay on 'Toxic Discourse', is the 'catalyst and … centrepiece' of the environmental justice movement (1998: 642).

*

Literature, popular cultural forms like cinema, especially in their apocalyptic version, documentaries and public discourses in general have for some time now been seized of the urgency of the climate crises, demonstrating the rise and impact of an ecological unconscious. This book is in broad agreement with Robert MacFarlane, Ursula Heise and numerous other scholars who see the literary imagining of disaster, hope, species and loss as central to the public response to and tackling of climate crisis.

The texts address disaster directly in many cases. Others examine specific themes, such as multispecies identities and engagements with or without climate crisis, as the backdrop. The rationale, then, for including creaturely texts is that the nonhuman is a key 'character' in climatological discourses. These texts also are implicitly addressing the theme of 'vulnerable earth' by pointing to the threats to and possibilities of more-than- or other-than-human species, speciesism, and species interactions. Such texts refuse to see vulnerability or potential in the human alone, although the overwhelming emphasis is on the human predations of or upon nonhuman life and the vulnerability of the nonhuman to human interventions. These creaturely texts also call upon us to rethink species boundaries, and examine the possibilities of multispecies becoming and belonging.

The themes and forms studied here from fiction, graphic novels and memoirs are an indicative rather than an exhaustive list because 'vulnerable earth' is a descriptor of much more than what this book covers although it hopefully captures the fragility and injurability of the, thus far only, home humanity and a host of nonhumans inhabit.

Notes

1. A large number of very readable works on the scientific evidence and analysis of climate change, from global warming to ocean pH levels, are available. See in particular Archer (2009), Archer and Pierrehumbert (2011) and Dessler and Parson (2021), among others.
2. The term 'Anthropocene', now central to the critical vocabulary on climate change – indeed often used interchangeably with 'climate change' – has been defined numerous times since its coinage by Paul Crutzen in the 2000s. A summary rather than a definition is as follows:

> This geological epoch [the Anthropocene] is the product of the last few hundred years of our history. The Anthropocene is the sign of our power, but also of our impotence. It is an Earth whose atmosphere has been damaged by the 1,500 billion tonnes of carbon dioxide we have spilled by burning coal and other fossil fuels. It is the impoverishment and artificializing of Earth's living tissue, permeated by a host of new synthetic chemical molecules that will even affect our descendants. It is a warmer world with a higher risk of catastrophes, a reduced ice cover, higher sea-levels and a climate out of control. (Bonneuil and Fressoz 2016, unpaginated)

3. Dipesh Chakrabarty has argued that the postcolonial critique of the subject 'was actually a deeper turning towards the human' (2012: 4). But the critique in both theoretical writings and literature has attempted to rethink the centrality of the human. Elsewhere, he also argues:

    > There could be no phenomenology of us [humans] as a species. Even if we were to emotionally identify with a word like mankind, we would not know what being a species is, for, in species history, humans are only an instance of the concept species as indeed would be any other life form. But one never experiences being a concept. (2009: 220)

    In her response to this statement, Catherine Malabou asks: 'I don't understand why the fact of becoming a geological form would have to remain entirely conceptual, and not produce a kind of mental phenomenon…. I would like to ask precisely why could we not be susceptible to experience mentally and psychically the indifference and neutrality that have become parts of our nature?' (2017: 6–7).

4. Essays in this volume draw attention to the politics around American farm policy, industrial fishing, garbage and waste management, carbon colonialism and others, thus providing a sweeping survey of the politics of and around environmental debates and deals.

2

Hydropoetics
Fluid Fictions

In Namwali Serpell's *The Old Drift* (2019), the mosquito chorus (called 'Moskeetoze') sings 'the story of a place is the story of its water, and the Kariba Dam is no exception' (78). The 'story of a place' and the 'story of its water' can be about either excess or scarcity, and the novels under consideration in this chapter deal with both effects of water. These novels are categorizable, after Sarah Nuttall, as 'pluvial novels' that are concerned with 'heavy rainfall and flooding, but also with the pluvial flows, ubiquitous wetnesses and manifold waters that pool, stagnate, drift and roil' (2022: 324). However, many novels dealing with water speak about the *scarcity* of water. I take this extended semantic scope of 'pluvial' from Nuttall herself, when she argues in her earlier work that

> [c]onceptually, the term [pluvial time] implies a material condition and a relation to time, and thus to geology and history, that we can refer to as 'pluvial time'. The pluvial lies at the centre of an accelerating climate change that exacerbates both drought and heavy rain. (2022: 324)

The fiction in this chapter, from literary novels to graphic texts, focuses on a crisis over or about water, a crisis often originating in and exacerbated by colonial history, postcolonial greed and models of development, human callousness and climate change. The novels are interested in not a single, cataclysmic event as much as a series of events and processes that lead to the crisis. These are not novels about the end of the world as much as an end-ing of the world some time in the future, and which is anticipated in the present, making them catachronistic in character and in their message.

Paolo Bacigalupi's *The Water Knife* (2015), structured as a climate thriller, is set in the near future where acute droughts brought on by climate change have rendered water an expensive resource. Water rights have been erased, and all water corporatized and guarded by militia hired by companies like the Southern Nevada Water Authority. The major agricultural areas, such as Imperial Valley, are becoming 'dust bowls', as one character puts it, due to the corporatization of water and protracted drought (70). There are water wars between these hydro-corporations, and people like Angel Velasquez (the 'water knife' of the title) are employed as spies, military personnel and regulators combined for the battles. Meanwhile, both the corporations and the resisters or dissenters are looking for the 'Pima' treaty, executed between the Native American tribes and the white man in a previous era, so that they can legally restore the water rights for Arizona. Their rights have been sold by the Native Americans themselves:

> Years ago they [the Pima nation peoples] made a deal with Phoenix to shift all their tribal water rights over to the city. The Pima had water rights to Central Arizona Project water.... Phoenix needed that water when the rivers around here started drying up.... Phoenix got the water it wanted ... and the Pima got a massive cash settlement.... (232)

Questions about the water crisis are at the centre of Cynan Jones' *Stillicide* (2019) too. The solution to the crisis is towing an iceberg from the Arctic all the way to water-strapped England. But for the Ice Dock to be prepared, it is necessary to demolish several residential areas, or what Jones describes as 'a gash cut through the city to steer the iceberg through' (19). This causes, understandably, deep social unrest and adds a new dimension to the water wars.

In Helon Habila's *Oil on Water* (2011), a petrofiction text set in contemporary Nigeria, British oil companies, like the European colonizers of old, exploit the land and the people. From a pastoral ideal, the villages have slid into chaos and violence. The native populations are divided among those who work for the company and those who believe the foreign presence is ruinous to the nation and the ecosystem. Resisters like Chief Malabo are arrested 'on charges of supporting the militants and plotting against the federal government' (39). Eventually, 'they [the locals] sold. One by one', so that the company took possession of the entire land (40). At the time the story begins, the wife of James Floode, the British oil engineer, is kidnapped and Rufus, an investigative journalist, goes into the jungles to find her. Across the region, civil unrest is commonplace as the citizens are caught between the militia, the oil company and the state, with rape and violence characterizing the postcolony.

In Namwali Serpell's *The Old Drift* (2019), a novel that begins in the early twentieth century, and the era of colonial exploration, and ends in 2023, the construction of the Kariba dam has resulted in the Zambezi flooding earlier and earlier each year. Serpell writes of the site:

> Despite the rain, it was crawling with men, fly-like amongst the beetling machines. It looked like a mammoth corpse, half-dissected or half-rotten. They had already lost so many men to it … a swirling thrusting deluge, red as blood because of the copper in the dust. (70)

Serpell's image of the humans who are 'fly-like' in the midst of both nature and the human construction is amplified through the voice of the chorus – sung by the mosquitoes – who underscore the futility of human enterprise:

> *The feckless bazungu continued building the dam. When the flood came again, it lifted four men, plastered them to the dam like insects. The concrete was wet; the workers were dead; in the end, they built the dam around them. Strange tomb!* (78, italics in original)

At the end of the novel, the Zambezi has overflowed the dam, and the entire region is flooded. In Amitav Ghosh's *The Hungry Tide*, he refers to the Sunderbans' history of colonization and the colonials' illusion that they could conquer the land. Hamilton had sought to domesticate a land, which, on the occasion when the waters came in, was not land at all (2004: 49). The British had hoped to make Canning a thriving town, where many homes and hopes could be built (49–53, 285–286). Yet, years later, 'catastrophe … [is still] … a way of life' here (79).

In Nathaniel Rich's *Odds Against Tomorrow* (2013), also a catachronistic novel, New York's growth and speculative capital has ruined the city, with fault lines and water bodies built over after ignoring warnings from geologists, environmentalists and scientists, and as a result the city is unprepared for the hurricane. Mitchell Zukor, a wizard at calculating risks, finds himself battling to survive in the floods that follow the hurricane. The city's social order collapses, as is expected in the event of a disaster, and survivors set up a commune far away in order to start life afresh – a commune to which Zukor eventually retreats. Here the narrative of imminent ecodisaster in New York references worldwide catastrophes, demonstrating the *global* ecology of disaster:

The weathermen … began to predict rain. They pointed to tropical storms in the Caribbean: imposing Irma, ominous Ophelia, promising Philippe – but all veered out to sea before making the Atlantic Seaboard. They pointed to a chain of hurricanes developing off the coast of Mauritania, another promising development. The Eurasian snow cover was higher than the previous year, broody cumulonimbus clouds were gathering just two hundred miles off Florida, and the sea surface temperatures in the tropics were at ten-year lows. (Unpaginated)

In all cases, the *event* of the disaster is subsumed under the *processes* that have brought, so to speak, the disaster.

This pluvial literature, which I rename the 'hydronovel' to gesture at the wider semantic scope of 'pluvial' to include both flood and drought conditions, emphasizes a unique feature of the Earth: that it is a 'blue planet', made principally of water. Adopting approaches from the blue humanities – Isobel Hofmeyer (2019), Sarah Nuttall (2020, 2022), Elizabeth deLoughrey (2018, 2019, 2023) and others – this chapter studies the fiction of Helon Habila, Paolo Bacigalupi, Amitav Ghosh, Stephen Baxter, Maggie Gee and graphic texts (Orijit Sen, Sarnath Banerjee, Subhash Vyam), as well as for their hydropoetics. 'Hydropoetics' as an overarching term is applied principally to 'deluge novels' (as Adam Trexler terms them, 2015) but also to drought novels. Later in the chapter, I examine a subgenre, the postcolonial graphic text that focuses on water and water-related crises. I use texts from the Indian subcontinent whose poetics works to link water crises, colonial histories and postcoloniality. Here the hydropoetics is in fact a hydro*gothic*.

The hydronovels brought together here engage with different sites of colonial legacies and the postcolony: the United States where the white man's profiteering ways were built upon the eviction of the Native Americans and Bacigalupi's explicit referencing of this history in *The Water Knife*; the history of development in the form of financial speculation and rampant urbanisms in *Odds Against Tomorrow*; and the postcolonies of Nigeria (Habila) and Zambia (Serpell) wherein colonial legacies haunt in the form of British oil companies and dams. The novels exhibit a shared purpose and points of similarity in their critique of these histories and in their 'location' of disaster within the social crisis stemming from these histories. These novels speak of the hydrocrisis as the cumulative effect of human interventions in terms of industrialization, techno-urbanisms, regulation of resources, specific historical forces and practices and 'imperial formations' (Stoler 2008). Due to this interest in the past and the legacy of imperial formations, the novels instantiate a decolonization of disaster studies. Such a decolonization, argues Anthony Carrigan, requires attention to be paid to historical forces and the

> social crises that have shadowed political decolonization – including war, genocide, and systemic poverty – [that] have been catastrophic for large numbers of people, radically transforming natural and built environments in ways that coincide with current forms of ecological imperialism. (2015: 117)

Decolonization of disaster studies demands that we pay attention to the 'connections between vulnerability production, imperialist practice, and cultural response' (Carrigan 2015: 122). This means attending to the 'historical vulnerabilities that are produced at the intersection of environment and society, and which cannot be disentangled from systemic power structure' (Anthony Oliver-Smith cited in Carrigan 2015: 122) and the 'repositories of vulnerabilities that ... last longer than the political structures that produced them' (Stoler 2008: 203). Carrigan adds that decolonizing disaster studies calls upon us to examine those 'postcolonial texts [that] challenge, reject, or reconfigure key disaster studies concepts such as resilience, risk, adaption, and vulnerability' (Carrigan 2015: 123). The latter calls for an unpacking of the aesthetic, rhetorical and narrative practices through which the catastrophic events are represented, because it is through these practices that our understanding of what we mean by 'disaster' is shaped. Such an unpacking has been undertaken by postcolonial environmental humanities scholars reading the cultural imaginings of climate change. Thus, for instance, Elizabeth deLoughrey et al. call for a 'new direction for tropical aesthetics that builds upon and complicates historical images of colonial landscapes and anticipates new futures' (2015: 1). Michael Niblett identifies a 'petro-magical realism' and 'saccharine irrealism' in Caribbean plantation fiction (2015). About the aesthetics of climate change fiction, Debjani Ganguly argues that an 'aesthetics of geoalterity' informs novels about climate change and planetary crisis (2020: 446). Others (Bracke 2018) have identified strains of the pastoral in climate change fiction.[1] My reading is in alignment with such interpretations of ecodisaster texts.

Setting their fiction in the contemporary or near future enables Habila, Serpell, Rich, Baxter and Bacigalupi to also emphasize an 'end period' rather than an end.

The Hydronovel's Catastrophic Realism

Catastrophic realism is a subset of the postcolonial novel's realist aesthetic. It demonstrates a commitment to norms of plausibility and verisimilitude, as Hamish Dalley has argued in the case of the postcolonial historical novel (2014: 9). Realism in the postcolonial historical novel, argues Dalley,

> is specifically *postcolonial* insofar as it constitutes an ethico-political and aesthetic response to the cultural significance of history in societies established on the basis of colonial occupation – places where memories of past violence fissure the imagined community, and, as such, become subject to contestation. (9–10, emphasis in original)

Where the realism of the catachronistic novel departs from that of the postcolonial historical novel is that while the latter enables a way of knowing the past, the former engages with the past as the *origin* of the crisis even as it projects this state of chronic crisis as the *future*. Catastrophic realism is a way of imagining, knowing and anticipating the future of ecodisaster, survivor cultures and living on in an end period even as it looks back at the past, especially practices and processes such as colonialism.

Catastrophic realism is a materialist aesthetic, focusing on local change, material loss and ontological disasters affecting human and nonhuman forms, the living and the non-living. It demonstrates how the material aspects of water systems become enmeshed in financial networks, producing entirely new evaluations of nature, which then break down.[2] The production of vulnerabilities is located in historical processes and cultural practices that create a particular, and inimical, hydro-social cycle.

The catastrophic realist aesthetic takes one of two routes. In the first, there are detailed, gritty and grim accounts of loss and ruin, generating an atmosphere of terror, revulsion and anxiety. In the second, a quantificatory method is employed to demonstrate scales of human power, greed and loss.

Grim Realism

Helon Habila describes a local topos thus:

> … the gnarled, hanging roots that grew out of the water like proboscises gasping for air. The atmosphere grew heavy with the suspended stench of dead matter. We followed a bend in the river and in front of us we saw dead

birds draped over tree branches, their outstretched wings black and slick with oil; dead fish bobbed white-bellied between tree roots. (2011: 9)

This local topography – or chorography, more accurately – is replicated throughout the region. As the narrator and his companions on the boat move along the river, they meet similar sights in *every* village: 'the next village was almost a replica of the last: the same empty squat dwellings, the same ripe and flagrant stench, the barrenness, the oil slick and the same indefinable sadness in the air' (9). Habila implies a flattening of the land and its people through environmental degradation.

In all descriptions, Habila focuses on three local material connections: militancy, the oil industry and the changing quality of the river waters. The oil company that begins by 'sending their men to the village to take samples of soil and water' (39) eventually comes to 'buy' the village lands, so that the inhabitants are forced to 'hea[d] northwards' (40). Then Habila elaborates the nexus between governments and corporate organizations that triggers environmental and social collapse:

[P]ipelines that have brought nothing but suffering to their lives, leaking into the rivers and wells, killing the fish and poisoning the farmlands. And all they are told by the oil companies and the government is that the pipelines are there for their own good, that they hold great potential for their country, their future. These people endure the worst conditions of any oil-producing community on earth, the government knows it but doesn't have the will to stop it, the oil companies know it, but because the government doesn't care, they also don't care. (107)

So the humans displaced, the river polluted and the life forms dead – all due to a hydro-social cycle inherited from the colonial era but now nativized, so to speak. This emphasis on material effects around water and oil enables Habila to make a crucial point: climate change has anthropocentric causes and posthuman (other than and beyond human) effects. Humans with their ruthless hydro-social cycle produce climate change whose effects expand beyond the human world to include the nonhuman and the non-living. The collapse is rendered more tragic through the invocation of a time-before, wherein Habila describes a chronotope:

Once upon a time they lived in paradise. It was a small village close to Yellow Island. They lacked for nothing, fishing and hunting and farming and watching their children growing up before them, happy. The village was close-knit, made up of cousins and uncles and aunts and brothers and sisters, and, though they were happily insulated from the rest of the world by their creeks and rivers and forests, they were not totally unaware of the changes going on all around them: the gas flares that lit up neighboring villages all day and all night…. For the first time the close, unified community was divided – for how could they not be tempted, with the flare in the next village burning over them every night, its flame long and coiled like a snake, whispering, winking, hissing? (37)

The passage embodies Habila's Arcadian discourse – which along with pastoralism is a constituent of much environmental writing in the contemporary era (Hannigan 2013) – and describes a world where humans and nonhumans lived together in a specific topos. The coming of the oil company effects an irreversible material transformation in that topos, producing both ecological and social collapse. This social collapse is an imperial formation as Stoler defines it: a legacy of the British Empire in the form of the oil company, which now operates with impunity due to the support offered by the postcolonial state. The ruins of the land and water are attributed in no uncertain terms to this toxic legacy in a doctor's account of his tests on the contamination, narrated to Rufus and others:

[W]hen people started dying, I took blood samples and recorded the toxins in them, and this time I sent my results to the government. They thanked me and dumped the results in some filing cabinet. More people died and I sent my results to NGOs and international organizations, which published them in international journals and urged the government to do something about the flares, but nothing happened. (Habila 2011: 92)

Habila's critique is aimed at multiple and uneven constituents of the imperial formation: the colonial empire, the postcolonial nation state, the international academia and the oil corporation. In the process of exploring the imperial formation that constitutes contemporary Nigeria, this catachronism also sketches the future, where the contaminated land and water will contaminate human bodies for an uncertain length of time.

The visceral accounts of bodies, stench, sights and texture of land, people, living and non-living suggest a material rhetoric in order to speak of ecological ruin.[3] Ruination is etched on the land, on the bodies of its human *and* nonhuman inhabitants, as well as the non-living embedded in material matter such as water and the land.[4] In the process, Habila displaces the human from or as the centre of the disaster – thereby decolonizing it of the human – in that it is the nonhuman and the non-living that seem to be more ravaged than the human (here I am in consonance with Feldner's [2018] and Olaoluwa's [2020] arguments).

If Habila's African setting demonstrates the human–nonhuman cohabitation, the city of London is also similarly drawn in Maggie Gee's *The Flood* (2004). The novel opens with this emphasis on the nonhuman at a time before the flood:

> The earthly city, down on the plain. Designed for humans. And pets, their playthings.… Billions of microbes. Snails and worms. And birds, of course; visiting the gardens: nesting, foraging. Quivering, flashing on the flowering quinces. Calling sharp warnings against the cats. Jackdaws, thrushes, pigeons, starlings with dark silk rainbows on the wing. On Daffodil Hill, near the City Zoo, you saw how many, how beautiful: sky-wide, skimming trapezia of starlings, smoking at the edges as they turn on the blue.
>
> And urban foxes. Twisting and fossicking, yipping and screaming mobs of red musk. Narrow-faced, amber-eyed, rufous, fearless. And swarming rats, and mice, and pigeons. (6)

Later, Gee emphasizes that the vermin survive, thus demonstrating their peculiar resilience:

> [T]he rats are there, just beneath the floor, in the U-bends of the staff lavatories, and round by the bins, in a frenzy of activity, sniffing and whiffling at the wonderful plenty, the prawn heads, the chicken skins, the lambs' feet, the creamy shell of cooling fat skimmed off the gravy.… (228)

In this fashion, by focusing on the nonhuman, Gee suggests that even in extreme situations, a vast volume of life survives, indeed thrives. Stephen Baxter's Nathan in *Flood* speaks of human resilience which will help them survive:

> Our forefathers split off and started evolving adaptations for open country. The chimps stuck to the forest fragments, and you know what, they were still there when the fucking waters rose up to drown them.… The new watery age, the Hydrocene, is just another rough moulding, and we'll come through it, smarter and stronger.… (2008: 523)

Baxter's Nathan sees humanity as surviving, in some form (it may also be noted that his account is strongly reminiscent of a *deep history* position).[5] In the novel, as the world drowns, gigantic arks are built that will sail the seas forever, and children will be born adapted to water, as they once adapted to land.

In *Odds Against Tomorrow*, Nathaniel Rich depicts New York City's (and Seattle's) economies of scale that transform the land into a disaster topos.[6] Researching the threat prospects for NYC, Mitchell Zukor discovers:

> With depleted salt marshes, narrower beaches, eroded soil, and a higher water table – the East River and the Hudson had each risen eight inches in the past twenty years – the city had never been more susceptible to flooding. (Rich 2013, unpaginated)

Rich then gives us a deep history of the water bodies and canals over which NYC had been built. In the process, he proffers a cultural chronicle of the disaster's origins, which lie in centuries of human exploitative economies.

> In the days when Times Square was a red maple swamp and St. Mark's Place a hickory forest populated by hawks and ravens, more than forty brooks and streams covered the island of Manhattan.... His old office at Fitzsimmons Sherman stood over a little body of water called Sunfish Pond.... For all he knew, the pond was still there beneath the Empire State Building, percolating below the subbasement....
>
> All of these waterways were buried when the city was built in the eighteenth and nineteenth centuries, but the water didn't disappear – it still pumped through the undersoil. (Unpaginated)

Beneath the city that greed built are waterways highly revered by the original settlers, the Lenape Indians, notes Rich in the same passage. The city's increasing vulnerability is linked to a culture devoted to financial profits, wherein one could 'plo[t] disaster and figur[e] out how to profit from it' (unpaginated). The vulnerability of today originates in a specific kind of history, and the disaster cannot be seen as an event but as the culmination of a process. Indeed, NYC embodies greed itself as virtue because it believes collectively that 'greed is good' (unpaginated).

Like Habila, Rich shows how the catastrophic flooding affects *other*, nonhuman lives, again in the language of gritty realism:

The birds had returned, at least some of them. Seagulls, kingfishers, even a few pigeons. In the absence of traffic and human voices, their calls filled the air. The melodies weren't particularly joyous – it was mostly a furor of confused squawking, their imbecilic brains having lost all sense of orientation. Still they were a reminder of a life that existed beyond the fog and the alien gray river. (2013, unpaginated)

The nonhuman life forms return to claim the land, but they have lost their bearings as a result of the ruined, waterlogged landscape. The nonhuman and the non-living are inheritors of an earth that can no longer sustain them, for the new hydro-social order created by humans has recolonized (destroyed) their habitats and their cognitive abilities. When the humans imperially expand their dominions, the nonhuman loses its grounds, so that when the flooding finally occurs, *both* humans and nonhumans are displaced.

Greed and exploitation as a systemic condition engendered by the state is everywhere in contemporary hydrofiction. Referencing this condition in the context of the USA, Paolo Bacigalupi says: 'a pile of unexploited water rights changed the game for half of the American West' (2015: 231). The control over natural resources determined the fate of civilizations: of the Native Americans but also of the white man who colonized the land and all the available water. In *Bangkok Wakes to Rain*, Pitchaya Sudbanthad speaks of the 'merchant galleon captains [who] paid the flooded grassland no mind as they floated upriver', no doubt in pursuit of riches (2019: 111). These were the same grasslands, notes Sudbanthad, that 'Burmese soldiers laid torches' to (111), once again linking land and ecological conditions to a history of trade and colonialism.

Arcologies are built in Bacigalupi's *The Water Knife* for a segment of humanity to survive without ever having to leave the building and encountering the sun, the drought or the dust of the world. But the arcology is a desperate measure in an era when most of the USA's water bodies have dried up and whatever water remains has been corporatized with militia employed to regulate supply and use. The water from 'Carson Creek, Cypress 1's fly-fishing river … cascaded through various levels of the arcology before being pumped back to the top of the system to run through a new cleaning cycle', writes Bacigalupi, again demonstrating how the ecosystem has been engineered to serve the arcology's luxury homes and offices (2015: 5). This ecosystem has replaced an older one, of the Pima tribes of the area: 'the Pima … descended from the Hohokam, who used to farm this area, back in the twelve hundreds' (231). Bacigalupi is pointing to historical vulnerabilities where development – symbolized in the arcologies – has replaced traditional Native American farming, just as the white man has replaced the Native American, in the process severely depleting the resources and monopolizing whatever was left.

The irony is, as Rich's novel indicates, such histories of previous instances of flooding and disasters are not even retained in the collective memory of the people. In Pitchaya Sudbanthad's *Bangkok Wakes to Rain*, he writes:

> Old memories of the flooded city had faded. It was simply raining hard, like it had always rained around this time of the year … the sun would soon appear and steam the roads dry, as it had always done. (2019: 196)

> Except the city wouldn't be rid of the puddles. The puddles soon turned curbs into ankle-deep streams … some spilled across major intersections … along canals stilt-house dwellers nervously eyed the waterline. Marks from previous years disappeared into the murky, dirt-stained flow beneath their homes. (196)

Sudbanthad's novel speaks of memories of disasters that are etched into houses and structures, and which ought to serve as cautionary texts about a future reiteration of the event but which people choose to ignore, until the next deluge.

Memories of disaster, Sudbanthad suggests, are erased, just like flood waters erase buildings and people. A similar image of erasure may be seen in *The Hungry Tide*, where an entire forest is drowned:

> Stretching away from them in every direction, as far as Piya's eye could reach, was a heaving carpet of leaves. Almost nothing was visible of the water's surface; the usual ripples, eddies and currents had disappeared under this layer of green. As for the island itself, it was entirely submerged, and its shape could be deduced only from the few thickets of trees whose uppermost reaches were still visible above water. These trees had a skeletal, forlorn look; few had any branches remaining and there was scarcely one that still had a leaf attached. (Ghosh 2004: 388)

If, as Adam Trexler argues, the rising river 'alters and erases not just geographical detail but also human connections to place' (2015: 107), so are signs of such events in the past. Water, then, levels terrain literally and metaphorically.

Quantificatory Realism

Nathaniel Rich in *Odds Against Tomorrow* (2013), even before he speaks of the flooding that drowns NYC and much of the USA, explores the economy of 'natural' disaster. The Fitzsimmons company's Board of Directors meets to ponder this question: 'If the Empire State Building fell, *how much* would it cost Fitzsimmons? Could we avoid paying as much as our friends in Seattle?' (emphasis added). Speculation on future catastrophes drives profits in Rich's novel. The company Zukor eventually joins, FutureWorld (headed by the drolly named Alec Charnoble), describes itself thus:

> FutureWorld is a private consulting firm.... We specialize in minimizing losses that may result from unforeseen or worst-case-imaginable scenarios. We will study your company's holdings, predict all possible future outcomes, highlight the most grievous, and explain what options might be available to you. Most important, we can indemnify you against liability claims brought against you in the wake of a catastrophe. (Unpaginated)

FutureWorld hires Zukor because he computes the odds of disaster for them to design insurance policies for those who are terrified by the odds. Zukor even seeks to calculate the odds of his own death: 'Odds-of-death chart (death by earthquake, 1 in 153,597; death by air accident, 1 in 5,862; death by accidental poisoning, 1 in 139)' (unpaginated).

And elsewhere:

> In the United States there were 900,000 elevators, each serving an average of 20,000 people per year. That meant eighteen billion passenger trips per year. These trips resulted in twenty-seven deaths. The chance of dying in an elevator accident was therefore one in 10.44 (repeating) million – about equivalent to the odds of dying from a dog bite, according to the National Safety Council odds-of-death chart he kept in his wallet.... (Unpaginated)

This quantificatory method, which gives a supposedly realist estimate of potential disaster, resource utilization and risk management, is employed by humans in Bacigalupi's text for a different purpose. He writes:

> Numbers flickering over the various catchment basins of the Rocky Mountains – red, amber, green – monitoring how much snow cover remained and variation off the norm as it melted. Other numbers, displaying the depths of reservoirs and dams, from the Blue Mesa Dam on the Gunnison, to the Navajo Dam on the San Juan, to the Flaming Gorge Dam on the Green. Over it all, emergency purchase prices on streamflows and futures offers scrolled via NASDAQ.... (2015: 6)

These, says Bacigalupi, are 'unforgiving numbers' (7).

But there are other unforgiving numbers too: the metered water that everyone buys. Digital meters fixed to the supply line indicate how much anyone can buy. The buyers celebrate as prices per litre fall:

> $5.85.
> $4.70.
> $3.60. (47)

Then the system discovers the falling prices and kicks back in:

> Already the price was rising. Kicking up as rich people's automated household systems caught the price break and started pumping gallons into cisterns. Or maybe it was the Taiyang Arcology getting in on the action, accelerating the buy as it realized the surplus was worth gorging on. The numbers flickered:
> $2.90 … $3.10 … $4.50 … $4.45…
> $5.50.
> $6.50.
> $7.05.
> $7.10.
>
> Order restored. (49)

The climbing numbers reflect a system of regulation, and the climactic phrase 'order restored' refers to the return of total control over the elements, concomitant with both commercialization and denial of the same to the poor of the urban area. The imperial cadastral survey and mapping projects (in the USA, South Asia and Africa) are a part of the postcolonial state too.

Quantificatory realism in these texts subjects the landscape, its features ('nature') and processes to rational or scientific assessment, involving close observation (with or without devices such as the digital meters in Bacigalupi), relating the parts to the whole and thereby making the condition of crisis – drought, flood – the condition of geological, financial and mathematical inquiry. Quantificatory realism is frightening because it captures in a narrative the *extent* of damage, control and social engineering at work. To adapt Ursula Heise's argument about vignettes of extinction in Mayra Montero's *In the Palm of Darkness*:

In texts such as these, the catalogs that accompany and complement the narrative evoke a numerical sublime of sorts, numbers too large to be contained by conventional storytelling procedures that focus on a discrete set of events, scenes, and characters. (Heise 2016: 56)

The inventories and numbers are also more in alignment with the call Michael Segal (2017) has issued: for the scientific narrative of climate change to enter the public discourse and debate around the phenomenon and process.[7]

If water shortage is quantified as numbers in Bacigalupi, it is excess water and its effects that is quantified in Rich's novel:

'How is it?' Jane asked Herman. 'In New York?'

'You know it's real bad', said Herman, 'because you can't see anything. I mean, there's news videos, things like that? I seen waves – I'm saying whitecaps – on Broadway. Right in front of Lincoln Center. Taxis – a dozen? Floating in a pack down First Avenue. Like a school of whales. Yellowback whales'.

'Have you heard any numbers?' asked Jane. (2013, unpaginated)

In the face of overwhelming human suffering – Rich speaks of people clinging to rooftops awaiting rescue – the culture that is the USA falls back on numbers again:

Behind the administration desk, set up on what had been public tennis courts, a large whiteboard listed neighborhoods next to their flood-depth figures. Every hour the numbers were updated by a woman…. (Unpaginated)

Ghosh's novel suggests that technology and its instrumental rationality fail in the face of the elements. Despite the Global Positioning System (GPS) and the phones, Piya cannot survive the storm but for the help of the native Fokir. Ghosh indicates that metropolitan knowledge fails, and what saves the human is the indigenous canny. The mystic version of the postcolonial – beyond maps, devices and quantification – however, is not a romanticization of the local. When the novel concludes, Ghosh has made a significant move: he integrates the 'rational' postcolonial with the 'mystic' one and proposes a newer humanist vision. When Piya proposes a database, a cyclone warning system and a greater commitment to local knowledge in Fokir's honour, we see a new postcolonial paradigm emerging, an indigenous canny that incorporates the spiritual-mystic within the technological modern. Piya's plans for the area are worth examining for this emergent postcolonial. Piya tells Nilima:

> All the routes Fokir showed me are stored here … Fokir took the boat into every little creek and gully where he'd ever seen a dolphin. That one map represents decades of work and volumes of knowledge. It's going to be the foundation of my own project. That's why I think it should be named after him. (Ghosh 2004: 398)

As I have suggested (Nayar 2010), Fokir is the ghostly data that will be, in Piya's words, the 'foundation' of her project. In a sense, then, Fokir is the spectre that returns to the body of data as incorporation. Both the uncanny and the tide country, unstable, uncertain, unreliable, and, therefore, lacking in strong 'foundations', suddenly move towards a foundation. The textual ghost of Fokir translates into the indigenous canny to be built upon by Piya and others in the imaginable future.

Grimy and quantificatory realism together communicate a sense of the disaster and its prehistory, but also its limitations in works like Ghosh's. Drawing on a common knowledge of such predictions of the future and incidents such as Katrina and other events in the past, the novels convey plausible scenarios and a familiar history of devastation. But this – the imperial legacy and the disaster – is not the only emphasis in the hydronovel, which also looks to the future and thereby constitutes its catachronism.

Catastrophic Irrealism

In Bacigalupi, the numbers or metrics already cited earlier also signal the corporatization of resources such as water, measured out in units and currency, but whose effects on humans – who fight for water – are unquantifiable. In Rich, speculations about disaster are in financial terms and probability statistics. There can be a mathematical magnitude to a disaster in terms of numbers of lives lost, the financial ruin, buildings collapsed, communities displaced, and so on. But there remains an unquantifiable aspect of the disaster: the human struggle to survive in the face of drought, floods and other cataclysmic events. This unquantifiable *sense* of disastrous effects is often captured in an aesthetic of what can be called catastrophic irrealism in the hydronovels.

Mitchell Zukor's account in *Odds Against Tomorrow*, when the storm finally hits NYC, gestures at such an aesthetic:

> I've spent a lifetime worrying about this moment, doing the calculations, taking the measurements, trying to render catastrophe in calculable, precise dimensions, and still I'm not prepared? But real catastrophe was like that. It was a form of genius. It astounded expectations, was unlike anything that came before. (2013, unpaginated)

Zukor is addressing the disaster that exceeds and defeats all calculations and speculations.

In more ways than one, Rich suggests, NYC is a 'centre of calculation' (Bruno Latour's term adapted by Tony Bennett (2004: 123) and which I use here in an ironic fashion) where capital and knowledge all flow towards the city, and it becomes the controlling centre of the world. Yet, when catastrophe finally arrives, the loss is *incalculable*, despite the amount of number crunching that corporations like Fitzsimmons or FutureWorld do.

The incalculability of the consequences of disaster is cast in multiple ways that I subsume under the term 'irrealism'. 'Irrealism' includes 'elements of the fantastic, the marvellous or the dreamlike' (Niblett 2015: 269). It generates 'some kind of minor disruption to an otherwise realist work' (278), and as a result the overall realist nature of the work may have an 'underlying sense of irreality' (279).

Irrealism manifests in the form of foggy memories and spectral manifestations in *Oil on Water*. Here is Habila's opening paragraph:

> I am walking down a well-lit path, with incidents neatly labeled and dated, but when I reach halfway memory lets go of my hand, and a fog rises and covers the faces and places, and I am left clawing about in the dark, lost, and I have to make up the obscured moments as I go along. (2011: 3)

Only when the mental-emotional fog lifts can even a recall of the disaster, the arson around oil refineries and the loss of lives become possible:

> The fog lifts as suddenly as it descended, and the sun shines brightly again, and once more I am on sure ground, but I know the fog can return again, get into memory's eyes, blinding it momentarily. (4)

Immediately *after* this account of the metaphoric fog, Habila describes the misty landscape in a passage that resonates with Marlowe's experience when travelling through Africa in Joseph Conrad's *Heart of Darkness* (1974):

> After a while the sky and the water and the dense foliage on the riverbanks all looked the same: blue and green and blue-green misty. The whole landscape was now a mere trick of light, vaporous and shape-shifting, appearing and disappearing behind the fog. (Habila 2011: 4)[8]

Water, which is the key site of the novel, is itself described in an irrealist way:

> the receding waterfront and the swath of white foamy furrow following in the boat's wake, curving when we curved, a soothing and mesmerizing sight that for a moment took my mind off whatever awaited us at our rendezvous. (67)

The elements – fog, the river and the land – possess an agency despite human presence (Liebermann and Neumann 2020: 159–160).

Perhaps the most effective irrealist account of the pluvial time and lands are to be found in Amitav Ghosh's *The Hungry Tide*. As I have argued elsewhere, the 'story' of the novel is inseparable from the shape, form, texture and history of the waterlogged Sunderbans land (Nayar 2010). The opening description of the landscape suggests both a setting and a metaphor:

> The rivers' channels are spread across the land like a fine-mesh net, creating a terrain where the boundaries between land and water are always mutating, always unpredictable.... When these channels meet ... at these confluences, the water stretches back to the far edges of the landscape and the forest dwindles into a distant rumour of land, echoing back from the horizon. In the language of the place, such a confluence is spoken of as a *mohona* – a strangely seductive word, wrapped in many layers of beguilement.
>
> There are no borders here to divide fresh water from salt, river from sea ... some say the water tears away entire promontories and peninsulas; at other times it throws up new shelves and sandbanks where there were none before.
>
> When the tides create new land, overnight mangroves begin to gestate.... (Ghosh 2004: 6–7)

Later Ghosh paints the land – which is effectively a land–water convergence – as unreadable, unpredictable and therefore uncontrollable:

> The freshly laid silt that bordered the water glistened in the sun like dunes of melted chocolate. From time to time, bubbles of air rose from the depths and burst through to the top, leaving rings upon the burnished surface. The sounds seemed almost to form articulate patterns, as if to suggest they were giving voice to the depths of the earth itself. (24)

Ghosh is gesturing at a prehuman time, the geological time of the earth itself, and therefore beyond comprehension by or for humans.

This is *terrain* rather than territory, to adapt Stuart Elden's formulation (2021; also Squire 2021). Elden has argued that we 'think about territory in relation to political-legal questions – where does the law apply, where does it cease to apply, and what kind of law is operable – and political-technical ones, including practices like surveying, measuring, cartography, and navigation' (2021: 174). Elden opts for the term 'terrain' and cites Gaston Gordillo's work where 'terrain' 'evokes material forms, volumes and textures that are not reducible to human control and appropriations'. Elden adds: 'while territory is shaped and made by human actions, the landscapes which those actions inherit, divide, command, and transform cannot be seen as entirely under their control' (2021: 175). Some-thing, Elden suggests, escapes human control.

In Ghosh's catastrophic irrealism, the land shapes the narrative even as the language constructs the land:

> The mudbanks of the tide country are shaped not only by rivers of silt, but also by rivers of language: Bengali, English, Arabic, Hindi, Arakanese and who knows what else … the tide country's faith is something like one of its great *mohonas*, a meeting not just of many rivers, but a circular round-about people can use to pass in many directions. (2004: 247)

The land, suggests Ghosh, is its languages, myths, stories – merging the material and the symbolic worlds.

Serpell's final scenes are catachronistic: 'Lake Kariba *would* soon become a river. The dam would become a waterfall. And miles away, the Lusaka plateau … would become an island….' (2019: 559, emphasis added).

Such passages, with their dream-like quality and blurred realities, contrast with the grimy realism of Habila's or Serpell's descriptions of the land and its victims. But Habila undermines the gritty realism with the irrealism of passages such as the above, suggesting that despite the land's best efforts in the form of the fog or the river, the human-inflicted damage marches on. Note, for instance, this scene:

The old man Tamuno saw the helicopter first. I couldn't see anything from where I stood, but I could hear the roar. The fog rose off the water and the mangrove leaves like smoke from wet kindling, blanketing the air and the sky for miles around. Then suddenly the helicopter appeared overhead, shrouded in its engine's riotous noise, the air pressure from its rotor parting the fog. It banked and cycled and hovered, its weight seemingly borne by the white fog, and I saw the huge oil-company logo on its side. From an open window a guard leaned down, his eyes covered in huge goggles, his machine gun poking through the open window. (Habila 2011: 42)

Despite the thick fog blanking out everything, the logo on the helicopter penetrates the landscape, the visual scene and the senses of Rufus and his companions. The helicopter, carrying armed soldiers, descends from the skies to meet the fog that 'rose off the water'. I suggest that Habila depicts the mystic power of the land colliding with the grim power of human weaponry as well as the symbolic power of the oil company's logo, a sign of neoimperial formations that have taken control over Africa's resources through a nexus of white capitalism and the postcolonial state. The logo is not concealable by Africa's fog or cloud cover – it scythes through all of that and imposes itself as a visual on the eyes and mind of the people. The gun poking out of the window is a supplement – in the Derridean sense – to the logo, for it completes the iconography of corporate conquest of the land, but is still an excess, because the logo is no less effective than a gun in demonstrating power over the land. The 'riotous noise' and the logo working in conjunction is the exact contrast to the state of being fogged in: the oil company's apparatus is a sensory assault itself. Thus, in Habila's catastrophic irrealism, the *unsettling* experience of being fogged in, which has once disrupted the realist mode of disaster description, is in turn disrupted by the techno-symbolic conquest of the air in the form of the machine and the logo that penetrates the fog surrounding the village.

My argument about catastrophic irrealism as an aesthetic that captures unquantifiable loss is reinforced towards the end of the novel when Habila writes:

I looked outside at the forest and the abandoned boats on the water, the few thatched huts, and I thought, what could fate possibly want with her on these oil-polluted waters? The forsaken villages, the gas flares, the stumps of pipes from exhausted wells with their heads capped and left jutting out of the oil-scorched earth, and the ever-present pipelines crisscrossing the landscape, sometimes like tree roots surfacing far away from the parent tree, sometimes like diseased veins on the back of an old shriveled hand, and sometimes in squiggles like ominous writing on the wall. Maybe fate wanted to show her firsthand the carcasses of the fish and crabs and waterbirds that floated on the deserted beaches of these tiny towns and villages and islands every morning, killed by the oil her husband was helping to produce. (2011: 175)

The crude reality of the oil pipelines cuts through the landscape. The comparison is to the natural phenomena of tree roots and the diseased veins of old people, but also to a metaphor: 'squiggles like ominous writing on the wall'. Catastrophic irrealism is here embodied in the portenting inscriptions – unsubstantiated, unquantifiable – of disaster. The images so juxtaposed are instantiations of a catastrophic irrealism where the brutal reality of the pipelines merges with the realist image of roots and veins, but then morphs into a surreal metaphor of the 'writing on the wall', thus gesturing at and portending the future (captured in the descriptor, 'ominous'). If Rich's novel spoke of speculations about the future, Habila – in a strange resonance of this theme about calculating disaster – speaks of the 'writing on the wall'.[9]

Catastrophic irrealism appears in a slightly different manner in *Odds Against Tomorrow*. The quantifier Zukor, who has come to know a Bruguda patient, Elsa, is appalled that she is unafraid of imminent death. He computes her chances as follows:

Mitchell had done the dreadful calculation. It could be reduced to a single number: 1 in 53, or 1.89 percent. These were the odds that a Brugada patient who had already had multiple syncopes would have a fatal attack in the coming year. That was exponentially more likely than the odds of dying from drug or alcohol abuse (1 in 10,837) or an accidental injury (1 in 2,454). There was no mathematical analysis that could make that 1 in 53 less frightening. When you broadened the time frame, the numbers only became uglier. The odds of a fatal syncope in two years: 3.7 percent; in five: 8.7 percent; by the time she turned thirty: 13.2 percent. But Elsa, like curious Sarah Axon in Iowa, seemed oblivious to fear.... (Unpaginated)

Elsa's refusal to be afraid is something Zukor is both afraid and admiring of and realizes that it is his attempt to quantify risk that is irrealistic. The danger and the catastrophe, like the company's logo in *Oil on Water*, erupt *through* and *despite* the numbers, the science and the beliefs. In other words, the catastrophe's occurrence may be computable in terms of likelihood and predictions – what Zukor likes to think of as 'order' and 'logic' – but incalculable in terms of loss of sense, identity and belongingness. And yet, Zukor not only mathematizes risk predictions of catastrophe, he also *dreams* them up:

> The way other people fantasize about surprise inheritances, first-glance love, and endless white empyreal pastures, Mitchell dreamed of an erupting supervolcano that would bury North America under a foot of hot ash. He envisioned a nuclear exchange with China; a modern black plague; an asteroid tearing apart the crust of the earth, unleashing a new dark age. Such singularities didn't frighten him, he claimed; they offered freedom. They opened wormholes to a sublime realm of fantasy and chaos. Worst-case scenarios, he said, were for him games of logic. How vast a nightmare could he imagine, and to what level of precision? What was possible? What should we be afraid of? (Unpaginated)

If irrealism is a mixture of the marvellous and the dream-like, Zukor's fantasies and terrifying nightmare visions, which he tries to convert into numbers, represent a catastrophic irrealism.

Gee's irrealism when speaking of the catastrophic drowning of London takes the form of a liquid aesthetics. She first paints the end of rains: 'After months of rain, the sun broke through' (2004, unpaginated). Then, as Adam Trexler has noted (2015: 112), even the waterlogged city has its own aesthetic moments: 'Water on roads, walls, bridges, washed the lights into long slurs of colour, peacock-eyed where traffic lights stared. Trapped motorists listened to their radios' (unpaginated). There is an air suffused with water and light in flooded London, lending a surreal aura to the city. The bricks-and-mortal reality is rendered visually blurred.

In Serpell, the mosquitoes, the hardy survivor-witnesses to the disaster of the dam, issue the warning to humanity: 'and so we roil in the oldest of drifts – a slow, slant spin at the pit of the world, the darkest heart of them.... We're an asterisk to nature, a law, a digression, a footnote, the drift, the diversion, the swerve, the clinamen' (2019: 563). The mosquitoes, who have intergenerationally witnessed the rise and fall of the dam, look forward to the scenes of final destruction:

> when atoms plummet like rain through the void, they detect just enough that their paths divert ... every small stray opens up a new way, an Eden of forking digressions.... Where you sought an origin, you found a vast babble and bubbling – which is also a silence: a chasm of smoke, thundering. Blind mouth! (545)

The mosquitoes capture the redundancy, indeed futility, of human instrumental rationality too: 'their blueprints were old, their calculations too tight, they'd made no concession to chance. Indeed, their mistake – the Error of Errors – was simply forgetting the weather' (562).

In each of these cited passages there is a failure or redundancy of instrumental rationality, or its subsumption under myths, errors and an air of unreality.

Catastrophic irrealism, I suggest, is a critique of the instrumental rationality of calculating and planning for the future risks, but also of the realist narrative mode through which an account of the disaster is provided. Irrealism is the clinamen, the swerve and the spin, as Serpell puts it, to the development narrative as well. In other cases, dreams of power and the illusions of risk management, for instance, are exposed as myths in Rich's novel. No calculation can prepare anyone for the disaster.

Other forms of preparedness for the coming disaster are also revealed to be inadequate. In Bacigalupi's novel, the super-rich who inhabit the arcologies are in fact living under the same illusion as the 'preppers' (who stock up essential goods like water and hope to outlast the catastrophic conditions in their town or region). This is what the 'water knife', Angel Velasquez, says about the preppers: 'Never could figure out why people would think they could survive all out on their lonesome like that. All of them sitting in their little bunkers, thinking they're going to ride out the apocalypse alone' (2015: 329). And to this Lily responds: 'Maybe they watch too many old Westerns' (329). Taken together, these two comments underline the delusional foundations of the 'prepper' way of life, drawn from myth and film equally.

Both, the arcology residents and the preppers, are marked by the same disconnect from the planet, withdrawing into their respective bunkers. Both of them *dream* of water:

In her dreams they were always vast lakes, deep underground, cooler and more inviting than any abandoned basement, huge caverns filled with water. Sometimes she dreamed that she rowed a boat across those wet cathedral spaces with stalactites phosphorescing overhead.... The roof of the cavern had glowed, and Maria had drifted across those dark reflecting waters, listening to water dripping, trailing her fingers in the soft cool liquid. (46)

Forced to drink their own urine due to the shortage of water, there is only the dream of water for most of the people in Phoenix. Catastrophic irrealism transforms the disaster into a nightmare, a blurred, unclear and yet threatening state of being.

All novels capture imperial formations from the past that continue into the present and, when projected into the future, have catastrophic effects. That is, the novel reappraises the past as determining the present and the future, a future whose exact contours are immeasurable yet proleptically communicate a sense of the future.

We see this most explicitly in texts like Rich's. Rich writes:

> New York would come back, certainly Manhattan and perhaps certain swaths of Brooklyn. But what about the long term? For the long term was now upon them. According to the scientists, these would become the presiding conditions. Over the next years and decades, things would not be as before. Things would be, for starters, a lot wetter. The floods would keep coming, more and more frequently. Soon the coastal cities would lose the will to rebuild the old seawalls and levees. No one would have to pay to hear about worst-case scenarios – they'd be living them night and day. The future would vanish as a preoccupation; the present would consume man's full energies. (2013, unpaginated)

As she reports on collapsing cities like Detroit and Phoenix (which Bacigalupi terms 'collapse pornography', 2015: 24), Lucy in *The Water Knife* realizes that '[she] had the feeling that she wasn't so much eroticizing a city's death as excavating a future as it yawned below them. As if she were saying, *This is us. This is how we all end. There's only one door out, and we all use it*' (26, emphasis in original).

Both Rich and Bacigalupi see the 'long-term' as already here. That is, the future is not something entirely incalculable in terms of catastrophe, because one can visualize the 'end'. Habila offers a metaphor:

> Now the worshippers were in the water, swaying and humming … I had felt the same optimism days ago when I looked back from the militants' boat at Chief Ibiram and his people. They were a fragile flotilla, ordinary men and women and babies, a puny armada about to launch itself once more into uncertain waters. (2011: 216)

The fragile flotilla is not perhaps just Nigeria but the planet itself. Habila calls it an armada – reminiscent of a moment in early modern Europe's imperialist tensions – but it could very well be an ark. The 'uncertain waters' are a symbol of the planet's precarious future.

In *Odds Against Tomorrow*, Zukor eventually abandons his calculations and logic and (re)turns to the land.[10] He retreats to a commune and learns to grow his own food (albeit supported by infusion of materials from the city and his former associate, Jane Eppler). This luddite-Thoreau vision with which Rich seeks to end the novel is itself catachronistic. As in the numerous Octavia Butler novels about post-apocalyptic earth, Rich's character has also romanticized a 'return' to the earth, learning to live off the land. Now that NYC, the 'empire city', has been ruined, this romantic community is all there is, in Zukor's view. This 'return and retreat' to the pastoral, notes Astrid Bracke, is a major theme in the climate change novel (2018: 60–61).

However, the pastoral ideal replicates class and social distinctions. In Stephen Baxter's *Flood*, there is a clear class distinction between those who sail on the luxurious arks and those pockets of humanity surviving on rafts and boats. Maoist (who, says Baxter, 'have borrowed notions of castes from the Hindus for a theoretical justification. Here the farming of people is systematic', 2008, unpaginated) and Khmer Rouge–like groups control large swathes of Asia. As Baxter puts it about a slum in 'an ageing Utopia':

> A slum was still a slum, however the world changed. The children who stared out at Lily were sunken-faced and big-eyed with hunger. These were people who had been poor in vanished cities and were poor here now, people for whom the flood meant only that they had swapped a slum in a river valley for one in the mountains. (272)

In *The Water Knife*, the community of survivors led by Maria and Lucy, assisted by Toomie and the reformed water knife, Angel, and armed with the treaty from the Department of the Interior which would secure the water rights for the region, head towards Phoenix. The document would, it is implied, start a revolution by exposing the imperial formations of the nineteenth century:

> Department of the Interior, Bureau of Indian Affairs, the signatures of tribal leaders…. Liquid promises. Symbolic compromises for a moment that no one expected to ever come. Millions of acre-feet of water. The missing piece to a puzzle that would allow the pumps of the Central Arizona Project to roar fully to life. With rights like these, they could dig new and deeper canals. Rechannel the Colorado away from California, away from Nevada. Pour water into a different set of deserts and a different set of cities. A few simple sheets of paper with the power to make Phoenix and Arizona the arbiters of their own fate instead of a place of loss and collapse. (Bacigalupi 2015: 363)

'Rechannel' is an anastomosing of past and present: an old treaty that can revive the future, where it is not water alone but rights, autonomy and lives that are being rechannelled away from the corporatized control back towards control by the people of the region.

The catachronistic novels clearly capture the historical vulnerabilities and the vulnerabilities engendered by historical processes such as colonization, urbanization and financial speculation. Refusing to see the disaster exclusively in terms of the event or accident (flood, climate change, hurricanes), the catachronistic novels call attention to prehistories of the event while also signalling that *this* (the catastrophe) is also the future. The rise of petroindustries (Habila 2011), urban planning (Rich 2013) and racially determined land use (Bacigalupi 2015) are all instances of ecological imperialism, and the novels ask us to recognize these origins of contemporary *and* future disasters.

By focusing on continuities that have imperilled the earth and produced the disaster, the catachronistic novels implicitly signal not the end but a continuum, or an 'end period'. Joshua Gunn and David Beard (2000) tell us, following the work of Frank Kermode, we are in a state of 'immanent apocalypse'. In such an apocalypse, we are dwelling in the end period (Kermode 2000: 272). In other words, the catachronistic novels do not look forward to a time when the world will end, but embody the 'weight of End-feeling', 'throw[n] on to the moment, the crisis' (Kermode 2000: 25). The catachronistic novel decolonizes disaster studies by pointing not just to imperial legacies that engender disaster but also portent a continuum of disaster.

I now turn to a subgenre of the hydronovel, a set of graphic novels from the Indian subcontinent, in order to delineate a different kind of hydropoetics, what I shall call the hydrogothic.

The Postcolonial Hydrogothic

As the world's largest user of groundwater, India is faced with country-wide water crises. Problems include: drought; inefficiency in water resource management; privatization; deteriorating water quality (one report, cited in Khullar 2022, places India at 120 out of 122 countries in terms of water quality); and – despite schemes such as the Jal Jeevan Mission – predicted severe scarcity by 2030 (Khullar 2022). Indeed, the efficacy and dangers of large dams (McCully 1996) and the effects of privatization practices are moving Indian water away from a potential hydrocommons and towards a network of hydrocommodities, as satirized in *All Quiet in Vikaspuri* (Banerjee 2015).

The texts studied here include Orijit Sen's *River of Stories* (1994); Sarnath Banerjee's *All Quiet in Vikaspuri* (2015); Subhash Vyam and Gita Wolf's *Water* (2018); Venkat Ram Singh Shyam and S. Anand's *Finding My Way* (2016); and Srividya Natarajan, S. Anand and Durgabai and Subhas Vyam's *Bhimayana* (2011). *Bhimayana* is based on the life and autobiographical notes of social reformer, activist and constitutionalist B. R. Ambedkar, and it employs water-based imagery and metaphors to brilliant effect. Bannerjee's *All Quiet in Vikaspuri* is set in New Delhi and gives a fictional account of water wars, privatization and myths around water resources that map real-world issues and impacts. Sen's *River of Stories*, often credited with being the first graphic novel in India, is a thinly veiled account of the Sardar Sarovar Dam on the Narmada river and the crisis of displacement its construction produced. Like Banerjee, Sen also depicts local myths and legends around the Namada river. Vyam and Wolf's *Water* is a short text dealing with forest-dweller tribes (*adivasis*) and their river fables, comparing and contrasting urban and tribal approaches to water and nature. Shyam and Anand's *Finding My Way* presents the life stories of the artist, Shyam, and his uncle, but also the story of their tribe and its setting. In fact, all of these graphic novels merge the biographical with the autobiographical and the prosopographical, especially *Bhimayana*, *Water* and *Finding My Way*. In the process of giving us an individual's or family's life story, the author-artist teams invariably make the storytelling about their *community*, its setting and locales, by weaving together water-linked anecdotes, myths, histories, songs and legends. In addition, being known for his satiric tone, Banerjee incorporates slogans, urban advertising rhetoric, government-speak and more general political discourse into his narration to help ensure the reader understands that his hydrotheme is deeply embedded in a larger socio-political context. Where Bannerjee's and Sen's graphic novels are relatively conventional texts, following the panel system of comics, both *Water* and *Finding My Way* make use of Gond art in their illustrations, producing not only a local visual aesthetic within a graphic novel form but also enabling a certain freedom in drawing (minus the panels, for example) that points to their expansive and liberational political ambition. Put together, these strategies point to an aesthetic of hydroterror.

Maria Beville has explained that 'Gothic and political terrors have overlapped' in contemporary times (2009: 33–34), that Gothic terror is the 'culture of fear' that is 'fuelled by 'the spirit of terror', and that Gothic terror functions as a manifestation – often expressed in the spectral appearance of ghosts and other Others – of our subjective, and collective, desire to explore 'the darker side of our known 'realities' (31–32). Other critics have noted that a nation's grappling with its colonial past and legacies has often been expressed with, or through, the Gothic – as a way of capturing the terrors and ghosts of history, and to help process a traumatic past and its continuing effects, especially within literary spaces (Punter and Byron 2004; Ilott 2019). Writing about the USA and its cultural investment in the Gothic as a way of grappling with its 'new nation' status, Marilyn Michaud explains:

> Early republicans mythologized their own national formations in much the same way as the British Whigs and, like their English counterparts, viewed their Gothic history in binary terms: one of light and liberty, the other dark and barbarous; one an ancient Elysium, the other a feudal nightmare. (2009: 2)

The visual dimensions of this binarized Gothic history are especially useful for graphic novels tackling the new nation's nexus of potentiality – as light – and the continuation of inequality, exploitation and destruction, especially ecologically – as layers of darkness – after empire has formally ended. Referring to the 'conjoined experiences of colonization and environmental destruction', Hanna Straß proposes that we need to look at contemporary environmental crisis in terms of a historical continuity to which new forms of uneven, unjust and unequal practices have been added in the form of 'development' or 'industrialization' (2016: 228). Such an idea underpins work on the postcolonial novel's rendering of Gothic toxicity, as a strategy for registering environmental pollution or crisis, colonial histories and contemporary political choices in the postcolony. In fact, water-bound terrors are omnipresent in the social realm – through the organization of water, and through the ways in which water organizes the lives of humans and nonhumans, materially and symbolically – and are often explored in the literary-cultural domain.

I suggest here that hydroterror operates through three principal modes in the graphic novels – hydrogothicity, hydro-mythopoesis and hydrocolonialism. I argue that hydroterror captures the chaos, guilt, injustice and anxiety lurking beneath the façade and rhetoric of growth that are said to guide a new nation. Hydroterror is a thematic and aesthetic working, in this fiction, through the nightmare that is post-imperial development within capitalist modernity in a postcolony.

Hydrogothicity

In the graphic texts studied here, the hydrogothic, and its terror, is a specific subset of ecogothic. Sharae Deckard usefully defines the ecogothic as

> expressing critique of the domination of nature in late capitalism, criticising dualist myths that separate notions of the human from nature rather than embracing humanity-in-nature, or summoning spectres of past ecological disasters in order to explore the complex causality of compound catastrophes. (2019b: 174–175)

Deckard also explains that the ecogothic can express criticism 'of the domination of nature in late capitalism' and can make use of 'spectres of past ecological disasters in order to explore the complex causality of compound catastrophes' (174–175). Such 'spectres of past ecological disasters' and their links to contemporary 'development' agendas under late capital in India are significant in Indian graphic novels. In such works the ecogothic-as-hydrogothic emerges from the hydrocolonialism that marks India's water wars and water crises.

We see this clearly in Banerjee's *All Quiet in Vikaspuri*. Documenting the erosion of the social order and lives of the people of the Tambapur township, Bannerjee's text pays particular attention to the local water filtration plant that had been 'abandoned' and, consequently, the water that 'had become toxic, leading to terrible diseases' (2015: 11). The region's 'water table fell drastically' and instead 'slimy ponds emerged everywhere' (11). Several features of the one-page panel documenting the crippling forms of hydrocolonialism at play deserve particular attention because they produce a Gothic hydroterror, with the water tank itself depicted as a monstrous embodiment of 'development' in the postcolony.

The water filtration plant lying decrepit with flotsam inside and outside it captures a near-Gothic erosion of an otherwise coherent structure. Cracks appear on the walls of the plant and branches stick out from it as though nature has encroached upon and through the human-made structure. Immediately below this is an image of a 'slimy pond' in an ecogothic representation. Two figures watch the pond. From the pond a hand with overgrown nails sticks out – whether this is of someone drowning or some kind of 'swamp thing' emerging is not clear. If the former, then it implies that the slimy pond swallows the living. If the latter – and this is my preferred interpretation because the emaciated hand with extra-long nails is reminiscent of typical horror-creatures – then the monstrosities of the deep have been dislodged and they have risen to the surface in a classic return of the repressed gesture. The image marks the contradictory relation to life that arises when water becomes toxic – in that life may come from the water but toxic water also brings death to all forms of life. In this way, Banerjee's employment of the image of water as toxic pushes the reader to see this contradiction as a kind of hydroterror. The image inverts the conventional values associated with water: water as cleansing, life-sustaining and regenerative. But in this case, water produces decay, deterioration and death – that is, it takes life and terrorizes the living.

Hydroterror also emerges from another figuration in *All Quiet in Vikaspuri*. In New Delhi, as the text makes clear, water is a precious commodity and battles are fought over it and ghettos arm themselves to defend their supplies. The Delhi Jal (Water) Board has been the centre of controversy ever since the management of its water supply and sewerage lines were set to be privatized, from 2005 onwards, and a Water Privatisation-Commercialisation Resistance Committee was formed by concerned citizens in the early days of the move to privatize water (see India Water Portal 2012). Banerjee situates his tale within water scarcity and the moves to privatize water. In *All Quiet in Vikaspuri* the quest for mythical and real water resources – such as the river Saraswati – is a key theme. In the subterranean recesses of the earth, Girish, the plumber, is searching for water at the behest of a water diviner when he encounters a large number of humans. These include corrupt government officials, a foreigner, a former army man and a water supplier. They are *all* humans who have battled to undermine or subvert the strict classification and organization of water. Awasthy cut down trees, Tanker Rajan procured water illegally, Philippa Jones wasted water, Gambhir stole water and Jagat Ram billed water usage incorrectly. Thus, the characters embody a critical questioning of the current water system. They force us to ask questions about water rights (as in the case of *The Water Knife*) and the legal and political jurisdiction over water resources.

Consequently, all of these characters are positioned as simultaneously human and 'Other' to the human-designed hydroregime of water supply and consumption they encounter and challenge. They exist on the border between the living and the dead, and are the kind of humans that might best be described as 'abhumans', that is, those whose loss of human specificity pushes them underground. Tracing the concept of the abhuman, Kelly Hurley describes how this figure 'retains vestiges of its human identity, but has already become, or is in the process of becoming, some half-human other – wolfish, or simian, or tentacled, or fungoid, perhaps simply "unspeakable" in its gross, changeful corporeality' (2002: 190). This mutation enables, as Hurley explains, the abhuman to become 'some unimaginable "thing" incorporating, mimicking, or taking on a human form, thereby constituting another kind of threat to the integrity of human identity' (190). In Banerjee's text, then, the underground dwellers seeking water are degenerate(d) humans, pushed to become 'abhumans' because of the dangers and difficulties involved in obtaining the life-giving powers of water. Living beneath the earth – which is also the originary site for water – the abhumans represent the chaos that surrounds water, at source, and their underground existence inverts the accepted order of life above ground. In this way, Banerjee's abhumans are hydro-abhumans and fit with Hurley's view of the gothic as 'the realm of disorder, wherein cultural ordering systems are revealed as always already having collapsed' – in this case the water- or hyrdo-ordering system – and as the mechanism whose chaotic possibilities can enable 'a certain gleefulness at the prospect of a world in which no fixity remains, only an endless series of monstrous becomings' (Hurley 1995: 28). These hydro-abhumans were abominations when alive, tampering with the water supply, corrupt and disorderly, and now they exist underground in a state or condition somewhere between the living and the dead. The 'water wars' of Banergee's text, then, involve the humans on the surface and these hydro-abhumans underground, with the 'Saraswati sena' entering the earth's depths to seek the mythical river and finding the death-in-life or life-in-death hydro-denizens of the deep. In this state, Banergee's hydro-abhumans signal a different form of life that cannot be entirely controlled by the capitalist world above and might be read as a version of Deckard and Oloff's (2020) 'oceanic weird'.

Where terror is typically bound to ideas of excess, the hydroterror of the graphic novel also emerges from a sense of excess, and while the presentation of gothic excess varies across the genre, it is often compounded by what Hurley calls a 'gratuitous Gothicity' (1995: 154) – that is, an indulged, extravagant and determined display of the gothic-in-excess. In fictional texts like *All Quiet in Vikaspuri* and *River of Stories*, the bureaucracy, the culture of development and urbanization are the sources of excessive and alienating hydro-regulation and hydro-commodification that are challenged through scenes of chaotic disorder as well as the abhumanness of those underground. In auto/biographies, real-life incidents are retold through terrorizing metaphors and images of excess that establish an over-determined sense of hydro-horror. For example, in a key incident in *Bhimayana*, Ambedkar and his travelling companions are refused water from the village water tank. The reader sees the tank, in the drawing, as filled to the brim, its border coterminous with the body of a fish. The tank also has – perched on its edge – a pair of feet pointing into the tank's waters, suggesting someone is looking into the water tank, but the rest of the human form is *not* drawn. The feet stand in isolation. Then, horrifyingly, a pair of detached hands float in the tank. The hands are drawn or positioned in such a way as to suggest they belong to the same body, or person, as the feet and the terrorizing effect of this water-determined dismemberment can be discerned through a reading of the text and image.

Ambedkar's experience, metonymic of the exclusion of specific communities from sources of water, is cast as an image of dismemberment. The illustration implies either a broken body or a dissolved one is within the water – and this establishes a gratuitous Gothicity, wherein all such representations are primarily excessive in terms of the plot movement, as Hurley argues. The disembodied hands and feet seem excessive because there is *no* corporeal violence in the anecdote, and, therefore, the broken or dismembered body appears to be a gratuitous image of structural violence as it becomes embodied. This idea is borne out in the accompanying text, which says '*Dheds*! Untouchables! They've polluted the tank!' (Natarajan et al. 2011: 85) Here 'pollution' – the key term in caste conceptions of untouchability – is deemed to occur via both physical contact and an immaterial, symbolic contact with the shadow of the 'Dalit' falling upon the upper castes. Hands that touch or shadows that 'fall' upon the cultural Other are instantiations of the tyrannical social order. But in the text they also signify something more. The dismembered hands and feet are mnemonic signifiers of the consequences of polluting the tank: the memory of historical violence that has always been inflicted upon the Dalits who dared quench their thirst at the (common) water resource. Thus, the text and the image are only gratuitous as part of an effort to capture the real-world excesses of exclusion of violence made obvious in relation to water. The dismemberment images occur at that point in the narrative where incidents of Dalits being beaten up for seeking water or digging wells have already been narrated (55). That is, the dismembered – materially and symbolically – 'untouchable' body evidences a hydroterror induced by our memories of the terrors inflicted upon Dalits for seeking their share of water. It is left to the reader to consider whether the 'untouchable' body has been drowned in the tank, or whether the body parts are scattered in it. This last interpretation is invited by the horrific news items from contemporary India documented a few pages later in the text. With the reports of 'Water wars, Dalit woman torched' and 'Dalit killed for digging own well' (47), the reader is reminded of the hydro-terrors facing Dalits in India and the manner in which their own bodies are part of a continual search for water in order to survive. At the same time, these moments of hydroterror also convey a sense of unfulfilled desire – for water, for equity and equality. The use of hydroterror becomes, then, a way to imagine and demonstrate a desire for what water *could* be or could enable, especially for those currently excluded and endangered.

Rather than the terrors characteristic of Gothic or noir writing, the graphic texts employ the aesthetic social realism in order to inscribe the fears, anxieties and threats associated with the consumption of water, the iniquitous social order, the politics of development and the modalities of state or corporate 'development'. Hydroterror emerges from the brutal victimization, predation and socio-political darkness connected to water and its consumption. Other than this form of corporeal and abject horror, one discerns another. This is the latent horror that we discern when, underneath the stories of progress, development and democracy lies the materiality of social inequity and injustice on an unimaginable scale. *Bhimayana* documents the caste-based privileges over water. Sen's *River of Stories* shows how tribals and others lose rather than gain from the hydel projects on their rivers. And in *Finding My Way* Shyam draws a knotted river, symbolizing the choking of the waters. Hydroterror, then, is the nightmare that is development. It captures the chaos, the guilt, the injustice, anxieties – as with Ambedkar's anguish at being denied water (Natarajan et al. 2011: 20–22) – beneath the façade and rhetoric of growth.

Hydro-mythopoesis

In a country where rivers are revered as goddesses by the Hindu population, a hydro-mythopoesis is almost inevitable in Indian literature in English, including its graphic literature. However, unlike the Hindutva propagandists who valorize all aspects of Hinduism unquestioningly, the graphic texts here very often point to the drawbacks, lacunae and explicit inequities within the religion. Thus, while Gond mythology shares the deification of water or nature with mainstream Hindu beliefs, texts like *Water* and *Bhimayana* signal how this water divinity has been instrumentalized and commodified so as to exclude the tribals, the Dalits and the poor more generally from accessing it or her. That is, there is no simplistic deification and acceptance of nature-as-divine because these texts focus on the social controls that separate water-as-a-resource from specific groups of people. Focusing on such inequalities enables these texts, particularly from Dalit/Adivasi authors-artists, to foreground the injustice that is inherent to the social order. They do so via a hydro-mythopoesis that communicates the horror lying latent, which we as readers detect when, underneath the stories of progress, development and democracy, social iniquity and injustice are revealed at an almost unimaginable scale.

In *Water*, Vyam and Wolf sketch what Hélène Cixous terms a 'mythic anthropology' with a 'foundation of gods and demons' (1976: 539). Vyam recalls how his mother told him and his siblings of the story of the seven sisters who made a pact with the lake that meant the youngest sister had to sacrifice her beautiful ring to the lake so that the lake would rise high enough for them all to collect water. But after acquiring the water, the sister and her siblings sought to retrieve the ring and were drowned in the lake. Vyam admits he did not like the ending of this story and 'would imagine that they were still living happily at the bottom of the lake' (Vyam and Wolf 2018, unpaginated). *Finding My Way* documents the Gond myths and legends, from creation to the role of Nature in the lives of humans (Shyam and Anand 2016). These myths and stories show a deeper connection and dependency of human relationships with the natural world (the Gond religion is called *koyapunem*, meaning 'the way of nature'). The forest dwellers treat their environment with respect and tenderness. In these same myths, invoking the supernatural and the divine, the landforms themselves are treated as the result of divine interventions, battles and divine–human interactions. For instance, Shyam and Anand narrate the Gond myth that all land masses are the result of a duel between Jalharin Mata, 'the water goddess', and Bada Deo, the maker of the world (unpaginated). The water goddess plunged into 'landlocked darkness' (unpaginated). So she 'forces her way up, breaking the land into fragments' (unpaginated). Thus, stories and histories of the land and its peoples are stories *of* natural elements such as water, of beings (human, animal and divine) dependent on, residing in, rising from water. Multiple hydro-linked beings intersect in determining the fate of the land and its inhabitants.

In *Finding My Way*, the river and its water-based creatures are instrumental in saving humankind. A fish in the river that the local washerman (*dhobi*) feeds every day when he does his washing warns him of the imminent end of the world and advises him to 'save himself and his loved ones' (Shyam and Anand 2016, unpaginated). As a result, the washerman gets into a wooden box with his sister and a rooster, and the fish ferries them to safety. Shyam and Anand write: 'After the apocalypse, when god searches for life on earth he finds the dhobi, his sister, the fish and the rooster – and the world is remade' (unpaginated). The accompanying image shows the fish carrying the humans and the rooster on its back, swimming across the river. The implication here is that Nature would rescue humanity. The text's didacticism suggests that these ancient stories and legends about nature-as-hope sidesteps, or even rejects, human solutions to the problems of both water scarcity and water excess. The fish's rescue of mankind just before the apocalypse so that the 'world is remade' gestures at the trans-corporeality that Stacy Alaimo (2016) theorizes as immanent to life on earth. The fish is prophetic and can see the coming apocalypse. Humanity, supposedly at the higher end of the evolutionary scale, cannot, and needs to be rescued from the water-dwelling life form. In Shyam and Anand's 'relational ecology' (Shelton 2019: 158) of the river, the union of human and nonhuman life is depicted as occurring through water on almost every page of *Finding My Way*. And, when the apocalypse arrives, the river and the fish, the humans and the rooster are linked in what Alaimo calls an 'evolutionary genealogy' (2016: 127), with their interlinking represented as crucial for the continuity of human life on the planet.

This kind of hydro-mythopoesis underscores a terraqueous history of the planet and of mankind. For instance, in Shyam and Anand's retelling of the Gond myths of creation, human history is 'terraqueous' (Shyam and Anand's term), underscoring the linkage of water, land and human life (Shyam and Anand 2016, unpaginated). Hydro-mythopoesis also links a precolonial (mythic, perhaps) past and the contemporary, thus making water the means of temporary connections resonant with the common metaphor of flow with time and water perpetually flowing. In fact, hydro-mythopoesis enables the author-artist to emphasize the connected histories of water and human life, from ancient times to the present, even when the present has, through its technocultural processes, transformed these 'connections' into unidirectional (from nature to human) and unjust (the resources denied to specific segments of the human and nonhuman populations) flows. Hydro-mythopoesis demonstrates a relationality, showing how contemporary humanity has alienated itself from the ecosystem in which it resides and with which it shares connections with antiquity. Finally, the hydro-mythopoesis also emphasizes the possibilities of the broken connections – of nature or water with humanity – becoming the causal factor in a large-scale tragedy. This is seen when people drown, crops are washed away and misery is inflicted upon the shore. In *Finding My Way*, Shyam and Anand write: 'The Narmada mostly blesses us with life, but sometimes curses us with death, eating up our goats and cows, crops and homes' (2016, unpaginated). Here, and in similar graphic works, myths can help provide a visual grammar of suffering and the tragic. The violence that informs the denial of water rights to the 'untouchable' is a subtext, not always spelt out, as in both *Bhimayana* and *Finding My Way*, and it constitutes what I have elsewhere described as a 'hidden history of violence' (Nayar 2016a: 481–482). The ellipsis in representation, the metonymy, gesture at the inequity, the injustice and the oppression are modes of signalling the tragic emanating from social factors and causes.

An important aspect of the mythicizing of water comes with the idea of healing. *Bhimayana* cites Namdeo Dhossal's poem 'Water', which talks of water's 'healing touch' (Natarajan et al. 2011: 23). And this idea of mythic hydro-healing recurs in Banerjee's *All Quiet in Vikaspuri*. Rastogi – the wealthy real estate dealer with criminal connections who now organizes the water wars – believes and argues that 'underground water extraction' is the future (Banerjee 2015: 17). Except that Rastogi links the contemporary technological with the mythic, saying, 'I fund expeditions into the earth's core, in the hope that one day we will discover the mother of all rivers, the mythical Saraswati' (17). In Sen's *River of Stories* (1994), the anthropomorphizing of the river Rewa and the local stories about the river cast it as a mother who nourishes the people living on her banks. This mythicizing of water as a healing element, though, is contradicted in Vyam's work when the marginalized Ambedkar – who has been denied the right to drink water at the school tap – mourns his loss:

> Boys at the well, even beasts at the trough,
> May drink till they burst.
> But the village turns a desert
> When I try to quench my thirst. (Vyam and Wolf 2018: 23)

The village does not become a desert, but with Natarajan, Anand and Vyams' illustrations art metaphorizes the entire landscape where the Dalit is denied water. Alluding to the fables where life forms change shape and nature, the metaphor of a land's desertification is the debunking of the myth that the environment sustains life. In fact, the Ambedkar incident suggests that the myth of water sustaining life is patently wrong when it comes to the Dalits because they are *denied* access to water. The double-page spread where this poem/anecdote is narrated shows a woman dancing before a pitcher (presumably of water), a man pouring water from a pitcher, animals drinking from a water body.

The man pouring the water is actually wasting the water, and the boy, Ambedkar, is holding out his palms for some water but does not receive any. The flow is also, undoubtedly, too fast for him to be able to collect it and drink. The man then prefers to waste the water rather than give it to Ambedkar. There is, evidently, adequate, maybe even surplus, water for some, and yet there is no water for many castes or communities. The terror here originates in the discriminating myths that are put in place to deny water to certain communities.

Later, after Ambedkar leads a campaign to make water bodies accessible to Dalits, the Brahmins seek to 'purify' the tank. The grotesque ritual, as *Bhimayana* describes it, is an exercise in excess: 'The Brahmins decided to "purify" the "polluted" Chavadar tank by pouring into it 108 pots containing a mixture of cow-dung and cow-piss, milk, ghee and curds ... to a soundtrack of Vedic chanting' (Vyam and Wolf 2018: 53). The accompanying image shows Brahmins pouring their grotesque concoction into the water, as they stand submerged in it. The fish stare at the action, and it is open to question whether the action purifies or pollutes the waters. The myths of purification are tragic, because they only signal the lack of concern for the life inside the water tank and for certain lives (Dalit) outside. Purification is contingent upon excluding certain communities from accessing the water – and once again gestures at the colonization of water and its accompanying socio-political terrors for those excluded from it.

The idea that water is a natural resource is also a *tragic* myth in the representations in *Bhimayana* and *Finding My Way*. If it were natural, it would be available to all, but as the Ambedkar story clearly shows, this is not the case. Shyam and Anand put it acerbically when they write, in *Finding My Way*, 'We lament the wasting of this earth by wasting it a little more. We produce the art of nostalgia, and we seem happy to produce art out of our critique of our nature to abuse nature' (2016, unpaginated).

The wasting of the earth or its resources – such as water – is the human counterpoint to the myth of 'natural' resources because it is human intervention that denies equal access to the resources. In other words, beyond even the message about social inequalities, *Bhimayana* and *Finding My Way* offer an environmental message about human control over natural resources. The Gond or tribal 'nostalgia' over unspoiled nature, the generosity of nature and the presumed human right to nature hinges on a myth about the roles and characteristics attributed to nature. The sustaining myths around water and nature, as in texts like Shyam and Anand's, embody a bioregional sensibility. The 'watershed aesthetics', as Lawrence Buell (2001) terms it, in *Water* and *Bhimayana* shows how the people are immersed in the ecosystem of the place. But this bioregionalism is not anthropocentric, since it involves paying attention to the nonhuman life forms sustained by the water or ecosystem as well. Hydro-mythopoesis, then, whether in the form of a retreat into a culture's folklore or a debunking of the myth of water as cleansing and life-sustaining, is a counternarrative to the myths of progress and development. This same mythopoesis points to the cultural shifts in the approach to water itself, and therefore constitutes a counter-history of hydro: the connectedness of all life forms with water, mutually sustained life, the careful attention to appropriate usage of resources, and others.

Hydrocolonialism

An idea of water-greed is repeatedly evident in Indian graphic novels, and exists in the context of the empire's approach to water and land acquisition as well as the hydrocolonial nightmares empire propagated. Hydrocolonialism is defined by Isabel Hofmeyr as

> (1) colonization by way of water (various forms of maritime imperialism), (2) colonization of water (occupation of land with water resources, the declaration of territorial waters, the militarization and geopoliticization of oceans), and (3) a colony on (or in) water (the ship as a miniature colony or a penal island). (2019: 13)

Hydrocolonialism revolves around the control and occupation of water and waterways. Deckard explains the contemporary coming together of social and financial modes of control when she writes that 'components of water systems and uncommodified elements of "the hydro-social cycle" are incorporated into financial networks as part of a fundamental shift in how "nature" is valued' (2019b: 109). In the postcolonial context, this incorporation of the flows of natural water into the social flows of people, capital and technology is examined in several of the graphic texts chosen here, in terms of a shift in the value-regimes that most often underpin hydrocolonialism and its terrors.

For example, hydrocolonialism is the key theme in Shyam and Anand's *Finding My Way*. They depict Bhopal as the site of the world's worst industrial disaster where, on 2–3 December 1984, the gas leak from Union Carbide killed thousands and left many with genetically transmissible mutations and illnesses because of the 'poison in its air, water and earth' (2016, unpaginated). Later, in the same text, Shyam and Anand explain that 'truckloads of [the] dead were being dumped into the Narmada', that villages were being submerged under water and that children were disappearing during the making of the Bargi dam (unpaginated). Marginally less destructive forms of hydrocolonialism are suggested in several other texts. In *Bhimayana* hydrocolonialism is explored through caste hierarchies. When the young Ambedkar and his siblings travel, they are denied water from a well, with a rude villager declaring: 'I've no water here. There is water on the hill, if you want to go and get it' (Natarajan et al. 2011: 41). Hydrocolonialism is first and foremost the caste-based control over water in the village well. The well itself is a spatial circumscribing of a resource. Second, the villager points his finger towards the distance, and the text accompanying the image gesture at a spatial distancing of the 'untouchable' boy in the process of ensuring the water in the well remains the material property of the upper-caste villagers. That is, hydrocolonialism is both material and symbolic: it works through a material-spatial separation of the resource and through the symbolic humiliation and discrimination perpetuated on the thirsty. *Bhimayana* constantly emphasizes this material-symbolic aspect of hydrocolonialism, beginning with the school incident where Ambedkar pleads to be allowed water from the school pump.

In Sen's *River of Stories*, the coming dam is discussed in relation to its hydrocolonializing effects, with 'our government' said to be 'planning to flood some of [... the] last remaining [tribal] villages out of existence' (1994: 42). Sen's depiction of trans-corporeality that is subject to the process of development is in the form of a *tableaux vivant* (50). The page is cut in half by the river flowing through it. Sen draws numerous fish in the waters, and writes 'some of the migratory fish species will disappear because of the dam', with the text like the fish cast in the middle of the river itself (50). On either side of the river, Sen lists the towns, cities and settlements on one bank and presents tiny figures representing multispecies lifeforms crowded on the other. The river seems to neatly divide and, simultaneously, bring together the different dependent lifeforms – human and nonhuman. Sen then writes:

> Forests provide food, wood for houses, implements and fuel, fodder for animals, gourds, resins, ropes & most other necessities for the people who live near them.
>
> Blackbuck, sambar, nilgai.
>
> Mixed deciduous forest.
>
> Parakeets, junglefowl, hornbills, etc and an as yet undocumented variety of insect species. (50)

Here the river feeds and supports all, and links between different species and the geological formations of hills, valleys and the river signal an ecological world view that does not segregate or discriminate between these life forms and others. What the dam will do is to choke the river, and Sen's inventory is a list of fungible and potential victims of hydrocolonialism.

In contrast, Vyam and Wolf's *Water* makes a case for a conservative hydrocolonialism with the text declaring: 'we would like some development to secure our basic need for water, but not in any way that would harm the place in which we live' (2018, unpaginated). In the context of the contemporary colonization of water through dams and other 'development' interventions, the emphasis in the texts of Vyam, Shyam and Sen is on precolonial ideas of water – as healing, as life giving, as divine. As *All Quiet in Vikaspuri*, *Water* and *Bhimayana* document, in their different ways, both environmental erosion and social tyranny proceed from the colonization of water. Critics like Hofmeyr (2019) see this kind of postcolonial hydrocolonialism as continuing the colonial era's regimentation of water and, as Vyam and others demonstrate, postcolonial development agendas regularly practice control over water resources as well.

Banerjee's *All Quiet in Vikaspuri* begins with the slow collapse of the copper mining firm Bharat Copper. With the downward slide in global copper prices, the company's losses mount. Residents across Delhi steal water, and water leaks from the supply lines. Water suppliers, like Tanker Rajan, confess that they 'drew water from nearby farmhouses', while others, like B.K. Gambhir, the ex-soldier, steal from the water tanks of neighbours (Banerjee 2005: 25, 28–30). Yet privileged others are reported as wasting water. This is given a large and explicit presentation when Carrey Jones asks for the swimming pool to be drained because her son has urinated in it (38). We see here how scathing Banerjee is in his account of 'development' in postcolonial India and in his depiction of the water wars as linked to the indifference of the super-rich (46), in their fortified buildings, when it comes to Delhi's water provisions and distribution. Banerjee writes: 'If you ask them where they get their water, they will say … "the building provides it!" They speak of their buildings as if they are self-contained ecosystems in the Amazon' (49, ellipsis in original). The image shows a monolith block of stone or metal (it is unclear what it is made up of), evidently a water reservoir. There are water tankers that have their pipelines hooked into the monolith, obviously getting filled with water. But there is a leak from beneath the tank and a gush of water from a pipe at the rear. The monolith is leaking water, and yet its anthropomorphic arms are raised in triumph. Banerjee captures hydrocolonialism's principal affective sources in the postcolonial era: greed and indifference. The resulting corruption, wastage and regimentation of water *is* the source of the 'water wars' of Delhi.

Hydrocolonialism also includes the 'militarization' of water. A water tank fitted with a machine gun is being rolled along in one image, and later Banerjee provides images and anecdotes on the 'heroes' of the water wars (45, 90–105). These images are cast in the visual trope of traditional battles. The troping of the Delhi 'water wars' through images sourced from and echoing traditional war films in Banerjee complicates the satire – the water wars are destructive, fought in absolute earnest. Banerjee's parody forces us to see the consequences of hydrocolonialism as akin to the territorial disputes and colonialisms that produced global as well as local crises. I suggest that this parody is not simply satiric when it appropriates an intertextual frame through its use of war movies. Adapting Simon Dentith's view of parody, I suggest that Banerjee's use of parody is 'the polemical allusive imitation of a preceding text' so that parody can have its 'polemic directed to the world rather than the preceding text' (Dentith 2000: 18). The war-Gothic invoked in the images of militarization, battles and deaths in *All Quiet in Vikaspuri* refers us to a colonizing past that has now, in the postcolony, shifted away from a war on or around territories and their populations directly and towards water and hydro-conflicts of internal population and citizenry. The humour and satire in Banerjee's depiction, then, reference how older forms of colonialism and colonial wars continue in slightly altered forms in a world experiencing water scarcity.

If scarcity is the state of hydro-linked lives in Delhi itself, Banerjee shows us over-hydration in other places. Banerjee draws a submerged village and notes how 'dams drown entire villages and destroy settled communities to produce unjustifiably low amounts of electricity' (2018: 56). Then there is the Yamuna river, 'sad, sluggish and thick with industrial effluents' (59). Dams, of course, figure prominently in the critique of 'development' in Banerjee, Sen and Shyam. Images accompanying these stories of various rivers, from the Narmada to the Jatadhari, show tracts of land submerged, as in *All Quiet in Vikaspuri*, and rivers choked in strangle-holds and knots and with watch-tower like constructions, as in *Finding My Way*. And the intentional drowning of entire ecosystems in the name of development is yet another example of hydroterror.

Technologies of collecting, distributing and consuming water are demonic in their destructive capacities and actions. In the place of supernatural terrors from aliens, demons and zombies, the graphic novel traces the source of all danger, threat and ruin to human-made hydrotechnologies. When Durgabai Vyam and Subhash Vyam draw the casteist people in *Bhimayana*, they assign scorpion tails to the latter's speech bubbles. The referent of the venomous scorpion points to the venomous thoughts, attitudes and actions of the Brahmins (and even the Muslims): refusing any rights to the Dalits or denying them water. By merging animal images as metaphors for human speech with the hydrotechnologies of water tanks and wells, *Bhimayana* shows how hydrotechnologies are political and reinforce the social distinctions among the users.

Hydrocolonialism cannot be seen as a ruination of the ecosystem of a particular place, but rather as a series of ruinations that are more transregional than bioregional. As Mitchell Thomashow argues, to fix the boundaries of an ecosystem or bioregion is itself likely to cause human suffering, as 'ideas and concepts move in and out of a particular place' and become expressions of 'an array of mediums, vectors, or paths – the landscape, air, water, the spoken word and modern technology' – of what is established is a set of 'mind regions' that 'cut through bioregional distinctions' (1999: 129). Interestingly, an inverted cosmopolitan bioregionalism in the graphic texts is discernible in terms of interconnected, plural and boundaryless ruination visited upon different ecosystems in different places and as perpetuated via water. Shyam and Anand's *Water*, for instance, tells us:

> The building I lived in had two huge water tanks up on the roof, and we had running water in the house, but only when the tank was full. In my neighbourhood, we often went without water, although not far from us there were rich houses with lawns and swimming pools.
>
> I discovered that you could buy water, if you had money. I never understood where this water came from. (2018, unpaginated)

At the foot of the page on which this quote appears, Shyam draws a picture of three cars, underscoring the city's dominant transportation regime. Facing this page is a drawing of a large suspended bird cage. The cage has sections, with each segment having some symbol of a life form – a bird, an eye, a human visage. Balanced on top of the cage are two pots of water filled to the brim. At the foot of the page a train of ants march, and hanging from the bottom of the cage is a bee hive. The cage is an ecosystem, self-contained and barricaded or protected from the world outside. The cage is linked to the water source, even if this source is unknown to the consumers of the life-sustaining liquid. The cage is a silo too and, as we have seen in *All Quiet in Vikaspuri*, nobody quite knows, or cares, where the water comes from, as they reside in their silos and prepare to fight for their share. In the city, the text's Shyam admits he does not know the source of the water supply. In *All Quiet in Vikaspuri*, Banerjee makes a similar point, as residents assume the 'building provides it' (2015: 49).

In Shyam and Anand's *Water* and Banerjee's *All Quiet in Vikaspuri*, this ignorance and assumption instantiates hydrocolonialism's inversion of cosmopolitan bioregionalism: the water is drawn from different regions, brought to the city and distributed at a cost. The 'mind regions' of Thomashow (1999) are inverted in the sense that people in most cities assume the same thing about their water supply. Further, hydrocolonialism is the exploitation of resources near and far, beyond bioregional boundaries and ecosystems. Shyam on a visit to his village is told of the coming dam: the dam 'was for making electricity for the city' (Shyam and Anand 2018, unpaginated). Thus, although people live in silos – embodied in the metaphor cage in *Water* – in very specific locations, hydrocolonialism ensures that their water, or electricity, comes from all over. Hydrocolonialism in the postcolonial graphic novel is Thomashow's cosmopolitan bioeregionalism inverted because it expands beyond boundaries and ecosystems to exploit even the most distant. If we see these graphic texts together, then we can see how hydrocolonialism has affected all rivers and peoples, from the Narmada to the Yamuna, from the waters of lakes and ponds of Gond villages to the massive Narmada dam. Hydrocolonialism, in short, is a national condition, or predicament.

Resistance

Texts like *Bhimayana*, *Finding My Way* and *River of Stories* refuse to be tied down to the idea that hydrocolonialism is overwhelming and unstoppable. In their emphasis on resistance, protest and resilience, whether in the form of *River of Stories'* representation of the anti-dam campaign or in *Bhimayana's* representation of Ambedkar as a reviving elixir of life, water is also the reason for insurgency and activism. The (re)turn to myth in *Finding My Way*, *Water* and *River of Stories* even offers up a different mythos to the dominant urban one of scarcity, regulation and commodification – one in which there is a greater respect and dependency that mark the human–nature relationship. Invoking myth, history, legends and stories conjoins the contemporary practices of development – which are instantiations of humanity's colonization of nature – with precolonial (but not necessarily romanticized) histories of the people, especially forest dwellers and the tribals. Within these histories, the author-artists locate a different worldview, even a means of resistance and rebellion.

It is also possible to see the invocation of antiquity in texts like *River of Stories*, *Water*, *Finding My Way* and *All Quiet in Vikaspuri* as suggesting a timescale not solely determined by contemporary (postcolonial) development agendas and myths of progress. Resonating with the 'pluvial time' that Sarah Nuttall proposes for fiction dealing with floods and droughts, the invocation of a hydrotemporality, the postcolonial's pluvial 'lies at the centre of an accelerating climate change that exacerbates both drought and heavy rain' (2021: 324). Where alternatives to the postcolony's hydrocolonialism are not proposed, symbolisms around the role of water abound to indicate resilience, recuperation and rejuvenation. And it is in this light that I turn to *Bhimayana* in order to propose a different role for water.

In *Bhimayana*'s stunning inversion of hydrocolonialism, we are shown Ambedkar speaking to his followers. His microphone ends in showerheads sprinkling water on people. Adjacent to this is an image of a set of people being sprinkled as they look up at Ambedkar (the faces are drawn angled upward). But what is more interesting than this rather obvious representation of water's (and Ambedkar's) refreshing power is the depiction of the water body. Throughout *Bhimayana* we are given news reports of the shackling of water, the injuries inflicted on Dalits who seek access to water and the social hierarchy that determines availability of water resources. The tanks are bounded in space. Symbolically, their walls are made of more than walls: the barrier is also a set of material-symbolic codes that disallows the Dalits from reaching into the tank, but in this particular representation, the tank has a wall on all but one side. A brick wall frames one side, a *digna* (the Gond equivalent of a fence or frame) the others. But on one side, the tank is open. The people listening to Ambedkar not only receive enlightenment and hope from his speech in the form of water, they are also drawn right at the open mouth of the tank. It is therefore an extraordinary image where the barriers around the tank have disappeared through Ambedkar's refreshing words metaphorized as water drops. Or, alternately, the people listening to Ambedkar no longer find themselves hemmed in by social or physical walls. Disrupting the wall and breaking free of the constraining structures of social hierarchies, the oppressed masses find themselves finally free.

*

The hydronovel is a preeminent form of the climate crisis novel. By constantly drawing attention to the past of nations, especially the colonial era, the genre ensures that we see today's crisis as stemming from a specific practice – exploitation – of the colonials. But by refusing to trace the crisis to *only* the colonial period and by demonstrating how the postcolony continues, even exacerbates, the iniquities and oppressions of humans and natural resources, the novel tells us that there is a resonance and a repetition of attitudes across the (raced) period of colonialism and native, independent nations. The horrors and terrors of postcolonial rule, whether democratic or totalitarian, generate social inequalities, reprise older ones and eventually may be found to affect, adversely, the environment.

Notes

1. The hydronovel suggests itself as the site for exploring the decolonization of disaster studies. The arguments here are in broad agreement with that of Astrid Neimanis' in *Bodies of Water* about the 'hydrocommons' that links all life forms. Neimanis calls for a relationality defined as liquid and fluid. Water, she writes, is an 'embodied *and* environmental materiality' (2017: 30, emphasis added). In contemporary global hydronovels, this materiality is in crisis, as human bodies, the body politic and the planet-as-a-body are all subject(ed) to hydrocrises of one kind or another. Then, linking the hydrocrisis across multiple sites and geopolitical regions resonates with a methodology that proposes that climate change 'requires the articulation of connections between events at vastly different scales' (Heise 2008: 205). Finally, floods and droughts are examples of how, very often, 'a whole world of ecological and climatic variation [is compressed] into a single, distorted disaster' (Trexler 2015: 90–91). Thus, the histories of the hydrocrises are not temporally or spatially isolated. Some find their origins in the colonial era, others in contemporary globalization, and some in nineteenth-century urban planning and development policies. Forms of resilience, resistance, adaptation to the hydrocrisis vary, just as the effects of the crisis vary from the USA in Rich and Bacigalupi to Nigeria in Habila, but when read together they demonstrate a disaster discourse that is *common* and probes the making, unmaking or prospects for a different, maybe more just, hydro-social order across the world, forming a 'global ecology' (Trexler 2015: 3).
2. Sharae Deckard speaks of this enmeshing of water systems in financial networks as the 'hydro-social cycle', and shows clearly the linkage of the material resources and capital (2017).
3. I employ the term 'material rhetoric' from Danielle Endres and Samantha Senda-Cook's work on the rhetoric of social protest movements. They write:

> material rhetoric not only focuses on material structures but also the symbols that are interrelated with these structures. Many protest events encompass this fluidity between the material and the discursive because they are held in places with symbolic meaning or are meant to alter or

challenge the dominant meaning of a place. While we consider how material structures are rhetorical, in part, because of their symbolicity, we also examine how these physical structures have material consequences. (2011: 262)

4. Sule Emmanuel Egya has commented on the manner in which Habila's novel shows how the 'afflictions to the environment translate as damage and injury to the humans inhabiting the environment, and this is manifest in the diminished bodies scattered throughout the narrative' (2017: 101).

5. Edward Wilson defines deep history as follows:

    Human behavior is seen as the product not just of recorded history, ten thousand years recent, but of deep history, the combined genetic and cultural changes that created humanity over hundreds of [thousands of] years. (1996: ix–x. See also Chakrabarty 2009: 213)

6. In the novel, Seattle is destroyed by an earthquake – and such an earthquake had been predicted but building laws for skyscrapers softened to allow 'development' (Rich 2013, unpaginated).

7. Segal writes:

    What does it mean for there to be a scientific consensus? How is the scientific method properly applied to a system that resists experimentation? What does a complex system look like? What is the nature of risk and probability?

    Each of these questions has a direct bearing on the climate change conversation without necessarily being about climate change. They, and others like them, constitute a suprascientific narrative that is necessary for science to become culture. (2017: 123–124)

8. Conrad writes in *Heart of Darkness*:

    What we could see was just the steamer we were on, her outlines blurred as though she had been on the point of dissolving, and a misty strip of water, perhaps two feet broad, around her – and that was all. The rest of the world was nowhere, as far as our eyes and ears were concerned. Just nowhere. Gone, disappeared; swept off without leaving a whisper or a shadow behind....

    ... in the hush that had fallen suddenly upon the whole sorrowful land, the immense wilderness, the colossal body of the fecund and mysterious life seemed to look at her, pensive, as though it had been looking at the image of its own tenebrous and passionate soul. She came abreast of the steamer, stood still, and faced us. Her long shadow fell to the water's edge. Her face had a tragic and fierce aspect of wild sorrow and dumb pain mingled with the fear of some struggling, half-shaped resolve. She stood looking at us without a stir and like the wilderness itself, with an air of brooding over an inscrutable purpose. (1974: 102, 136)

9. I have argued that Ghosh relies extensively on the visual metaphors to describe the Sunderbans area and its effect of an epistemological uncanny (Nayar 2010).

10. Such a renewed community, and community feeling, which survives the flood is also the conclusion of Maggie Gee's *The Flood* (2004). Children at play, the sun out and 'no one is mad here, no one is angry', writes Gee (unpaginated). The opening lines of the novel, since the rest of it is all about how the unnamed narrator came to be in this community, is an even more explicit representation of the new moral order:

> I am going to tell you how it happened. How I came to be here, with many others, in this strange place I often dreamed of, or glimpsed in t distance, across the river, the lit meadows, the warm roof-tops, caught those narrow shafts of sunlight, in this moment that lasts for ever. A hovering over the darkness. Above the waters that have covered the ear stained waters, rusty waters, pulling down papers, pictures, peoples; a patch of red satin, a starving crow, the last flash of a fox's brush. A place which holds all times and places. And we are here. We are all still here. (Unpaginated)

Other novels do not quite replicate Gee's representation of the 'paradisiacal spatial and temporal space', as Sarah Dillon puts it in her study of the novel, but do suggest a certain romanticized pastoral idyll (Dillon 2007: 377).

3

Extinction
After/Lives

In the introductory remarks to her *The Book of Vanishing Species*, Beatrice Forshall writes: 'In the eighteen months it has taken me to research this book, 107 species have been declared extinct…. We are depriving ourselves of the raw material of poetry' (2022: 13). Charlotte McConaghy opens her novel *Migrations* with the statement: 'The animals are dying. Soon we will be alone here' (2020: 3). James Bradley's *Clade* depicts a slow, incremental loss of species, as the earth itself implodes.

> Most of the birds are gone now. She is not sure when they began to disappear: elsewhere there have been huge die-offs, great waves of birds falling from the skies, yet here the process has been more gradual, species slowly disappearing, those that remain less numerous with each passing year. (2017: 43)

Forshall mourns the passing of species, a passing that is irreversible and the species irretrievable. McConaghy suggests that when the nonhumans disappear, humanity will be left all alone. The excerpts are rooted in a history of vanishing species, which is then projected as the imminent future in the characteristic catachronism of the contemporary climate crisis novel, but with the exception that in this future, mankind is likely to disappear too, a literary theme Greg Garrard terms 'disanthropy' (2012).

The death of entire species, including the human, has been the subject of considerable literary interest in the era of climate crisis. Although Mary Shelley postulated an earth without humans in *The Last Man* (1826) and the planetary apocalypse that wipes out humanity is the subject of a novel as early as *On the Beach* (Nevil Shute 2010 [1957]), the concern with vanishing species has amplified. This decline narrative is everywhere: in different forms of literature;

non-fictional works such as Elizabeth Kolbert's *The Sixth Extinction* (2014); studies of individual species vanishings such as Joel Greenberg's *A Feathered River Across the Sky* (2014) on the passenger pigeon; collections on vanished species such as Christopher Cokinos' *Hope Is the Thing with Feathers* (2000); thought experiments like Alan Weisman's *The World Without Us* (2007); graphic texts like Brian Vaughan and Pia Guerra's *Y: The Last Man* (2002–2008); and the IUCN's Red List of endangered species arranged in a rising scale of risk and vulnerability, among others. Artwork on endangered species and extinction has also flourished as seen in Isabella Kirkland and the Extinction Art Project.

Often bordering on the apocalyptic and the cataclysmic – a key form of literary and popular climate discourse where an event of unimaginable magnitude wipes out the planet's life forms – extinction discourse is tragic in tone (Heise 2016: 12). For instance, Diane Ackerman writes in her *The Rarest of the Rare: Vanishing Animals, Timeless Worlds*: 'There was a time when dinosaurs grazed in this same region, and I lament their passing' (1995, unpaginated), and elsewhere:

> [T]he last recorded Caribbean monk seal was spotted in 1952. I was four years old, growing up in a small town in Illinois, playing in the plum orchard across from my house, and learning to count. I didn't know that an animal that had survived for fourteen million years was at that moment becoming extinct, nor that I would one day lament its passing. (Unpaginated)

This chapter examines extinction discourse in texts, both fiction and non-fiction, dating from the late twentieth century to the present. While I am in broad agreement with Heise's interpretation of extinction discourse and reading of the IUCN's Red List as an 'ecological epic' drawing on the database (Heise 2016: 15), I discern features beyond the lament that Heise identifies. The extinction narrative, I argue, is a eulogy narrative. This eulogy narrative exhibits three specific features: the desire for plenitude and presence; the 'making visible' of species in specific ways; and multiple temporalities that also encode an anticipatory nostalgia for species and life forms. Eulogy narratives about vanished species and the *vanishing* of species daily, weekly or annually point catachronistically to the future that is already here, and thereby indicate the multiple temporalities coexisting in the present. This anthropogenic extinction where humanity is the apex predator marks many of the extinction narratives.

It is in a context of rapid and devastating changes such as described by James Bradley in *Ghost Species* – 'much of southern Europe is now deserted, as is south-west Australia, subequatorial Africa, India. To the north the ice is melting faster and faster. The deserts are spreading, growing' (2020: 242) – that the de-extincted species also arrive or return. Bradley leaves it open-ended as to whether the Neanderthals resurrected will survive the global disaster. The last section of the chapter deals with another prominent theme in the writings of the twenty-first century: de-extinction and rewilding. Novels such as *Ghost Species*, *Jurassic Park*, the widely publicized projects such as Dolly the (cloned) sheep, the Pleistocene Park and the woolly mammoth project are accompanied by popular science writing on rewilding and de-extinction.

Plenitude and Presence

In the opening pages of *The Song of the Dodo*, David Quammen writes: 'Passenger pigeon, great auk, Steller's sea cow, Schomburgk's deer, sea mink, Antarctic wolf, Carolina parakeet: all gone' (2004, unpaginated). Before he embarks on his island biogeography, Quammen lists the species that have disappeared, or are reduced to the last living specimens, in Mauritius, Java, Santa Catalina, New Zealand, Aldabra, St. Helena and other islands. Speaking of islands as 'laboratories of extravagant evolutionary experimentation', Quammen argues that the progress of both evolution and extinction, and the status of biodiversity can be best studied on islands (unpaginated). Quammen is speaking of the erosion of biodiversity as an erosion of plenitude.[1]

Elizabeth Kolbert writes of the golden frogs of Panama:

As recently as a decade ago, golden frogs were easy to spot in the hills around El Valle.... One creek not far from El Valle was nicknamed Thousand Frog Stream. A person walking along it would see so many golden frogs sunning themselves on the banks that, as one herpetologist who made the trip many times put it to me, 'it was insane – absolutely insane'.

Then the frogs around El Valle started to disappear. (2021, unpaginated)

Diane Ackerman, in a poetic vein, mulls over the consequences of this loss of diversity: 'As more and more species become rare, angles of color will be deleted from this living kaleidoscope, reducing the possible combinations. Variety is not only the spice of life, it's the indispensable ingredient' (1995, unpaginated). In Bradley's *Clade*, entire bee colonies, we are told, are disappearing.

In these narratives, we discern not just the praise of diversity and variety of plant and animal species, but a desire for plenitude and presence as the preferred condition of the planet. A former plenitude and presence is recalled with a simultaneous expression of a yearning for the return to that state. These texts also note that extinction is never of one species alone: the loss of one species results in the consequent loss of another (co-extinction) and a concomitant flourishing of another. When, for instance, Sandra Steingraber speaks of rising levels of carcinogens in the air, water and soil in her memoir, *Living Downstream* (2010), she notes that animals across species also receive high doses of these carcinogens and die (see chapter 6, 'Animals', in which Steingraber juxtaposes her bladder cancer with transitional cell carcinoma among the beluga whales of the North Atlantic).

I characterize such accounts as eulogistic, following James Martin, who argues that the eulogy 'speaks in response to the loss of presence' (2023: 483). The eulogy narrative, James Martin argues, exhibits a desire for plenitude and presence through the evocation of memory (478). It is also epideictic because it 'uniquely invites the audience to be a witness to an event, thereby fostering communal recognition of what is', that is, it makes visible an event or set of events that forces us to recognize what is going on or has happened (482). Epideictic discourse 'intensifies the present moment, revealing it to be not a discrete, passing instance between the past and future but, rather, a point of convergence that discloses an underlying precondition' (483). But this is also impossible because, as Martin notes, 'there is an urgent desire to reconstitute the presence of the deceased, to recollect their character, state their accomplishments'. But accompanying this desire is the 'anguished awareness that such recollection cannot restore what was lost' (483).

Extinction discourse is a memory discourse that highlights the value of what is lost, the singularity of each species that has disappeared. One way in which the desire for plenitude and presence and acts of memory appear in these texts is in the form of an enumerative discourse.

The Enumerative Sublime of Extinction

Writing about the passenger pigeon, Joel Greenberg recounts statistics: the area covered by roosting pigeons, approximate numbers of pigeons killed, fledglings found, and so on. He often foregrounds, first, the acreage the roosting pigeons occupy, where such passages signal nothing less than an avian sublime:

> The largest roost known in Maryland was used from at least 1862 to 1872. Located in Allegany County, the site claimed six acres of alder swamp and was thought to draw birds from as far as fifty miles away. The place was

packed: 'So great was the number of birds that they were piled upon each other, in places, from one to two feet in depth'....

Western Kentucky hosted two major roosts of between four thousand and five thousand acres, plus several smaller ones....

The 1878 Petoskey, Michigan, nesting encompassed over 200 square miles, and another in Huron County, Ontario, around 1870, was almost square at thirteen miles by eleven miles. And in 1823, a nesting of 180 square miles took place in upstate New York. (2014, Unpaginated)

Jeff Corwin notes that the 'plight of the 16,928 species threatened with extinction is largely due to devastating man-made ecological changes such as habitat loss, pollution, climate change, and unsustainable exploitation' (2009, unpaginated). And elsewhere: 'with 3,246 of the world's animal species classified as critically endangered' (unpaginated). About Africa he writes: 'Since the 1970s, the human population has grown 600 percent in Central Africa; meanwhile, the African elephant population has dropped from 1.3 million to an estimated 470,000 to 690,000'. And further: 'Only 7.3 million square miles of natural habitat are protected worldwide – approximately 13 percent of Earth's total land mass ...the world's forests are vanishing at a rate of 44,400 square miles a year' (unpaginated).

Such an enumerative modality serves the purpose of memory, as 'a numerical mnemonic ... gives structure to information which is otherwise disordered' (Crump 1990: 29). However, even these numbers do not enable a full comprehension of the scale of loss. The approximation of the mathematical sublime (an aesthetic that refers to the impossibility of capturing, say, the magnitude of the universe) is an attempt to give us comparative scales and measurement.

Foregrounding the anthropogenic causes of extinction, Greenberg provides such data as the following:

[I]t was estimated that, in 1880, 62,868 passenger pigeons were shot at and 44,668 killed....

New York State Sportsmen's Association ... Their 1874 extravaganza claimed forty thousand to forty-five thousand passenger pigeons. Another of their matches held in Syracuse in 1877 used twenty thousand. And then there was the contest put on as part of the Sportsmen's Association annual meeting in June 1881. It took place on Coney Island and involved twenty thousand to twenty-five thousand birds.... (2014, unpaginated)

He also underscores the scale of human effort:

> Benzie County was inundated with three thousand hunters, described as running the gamut: 'Professionals, amateurs, mossbacks, city sports, young bloods, and greenhorns had invaded the country from all directions, surrounding and penetrating the pigeon grounds.' (Unpaginated)

Even the fledglings and eggs were not spared, thanks to the thoroughness of human efforts, also captured in numbers:

> More pernicious was the unnamed C, a former member of the Wisconsin legislature…. He hired two hundred Ho Chunk tribesmen to systematically go from nesting area to nesting area collecting squabs…. In this way not only the young are killed but the eggs are broken. In two days this operation reportedly reaped 27,060 squabs. (Unpaginated)

The impact of humanity on the species is incalculable, even though we try to compute the number of killings, as Greenberg's narrative underscores.

Charlotte McConaghy in *Migrations* gives us the geomorphic role of humans in explicit detail:

> They [the Bermuda Petrels] did not survive our second attack. This one was crueler, far more pervasive. With the burning of fossil fuels we changed the world, we've killed it. As the climate grew hotter and the sea levels rose, the Bermuda petrels were washed from their burrows and drowned. That is one species of a very great many. And it's not only birds that suffer – as I've said, birds tend to be the most resilient. Polar bears are gone, thanks to that rise in temperature. Sea turtles have gone, the beaches where they once lay their eggs eroded by those same rising seas. The ringtail possum, which could not survive temperatures above thirty degrees Celsius, was decimated by a single heat wave. Lions perished in never-ending droughts, rhinos were lost to poaching…. Creatures that have learned to survive anything, everything, except us. (2021a: 44)

Greenberg and others generate a numerical mnemonic, highlighting the loss in some *calculable* form. What Ursula Heise calls 'elegiac' and I have qualified as eulogistic is this sense of incalculable loss that must, ironically, be comprehended in terms of the mathematical-statistical enormity of anthropogenic extinction. The paradox of incalculable loss stems from the very nature of a eulogy to the dead species. As James Martin puts it, the eulogy's epideictic discourse's 'attention to the present … to the event of the here and now … uniquely invites the audience to be a witness to an event, thereby fostering communal recognition of what *is* … a singular, unrepeatable loss to the community' (2023: 483, emphasis in original). When we recall the extinct species, 'there is an anguished awareness that such recollection cannot restore what was lost, that the singularity of the deceased … cannot be restored and is gone forever' (483). Martin is speaking of humans, of course, but – at the risk of anthropocentrism rearing its head – the same argument could be made of nonhuman species.

Arcadian Discourse

The enumerative sublime gestures at the sheer incomprehensibility of extinctions and their magnitude, but another component of the eulogistic narrative of extinction also draws attention to the value lost when species die. When Léa asks Franny Lynch in *Migrations*, 'why does it matter where they die, those birds? Because they'll die one way or another, no? And what does it even matter if they do? Makes no difference to us', Franny records that she is left 'breathless' (McConaghy 2021a: 144). The apathy is beyond belief because, for Franny, it is not the number of individual deaths but the fact of an entire value that has disappeared – which is incalculable.

In Quammen's *The Song of the Dodo*, he signs off the narrative with a meditation on what the loss of biodiversity and extinction in general might mean. Quammen writes:

> Within a few decades, if present trends continue, we'll be losing a *lot* of everything. As we extinguish a large portion of the planet's biological diversity, we will lose also a large portion of our world's beauty, complexity, intellectual interest, spiritual depth, and ecological health. (2004, unpaginated, emphasis in original)

Christopher Cokinos, implicitly attributing extinction to European world views, draws attention to Native American attitudes towards Nature when he records:

> For Native Americans, birds exuded spiritual importance. Creatures and forces of Nature were gods to this continent's indigenous cultures; these things, including parakeets, manifested a sacred cosmos … the European settlers of the Atlantic coast and eastern forests (and the Spanish in the Southwest and Florida, for that matter) not only rejected such pantheism, they used its existence as proof of Christian and rational Enlightenment superiority. In turn, this justified genocide…. (2009, unpaginated)[2]

One of the most powerful accounts of a certain idealizing discourse when speaking of Nature is to be found in Diane Ackerman's *The Rarest of the Rare*. First, Ackerman presents the forest's and, by extension, the planet's diversity of life forms as the antidote to humanity's various ills:

> In a burst of spirituality, it's tempting to picture this as a sort of rigid morality play: multitudes of plants, insects, and fish put on earth to provide the perfect antidote to specific human diseases. (1995, unpaginated)

Then, she writes of the wilderness as Edenic, full of plenitude, diversity and presence:

> In the rain forest, no niche lies unused. No emptiness goes unfilled. No gasp of sunlight goes untrapped. In a million vest pockets, a million life-forms quietly tick. No other place on earth feels so lush. Sometimes we picture it as an echo of the original Garden of Eden – a realm ancient, serene, and fertile, where pythons slither and jaguars lope. (Unpaginated)

What emerges from these brief excerpts is the romanticization of Nature, a valorization of its supposed purity, intrinsic value and even spirituality. These constitute what Karin Gustafsson, following John Hannigan in *Environmental Sociology*, has identified as the 'Arcadian discourse' of environmentalism (Gustafsson 2013).

Humanity in the Arcadian discourse of these texts has reneged on its foundational relationship with Nature, where humans are embedded in, rather than being the masters of, the diversity of the planet, sharing space and life with other life forms in an *integrated* universe. Thus, presuming that Nature cannot and ought not to be dominated by any life form, Diane Ackerman says of the human:

> Mining projects, rubber plantations, massive ill-fated cattle-growing projects, hydroelectric dams, highways, and an attempt to burn and dominate the land just because it is frontier and human beings can't abide an unowned space. (1995, unpaginated)

Jeff Corwin writing of the forest habitat of the Indian rhino says:

> Very few natural places are isolated from man and his assaults on the last remaining wilderness. In Chitwan, when you're beneath the tree canopy and

surrounded by mountains, it's easy to believe that you're walking through pristine wilderness, but the illusion is soon shattered by the sound of rushing tires on a roadway nearby or the droning engine of a low-flying plane overhead. The dense, once-uncharted forests that inspired the poetic nickname green mansions are now more like small apartments clinging to existence on the outskirts of civilization. (2009, unpaginated)

Corwin is particularly fond of the descriptor 'pristine'; elsewhere he would describe as Hawaii in similar terms.

The impact of humankind on the pristine environment of a new frontier has almost always been catastrophic for indigenous life. The ecological impact that results from the human colonization of an unspoiled habitat isn't unlike the pathological damage that a parasite imparts on its unwitting host. For the Hawaiian Islands, human colonization represents the definitive story of paradise found and, ultimately, destroyed. (2009, unpaginated)

The representation of Nature and wilderness as pristine is primarily an expression of the longing for an uninhabited-by-humans Nature. But such a landscape becomes a place humans go or retire to for isolation from their species, as seen in Cokinos' account of bird watchers entering the forested areas of Tallulah: 'The ornithologists felt a bracing isolation. This was wilderness. Allen called it a "jungle." The forest vibrated and echoed with the songs of warblers and wrens' (2009, unpaginated). David Quammen records how Abel Tasman viewed the islands he came to: 'Abel Tasman didn't give the island much attention. It looked unpromising, a wilderness without sign of advanced human culture or valuable produce ... although notched trees and traces of cooking-fires were seen....' (2004, unpaginated).[3]

Humans have not only reneged on their responsibilities towards Nature (a major feature of Arcadian discourse, Gustafsson 2013: 47–48), they have actively set about destroying it through exploitative mechanisms and the urge to dominate any and all 'unowned space' (48). The urge to be sovereign over an ecosystem which demands, in sharp contrast, a balanced and mutually dependent relationship, implies Ackerman, has set us on the route to anthropogenic extinction. In the process, Ackerman and the others set up Nature as entirely external to and outside of the human world: distinct and pristine.

This Arcadian discourse is also shot through with more than just the ideal, romanticized version of Nature. In cases like Ackerman's, Nature is also panic-inducing and violent and therefore, as Simon Schama noted in his classic *Landscape and Memory* (1995), primitive. Thus, immediately following the account of Nature as a Garden of Eden, Ackerman qualifies this 'garden': 'it is mainly a world of cunning and savage trees. Truant plants will not survive. The meek inherit nothing' (1995, unpaginated). She then goes on to describe how plants vie for sunlight and even destroy the weaker species. Later, she ascribes cunning to them: 'plants lure hummingbirds, bees, bats, butterflies, moths, insects. Plants are willing to dress up in animal disguises…. They are promiscuous, and they will stoop to every low-down trick. They would dress up in a gorilla suit if they could' (unpaginated).

Ackerman places humanity in an antagonistic relationship with the wilderness, going so far as to propose that it is in the wilderness that Nature reminds us of our position within the world:

I like being reminded what frail outposts we construct in the wilderness, as if plaster, metal, and linoleum really could keep Nature away from us, even temporarily. Nature always waits awhile, then sends in its platoon of ant, gecko, bird, or beetle – the where-you-least-expect-to-find-them brigade, specialists in remote places. (1995, unpaginated)

The wilderness, she suggests, enters the human world too:

I don't mind ants in my bed here [in the rain forest], any more than I minded, only a week ago, finding a garter snake basking on a potted chrysanthemum at my living-room window in upstate New York. It's nice to be reminded occasionally that borders are arbitrary, and that absolute categories such as 'outside' and 'inside' can just as easily reverse. (Unpaginated)[4]

The relationship between cultivated gardens and 'the wild' is constructed to suit human needs, as these texts that valorize the wilderness suggest.

Ecological Modernity and Its Connections

In addition to the depiction of Nature as a praiseworthy, pristine wilderness that has its share of the primordial and the primitive, the eulogistic discourse of plenitude and presence also foregrounds Nature's diversity.

Biodiversity, especially since the 1990s, has been at the centre of conservationist debates and campaigns. The biodiversity campaign relies, as Arturo Escobar (1998), Geoffrey Bowker (2000), Ursula Heise (2016) and others have shown, on a data-driven movement to document, classify and then narrativize at the level of species, and demonstrates a form of biopolitics. It also feeds into a discourse of ecological modernity where, as Karin Gustafsson proposes, the loss of biodiversity is often projected as a socio-economic tragedy, thus calculating the impact of biodiversity loss in monetary terms. Further, she continues, 'Nature is argued to hold solutions to a diverse set of problems, solutions that could be of great value to human society and that will be lost if parts of Nature are extinguished' (2013: 48–49).

There are several parts to this theme of biodiversity within the discourse of ecological modernity.

The first and foremost topic when extinction narratives speak of biodiversity is to highlight the role of diversity in the production process. Take, for instance, Barbara Forshall's account of the wisent (bison). Forshall writes:

> With their bulk and numbers, they change their environment. Churning soil, rubbing off bark, pushing over trees, feeding on saplings, they create glades, letting in light for other plants. The fallen timber rots, increasing biodiversity by attracting insects on which birds feed. These use the bison's fur to build nests. Harebell, heather and rosebay willowherb grow out of the bison's sand baths. By eating scrub and undergrowth, wisent reduce the risk of forest fires and, for this reason, are being reintroduced into Spain. (2022: 142)

Elsewhere, speaking of fungi, she writes: 'We are beginning to realise that fungi reduce the need for fertilisers and pesticides because of their defensive properties and the way they help to feed plants' (138). In *Ghost Species*, James Bradley's entrepreneur-scientist, Davis, speaks of geoengineering, in which 'If we're going to do this [resurrect extinct species] we need to do more than resurrect individual animals, individual species, we need to reconstruct entire ecosystems' (2022: 22). Such a geoengineering project is precisely what the Simovs undertake in Pleistocene Park (https://pleistocenepark.ru).

Diane Ackerman makes the link between conservationist-biodiversity efforts and ecological modernity's economic and utilitarian world view when she writes:

Drug companies help protect some rain forests because of the medicinal plants there.... Obsessed with sex, poison, and death, insects live like lilliputian Lucrezia Borgias and Machiavellis, wielding sophisticated weapons, concocting lethal potions, refining aphrodisiacs. Their scourge or weaponry sometimes works as a tonic for us.... Merck and Company has agreed to protect the rich Costa Rican rain forest for 'chemical prospecting' – a conservation coup. (1995, unpaginated)

In much the same fashion, Niall the conservation scientist in Charlotte McConaghy's *Migrations* lectures on the loss of life:

Eighty percent of all wild animal life has died. They say most of the rest will go in the next decade or two. We'll keep farmed creatures. Those will survive because we must keep our bellies full of their flesh. And domesticated pets will be fine because they let us forget about the rest, the ones dying. Rats and cockroaches will survive, no doubt, but humans will still cringe when they see them and try to exterminate them as though they are worth nothing, even though they are fucking miracles. (2021a: 208)

Niall is pointing to the value humans assign to forms of life. The socio-economic role of the life form, he suggests, determines how we perceive the species: not as life forms in and of themselves valuable but as an economic resource. Even conservationists and scientists are driven by the utilitarian impulse. Niall thinks:

Saving specific animals purely on the basis of what they offer humanity may be practical, but wasn't this attitude the problem to begin with? Our overwhelming, annihilating selfishness? What of the animals that exist purely to exist, because millions of years of evolution have carved them into miraculous being? (211)

Writing about the diversity of frog species alone, Jeff Corwin says:

There are numerous frogs whose skin secretions contain antimicrobial peptides – molecules consisting of two or more amino acids – that do have medicinal uses for humans. Among many others, there's the Oriental fire-bellied toad, a brilliantly colored frog whose peptides can lower blood pressure by dilating blood vessels; the Australian green tree frog, a strapping, long-lived species that secretes peptides that block HIV infection without harming vital white blood cells; the African clawed frog, which can escape stretches of dry weather by digging deeply into mud and whose skin secretions can cure foot ulcers resulting from diabetes; and the waxy monkey tree frog, an especially slippery species whose peptides have antifungal properties and can be used to treat antibiotic resistant staph (Staphylococcus) infections. There's also the crucifix toad, a baseball-size species whose sticky proteins serve as a glue to hold it and a partner together during mating. This same glue is also used as a medical adhesive that can bind together human cartilage. (2009, unpaginated)

He concludes this inventory with the following statement:

The more we learn, the more we realize that there's much we haven't yet discovered about amphibians and the many ways that keeping them alive – and well – can benefit the world. If we allow them to vanish forever, the ramifications will be profound for the planet's ecology and, quite possibly, the survival of the human species. (Unpaginated)

In the course of the debate in the conservation station that Niall and Franny go to in *Migrations*, they hear only utilitarian views:

They had to choose the more important animals, the ones we need and those with a chance of survival, letting the no-hopers fade into extinction. Interestingly, insects are high on their list – bees, wasps, butterflies, moths, ants, and some types of beetles, even flies. As are hummingbirds, monkeys, possums, and bats. All these animals are pollinators; without plant life we are truly fucked. (McConaghy 2021a: 211)

This is precisely what Karin Gustafsson identifies as a marker of ecological modernity: there is a clearly utilitarian and socio-economic advantage for the humans if biodiversity is encouraged and made to flourish.

In contrast to this utilitarian view, some of the writings suggest, Nature and its forms need to be valued in and for themselves. Thus, mapping the growth of human settlements in Malagasy, David Quammen at once romanticizes the indigenous people and foregrounds an ecological modernity that valorizes Nature as essential to human progress:

[The] traditional knowledge of the sort by which village people had once connected themselves, physically and emotionally, with the forest. Throughout most of Madagascar that knowledge has been lost, as the forest itself has been lost…. Ranomafana was still on the cusp between primordial landscape and agricultural settlement. (2004, unpaginated)

The indigenous peoples, he implies, had a different connection with Nature, valuing it for itself.

However, it is not just a utilitarian and primarily economic vision that informs the biodiversity discourse within extinction texts. Even as these texts speak in terms of the 'uses' of biodiversity, they emphasize, especially since the 1990s, a vision of the planet as a set of mutually dependant, co-created and symbiotic networks. In such a view, extinction is

> the loss not of a single fixed 'kind,' but of a potentially limitless set of emergent and branching flight ways from the present into the diversity of the future ... what is lost in extinction is not 'just' the current manifestation of a flight way – a fixed population of organisms – but all that this species has been, as well as all that its past and present might have enabled it to one day become. (van Dooren 2014: 38–39).

As Matthew Chrulew and Rick de Vos in their gloss on van Dooren put it, 'extinction [is] a slow falling apart of entangled ways of living, interacting and surviving, an undoing with drastic implications for future generation' (2018: 187).

Building on the work of Paul Shepard, Dominique Lestel argues that the disappearance of a species should not be read as extinction in a hermetically sealed sense. Rather,

> [w]hen we exterminate these cohabiting species, we reduce our imagination dramatically and drastically limit our existential potential to become constantly actualized human beings. *Each species that disappears is a part of our imagination amputated perhaps permanently and irreversibly* ... today's collapse of biodiversity ... is also, and perhaps above all, an existential catastrophe that substantially reduces the extent and complexity of our imagination and consequently of our humanity itself. (Lestel 2013: 311, emphasis in original)

What becomes extinct, in short, is *shared* life.[5]

This emphasis on the web of life, the network that constitutes the fabric of the planet is a favourite theme in extinction and in some sci-fi texts. Charlotte McConaghy, in lines already quoted, speaks of humanity left alone once the animals are dead. The poet Mary Oliver writes of the connections between and across life forms in her poem 'Winter Hours':

I would say that there exist a thousand unbreakable links between each of us and everything else, and that our dignity and our chances are one. The farthest star and the mud at our feet are a family; and there is no decency or sense in honoring one thing, or a few things, and then closing the list. The pine tree, the leopard, the Platte River, and ourselves – we are at risk together, or we are on our way to a sustainable world together. We are each other's destiny. (2000, unpaginated)

Ray Bradbury's short story 'A Sound of Thunder' is set in 2055. In the story, one can go back in time to any period in earth's history and shoot an animal of his or her choice. But there are restrictions on which animals may be shot. As the tour organizer Travis tells one such hunter, Eccles:

Not knowing it, we might kill an important animal, a small bird, a roach, a flower even, thus destroying an important link in a growing species … say we accidentally kill one mouse here. That means all the future families of this one particular mouse are destroyed, right? … And all the families of the families of the families of that one mouse! With a stamp of your foot, you annihilate first one, then a dozen, then a thousand, a million, a billion possible mice! … what about the foxes that'll need those mice to survive? For want of ten mice, a fox dies. For want of ten foxes a lion starves. For want of a lion, all manner of insects, vultures, infinite billions of life forms are thrown into chaos and destruction. Eventually it all boils down to this: fiftynine million years later, a caveman, one of a dozen on the entire world, goes hunting wild boar or sabertoothed tiger for food. But you, friend, have stepped on all the tigers in that region. By stepping on one single mouse. So the caveman starves. And the caveman, please note, is not just any expendable man, no! He is an entire future nation. From his loins would have sprung ten sons. From their loins one hundred sons, and thus onward to a civilization. Destroy this one man, and you destroy a race, a people, an entire history of life. It is comparable to slaying some of Adam's grandchildren. (Bradbury 1952, unpaginated)

All extinction, then, is *co-extinction* of other species as well.
In *Where the Wild Things Were*, William Stolzenburg writes:

[T]he base of the oceanic food chain – with the infinite masses of photosynthetic plankton called diatoms – feeding great planktonic herds of diatom grazers, they in turn feeding the little fish and krill destined for the beaks of landward-bound seabirds. Inland of the tundra wildflowers, he saw the chain stretching even further, to insects and spiders, to the beaks of buntings and the jaws of foxes. It was more than a chain of food; it was of web of interactions, ultimately transforming the face of the land. The pastures of the sea were fertilizing terrestrial gardens. And animals were doing much of the heavy lifting. (2008, unpaginated)

Proposing a more widespread sense of connection with not just lifeforms but the ocean itself is Diane Ackerman:

[W]e are also drawn to the ocean; we like to vacation beside it, staring for countless hours at its hypnotic pour and sweep. It's both mesmerizing and narcotic. An impulse ancient and osmotic connects our fluids with the ocean's. I suppose we feel drawn to it because we ourselves are small marine environments on the move. (1995, unpaginated)

Christopher Cokinos, speaking of the extinction of heath hens, meditates on the connections forged between humans and the natural world but which have been ignored or even frayed by humans themselves:

Every action on the lek brought to mind Heath Hens, the details of their lost lives, and the attachments I felt to them. History's rhizomes may not be as tough as those of switchgrass, but they run beneath the surface of our lives in places. They hold the soil, too, if we choose. They remind us of connections that span a continent and the years. (2009, unpaginated)

Cokinos' veiled eulogy for the time when humans and the natural world had better interconnections is a vision of ecological modernity that yearns for these connections. This vision is what drives Thom van Dooren in *Flight Ways* to speak incessantly of the 'entangled' lives of species (2014).

In many narratives, ecological modernity's vision is cast in terms of a very local and spatially circumscribed set of connections of humans and nonhumans, particularly animals. However, this 'faunal endemism' often aligns indigenous cultures and their extinction with that of the local fauna. There is forged in such narratives larger questions of territorial cultural rights and sovereignty, globalization – whether of tourism or extinctions – identity, for humans and local animal populations alike. As Genese Marie Sodikoff puts it in the introduction to *The Anthropology of Extinction*: 'Indigeneity and endemic biodiversity are analogous; their intrinsic value intensifies as they are perceived to be endangered' (2012: 13). An example of such a faunal endemism is explored by Tracey Heatherington writing about the cloned mouflon in Sardinia:

her Sardinian citizenship was constructed through metaphors that conflated biological heritage with indigeneity.... The mouflon is now simultaneously an emblem of distinctive national heritage and identity, proof of living national wealth in biodiversity (a commodity likely to escalate in value for ecotourism as extinction events proceed), and the embodiment of national achievement in science and technology, with all their implicit economic potential. (2012: 44, 50)

In other words, extinction, conservation and rewilding are undertaken within ecological modernity as a part and parcel of local, even national cultural identity-making processes to which the local animal species are instrumentalized.

In David Quammen's account of the thylacine (misnamed popularly as the Tasmanian tiger, when it is actually of the wolf family), he notes how the sacred Aboriginal sites had art work on the animal: 'Ubirr ... fifty feet up on a sandstone wall is an unmistakable pictograph: a slim, doglike creature with dark vertical stripes.... Aborigines on the mainland ... had seen thylacines ... the artistic record is confirmed by the subfossil record' (2004, unpaginated). Quammen makes the connection between the indigenous human and faunal populations tragically clear when he observes a certain pattern in the European settlement of the region. He writes:

[T]he tendency among British settlers to see the Tasmanian Aborigines in the same terms as they saw the thylacine: as a distinct species, inconvenient to current circumstances and requiring removal. The bounty rates for Aborigines were more generous than for thylacines, five pounds per adult and two pounds per child. (Unpaginated)

Later, writing about an Aborigine survivor, Quammen says:

At the end, in 1876, she [Truganini] was the only surviving full-blooded Aborigine from all those 'conciliated' by George Augustus Robinson. She had witnessed, almost from start to finish, the destruction of her people. At the time of her birth, in 1812, Tasmania had been a glorious green wilderness harboring native tribes, thylacines, and uncountable kangaroos, though already the first Europeans had arrived and the transformation was under way. (Unpaginated)

Quammen is making a point about the march of European 'civilisation' in Australia and Tasmania: a march that cost the lives of animals and humans alike. As David Owen states baldly in his *Thylacine: The Tragic Tale of the Tasmanian Tiger*: 'The thylacine *is* Tasmania. To that extent alone, it lives on' (2003: ix, emphasis in original). Julia Leigh's *The Hunter* also hints that the extinction of the thylacine was akin to the erasure of the 'local aboriginal people' (2000: 56). But the contemporary hunter has no remorse for such a history:

> It was hopeless, said the zoologists, because the animal was extinct: a combination of habitat fragmentation, competition with wild dogs, disease and intensive hunting had forced their demise. But this history does not discourage M: there is always new history to be made. Today he is acting upon new information, so today the hunt begins afresh. (37)

Places and regions begin to be described in such extinction narratives in terms of the endemic fauna. Thus, Elizabeth Kolbert says of Hawaii: 'Hawaii was, in its prehuman days, home to thousands of species that existed nowhere else on the planet, and many of these endemics are now gone or disappearing' (2014, unpaginated).

Writing about the Nagas of northeastern India, Beatrice Forshall notes that they hunted the Amur falcon relentlessly, 'catching as many as 12,000 birds a day' (2022: 186). After the reports of such large-scale extermination became public in 2012, Forshall writes, the local communities imposed penalties on hunting the birds. The very next year 'not one falcon was taken around the Doyang reservoir' (186). Forshall goes on to observe: 'The contribution that hunting … made to the Nagas, was considerable. Yet a year later they were confirmed conservationists' (187). Forshall here underscores local or indigenous cultural identity and sovereignty when speaking of their conservationist efforts. In the process, she implies that faunal endemism is not a matter of protecting dying species but of defining human communities themselves *in terms of the lifeforms* they protect and prevent from dying.

Making Visible in the 'Intensified Present'

The eulogy's epideictic Nature 'makes visible what is there that, otherwise, might be missed' and 'magnifies attention to the current event'. It also 'encourages audiences to find there a source of communal affirmation – whether that is the accomplishment of great deeds, the union of friends, or the passing of a life' (J. Martin 2023: 482–483). In the process, the narrative 'intensifies the present moment revealing it to be not a discrete, passing instance between the past and future but, rather, a point of convergence that discloses an underlying precondition' (483). It is to this quality of eulogistic narratives around extinction that I now turn.

Texts like McConaghy's *Migrations* make visible and encourage us to recognize that something spectacular is about to pass away from the planet, and highlights the courage of either individuals or the species as a collective. The purpose, it appears, is to point to the *singularity* of the lifeform, a singularity that is doomed to disappear from the earth. This singularity is recorded in different ways in the extinction narratives.

Franny Lynch, when we meet her very early in the novel, is struck by the sheer fragility of the tern (McConaghy 2021a: 4). The courage of the Arctic terns that undertake the most arduous migration of any species on earth is, Niall and Lynch note, unmatched. Franny lectures the ship's captain, Ennis, on this subject:

> The Arctic tern has the longest migration of any animal. It flies from the Arctic all the way to the Antarctic, and then back again within a year. This is an extraordinarily long flight for a bird its size. And because the terns live to be thirty or so, the distance they will travel over the course of their lives is the equivalent of flying to the moon and back three times. (23)

McConaghy writes of the silence following this speech: 'We share a silence filled with the beauty of delicate white wings that carry a creature so far. I think of the courage of this and I could cry with it' (23).

Later, Niall and Franny ponder of the moment when the last of the terns would die: 'What happens when the last of the terns die? Nothing will ever be as brave again' (208). The novel revolves around the resolve of the birds to make the trip, 'an exhausted little bird who has flown across the entire world with hardly a thing to eat … because we have made the world impossible for them' (223). Franny recognizes that the terns demonstrate something truly spectacular:

> Hundreds of Arctic terns cover the ice before me. Squealing and creaking their cries, dancing upon the air with their mates, caterwauling joyously. Sea swallows, they are called, for the grace of their dips through the water, and I see it now as they dive hungrily for fish, in a sea thriving with what must be millions of scales.
>
> I sink awkwardly to the ground and weep.
>
> For the journey they have made. For the loveliness left behind. (249)

The terns are, in short, incomparable in the lesson they teach Franny. When Franny and Ennis reach Antarctica, they are astounded to see that the terns have indeed survived the longest migration on the planet and arrived at the South Pole. Yet, despairing of ever being able to accomplish anything, Franny decides to drown herself. Then she has what she thinks are final thoughts as her body begins to freeze: 'We are not here alone, not yet. They haven't all gone and so there isn't time for me to drown. There are things yet to be done' (254). This sustained meditation on the heroic journey made by the delicate terns highlights the special features of the species: features that would disappear when the last terns die.

In other cases, the extinction narratives focus on other unique features – the singularity – of the species. Jeff Corwin speaks of the adaptation of the polar bears to the coldest regions on the planet:

> Polar bears have spent their entire evolutionary history adapting to the sea-ice environment. Less than 300,000 years ago, they diverged from brown bears … and began adapting to their frigid climate…. Their huge feet also act like snowshoes when the snow is soft underfoot. And their fur functions as a superefficient insulating and heating system…. Polar bears are graced with a keen sense of smell – they can trace the scent of a seal that's under 6 feet of snow from a few miles away. They've adapted so well to their icy environment, in fact, that now they can't survive without it … as the sea ice diminishes, so, too, does our capacity to secure the survival of this remarkable species. (2009, unpaginated)

David Quammen writing about a species of lemur describes it as 'most spectacularly peculiar', then proceeds to spell out the uniqueness of the creature: 'it moves through the forest without touching the ground…. This mode of locomotion is astonishing' (2004, unpaginated). About the golden lion tamarin, whom she dubs 'the most beautiful monkey in the world, a sunset-and-cornsilk-colored creature that lives nowhere else on earth', Diane Ackerman writes:

> A global effort is under way to save them, in part because they are what's called a flagship species. Like the panda or koala, golden lion tamarins live in an endangered ecosystem. Not only they but their entire world may go extinct. (1995, unpaginated)

In each of these cases, the singularity of the species, dead and/or dying, is underscored, in addition to the above identification of unique traits, through their narrative transformation into specimen *and* spectacle.

As *specimens*, the species and any surviving member become the object of inquiry. Such inquiries appear in the form of details about the species in anatomical, physiological or ethological terms. As *spectacle*, the individual members or the collective become the object of the gaze, of the scientist as well as the lay person.

The fossil record and the museum samples of stuffed animals serve as both specimen and spectacle. Fossils, notes Simon Knell, are 'scientifically significant objects' that circulate and are embedded within systems and processes – from individuals to learned societies – of knowledge production (2007: 28). Writing about the significance of fossils in paleoanthropology, M. J. S Ruddick argues: 'The study of human origins is a highly speculative hybrid discipline ... based on a very small body of physical evidence. The accidental discovery of one or two fossil bone fragments has the potential to bring about a revolution in the field' (cited in Herbrechter 2022: 31).[6]

References to specimens and spectacles abound in extinction texts. David Quammen describes how fossils, stuffed animals and animal remains arrived in various European museums from the nineteenth century. Descriptions such as the following occur: 'The animal [the komodo lizard] was stuffed after its death in 1933, and it now stands on display at a park in California, with its tongue dangling out like a barbecue fork' (2004, unpaginated).[7]

Then there are accounts of the *last* specimen of a species – the endling.[8] Jeff Corwin gives an example of such an endling:

> George is the last living member of a subspecies of giant tortoises called the Abingdon Island tortoise (*Geochelone nigra abingdoni*). This gentle giant was discovered in 1971 on the island of Pinta (also called Abingdon), one of the Galápagos Islands, and quickly became a symbol for world wildlife conservation ... he remains a poignant image of the last of his kind, a solitary sentinel of extinction. (2009, unpaginated)

About the heath hen he records:

> In 1927, only a dozen heath hens survived, and just two of them were females. The following year, only one male danced in the lek. He boomed out his mating call again and again, unaware that there were no others of his kind to hear him. Known as Booming Ben, he heralded the spring for 4 more years as locals hoped against hope that perhaps a female would present herself. But she never did. And on March 11, 1932, the last living heath hen made his final appearance. (Unpaginated)

Christopher Cokinos writes about Martha and George, the last passenger pigeons, and their lives in the Cincinnati Zoo:

> George died on July 10, 1910. His body was not preserved because the plumage was in a 'poor state', according to one naturalist. Martha was now alone. Probably she could not have missed George in what we'd call memory, though who can say? Certainly she lived in the insistent alone-ness of each moment after George's death. Her eyes saw cages, concrete, seeds, passing flits of birds beyond. She saw none of her kind, and this may have been a kind of anxiety in a bird as intensely social as the Passenger Pigeon. (2009, unpaginated)

Speculating on Martha's memory, emotional and psychological responses to the setting, Cokinos heavily underscores the lastness – and concomitant 'alone-ness', as he calls it – of Martha, the last of a long line of a species.

One notes that these deaths are deaths in human-controlled spaces: zoos, conservation sites, sanctuaries. The deaths of their siblings or ancestors in the wild went unobserved, and these unnoticed deaths is the subtext to the detailed recording of the final exit of the 'last living' specimen. An attempt is made to record the time and date of death. For example, Joel Greenberg writes of Martha, the last passenger pigeon: 'Forty years later the species was almost extinct, and by late afternoon on September 1, 1914, it was completely extinct when Martha, the last of her species, died in the Cincinnati Zoo' (2014, unpaginated).

Citing records of the last thylacine, David Owen writes:

> [T]he animals [in the Hobert zoo] were increasingly neglected. There could only be one outcome:
>> With genuine distress in her voice, Alison recalled to me the last weeks of her life at the zoo in 1936. Powerless, keyless and shortly to be dismissed from the zoo and turned out of her home, she listened at night to the distress calls of the zoo's remaining carnivores: the last thylacine, a Bengal tiger and a pair of lions, all too frequently locked outside in the open to face the cold, rain and snow of the Hobart winter.
>
> There exists 62 precious seconds of film footage of that thylacine, taken by David Fleay (who was bitten on the buttock while filming). The thylacine died on the night of 7 September 1936. (2003: 133–134)

Owen captures a historic(al) moment: the moment of death of the last specimen of the species.[9]

The last living specimen is a spectacle that merges time frames, but also moves between the unique individual and the species that it metonymically represents. As Ursula Heise puts it, 'The focus on species decline, on last specimens and the value of biological rarity, links the Red List to the species elegy and highlights that they are different cultural forms expressing the same underlying perspective' (2016: 75–76). The rhetoric of lastness in these narratives is in fact an 'outlastness', as 'an outlasting that is both blessing and curse', in Ben Hutchinson's words on European Romanticism's obsession with lastness and lateness (2016: 44). Hutchinson adds:

> Lastness refers to the final link in a teleological chain, a linear development that is now viewed retrospectively as having reached its conclusion … lastness is generally tied to an individual, to the 'last man' … lastness is invariably narrated in the first person, since the conceit is generally that the narrator is the only survivor. This heightened pathos and urgency make the last man an emblem of extreme subjectivity … the last man may be the conclusion, but he is also the *culmination* of a given tradition or race. (46, emphasis in original)

Thus, the last specimen represents not just a final individual but the culmination of an entire species way of life which cannot, hereafter, as Dominique Lestel (2013) has argued, be ever retrieved, remembered or reproduced. The lastness adds a singularity that is outstanding: both for having outlasted the others of the species, but also being this culmination of a teleology that began thousands of years ago. The emphasis on the lastness of George, the Abingdon Island tortoise, as a 'poignant image of the last of his kind' in Jeff Corwin's account approximates to what Ben Hutchinson terms 'an aesthetic of individuation' (2016: 74), focusing on the self of the last individual of the species.

Museum collections of a single specimen standing in for a species, notes Heise, 'often isolate the subject to the point where it appears artifactual and decorative rather than biologically embedded'. Such images, she adds, 'give no sense of habitat or ecosystemic connectedness, a strategy that may seem at odds with the environmentalist emphasis on locality and rootedness' (2016: 82–83). However, the Anthropocene extinction narratives do not just employ museum specimens to meditate on a natural process of life and death. Jeff Corwin, David Quammen, Diane Ackerman and others imply that these are specimens that embody what Kathryn Yusoff (2013) calls humanity's 'geomorphic role': humanity's role that causes extinctions through either direct hunting-and-killing of animals (the dodo and the thylacine are instances of this mode) or indirectly through the systematic alteration of the world's climate, multispecies encounters, geology and other conditions so that the animals cannot live in the world any longer.

Talking to Lewis Cross, a local, who remembers seeing passenger pigeons in his youth (and having shot and then stuffed one himself), Joel Greenberg records:

> One of his [Cross'] most striking passenger pigeon paintings and the actual stuffed bird on which they were based are well displayed in the Lakeshore Museum Center in Muskegon.

> Like most of his contemporaries, he rejected the notion that humans alone could have wiped the species out, despite the killing he himself witnessed. (2014, unpaginated)

Greenberg's text is full of anecdotes about similar specimens in museums and collections across the USA, even as he notes that humans shot the pigeons who now appear in the form of specimens:

> Yet another pigeon ventured into Lake County, Illinois, this time reaching the tony suburb of Lake Forest. It was killed by a boy on August 7 using a rifle ball that mutilated the carcass. Fortunately, the young man brought the bird to a neighbor, John Ferry of the Field Museum, who, realizing its significance, preserved the skin anyway. (Unpaginated)

David Quammen writes:

> In a ramshackle museum in Antananarivo, I've seen its skeleton; I've seen its two-gallon egg. Paleontologists know it as *Aepyornis maximus*. The species survived until humans reached Madagascar, just within the last few millennia, and began hunting it, harrying it, transforming the ecosystem it was part of, scrambling those bounteous eggs. (2004, unpaginated)

Similar examples could be multiplied across Quammen and Greenberg.

Elizabeth Kolbert reading absences and a fragmented fossil record writes about the Cincinnati Zoo and the Big Bone Lick bones-and-fossil collections:

A second sign noted that among the remains found at the Lick were 'those of at least eight species that became extinct around ten thousand years ago'. As I continued along the trail, I came to still more signs. These gave an explanation – actually two different explanations – for the mystery of the missing megafauna. One sign offered the following account: 'The change from coniferous to deciduous forest, or maybe the warming climate that brought about that change, caused the continent-wide disappearance of the Lick's extinct animals.' Another sign put the blame elsewhere. 'Within a thousand years after man arrived, the large mammals were gone,' it said. 'It seems likely that paleo-Indians played at least some role in their demise.' (2014, unpaginated)

The specimens, these signs indicate, were produced in certain contexts, whether climate change or human presence and behaviour. In other cases, humans introduced predators and vectors that ensured the extinction of indigenous species. Jeff Corwin writes about '[t]he last surviving po'ouli [who] died of complications related to advanced age at the Maui Bird Conservation Center':

While the case of malaria it was carrying at the time was benign, the disease had no doubt played a large role in the events that decimated the species. That's what happens when worlds that Nature never intended to meet collide. The po'ouli was native to the Hawaiian Islands; the mosquito is not. How, then, did this bird become the target of an alien parasite? The answer can be traced back to what was probably the first nonnative species to arrive in the Hawaiian Islands, more than 1,300 years ago: *Homo sapiens*. (2009, unpaginated)

Lastness adds a specific spectacular value to the individual. Jeff Corwin captures the moment of his encounter with one such last surviving member of a species:

I looked at Lieberman and, unable to entirely keep the sarcasm out of my voice, asked, 'So tell me, what makes the puaiohi different from any other species of thrush? What's the big deal about this bird, I mean?'

He paused for a moment, and when he spoke, the words were simple but astonishing: 'He may be one of the last of his species'.

I looked at the puaiohi again, and it had transformed into the most vivid bird I'd ever seen. Every little feather, every twitch of its head seemed as vital an expression of life force as I'd ever witnessed. (Unpaginated)

Corwin's entire attitude towards this living specimen, as seen in these excerpts, is altered when he discovers its lastness. It is the iconic lastness, then, that produces a certain value for the bird's body.

Museum and conservation campaign specimens are interpreted within biological, social and geological frames, to constitute a 'geologic corporeality', as Kathryn Yusoff terms fossils (2013: 788). Geologic corporeality is embodied in the specimens and in the narratives around the 'last' of the species, where the account of a Corwin or a Quammen, one could argue, is an attempt to keep alive in discourse the species, a 'broader narrative of aesthetic recuperation' (Hutchinson 2016: 55). There are the geological timeframes of origins and extinctions, there are the timescales of human intervention and approaches to fauna and flora, and then there are the biological factors of the species on bodies and food-availability that determine how we view the last specimen in the extinction narrative.

The epideictic nature of the extinction narrative ensures that we recognize we are, as residents of the planet, called upon to be witness to an event or series of events in which parts of the connected family of lifeforms on earth have disappeared, leaving the rest partial, incomplete. The tone in these narratives is quite often melancholic, wistful and the genre itself may be thought of as 'extinction elegies' because 'endlings' are 'creatures steeped in pathos, gravitas, and tragedy' (Pyne 2022: 8).

Lineages of the Future and Anticipatory Nostalgia

As should be clear from the foregoing discussion, extinction narratives document and speculate on multiple time frames: the geological time of species origin, dispersal and death, the present era of climate change, and the foreseeable future – or lack of it – for various species. To study extinction, argues Thom van Dooren, is to study multiple temporalities (2014: 34).

James Bradley's Eve, seeking her true ancestors, finds them, or rather their metonymic versions, in a video about submerged caves, whose walls have handprints from prehistoric times.

> Only when she is done, and she walks deeper into the cave and finds the handprints, that she finally understands. For there, in that pale-walled gallery, where once firelight flickered, illuminating this record of so many lives, of so much time, she lifts a hand and places it on one of them, suddenly aware that it fits, time telescoping in a rush like wind. (2020: 169)

Eve, as she discovers, is the very embodiment of multiple temporalities: her very contemporary present and, within her own body, an ancient being/person.

In *Where the Wild Things Were* Christopher Cokinos writes of the Carolina parakeets: 'Although tamed, the parakeets seemingly could not quite forget their wild origins' (2009, unpaginated). And elsewhere: 'She [Martha] would stay in Cincinnati surrounded by hills where her ancestors had once flocked' (unpaginated). Such origin stories are common in extinction narratives.

In many cases, origin stories are demographic accounts, going to show how widespread or localized a species was, and how this space has either shrunk or disappeared, and the population has diminished. Note, for example, Jeff Corwin's account of the Chinese alligator:

> the Chinese alligator (*Alligator sinensis*) … [the] smaller cousin of the American alligator originally flourished throughout much of China, but in recent years, it has retreated to the last viable wetlands connected to the Yangtze. Unlike its American cousin, whose dorsal surface is covered with bony protective plates known as scutes, this alligator bears armor on both its dorsal surface and its belly. Unfortunately, that's not the kind of protection that can ward off extinction, even for a formidable creature whose local name (Yow-Lung or T'o) means 'dragon'. The defense it really needs is an ironclad commitment to conserving its remaining habitat along the Yangtze from further development.
>
> Fewer than 200 Chinese alligators – only about 50 of which are mature – exist in an area consisting of little more than a handful of ponds. (2009, unpaginated)

Corwin captures the synthetic, and shrinking, ecosystem for the alligators. Joel Greenberg writes about the nesting grounds of the passenger pigeon in nineteenth-century USA:

> L-shaped, it spread across 850 square miles, although not every bit of that area contained nests. The 1878 Petoskey, Michigan, nesting encompassed over 200 square miles, and another in Huron County, Ontario, around 1870, was almost square at thirteen miles by eleven miles. And in 1823, a nesting of 180 square miles took place in upstate New York. (Unpaginated)

The catachronistic lineage of a species is crucial to the extinction narrative because, as Thom van Dooren puts it:

Each species lineage embodies a particular *way of life*, a particular set of morphological and behavioral characteristics that are passed between generations. But this is also not a static way of life. More than the sum of those individuals currently living, species are engaged in an ongoing intergenerational process of *becoming* – of adaptation and transformation – in which individual organisms are not so much 'members' of a class or a kind, but 'participants' in an ongoing and evolving way of life.

In this context, any individual bird is a single knot in an emergent lineage: a vital point of connection between generations – generations that do not just happen, but *must be achieved*. (2024: 27, emphasis in original)

Deborah Bird Rose in like fashion speaks of 'knots of embodied time', indicating the multigenerational nature of any individual of a species (2012: 128–131). What critics like Rose and van Dooren point to is 'in our time … so many other species, may be coming to an end'. They attribute this to the fact that these species' 'paths cross our [human] ever-expanding, ever-more-widely circulating, impacts and demands on life systems' (van Dooren 2014: 29). That is, extinction is the coming-to-an-end not of an individual but an entire timeline, ways of life, nesting and mating behaviours, whose origins often predate humanity's appearance on earth. Two different timelines, human and animal, converge and, as a consequence, the latter begins to be erased. These writings capture an imminent future even as they reflect on past extinction events.

Ending-time, rather than end-time, marks the extinction narrative, even as it documents the complete erasure of a species. Frank Kermode has argued that we live in the time of an 'immanent apocalypse' (2000: 272). Kermode argues: 'we think in terms of crisis rather than temporal ends' (30) and the 'weight of End-feeling' is 'throw[n] on to the moment, the crisis' (25). Extinction narratives capture this 'End-feeling' as no other genre in contemporary literature does.

Solastalgia and the Present

Much contemporary fiction, especially the apocalyptic variety, speaks of flooded cities and rising waters. Maggie Gee, Nathaniel Rich, J. G. Ballard (who pioneered the deluge novel in *The Drowned World*), James Clade, Stephen Baxter and a host of other writers envision a flooding of the planet as temperatures and water levels rise. As habitats of most life forms collapse, the residents (human and nonhuman) see their homes and cognate spaces disappearing. This erosion of the spaces of comfort, of solace, as cities and homes collapse, generates anxiety, despair and unleashes violence among survivors – psychological conditions directly related to the loss of home, and from a recognition that the earth-as-home is no longer a *locus amoenus*, a place of amenity, and cannot provide a sustainable environment for life.

'Must we simply accept our loss of beloved buildings and cities to the floods and rising seas of climate crisis?' asks Thijs Weststeijn in an essay about the future of Amsterdam's historic buildings with climate change and rising sea/water levels (2021, unpaginated). Weststeijn's rhetorical question is about a present whose future is potentially risky, disastrous and uncertain. It reflects a consciousness of the crisis that permeates the present and therefore unsettles and prevents any experience of enjoying the pleasures of the home-place.

The awareness that the current ecosystems humanity shares with plants and animals are toxic, ruined and unsustainable generates a form of sickness, often called somaterratic illness. Glenn Albrecht in a 2003 pathbreaking paper would narrow the focus of such a sickness to what he calls 'solastalgia', Albrecht et al. define it as

> the pain or distress caused by the loss of, or inability to derive, solace connected to the negatively perceived state of one's home environment. Solastalgia exists when there is the lived experience of the physical desolation of home. (2007: S 96)[10]

Extinction narratives foreground an anguish experienced when humanity encounters the indisputable fact that (*a*) humanity is the apex predator on earth and (*b*) the place humanity calls home has seen the disappearance of numerous species, whether in the form of climate-driven or anthropogenic extinction.[11] This loss of an origin(al) biodiversity, even where evidence is sketchy, informs a certain affective response to the present into which are read absences, loss and ruin. It is a world that offers no solace of biodiversity, or of a balanced Nature.[12]

For instance, about the iconic aurochs, Ronald Goderie et al. write in their rewilding narrative, *The Aurochs: Born to Be Wild – The Comeback of a European Icon* (2022):

> Animals like aurochs and wisent suffered drastic declines. At the end of the period, both species were confined only to the present-day Poland, where they survived in very small numbers on hunting reserves protected by the higher nobility. Although protected, they still suffered from further

hunting, poaching, domestic cattle diseases, war, famine and neglect. Numbers continued to dwindle rapidly until the last aurochs cow died in 1627 AD and the bison were eradicated from the wild in 1927. The aurochs, the King of the Wilderness, who had once dominated and shaped the vegetation of the landscapes all-across Europe, was no more. (53)

Diane Ackerman writes in her typical elegiac fashion: '[T]he photograph of Africa reminds me of the giant animals caged forever in the past. The large animals we associate with Africa – elephants, giraffes, hippos, ostriches, and others – are dwindling remnants of the massive creatures that once flourished' (1995, unpaginated). Ross Andersen contemplating the Arctic wastes in which the Zimovs are building their Pleistocene Park writes: 'it was easy to envision huge herds of these animals clearing the steppes of Eurasia and North America during the Pleistocene' (Anderson 2017).

Justin Quinn, working with geneticist George Church on the woolly mammoth project, observes to Ben Mezrich:

As the last ice age ended, human populations moved northward. Hunting parties decimated the native populations of herbivores and predators. Though the science was still a bit controversial, the Russian experiments – the resettled animals, the tank turning over the soil, the pile drivers – were meant to provide proof that it wasn't just the changing environment that had caused the mass extinctions. In large part, it was the other way around.

At first, we were like every other predator in this place. We hunted what we needed. But we never get full. We never stop hunting. We aren't just another predator – we are the Apex Predator. (Mezrich 2017, unpaginated)

Paul S. Martin cites nostalgic accounts of a lost animal paradise: 'We yearn for "a home where the buffalo roam, where the deer and the antelope play"…. Native glyptodonts, ground sloths, and proboscideans go unmentioned' (2005: 186). And elsewhere: 'I view the loss [of megafauna] as horrendous. It deprives us of a full measure of the wildness…. Without the large mammals, the land is tame; much of the emotion of the out of doors is drained' (201).

These are not just accounts of loss: they attribute *causes* for the loss. What Quinn is gesturing at is the ruination of the home-place – Planet Earth – by inhabitants such as humans. Some of this ruination is linked directly to the loss of other forms of life as well. Thus Li Lijuan in *Clade* writes up a list of losses:

Birds

Bananas

Tigers

Frogs

Bees

Coffee

Polar bears

Coral (Bradley 2017: 148)

The solastalgia in these texts stems from a loss of fellow residents of the home-place, as James Bradley shows through the lives of Adam, Ellie and others, as they watch various species around them disappear.

Lineages of the Future

Extinction narratives look at the vanishing of any species as an index not only of the past but of the future: that there will be, one day, no animals. As Deborah Bird Rose says, 'while people cried for the memory of their dogs, there would perhaps be no one left to cry for them. They were looking already into the possibility of their own extinction' (2011: 19).

This is the anticipation of human extinction, being read into the signs of animal extinction.

Beatrice Forshall speaking about the European turtle dove writes: 'If we do not allow room for Nature in our farming, the turtle dove may no longer take its annual message of summer to the misty north. My generation might be the first to lose its song' (2022: 145). Forshall is not speaking of an absolute finitude and the last specimen. Rather, she is drawing up a lineage of the future in the present, speaking of the immanent apocalypse of species, a 'slow violence' (Rob Nixon's evocative phrase, 2011) of lives extinguishing, one by one. If, as Molly Wallace argues about nuclear criticism which is 'necessarily oriented toward the future, but in a way that also required imagining the future's nonexistence' (2016, unpaginated), extinction writing is also oriented towards the future, but one in which several species we encounter, read of or know of today will *not* have a future. In other words, the end of a species line is a lineage of the future disappearance of the line itself. This alignment of lineage with memory and a future-oriented reflection on the memory is anticipatory nostalgia in extinction narratives.

The texts may conflate multiple species extinctions with human extinction, as in Mahaswetha Devi's story 'Pterodactyl, Puran Sahay, and Pirtha' (1995):

> What does [the pterodactyl] want to tell? We are extinct by the inevitable natural geological evolution. You too are endangered. You too will become extinct in nuclear explosions, or in war, or in the aggressive advance of the strong as it obliterates the weak, which finally turns you naked, barbaric, primitive, think if you are going forward or back. Forests are extinct, and animal life is obliterated outside of zoos and protected forest sanctuaries. What will finally grow in the soil, having murdered Nature in the application of man-imposed substitutes? (157)

A list of such 'man-imposed substitutes' is then given: 'Deadly DDT greens, / charnel-house vegetables, / uprooted astonished onions, radioactive potatoes / explosive bean-pods, monstrous and misshapen / spastic gourds, eggplants with mobile tails / bloodthirsty octopus creepers, animal blood-filled / tomatoes?' (157). Dominic O'Key reading this text argues: 'The pterodactyl thus conjures up a kind of memory of the planet which, by predating humanity, unsettles "modern man," reminding him that he is not exempt from extinction' (2020: 88). That is, the memory of species erased from earth prepares humans for a *future* loss, of themselves, too, as argued earlier. David Quammen fantasizes a scenario:

> Eons in the future, paleontologists from the planet Tralfamadore will look at the evidence and wonder what happened on Earth to cause such vast losses so suddenly at six points in time: at the end of the Ordovician, in the late Devonian, at the end of the Permian, at the end of the Triassic, at the end of the Cretaceous, and again about sixty-five million years later, in the late Quaternary, right around the time of the invention of the dugout canoe, the stone ax, the iron plow, the three-masted sailing ship, the automobile, the hamburger, the television, the bulldozer, the chain saw, and the antibiotic. (2004, unpaginated)

This is a nostalgia-in-the-making, or an anticipatory nostalgia.

Krystine Irene Batcho describes anticipatory nostalgia as 'aligned with thinking of the future, emotional distancing, difficulty enjoying the present, and a greater tendency to sadness and worry' (2020: 36). It is about 'missing aspects of the present before they are gone, as mental time travel allows a person to imagine the present from a vantage point in the future' (36). Writing about conservation and anti-pollution campaigns, Jennifer Ladino argues a case for 'counter-nostalgia': 'Viewers are instructed to look to the past – to what "was once this country" – to find natural beauty and to use that ideal as motivation for present-day preservation efforts' (2012: 121; see also Jacobsen 2020). Steven Ostovich writes of nostalgia as 'an affect in which what matters is the feeling about the past I have now, not what happened then', and thereby underscores the affective nature of memories (2020: 103). It is this affective intensity that informs the anticipatory nostalgia about species death and human mortality in extinction elegies.

When extinction narratives recall lost and vanished species they are in effect enacting a cultural memory, which has a powerful affective component. Christopher Cokinos captures this aspect well:

> The more I learned of the Carolina Parakeet's life, its extinction and its erasure from our memory, the more I wondered: How could we have lost and then forgotten so beautiful a bird? This book is, in part, an attempt to answer those questions and an effort to make certain that we never again forget this species nor the others of which I write. (2009, unpaginated)

'Nature', writes Pola Oloixarac in her novel *Dark Constellations*, 'is horrifying precisely because it bears witness to the vileness of humankind; it waits, arms crossed, for our extinction' (2019: 76). The anthropomorphosis notwithstanding, Oloixarac is pointing to an inevitability: human extinction. When David Quammen encounters a tiny bird, weighing about 10 grams, he speculates on the possible future for such a delicate bird:

> Peggy opens her hand. For a moment the dainty brown spadebill sits dazed on her palm, heart pumping furiously, and I have time to wonder about its future. How long can *Platyrinchus saturatus* maintain itself in a hundred-hectare reserve? Will this species eventually disappear, like the margay cat and the golden-handed tamarin? Will it follow the birds that follow the ants? Will it prove to be ecologically desolate in the absence of solitary bees? Will it suffer terminally from the rupture of some other mutualistic relationship? Will it die back to a state of precarious rarity, then damage itself with inbreeding, lose its adaptive vigor, and be finished off by a minor accident? Or is one hundred hectares of insularized habitat all the universe that a population of cinnamon-crested spadebills will ever need? (2004, unpaginated)

Jeff Corwin seeing polar bear cubs writes:

> Although I'm well aware that these are wild animals with sharp claws and teeth even at a young age, seeing them in this vulnerable state, without their mother's protection, instinctively tugs at my heart. I want them to live long and healthy lives in their natural habitat. In this moment, I don't allow my mind to dwell on the difficult future these cubs are destined to endure as their home melts away beneath their paws. (2009, unpaginated)

Joel Greenberg documenting the last nestings of the passenger pigeon writes:

> Although these firsthand accounts are invaluable, data based on the memory of events that took place four or more decades earlier are apt to contain inaccuracies. In addition, the value of a recollection related to the size of a nesting is limited not only by memory but the subjective Nature inherent in that kind of assessment. (2014, unpaginated)

The data is incomplete, fragmented, speculative. The memory of vanished species, even with a fossil record and documentation, is partial and speculative too, as the extinction narratives indicate. But when Cokinos describes his own feelings over even this partial record of vanished species, when Greenberg speaks of the 'subjective Nature' of assessing memories, and when Corwin and Quammen witness the vulnerable cubs and tiny birds, they respond sentimentally to the sights and experience, even as these moments produce an interest and concern – and an interrogative – over the future of many species.

Extinction narratives speculating on the causes, quantum and exact moment of a species disappearing – especially in cases where the 'last' specimen who died in the wild is not on record – highlight the intense *feeling* of loss. Then Cokinos admits it is mediated memory that we have of the vanished species: 'Our memory of Passenger Pigeons, now mediated through words' (2009, unpaginated). Towards the end of his work, he writes:

> I have learned much from this history and have realized, finally, that sadness at loss is our best *first* response. It should not be our only response. We know the world gives us life, beauty and solace. We would be ungrateful if we failed to give that back. (Unpaginated, emphasis in original)

Here Cokinos uses the affective memory of lost species to argue a case for the *future* ('give back' to Nature). In Jeff Van derMeer's *Hummingbird*

Salamander, 'Jane Smith', the pseudonymous protagonist, writes about a specific species:

> Not just rare, then, but presumed extinct. Last seen in 2007. I felt a pang of emotion, as if this was a twist. But a twist that you could have seen coming. And after the pang – it took no time at all – that emotion began to recede from me. Couldn't hold on to it. Self-inoculation. (2021, unpaginated)

The data is speculative ('presumed extinct') but the emotions that respond to the data are real. David Quammen writes, mapping a teleology for future extinctions:

> Species of rare ape will disappear, and no new ape species will arise. Species of feline will go extinct, and no new felines will evolve. Species of dipterocarps, the great hardwoods of Asian rainforests, will be lost and not gained. The world will be an emptier, lonelier place. Still, we humans can probably look forward to sharing the future with a fair number of beetles, tapeworms, fungi, tarweeds, mollusks, and mites. Dandelions and silverfish are also a good bet.
>
> The whole idea is profoundly gloomy, important, and persuasive. (2004, unpaginated)

These are instantiations of anticipatory nostalgia where affective memories of the past lay the foundations for not just anticipating a 'gloomy, important, and persuasive' vision of human extinction but also, in some cases, a plan of action for the future.[13]

Such an anticipatory nostalgia also produces both a new science and a new social imaginary: the revival of extinct species, or de-extinction.

Rewilding and De-extinction

> This place will overflow with life once again. Our original sin will be wiped clean. And if, in doing all this, we can save our planet and ourselves, that will be the stuff of a new mythology.

This is Ross Andersen on the potential of the Pleistocene Park, in which the Zimovs are trying to bring back extinct species (2017, unpaginated). In *Ghost Species*, Davis, who heads the de-extinction project, says to the scientists, Jay and Kate: 'We need to reconstruct ecosystems all over the planet. Rebuild what's been lost. What we've destroyed…. [I]t gives us the chance to undo the wrong that was done when they were wiped out' (Bradley 2020: 24). What they create in the lab is a Neanderthal, Eve.[14] Ian Malcolm in *Jurassic Park* does not believe that the planet is in jeopardy: '*we*', he says, 'are in jeopardy' (Crichton 1990: 369, emphasis in original).

Andersen's and Bradley's wishful thinking envisions a landscape that is at once contemporary, technologically crafted and controlled, and simultaneously 'old world'. It is, in effect, a summary of both solastalgia – which Andersen defines as 'existential grief for a vanished landscape, be it a swallowed coast, a field turned to desert, or a bygone geological epoch', and which he believes the senior Zimov, Sergey, suffers from – and utopian techno-futurism. It is also a pithy account of two developments that mark the contemporary age's efforts to stop, slow down, or even reverse extinction: rewilding and de-extinction.

Rewilding is defined as

> restoring species and, more important, ecological processes that are absent from contemporary landscapes – especially predation, grazing, succession, dispersion, and decomposition … a desire to shift the target baseline for conservation away from premodern agricultural archetypes toward the pre-historical ecological conditions that characterized the northern hemi-sphere at the end of the Pleistocene…. The aim is to create analogs of what emerged after the retreat of the glaciers and before agriculture, forestry, and animal domestication. (Lorimer 2015: 100–101)

The 2020 *Global Charter for Rewilding the Earth* puts it thus:

> Rewilding means *helping Nature heal*. Rewilding means giving space back to wildlife and returning wildlife back to the land, as well as to the seas. Rewilding means the mass recovery of ecosystems and the life-supporting functions they provide. Rewilding means restoring and protecting specific places – on land and in the ocean – where Nature is free to direct the ebb and flow of life. Rewilding is about allowing natural processes to shape whole ecosystems so that they work in all their colorful complexity to give life to the land and the seas. Such wild lands and waters are critical to sustain ecological vitality by supporting intact food webs and natural processes. (5)

De-extinction is 'the ability to bring species that have already disappeared back to life with the goal of one day reintroducing them to their historical range' (O'Connor 2015, unpaginated). It has been given an ethical colour, as O'Connor notes: 'These attempts to repopulate the modern landscape with extinct fauna rest on an intriguing ethical argument: that humans have a moral responsibility to make amends for overexploitation by our ancient and recent ancestors' (unpaginated). Richard Stone records how the Maoris, when discussing the possibility of de-extincting the endemic huia bird, argued that 'since humans drove the bird to extinction, they were obliged to try to resurrect it through clonings' (2002: 166). Leading de-extinction scientist Beth Shapiro writes: 'De-extinction aims to resurrect, via cloning, identical copies of extinct species.... Most likely, it will mean that specific traits and behaviors of the extinct species will be genetically engineered into living species' (2015, unpaginated). As Harvard geneticist George Church puts it in his co-authored book *Regenesis*: 'extinction, supposedly, was forever ... an extinct species could be resurrected, not by magic or miracles but by science' (Church and Regis 2012, unpaginated).

Fictional works like *Jurassic Park* (Michael Crichton) and more recently *Ghost Species* (James Bradley), non-fiction such as *Mammoth: The Resurrection of an Ice Age Giant* (Richard Stone), and popular cinema have contributed to the social imaginary of de-extinction, of bringing back, selectively, vanished species. In the process, it reverses evolution and time.

The extinction of a species need not be taken as a final story, of finitude, because, 'species like woolly mammoths and Neanderthals are not lost after all, but continue to exist as the genetic codes residing in their remains' (Turner 2007: 58). Thinking in terms of 'genome time', Turner adds:

> The phenomenon [of genome time being perpetually present] articulates mythic elements in extinction studies, such as nostalgia for an idealized past, the association of homeland with destiny, the perilous quest for the rare beast, and ritualized atonement for transgression. (59)

Turner terms it the 'peril and recovery' dialectic, and demonstrates how the dialectic has a moral subtext to it: because *Homo sapiens* were responsible for the extinction of animals like the thylacine, *Homo sapiens* should take the responsibility of reviving them (63). That said, it is not clear whether extinct lifeforms have the same right to life as current ones, following from which is the thornier question: should we then revive them? (Littmann 2014).[15] For many scientists and lay persons, Richard Stone admits, such a resurrection 'spells doom', but for others it is 'the start of a spectacular scientific drama' (2002: 13). But beyond the scientific drama is something more dramatic: and that is of life coming alive for, as Ian Malcolm says in *Jurassic Park*: 'you cannot make an animal and not expect it to act *alive*. To be unpredictable. To escape' (Crichton 1990: 284, emphasis in original).

In *Ghost Species*, when Eve is 'born', her difference from humans is palpable. Later, in a chapter titled 'I Was a Teenage Neanderthal', Eve, troubled by her ancestry as well as her contemporaneity – she is after all a product of the science of the age – seeks information about her kind:

> They were violent, brutal, cannibals. They were simply less successful, were outcompeted. They were exterminated. There is a story she returns to more than once, of the last population of her kind, trapped on the edge of the Iberian peninsula. A dying community. Sometimes she tries to imagine their lives. What was it like to be so alone? Did they know they were the last? (Bradley 2020: 167)

She understands who she is when she sees, expectedly, mirror images of herself:

> One evening she calls up a virtual tour of the Natural History Museum, steps into its Hall of Mankind. The figures that populate it are so lifelike it is unsettling, but though she recognises their thick hair, the large eyes and wide noses from her own mirror, she cannot bear to approach them. (167)

And, like Doris Lessing's Ben in *The Fifth Child* which *Ghost Species* resonates so powerfully with, Eve 'seeks out other movies, not just about cavemen but about robots and monsters and patchwork people, all the uncanny golems of the Gothic imagination' (Bradley 2020: 168).

Both rewilding and de-extinction narratives rely heavily on what we could call de-extinction icons (as contrasted with extinction icons such as the dodo): the woolly mammoth, the thylacine, the dinosaurs and of course the Neanderthals.[16] Both rewilding and de-extinction encode their own biopolitics. Both are also proposed not only as solutions to retrieving the lost, but also as a way of restoring a balance to delicately poised parts of the earth like the Arctic where the permafrost is melting fast and the release of the trapped carbon dioxide could render the planet itself a greenhouse. Sergey Zimov, founder of the Pleistocene Park, outlines the need for rewilding and cloning or creating the extinct herbivores in the tundra (the Zimov talk is summarized as George Church recalls it), in *Woolly*:

During the last ice age, the last great global freeze which marked the tail end of the Pleistocene Era (which stretched from 2,588,000 years ago to 11,700 years ago, when our anatomically modern human ancestors emerged), the tundra wasn't a scarred bed of moss and lichen; it was a lush refuge of high grass. Megafauna – herds of giant, furry herbivores, from horses and buffalo to reindeer and Woolly Mammoths – populated the steppes in huge numbers, continually trampling and turning the topsoil above the world's largest biome as they grazed. Even as the ice age ended and the world began to warm, the herbivores naturally tilled the earth, churning the soil to expose the frozen ground beneath to the even colder air, keeping the permafrost perpetually chilled.... By the end of the Pleistocene Era, a mass extinction had begun. The megafauna were hunted to extinction, and with them went the ecology of the finely balanced system. The grasslands withered and died. The moss and lichen took over. Trees sprang up haphazardly between the weeds. And over time, the permafrost began to melt.

The time bomb began to tick. (Church 2017, unpaginated)

Ross Andersen in his account of the Zimov project writes:

If this intercontinental ice block warms too quickly, its thawing will send as much greenhouse gas into the atmosphere each year as do all of America's SUVs, airliners, container ships, factories, and coal-burning plants combined. It could throw the planet's climate into a calamitous feedback loop, in which faster heating begets faster melting. The more apocalyptic climate-change scenarios will be in play. Coastal population centers could be swamped. Oceans could become more acidic. A mass extinction could rip its way up from the plankton base of the marine food chain. Megadroughts could expand deserts and send hundreds of millions of refugees across borders, triggering global war. (2017, unpaginated)

Bradley's *Ghost Species* echoes the Zimovs almost word-for-word:

'[A]s the permafrost melts, the methane that is locked up in it is being released, hastening the warming that's already taking place. If we can't slow that down, it's game over for the climate ... if we can reintroduce large herbivores we can re-create the conditions of the last Ice Age and keep the forest at bay'.

'Thereby slowing or even preventing the release of the greenhouse gases in the permafrost', Jay says. (2020: 24)

Thus, rewilding and de-extinction are not attempts to simply revive lost animals: they are projected here as attempts to save the earth itself:

> Nikita [Zimov] will need to import the large herbivores of the Pleistocene. He's already begun bringing them in from far-off lands, two by two, as though filling an ark. But to grow his Ice Age lawn into a biome that stretches across continents, he needs millions more. He needs wild horses, musk oxen, reindeer, bison, and predators to corral the herbivores into herds. And, to keep the trees beaten back, he needs hundreds of thousands of resurrected woolly mammoths. (Andersen 2017, unpaginated)

Fictionalizing these sentiments and aspirations is Charlotte McConaghy in *Once There Were Wolves*:

> What we have here in Scotland … is an ecosystem in crisis. We urgently need to rewild. If we can extend woodland cover by a hundred thousand hectares by 2026 then we could dramatically reduce CO_2 emissions that contribute to climate change and we could provide habitats for native species. The only way to do this is to control the herbivore population, and the simplest, most effective way to do that is to reintroduce a keystone predator species that was here long before we were. The vital predation element of the ecosystem has been missing in this land for hundreds of years, since wolves were hunted to extinction. Killing the wolves was a massive blunder on our part. Ecosystems need apex predators because they elicit dynamic ecological changes that ripple down the food chain, and these are known as 'trophic cascades'. With their return the landscape will change for the better – more habitats for wildlife will be created, soil health increased, flood waters reduced, carbon emissions captured. Animals of all shapes and sizes will return to these lands. (2021b: 23)

The return of the keystone species is not, then, about nostalgia for the extinct animals but a necessity directed at a future, making it a catachronistic text, but one of hope. In McConaghy, of course, a certain bioregionalism is at work. When Inti and her team seek to convince the Scots of the uses of rewilding by wolves, they encounter resistance from the locals. Later, Inti is embarrassed to discover that the locals themselves have embarked on a rewilding project, as Mrs Doyle explains:

> She tells me, slowly so I can follow her, of the four thousand hectares of the estate's land that are being rewilded, of the millions of trees planted …

when we first realized our forest clearing had brought us down to a few pathetic groves of Caledonian pines. Instead of planting natives our forest management planted groves of non-native conifers! The lunacy! Just terrible for the native wildlife. In any case, we started getting back on track and began to plant the natives and reintroduce the poor lost animals. (McConaghy 2021b: 188)

The point Mrs Doyle makes is of *local* agency cultural identity, decision-making and of course species. Bioregionalism here accounts for all of these, and does not rely on external organizations to attain the necessary results.

In other cases, however, the purpose and intent is simply entertainment and profit.

In *Jurassic Park*, Crichton's pioneer de-extinction investor, Hammond (played on screen by the redoubtable David Attenborough), calls the genetically manufactured animals – he carries a tiny elephant in a cage to investor meetings, to demonstrate the possibilities – 'consumer biologicals'.[17] But this was not a genetically manufactured creature, Crichton tells us: 'Atherton [the geneticist] had simply taken a dwarf-elephant embryo and raised it in an artificial womb with hormonal modifications.' But the key point is the investment in biological matter. Ashley Dawson (2018), Melinda Cooper (2008), Kaushik Sunder Rajan (2012) and others have argued that biocapitalism is the next stage of capitalism with its huge investments in biological matter, from embryos to entire, patentable, life forms. Focusing on de-extinction, Dawson argues: 'The fundamental problem with de-extinction is that it relies on the thoroughgoing manipulation and commodification of Nature and, as such, dovetails perfectly with biocapitalism' (2018, unpaginated).

Jurassic Park and *Ghost Species* embody biocapitalism's interest in creating and profiteering from (renewed) life forms.

First and foremost, Hammond in *Jurassic Park* envisions de-extinction as a revenue generating 'amusement park':

The most advanced amusement park in the world, combining the latest electronic and biological technologies … we set out to make biological attractions. Living attractions. (61)

In Hammond's vision, bringing back extinct species, such as dinosaurs, is utilitarian and driven by the profit motive. The question that underlies Ian Malcolm's opposition to the entire project is not simply drawn from the scientific principles of the operation, but from moral and ethical ones such as the ones Greg Littmann lists:

> Do extinct species, like the tyrannosaurus, have a right to live, and if so, does this give us a moral duty to revive them if we are able? Do our duties to an extinct species depend on whether the species was driven to extinction by human beings – like the Neanderthal, the Dodo, and the Tasmanian Tiger – rather than killed off before humans arrived on the scene, like the dinosaurs? (2014, unpaginated)

Further, if the purpose of bringing them back is entertainment and amusement for the *humans*, have we pushed our (human) commodification – 'rendered', to use the term from Nicola Shukin (2009) – to previous species as well? One of the lawyers is sure of the project's financial success: 'We're gonna make a fortune out of this place' (Crichton 1990: 79).[18] Bodies and organizations that monitor, fund and regulate biotech developments fall prey, Crichton implies, to the profit motive.

Then, there is an aesthetic element to the book – and the movie – although it is essentially a monster tale. Note here Crichton's account of the first sights of the dinosaurs:

> Her first thought was that the dinosaur was extraordinarily beautiful. Books portrayed them as oversized, dumpy creatures but this long-necked animal had a gracefulness, almost a dignity about its movement.... The sauropod peered alertly at them, and made a low trumpeting sound, rather like an elephant. A moment later, a second head arose above the foliage, and then a third, and a fourth. 'My God' Ellie said again. (1990: 79)

And this is where the question of animal appeal comes into play. Animals that serve economic purposes, such as the *Tyrannosaurus rex*, or *T. rex*, would of course be a priority for being resurrected, because it would be a star attraction in the Park. As Jamie Lorrimer and others have noted about the conservation campaigns – arguments that can be extended to de-extinction projects (Kadonaga 2014) – a certain cuddly and cute animal like the panda is likely to receive greater funding for conservation initiatives than, say, frogs. As Lydia Pyne phrases it, 'charismatic animals' like parrots, thylacines, rhinoceroses, ibex, river dolphins, and even parakeets have 'popular appeal' and so 'it's easy to want to save panda bears and elephants', but more difficult to 'convince people to care as urgently about the critically endangered venomous Sahul reef snake' (2022: 55). That is, there will be a specific set of attributes that visitors to the Park will want to see among the resurrected animals – and this set of attributes, carefully calibrated, will be a part of the calculations when the choice of animals for resurrection is being deliberated. In Crichton, clearly, the choice is made: the most famous of the predator dinosaurs, *T. rex*, is the Park's centrepiece. And since 'genetically engineered animals can now be patented', as Dodgson the lawyer puts it in the novel (Crichton 1990: 68), the ancient *T. rex*, revived, would become the property of InGen (Hammond's company in the novel).

The island itself is described as a biodiversity marvel. In a tone reminiscent of island biogeographies, Crichton presents a magical place:

> Only seventy-five miles wide at its narrowest point, the country was smaller than the state of Maine. Yet, within its limited space, Costa Rica had a remarkable diversity of biological habitats: seacoasts on both the Atlantic and the Pacific; four separate mountain ranges, including twelve-thousand-foot peaks and active volcanoes; rain forests, cloud forests, temperate zones, swampy marshes, and arid deserts. Such ecological diversity sustained an astonishing diversity of plant and animal life.... New species were being discovered all the time.... So a new species was perfectly possible.... (21)

But this biodiversity marvel is transformed into a multinatural space by human entrepreneurship. Jamie Lorimer describes a multinatural space thus a 'hybrid' world in which 'science will be complicit in this modification' and 'the result is a proliferation of knowledge controversies … there is no single Nature or mode of Natural knowledge…. The Anthropocene is multinatural' (2015: 2).

Ian Malcolm observes about the physical space that is the Park, on the island off Costa Rica:

> 'Zoos don't re-create Nature,' Malcolm said. 'Let's be clear. Zoos take the Nature that already exists and modify it very slightly, to create holding pens for animals. Even those minimal modifications often fail. The animals escape with regularity. But a zoo is not a model for this park. This park is attempting something far more ambitious than that. Something much more akin to making a space station on earth … everything about this park is meant to be isolated. Nothing gets in, nothing out. The animals kept here are never to mix with the greater ecosystems of earth. They are never to escape.... Such isolation is impossible,' Malcolm said flatly. 'It simply cannot be done.' (Crichton 1990: 90)

Crichton underscores the point that when we recreate species, we do not know how they will behave, since they come from a prehuman period into today. Conservation projects about rewilding, Jamie Lorimer argues, are often 'wild experiments' where 'rather than seeking to test explicit theories and hypotheses framed by transcendent archetypes of Nature', the laboratory is 'interested in emergent properties ... an experimental epistemology grounded in an acknowledgment of uncertainty and contingency' (2015: 102). This means, Lorimer continues, that 'the speculative, inductive, experimental systems established by wildness on reserves ... frame these sites as uncertain epistemic "wild things"', and hence put 'accepted knowledge at risk' (109)

The Park in Crichton is a constant source of surprises: from the gender switching of creatures to the forms of behaviour that they exhibit. Unpredictability, Malcolm underscores, is the one predictable feature of the Park. This is because the Park is an emergent space/condition and whatever knowledge the humans who revived the dinosaurs possessed, it was open to scrutiny and erosion. Here is a passage from Crichton:

> [T]he danger existed because they still knew so little about the animals. For example, nobody even suspected the dilophosaurus were poisonous until they were observed hunting indigenous rats on the island-biting the rodents and then stepping back, to wait for them to die. And even then nobody suspected the dilophosaurus could spit until one of the handlers was almost blinded by spitting venom.

> After that, Hammond had agreed to study dilophosaurus venom, which was found to contain seven different toxic enzymes. (1990: 146)

As the novel proceeds, the tension arises partly because the humans have no idea about the behaviour of these ancient-yet-recent reptiles. Although the habits of the dinosaurs, Grant recalls, had been studied and documented through consultations with palaeontologists, there was much that they did not know, as Grant observes:

> We know these animals [raptors] hunted in packs, but we don't know anything about their social behavior in a group. (Crichton 1990: 57).

This ignorance about dinosaurs is repeated several times in the novel (290, 305–306, 334). He then thinks:

They [humans] knew so little about dinosaurs, Grant thought. After 150 years of research and excavation all around the world, they still knew almost nothing about what the dinosaurs had really been like. (58)

That is, the social and collective behaviour of the revived dinosaurs in the Park cannot be predicted because they have not been studied *in their original habitat*, which was before humans appeared on the scene. As B. A. Minteer argues:

> [D]e-extinct organisms will not have evolved in relationship to other species within a natural habitat over millennia. And that unique co-evolutionary and ecological narrative is … an important part of how and why we value wild species…. (Cited in Diehm 2017: 27)

Ellie Sattler the paleobotanist is horrified at the kind of plants John Hammond and his team had put (back) into the Park:

> [W]hoever had decided to place this particular fern at poolside obviously didn't know that the spores of veriformans contained a deadly beta-carboline alkaloid. Even touching the attractive green fronds could make you sick, and if a child were to take a mouthful, he would almost certainly die-the toxin was fifty times more poisonous than oleander. (Crichton 1990: 85)

And this incongruity and dissonance of the dinosaurs as a species and as a collective rather than as individuals is what produces the chaos of *Jurassic Park*. In Crichton's words:

> People who imagined that life on earth consisted of animals moving against a green background seriously misunderstood what they were seeing. That green background was busily alive. Plants grew, moved, twisted, and turned, fighting for the sun; and they interacted continuously with animals-discouraging some with bark and thorns; poisoning others, and feeding still others to advance their own reproduction, to spread their pollen and seeds. It was a complex, dynamic process which she never ceased to find fascinating. (86)

In *Ghost Species*, bringing up Eve the Neanderthal is, like in the case of the dinosaurs, a fraught exercise, because the question is whether humanity should bring her up based on *homo sapiens* norms or the norms we assume the Neanderthals possessed *in their time*:

Jay and the rest of the team set about devising a program to help Eve extend her abilities in those areas where she has deficits. At Kate's insistence they also formulate a plan to allow her to develop herself in those areas in which she exceeds the normal sapient range. 'Why should we limit her education with sapient standards of normality?' Kate argues. 'By that reasoning *we* should be being trained to improve our visual memory until it equals Eve's'. (Bradley 2020: 119, emphasis in original)

Since we do not know the original contexts in which the Neanderthals nurtured their young, their cognitive abilities or their social behaviour, the ideas of 'development' or nurture become crisis points. Kate's question about the 'sapient range' is aligned with Bradley's implicit suggestion that the Neanderthal has 'deficits' because we view her from the sapient point of view.

Jurassic Park and *Ghost Species*, in contrast with the attempts in real life to bring back endemic species – such as the woolly mammoth – constitute a fiction of cosmopolitan rewilding. In the case of the woolly mammoth, its resurrection became, Matthew Chrulew argues, a subject in the discourse of 'bioregional purity':

> The attempt to reimagine elephants as flagship species of North America, of enormous symbolic as well as material worth, thus draws on this long-held desire to restore to American Nature – and thus to the overall health, vitality, and esteem of the people and nation. (2011: 15)[19]

The Parks (the fictional Jurassic and the real-life Pleistocene Park in Siberia) are multinatural, as noted earlier, bringing together technology and Nature in unexpected ways.

Defending the revival of megafauna such as the mammoth, Josh Donlan et al. (2006), in a justly famous essay in *The American Naturalist*, speak of the ecological necessity of bringing them back:

> A variety of evidence indicates that the functional roles of large carnivores and megaherbivores are often significant…. [M]any extinct large mammals must have shaped the life histories of extant species and ecosystem characteristics through the selective forces of strong species interactions…. (662)

As an example, they document the role of such megafauna on a species of plant: 'the loss of proboscideans and other megaherbivores capable and suspected of dispersing the large fruits of these trees may have caused or contributed to the extinction of the other *Maclura* species' (662; also see the case made for the gray wolf, 662).

Jurassic Park, Woolly and other de-extinction texts rely on a specific model of extinction, what the philosopher Leonard Finkleman, following the work of Julien Delord calls, demographic extinction:

> Demographic extinction follows the death of all organisms in a species; however, the means for perpetuating the species – intact genetic material, for example – may survive. A species is extinct in Delord's 'final' sense only when all means of perpetuating the species have totally disappeared. (Finkleman 2018: 31)

Finkleman also asks whether such a revived species in the form of their latter-day clones have the same properties of the original-but-extinct species. In other words, does a backengineered, cloned or resurrected *T. rex* have the same properties as the original *T. rex*, and how would we know?

The problem Crichton turns the spotlight on is the Park's very idea of a life form as embedded solely in its genetic materials and/or morphological similarity – or what humanity now, from paleontological evidence considers similarity – to their now-extinct ancestors.[20] The dinosaurs being revived are deemed to be true to their species characteristics – about which we know little, in the first place – as though their genetic material is adequate, in the present, to bring back these characteristics. This pointedly ignores the dinosaur species' interactions with (*a*) predators and other species and (*b*) the larger ecosystem. As Ed Regis tells Alan Grant in the novel: 'these creatures are not of our world. They come from a time when there were no human beings around to prod and poke them' (Crichton 1990: 110). Since the properties of the species evolved over thousands of years and in close interaction with predators, ecosystems, within symbiotic relationships and the food chain, how does the contemporary *T. rex* behave? Further, having placed these newly created creatures in an environment closely resembling zoos (and not the Cretaceous period's ecosystem), they would, Hammond and his team believe, behave like animals in zoos anywhere. They would learn the regularities of their care, and they would respond' (Crichton 1990: 140). Except that they do not. Ian Malcolm explains the flaw in this arrangement:

> This stegosaur is a hundred million years old. It isn't adapted to our world. The air is different, the solar radiation is different, the land is different, the insects are different, the sounds are different, the vegetation is different.

Everything is different. The oxygen content is decreased. This poor animal's
like a human being at ten thousand feet altitude. (Crichton 1990: 159)

In other words, the Park becomes emblematic of a genetic determinism and
biological essentialism, decontextualizing the species and its individuals. In
such a decontextualized Park, Crichton's novel poses two points about the
authenticity of the creatures. One, if we say the *T. rex* reborn is not an authentic
T. rex, it implies that it is not *T. rex* but only a creature that *resembles* a *T. rex*.
Two, if we say that the reborn *T. rex* is not an authentic *T. rex*, it can mean
that it is a certain kind of *T. rex* but *not* the original kind (this of course brings
back the original *versus* copy dialectic, as Helena Siipi suggests, 2014). As Paul
Martin puts it in his account of the rewilding projects:

> Some may object that the introduced tortoises are not genetically identical
> to those eliminated hundreds of years ago. It is, of course, possible that the
> reintroduced animals will not prove adaptable. However, I would argue that
> these reintroductions are the closest we can come to true resurrection, and
> infinitely better than continual attrition…. Some of these creatures no longer
> have close living relatives; in these cases we should consider proxies for them
> that perform the same ecological functions. The Bering Land Bridge should
> not be shut down forever in the interest of imagined faunal purity. (2005:
> 204–207)[21]

The question of the authenticity of species so revived also begins to haunt Kate
in *Ghost Species* when she sees what they have created in the laboratory:

> even a superficial glance is enough to reveal she is not normal. Beneath
> the thick red-brown hair plastered against her scalp her head is larger, the
> face more simian, the rounded cheeks and jaw reminiscent of those of a
> chimpanzee, her subtly shorter forehead emphasizing the unusual largeness
> of her eyes.
>
> Yet it is not these differences that strike Kate most forcefully, but her fragility,
> the wonder of her. She is them but not them, human but not human, extinct
> yet somehow here, in the world. But most of all she seems to embody a kind
> of possibility, something both dizzying and terrifying to contemplate, her
> presence in the world changing everything. And nothing. (Bradley 2020: 62)

This, in short, summarizes the de-extinction project: what is created in the
laboratory and the petri dish as a way of repopulating the planet is at once

human and not-human. As Crichton puts it in *Jurassic Park*, 'there's no point getting starry-eyed about these animals. It's important for everyone to remember that these animals are created. Created by man' (1990: 128).

*

The climate crisis clearly motivates and inspires end-of-the-world scenarios, but also speculates on a retrieval, restoration and resurrection of the old world and its inhabitants. Extinction texts mourn the loss of biodiversity, even as the fictional and non-fictional accounts of worlds without mammoths or humans speculate on a future without humans, or fewer birds and commonplace animal life.[22] Yet others believe a rewilding is both possible and necessary, as a move to save the earth and restore a measure of balance to Nature through, ironically, technocultural interventions. Whether the revival of a species, dinosaurs, mammoths or Neanderthals, restores the balance to 'Nature', the ethics of this regenesis, and of course the problem of comparison and authenticity infuses the debates and writings, fiction and non-fiction, around de-extinction. Comparisons and the authenticity question, James Bradley suggests in *Ghost Species*, are inevitable, especially if we revive beings close to *Homo sapiens*. Kate, mothering Eve in the novel, ponders:

> Even the terminology makes her uneasy. To speak of *Homo sapiens* and *Homo neanderthalensis* is clumsy, yet still preferable to depending on the term 'human', and its implication that Eve is not. Better again is the distinction she has taken to drawing between sapient and Neanderthal, though even this makes her uncomfortable. (Bradley 2020: 71)

Notes

1. 'Biodiversity' is now 'a symbol or metonymy for the environmental concerns at large' and 'combines and articulates in a new way previous environmental concerns, such as the extinction of species and the protection of wilderness by giving them a scientific grounding' (Väliverronen 1998: 28–29).
2. The romanticization of indigenous practices, whether in hunting or agriculture, in such discourses is, as commentators have noted, built on the erasure of the true extent of the practices' consequences. For instance, Andrew Isenberg's *The Destruction of the Bison* (2000) notes how the Native Americans were also a major bison-hunting culture across America. In similar fashion, Joel Greenberg (2014) documents how the Native Americans too massacred the passenger pigeons.

3. There is, William Cronon has noted, the transformation of Nature into scenery achieved through the erasure of the indigenous inhabitants of the place:

    > [N]arrative revalue Nature by turning it into scenery and pushing to its margins such characters as Indians who play no role in the story-or rather, whose roles the story is designed to obscure. (1992: 1354; see also Cronon 1996)

4. Martin Puchner argues: 'It is striking how consistently (though variously) literature draws a line between civilization and wilderness' (2022, unpaginated).

5. Scientific evidence points to the large-scale losses and ecosystem damage when species – and not just keystone species – go extinct. For instance, Felisa Smith et al. (2023) demonstrate that the loss of megafauna like the mammoth left legacies across the geosphere, the hydrosphere, the modern atmosphere and the biosphere.

6. Ruddick also admits that paleoanthropology is an ideologically fraught field. He writes:

    > [W]e can, however, say that the truth that humanity is one species is more likely to conduce to our survival – and is therefore more important and valuable – than the truth that individual human beings show great phenotypic diversity. Similarly, pf (or indeed any artistic product) that affirms that, despite our differences, all human beings are united in their fundamental humanity, is likely to be more culturally valuable and aesthetically praiseworthy than counterclaims that our differences are unbridgeable because of primal racial incompatibilities. (Cited in Herbrechter 2022: 31)

7. Pauline Wakeham has argued that the presence of both indigenous bodies *and* stuffed animals in natural history museums mix racial and species discourses into what she calls 'narratives of disappearance and extinction' (cited in Bezan 2021: 482).

8. The term 'endling' was coined in 1996 by Robert M. Webster and Bruce Erickson in a letter to *Nature*, and is now used to describe nonhuman organisms, mostly animals and some plants, that have been identified as 'the last vestige of their species' (Pyne 2022: 5).

9. Ricardo De Vos writes of this rhetoric of the last individual specimen:

    > [T]he notion of the last of the species, a notion which is established using historical evidence to identify a specific time, space and specimen, is

merged with that of an ideal state such as 'the thylacine' as species, a category invoking an ontological or metaphysical presence.... The last animal provides a singular body and a singular moment ... [and] is presented as both real and ideal in an enunciative present, one which is separated from both the past, a time of presence, and the future, a time of absence. (2007: 189–190)

10. Other commentators have expanded the term:

Placebased distress when still in place (solastalgia) emerges in the nexus between the biophysical, social and ontological, and is closely intertwined with matters of power and autonomy to determine the interpretation of the past and imagination of the future.... The anguish ... is manifold. It concerns the destruction of a known environment, of a place with continuity and narratives; an ending of long-standing social relations; and, a loss of trust in the social institutions that are supposed to protect and secure people and their place in society. (Askland and Bunn 2018: 21)

11. Incidentally, James Bradley suggests that even if we were to manage to revive the extinct creatures, humanity would remain an apex predator, and thus pose threats to the resurrected lifeforms. In *Ghost Species*, Eve, searching for her kin, comes across a carcass of a woolly mammoth somewhere in Europe and immediately wonders: 'what happened to it? She has heard stories about humans hunting the *new* beasts, killing them' (Bradley 2020: 241, emphasis added).

12. George Church defines Nature as prehuman:

Even though humans and our works are part of Nature, 'natural' could be defined as prehuman. (2017)

13. Other commentators have also argued that nostalgia can serve the purpose of social reform (Slovic 2008).

14. There are clear parallels between Bradley's work and Doris Lessing's *The Fifth Child* (2001 [1998]; and its sequel, *Ben, In the World*, 2000). In Lessing's novel, the Neanderthal is not engineered into existence. In Lessing too, Ben seeks people of his own kind, and finds them in cave paintings. Described as a 'throwback', Ben is an anomaly who reminds his family and others of humanity's ancestors.

15. There are three modes of reviving the extinct animal: back-breeding, cloning and genetic engineering.

16. George Church attracted controversy due to his alleged claim about the possibility – very real – of reviving Neanderthals.

17. That *Jurassic Park*'s foundational premise – of cloning a dinosaur from DNA extant in amber – is flawed scientifically has been stated several times. Ben Mezrich writes in *Woolly*:

> Dinosaurs had died out 65 million years ago, which meant there was no such thing as extant dinosaur DNA to be found in our modern era. No genetic material could survive even a fraction of that length of time. It would have been continuously bombarded by cosmic radiation or consumed by enzymes in the soil, which would destroy the DNA. No dinosaur fossils ever found had any genetic material. There was nothing at all to sequence. And no dinosaur fossil that would be found could contain any. An insect trapped in amber for millions of years became, at a cellular level, simply amber. It might look like a prehistoric insect, but it no longer contained any DNA. (2017, unpaginated).

18. About the *Jurassic Park* films, John Karavitis notes that the first film 'presents the view that animals are property … and they don't have any rights'; the second film, *The Lost World: Jurassic Park*, 'presents the view that animals are due some moral respect, but only indirectly'; and the third, *Jurassic Park III*, 'presents the view that animals not only deserve our respect, but that they also have rights – most importantly, the right to be left alone' (2014, unpaginated).

19. This discourse was also applied to the Pleistocene Project in northern Siberia, wherein 'Siberia is conceived as the mammoth's homeland, haunted by an extinct creature who belongs to the landscape, a terrain that is incomplete without its flagship species' (Chrulew 2011: 15).

20. Markku Oksanen and Helena Siipi in their introduction to *The Ethics of Animal Re-creation and Modification* write:

> a species consists in genomes and/or a species membership that is determined by a morphological similarity with other (past) members of the species. An animal's lack of ecological interactions with its (native) biophysical environment, social relations and the way it came into existence is seen as insignificant to its species identity. (2014: 11)

21. Elsewhere Martin would outline a spatialization of de-extinction:

> Where there are closely related survivors, the approach is simple (if, on occasion, politically problematic). Especially when fossil records indicate extinction within the last few thousand years, any surviving populations of taxa on the brink of extinction should be spread back into their former ranges by any means possible. Even relatively modest

efforts in this direction may have gratifying results. For example, the giant tortoises of Aldabra could be restocked in Madagascar, the Comoros, and other small islands in the Indian Ocean, as has been done in at least a few cases. Galapagos tortoises could be returned to islands emptied of giant tortoises, as has been done on Santa Fe, where the original population was eliminated by whalers and pirates. A more venturesome reintroduction would be to return giant tortoises from the cactus-clad islands of the Galapagos to similar habitat in Ecuador. This is an opportunity for restoration of one taxon of continental megafauna, at least in protected reserves. (P. Martin 2005: 204)

22. The one exception that I am aware of where an extinction narrative is written in a humorous – some may think it, justifiably, uproariously funny – is Douglas Adams and Mark Carwardine's *Last Chance to See* (1990). While Adams – an established author of quirky and comic science fiction – laughs mainly at his own incompetence when in Bali or Madagascar, he also laughs at the creatures he witnesses: creatures on the very edge of extinction. Yet, despite the humour, the work communicates a sense of urgency about the subject of biodiversity loss.

4

Creaturely Texts
Multispecies Encounters

In Richard Powers' *The Overstory*, Patricia Westerford writes about trees and their effect on humans in their midst:

> Trees know when we're close to by. The chemistry of their roots and the perfumes their leaves pump out change when we're near…. When you feel good after a walk in the woods, it may be certain species are bribing you. (2018: 424)

Westerford publishes these claims about vegetal communications to the mockery, initially, of the scientific establishment:

> When the lateral roots of two Douglas-firs run into each other underground, they fuse. Through those self-grafted knots, the two trees join their vascular system together and become one. Networked underground by countless thousands of miles of living fundal threads, her trees feed and heal each other, keep their young and sick alive, pool their resources and metabolites into community chests…. There are no individuals. There aren't even separate species. Everything in the forest is the forest. (142)

Westerford's efforts, and that of the novel's principal characters, are directed at establishing that vegetal communications as the collective agency of plants respond to their environs and shape them in ways that humans have refused to understand or even acknowledge. In Charlotte McConaghy's *Once There Were Wolves* (2021b), the father teaches the twins, Aggie and Inti, the basic facts of vegetal communication:

> This is how the trees speak with and care for each other. Their roots tangle together, dozens of trees with dozens more in a web that reaches on forever,

and they whisper to each other through their roots. They warn of danger and they share sustenance. (15)[1]

Neil Abramson's *Unsaid* is a quasi-ghost story narrated from the perspective of a dead woman, a vet, Helena, who when alive was adept at reading animal behaviour. Helena notes how her favourite dog, Skippy, stares at her picture after her death:

> Skippy's eyes show recognition and then he makes a sound. Perhaps it is my imagination, but to me it sounds like a sigh. (2011: 159)

To turn to a different theme, contemporary biomutation texts examine the ontological segregation of the human from other lifeforms and explore the possibilities of crossing this border. In Tania James' *The Tusk That Did the Damage* (2015), a boy steals ivory from the elephants' graveyard and finds himself metamorphosing into an elephant. In Marie Darrieussecq's *Pig Tales* (1996), a woman is transformed into a pig. In Greg Bear's *Darwin's Children* (2003) and Jeff Lemire's *Sweet Tooth* (2021), children born after a virus has ruined the earth are hybrid, humanimals. In Pola Oloixarac's *Dark Constellations* (2019), we are told of plant–insect hybrid or trans-species forms that existed as 'dark patches distributed en masse among humans and nonhumans alike, on a spatiotemporal scale invisible to the eyes of men' (12).

Shared vulnerabilities of humans and nonhumans is a theme in much contemporary literature. Yann Martel's celebrated *Life of Pi* (2004) is the story of a human's cohabitation, on a boat, with a tiger. Paula Cocozza's *How to Be Human* (2017) details the relationship between a woman, Mary, and a fox in the heart of London, and Amitav Ghosh's *The Hungry Tide* (2004) is an exploration of a landscape that pits tigers against humans, where both are victims of a state-driven politics of dispossession and control. Julie Leigh's *The Hunter* (2000) traces the killing of the last Tasmanian tiger by a man identified only as 'M', who is hired to extract the animal's blood so that its DNA can be used to clone more such tigers:

> By studying one hair from a museum's stuffed pup, the developers of biological weapons were able to model a genetic picture of the thylacine, a picture so beautiful, so heavenly, that it was declared capable of winning a thousand wars. Whether it will be a virus or antidote, M does not know, cannot know and does not want to know, but there is no question the race

is on to harvest the beast. Hair, blood, ovary, foetus – each one more potent, each one closer to God. (40)

The possibilities of the biopolitical paradigm are ever-expanding *across* species. Mayra Montero's *In the Palm of Darkness* (1997) shows how animal species and humans are both at the mercy of human politics in Haiti. In Ibrahim al-Koni's *Gold Dust* (2008) too, a link between European colonialism that forced the exile of the natives from their homeland and the natives' extermination of the local fauna is forged: 'he [Ukhayyad] knew this from having often gone hunting gazelles in nearby valleys during easier years – back before the Italians invaded the country and drove the various tribes into exile' (157).

This brief inventory of the contemporary canon of creaturely texts has a prehistory in literature from different parts of the world. Animal fables and stories in all their variety, from Anna Sewell's *Black Beauty* to Richard Adams' *Watership Down*, the ancient Indian texts of *The Hitopadesha*, the *Panchatantra* and *Jataka Tales* have centred animal voices, demonstrated their role in human identity formations and offered moral lessons (see Srinivasan 2021). Thus, it is a moot point whether literature has been cognizant of the human–nonhuman shared worlds in a predictive *anticipation* of contemporary science. Susan McHugh certainly thinks so in her *Animal Stories*: 'best-selling ethological narratives of life in the field influence broader imaginative engagements with elusive species like the great apes … such stories promote instead popular ethologists themselves as skillful storytellers'. She adds: 'in so doing, they also forge links in chains of literary influence, raising questions about how this pioneering scientific field traces its roots back to fiction' (2011: 212). And elsewhere, she posits a '"narrative ethology" … in which ethology and fiction alike proceed from the complicated operations of affect, and leads to an ethics premised on feelings honored as concrete, intense, and shared' (217–218). Sharing this sense of literature as a narrative ethology although he does not employ the term, Ben De Bruyn cites the work of Mario Ortiz Robles to argue that '[literature] has noticed animal sounds from the start, in line with the fact that no textual feature is "more visibly literary, nor more visibly discredited" than "the giving of voice to animals"' (De Bruyn 2020: 6).[2] More recently, advocates of multispecies ethnography, such as Anna Tsing, have called for attention to 'how humans and other beings build worlds together' where, for instance, the mole, the rabbit and the potato, among others, are not just 'tools or blocks for human projects' but instrumental in 'world-making projects' of their own (Tsing 2023: 1).

This chapter is in resonance with the argument proffered by David Herman in *Narratology Beyond the Human* that 'narratives ostensibly centering on human protagonists can nonetheless raise important questions about the scope and limits of selfhood in a wider world of selves, nonhuman as well as human' (2018b: 34).[3] Herman cites Val Plumwood's famous argument that 'cross-species representation, like cross-cultural representation, is not automatically colonising or self-imposing, and may express motives and meanings of sympathy, support and admiration' (Herman 2018b: 6). These texts, in Herman's words, represent and embody 'a fuller range of relational ties to others, human and nonhuman alike. The relational ties are identity-constituting' (63). Or, as Suvadip Sinha puts it in his reading of texts from India, 'the fictional world expects us to think like an animal, behave like an animal, and emote like an animal.... [I]t is a call for going beyond the limit of the subject and reach for the approximate open' (2023: 58).

Herman's 'narratology beyond the human', Anat Pick's 'creaturely poetics' (2011), McHugh's 'narrative ethology' (2011) draw upon a considerable body of work on the nonhuman Other, notably Edward Kohn's (2013), Günther Witzany's (2006) and Anna Tsing's (2017) on plants and fungi, the developments in ethology with respect to animal communications (Couzin 2006), philosophical works on plants, science and literature (Galgiano et al. 2017) and posthumanism (Braidotti 2012; Alaimo 2010, 2016; Haraway 2008, 2016). Much of this critical work, while alert to colonizing politics, anthropocentrism and speciesism focus on the linkage and mutually constitutive relationships and identities of the human and nonhuman, also suggest that the human sense of the self has been destabilized in favour of multispecies belonging and identity, and in the process offered critiques of contemporary human society and its treatment of the nonhuman Other. For Ben De Bruyn, the 'failure in cross-species communication [is] rooted in the poor listening skills of absent-minded humans' (De Bruyn 2020: 2).[4] Similar cautionary notes have also been issued by feminist anthropologists working with multispecies intersectionalities, suggesting that we need to keep in mind the 'asymmetry in the intersecting power relations that are most salient in shaping individuals' experiences and possibilities between species' (Petitt 2023: 30). As Andrea Petitt argues, one must note the 'connection between animal breed and human categories of power' (24).[5] Sundhya Walther's work argues that 'nonhuman voices expose forms of multispecies living that challenge dominant understandings of space, nation, narrative' (2021: 13).[6] Walther's call for 'multispecies subaltern alliances' hinges on affective responses and relations, which 'refuse the sovereign human subject and enact agential forms of inhuman relationality' (16). Amitav Ghosh speaks of a certain uncanniness of human presence on earth:

> No other word comes close to expressing the strangeness of what is unfolding around us. For these changes are not merely strange in the sense of being unknown or alien; their uncanniness lies precisely in the fact that in these encounters we recognise something we had turned away from: that is to say, the presence and proximity of nonhuman interlocutors.... Our gaze seems to be turning again; the uncanny and improbable events that are beating at our doors seem to have stirred a sense of recognition, an awareness that humans were never alone, that we have always been surrounded by beings of all sorts who share elements of that which we had thought to be most distinctively our own: the capacities of will, thought, and consciousness. (2016: 30–31)

This chapter looks at a multispecies relationality in contemporary creaturely texts, which I define as texts where the 'intersections or interrelations between the experiential worlds of humans and of other kinds of animals structure, more or less explicitly and overtly, the unfolding of events' (Herman 2018a: 2). Following Herman's lead in *Narratology Beyond the Human*, it does not focus on texts in which nonhumans are agential actants from the very beginning, but examines themes and texts in which the human–nonhuman boundary is breached in significant and mutually constitutive ways. It assumes, with David Herman and others, that the human–nonhuman exchanges are instances where the human self is refused primacy and is characterized by a distributed self and a relationality with other lifeforms. This latter takes the form of a 'creaturely poetics' in the fiction examined in the chapter. Alex Lockwood defines 'creaturely poetics' thus: '[T]o take a creatural path is to place one's body into an encounter with the creaturely, and the creaturely other. It is to be "thought by" the nonhuman other. It is, at its heart, a corporeal reckoning with our bodily alienation from the nonhuman world' (2022: 33).

Attending to creaturely poetics, species encounters have specific meanings, as Anat Pick's approach indicates. The first is to recognize that 'being human is grappling with what is inhuman in us' (Pick 2011: 6). Then, it calls for us to 'trac[e] the logic of flesh in examples across image and text that reveals how culture makes sense (and use) of the body as a wager of species identity' (6). In Pick's own work, she enmeshes two strands of thought that inform animal studies today:

[E]xtensionism (an essentially liberal ethics of extending moral consideration to animals based on their shared capacities and characteristics with human beings) and the more decidedly posthumanist project to tackle and alleviate what Cary Wolfe called the 'fundamental repression' ... of nonhuman subjectivity. (2)

To this end, the chapter examines spaces of shared embodiment in 'landscapes of fear' (Farina and James 2021) and the consequent shared but differentiated and unequal vulnerabilities of humans and nonhumans. This scrutiny of locations and spaces of fear and vulnerability is an attempt to underscore the biomes that humans and nonhumans occupy, interact with, and within which they develop their shared identities and vulnerabilities. Then the chapter moves on to specific modes of human–nonhuman interactions, studying what McKenzie Wark in a different but assimilable context called 'xenocommunications' (2014). Finally, I turn to select contemporary biomutation texts – whose origins, of course, lie in animal fables, Gothic and horror tales and classic works such as Franz Kafka's *The Metamorphosis* (2016 [1915]) – which seem to indicate a different creaturely poetics.

One line of criticism regarding creaturely texts has argued that humans have reduced animals and plants to symbols (from the famous nightingales of English Romantic poetry to the 'pig' of William Golding's *Lord of the Flies,* 2009), as indices of a specific indigenous landscape, or 'assimilating it [animal sounds] to their human purposes, figuratively "caging" the animal in rhyme, convention, and allegory' (De Bruyn 2020: 6). Further, and aligned with the anthropocentrism of such animal narratives, we can discern in such texts the risks of re-enacting human domination of the planet so that colonial capital's logic has informed both species and races (Huggan and Tiffin 2010; Ahuja 2009, 2016).

The debate over nonhuman agency continues to rage, of course, between the (posthumanist) valorization of the agentic role of the nonhuman and their (presumed) responses to human interventions and presence. Alf Hornborg (2016) and Panos Kompatsiaris (2022), to mention just two, have both cautioned against the ready acceptance of illusions and myths of nonhuman response and 'plural relating' (Kompatsiaris 2022). Even if we concede the agentic role of the nonhuman in multispecies biomes, questions remain over this role. Kompatsiaris persuasively argues: 'under the banner of "inclusivity", the agentic capacity is said to equally exist in humans and nonhumans, from animals to objects, who are seen as having the power to act in the world' (11). He cautions:

Animals in these settings are entirely defined and dominated by the human logic, will and aims; even if they respond somehow it does not mean that we should overlook the massive apparatus of domination that dictates their responses. Slaves, people in concentration camps and colonised peoples were also responding *somehow* so that they could continue to live. This romanticisation of agentic capacity can offer an intellectual alibi for reproducing structures of domination: since the controlled populations participate, or are made to enjoy, we are entitled to not even speak about domination. (11, emphasis in original)[7]

In other words, are the nonhuman responses not an index of their acculturation by or with *humans* so that they (the nonhumans) can continue to live? Does this imply agency or tutoring? Alf Hornborg is even more categorical:

Non-living objects do not have agency, but they can impact on their surroundings (that is, have consequences for them) in at least four ways. First, they can form physical constraints on the agency of living entities, for instance, by restricting their movement. Second, they can serve as catalysts, prompting them to respond, for instance, to weather events. Third, they can be delegated specific functions, as in the famous example of the door stop and other human artifacts and technologies. And, fourth, they can be attributed agency, as when artifacts or other entities are perceived as having autonomous agency that they do not have … in no case is it justified to dissolve the crucial difference between purposive agency and merely having consequences. When a fetishized object has the appearance of having agency, it is the perception of the object which influences human agency, not the object itself that acts. (2017: 4–5)

These misgivings about anthropocentric 'projections' of the human will, desire and aspirations for the nonhuman remain a subtext to our reading frame when we read contemporary literature about multispecies.

The focus of creaturely texts, then, is the mutually constitutive nature of human and nonhuman identity, and the openness of human subjectivity, identity and ontological state to other lifeforms.

'The World of Sensible Seasons Had Come Undone'

In *The Overstory*, Olivia and Nick protest against the lumber industry by climbing up and living on a tree that is destined for cutting. Living dangerously several feet off the ground, the two protestors literally embrace the tree they seek to protect. The tree *provides*, and when Nick suspects that the loggers are trying to 'starve [them] out', Olivia assures him: 'Hold out.... The huckleberries will be fruiting again before we know it' (Powers 2018: 291). But this is only one aspect of their existence up the tree: the destinies of the humans and the tree are forcibly enmeshed, because Olivia and Nick have decided that they would protect the tree with their lives. The fact that the trees are bound for felling means that their lives on the tree are also at stake, as they soon find out.

In Margaret Atwood's *The Year of the Flood* she writes of mutual dependencies of life forms:

> Consider also His workers in the Earth! Without the Earthworms and Nematodes and Ants, and their endless tilling of the soil, with-out which it would harden into a cement-like mass, extinguishing all Life. Think of the antibiotic properties of the Maggots and of the various Moulds, and of the honey that our Bees make, and also of the Spider's web, so useful in the stopping of bloodflow from a wound. For every ill, God has provided a remedy in His great Medicine Cabinet of Nature!
>
> Through the work of the Carrion Beetles and the putrefying Bacteria, our fleshly habitations are broken down, and returned to their elements to enrich the lives of other Creatures. (2010 [2009]: 193)

In Nick Hayes' *The Rime of the Modern Mariner* (2011), a set of powerful images present the link humans have with the earth. The image accompanying the text about compacted bones, shows the mariner in silhouette. The odd thing about this human silhouette is that it is drawn as geological lines, traditionally used to depict the strata of the earth. The strata represent geological timelines as well. The mariner's feet in this silhouette flow into the soil, and one cannot separately identify his feet: it is one mass merged with the top layer of the earth. Hayes' image is evocative, showing a different form of embedding from the earlier one of the man's hand merging with Nature embodied as vegetation. Here the man *is* the soil, the soil makes the man. The image could be read as the soil climbing up into the man, becoming his very constituent. Man is of the elements here: he *is* earth. In the next set of images, Hayes builds on this theme of man being *made* of the elements. His feet, says the mariner, 'dug down like wooden roots', his 'fingers felt like leaves'. He then 'drew upon the earth and air, like every living tree'. All his breath is part of the natural setting, his 'budding alveoli inhaled in perfect time', like the trees. Even his neurons are like 'mycelium' and 'exhaled in hopeful spores'. The elements are older, a part of the world the human race inhabits, in which humanity is a relatively recent entrant. By depicting the mariner's revival within Nature, Hayes implies that it is only a return to ancient connections, with Nature, that can help man redeem himself. This return to the ancient connections is implicitly a comment on the precarious nature of the human–earth link in today's age (Nayar 2019: 57–58).

Landscapes of Fear

For Dellarobia in *Flight Behavior*, the unusual spectacle of monarch butterflies on the mountain in her own backyard – which she only sees, as she admits, because she was 'running away from things' (Kingsolver 2012, unpaginated) – communicates a profound message to her (but not to others in her family or community): '[I]t felt like a dream to see that cold fire rising. It was impossible to believe what she saw was real. The end of the world, as good a guess as any' (unpaginated). Everything has changed, and the nonhumans feel and demonstrate this change. Kingsolver writes:

> Dellarobia couldn't remember a sadder-looking November. The trees had lost their leaves early in the unrelenting rain. After a brief fling with coloration they dropped their tresses in clumps like a chemo patient losing her hair. A few maroon bouquets of blackberry leaves still hung on, but the blue asters had gone to white fluff and the world seemed drained. The leafless pear trees in Hester's yard had lately started trying to bloom again, bizarrely, little pimply outbursts of blossom breaking out on the faces of the trees. Summer's heat had never really arrived, nor the cold in its turn, and everything living now seemed to yearn for sun with the anguish of the unloved. The world of sensible seasons had come undone. (Unpaginated)

It is not a spectacle in that sense for, as Ovid Byron, the lepidopterist, explains to Dellarobia:

> 'We are seeing a bizarre alteration of a previously stable pattern,' he said finally. 'A continental ecosystem breaking down. Most likely, this is due to climate change.... Climate change has disrupted this system. For the scientific record, we want to get to the bottom of that as best we can, before events of this winter destroy a beautiful species and the chain of evidence we might use for tracking its demise. It's not a happy scenario.' (Unpaginated)

He informs her of the cause of this migration: the monarchs extend their migration range further and further north. They also are forced to leave their roosting sites earlier with each passing year (unpaginated).

The butterflies signify the end of the world, although Kingsolver does not carry through the ecoapocalyptic mood, opting instead for a measured, and slow, pace of disruptive and dangerous change, and ending on a note of optimism where the butterflies take a calculated risk and fly out seeking another habitat.[8] Climate change that causes habitat destruction for humans and nonhumans, transforms the landscape in which these lifeforms are embedded.

Humans and the nonhumans occupy, with different degrees of vulnerability and agency, 'landscapes of fear' in contemporary literature. Kaitlin Gaynor et al. (2019) define a landscape of fear as 'the spatial variation in prey perception of predation risk' (3). They add: 'For animals with advanced cognition, the landscape of fear may exist as a "mental map" that an animal proactively responds to, but the landscape of fear can also occur in real time as an animal navigates and responds to a landscape of heterogeneous risk' (3). Almo Farina and Philip James, building on the work of Gaynor et al., focus on the fear of humans that alters the behaviour of medium-sized predators, thus producing a landscape of fear: 'the fear of humans as apex predators modifies the perception of the surroundings and several consequent actions' (2021: 423). While the work of Gaynor, Farina and others deal with vast landscapes in which they track animal behaviour, contemporary literature highlights this role of humans as apex predators in multiple settings, from the confined to the forest.

Speaking of the Pacific islands, David Neiwert in *Of Orcas and Men* writes of a vast oceanscape of fear for the lifeforms in the area:

> In ancient times, the Kwakwaka'wakw say, men and killer whales could talk to each other. Unfortunately, they were also at war. The myths do not say why, but for many years, orcas and men hunted and killed each other. One of the dances performed at the lodges tells the story of how the depredations of the orcas became so great that the people prayed to the spirit of the mighty Thunderbird to save them. In the dance, the Thunderbird and the Max'inuxw do fierce battle until finally the Thunderbird strikes a mighty blow, and the Killer Whale lies dead. (2015, unpaginated)

Later, Neiwert explains exactly why and how the oceanscape emerges. The first reason, he notes, is the role of the captive-orca industry set up by humans: '[Y]ou will never, ever hear about the endangered population of killer whales in the Pacific Northwest and most certainly not about the outsize role played by the captive-orca industry in driving those populations to the brink.' This entire project of whale captivity in the name of conservation, he notes, is 'rationalized':

> as a means of rationalizing the continued captivity of killer whales by theme parks, you may be told that whales face all kinds of survival challenges in the wild and often do not survive them. You will be told the oceans are a scary place (as proven by the difficulties whales face in Puget Sound) and that the parks can provide the whales better food and care than they can get in the wild, you may be told that their orcas live longer in captivity than do whales in the wild. (Unpaginated)

This last, he notes, is an outright lie:

> Captivity has been a catastrophe for most killer whales taken from the wild. Study after study has demonstrated that whales in captivity are more than two and a half times more likely to die than whales in the wild. All the care in the world cannot compensate for the stress brought on by placing a large, highly mobile, highly intelligent, and highly social animal with a complex life into a small concrete tank. (Unpaginated)

Neiwert is in fact mapping the transformation of a habitat into a landscape – oceanscape, to be exact – of fear where humans make a case for captivity in a 'small concrete tank' as a safer option for the orcas. The ocean is 'scary' but cages and ponds are safe (for the whales), in the twisted logic of conservation and preservation. There is another aspect of the landscape of fear in Neiwert's work. He points out that

> [e]ven though they have been observed countless times over the centuries devouring species ranging from humpback whales to sea lions to moose, there have been only a few recorded attacks on humans by orcas in the wild, and those mostly against boats carrying humans. (This benign relationship with humans cannot be said of orcas in captivity, but that is another part of our story.)… Recorded attacks on humans by killer whales in the wild could be counted fewer than the fingers of one hand…. (Unpaginated)

Thus, the evidence for killer whales attacking humans is, Neiwert argues, rather thin. The oceanscape, then, is a mythic landscape of fear, and adds to the grand narratives of dangerous predators. If we juxtapose the two arguments

Neiwert makes about captive spaces and the wild, we see that the 'fear' is the consequence of human activity in the wilds.

Acknowledging that humans produce such landscapes of fear – under various pretexts, as Neiwert shows in the case of orcas – is itself an impossible task, as Patricia Westerford discovers when she argues the case for forests in *The Overstory* (Powers 2018). She calls the forest 'a threatened creature', in the singular, implying that the forest whose multiple forms of life crisscrossing its lands, is one single, coherent, organism. Powers suggests that the construction of landscapes of fear, such as the forest, is a strategy humans have developed to propose control and 'management' of the wild. In Westerford's meditations on the forest, we uncover Powers' critique.

First, Westerford offers a critique of human vanity:

> *People aren't the apex species they think they are.* Other creatures – bigger, smaller, slower, faster, older, younger, more powerful – call the shots, make the air, and eat sunlight. Without them, *nothing*. (Powers 2018, emphasis in original)

This apparent inversion of the landscape of fear where humans are the apex predator is not as simple as it first appears because it indirectly references what animal studies scholars have identified as a key methodological and political question: 'At what scale should politics be enacted: the individual animal or the collective?' (Collard and Gillespie 2015: 10–11). R. J. White argues that the animal geographers are driven by a 'desire to reject the undifferentiated and impersonal collective (*species, herds, "farmed" animals*) and emphasize the individual and unique natures of those sentient beings' (2015: 21). Powers through Westerford's meditations is calling for the apprehension of landscapes of fear as spaces of cohabitation of species collectives, but also to see collectives such as the forest as *one* organism because it unites everything – multiple life forms, processes, output – into itself. In other words, when Westerford believes that other species than humans *within* the forest have 'call[ed] the shots' by producing the air and the food on which all species depend, she has conflated the individual and the forest, pointing to the inevitable and mutually dependant cohabitation of companion species within it. As Westerford conceives it: 'For every large trunk, a few hundred seedlings huddle in the litter. Sword fern, liverworts, lichen, and leaves as small as sand grains stain every inch of the dank, downed logs' (Powers 2018: 134). While each species within the forest possesses distinctive ontological characteristics, this in no way denies or rejects the situated relations that make such characteristics possible.

Later, Powers' Westerford inverts the cultural meanings the forest and its decaying life are invested with by humans. Decay and rot are reconfigured in the narrative in an extended passage worth citing in full:

A bit of bushwhacking reveals the extent of the prodigious rot. Crumbling, creature-riddled boles, decaying for centuries. Snags gothic and twisted, silvery as inverted icicles. She has never inhaled such fecund putrefaction. The sheer mass of ever-dying life packed into each single cubic foot, woven together with fungal filaments and dew-betrayed spiderweb leaves her woozy. Mushrooms ladder up the sides of trunks in terraced ledges. Dead salmon feed the trees. Soaked by fog all winter long, spongy green stuff she can't name covers every wooden pillar in thick baize reaching higher than her head. (134)

Westerford then meditates on the cultural meaning of rot that invests the landscape as a space of fear alone:

Death is everywhere, oppressive and beautiful. She sees the source of that forestry doctrine she so resisted in school. Looking at all this glorious decay, a person might be forgiven for thinking that old meant decadent, that such thick mats of decomposition were cellulose cemeteries in need of the rejuvenating ax. She sees why her kind will always dread these close, choked thickets, where the beauty of solo trees gives way to something massed, scary, and crazed. When the fable turns dark, when the slasher film builds to primal horror, this is where the doomed children and wayward adolescents must wander. There are things in here worse than wolves and witches, primal fears that no amount of civilizing will ever tame. (134–135)

Powers shows that rot and death are sources of life itself: that one cannot have life without death. The myths and primal fears that the forest's dead mass induces in the human imagination and narratives effectively make the landscape a means of threat, not life. In the death of the tree, the lower-level plants and the animals, Powers suggests, there are the sources of life. Since 'each of us is a species multiple', as Thom van Dooren, Eben Kirksey and Ursula Münster (2016: 14) describe it, the decaying matter of or in a forest is a zone of multiple life forms who flourish precisely because some lives end. As Powers puts it, 'dead logs are far more alive than living ones' (2018: 139). A fuller description of this life-from-death occurs elsewhere in the novel:

[T]he temperate jungle's million invisible tangled loops need every kind of death-brokering intermediary to keep the circuits coursing. Clean up such a system, and the countless self-replenishing wells run dry. This gospel of new forestry is confirmed by the most wonderful findings: beards of lichen high in the air, that grow only on the oldest trees and inject essential nitrogen back into the living system. Subterranean voles that feed on truffles and spread the spores of angel fungi across the forest floor. Fungi that infuse into the roots of trees in partnerships so tight it's hard to say where one organism leaves off and the other begins. Hulking conifers that sprout adventitious roots high in the canopy that dip back down to feed on the mats of soil accumulating in the vees of their own branches. (141)

Deeply resonant with Powers' vision is Alexis Smith's *Marrow Island* (2016) where fungi redeem the earth of the land after it has been thoroughly contaminated. Lucie is introduced to the 'remediating' project, as the Marrow Island commune calls it – 'removing toxins from the ecosystem' (unpaginated) – by Tuck:

The mushrooms … go on for miles just under the soil, taking up what's there – vegetation, animals, mineral – breaking it all down, leaving soil the plants can thrive in. We've been inoculating different parts of the forest with different species. (Unpaginated)

The mycelia 'expedite soil restoration', Tuck informs Lucie (unpaginated). We see a similar account in *The Hungry Tide* where Ghosh (2004) presents the crabs as absolutely essential elements in the ecosystem. The crabs emerge at dawn and at dusk 'to salvage the rich haul of leaves and other debris left behind by the retreating tide' (114). They form a 'fantastically large proportion of the system's biomass' and constitute 'the keystone species of the entire ecosystem' (142). And, as lifeforms that keep 'the mangroves alive by removing their leaves and litter', they enable further life (142).

This landscape of fear where predation is spatially organized and responded to is also treated as a space to be cleared of the dead. Speaking of 'forest health', Westerford and the researchers in the forest point to the fallacies that project humans as the persons who need to save the forest:

'When I was a student, my teacher told us that fallen trunks were nothing but obstacles and fire hazards.'

The man on the ground looks up at her. 'Mine said the same thing.'

'"Clear them off to improve forest health.'"

'"Burn them out for safety and cleanliness. Above all, keep them out of streams.'"

'"Lay down the law and get the stagnant place producing again!'"

All three of them chuckle. But the chuckle is like pressing on a wound. Improve forest health. As if forests were waiting all these four hundred million years for us newcomers to come cure them. Science in the service of willful blindness.... (Powers 2018: 138)

As the conversation indicates, it is useful for humans to think of themselves as the newcomers who manage forest health by clearing out the dead wood (literally), forgetting that dead wood is what generates life. The humans, Powers suggests, laughably assume they can 'cure' whatever ails the forest.

Finally, the individual human in the forest, when alert to the true nature of the forest, does not discern a landscape of fear. Patricia Westerford sees the forest as contributing to her sense of self. Over time, so do the protestors, Nick and Olivia, up in the tree and the rest of the protestors. Powers suggests a powerful decentring of the human when Westerford, 'disentangles herself from a reactive, defensive self-narrative and moves toward a new story of the self as one living creature among others, embracing new possibilities of biocentric becoming', to borrow David Herman's phrasing (Herman 2018b: 35). That is, the scale and scope of predation is not the focus of Westerford's becoming: rather, she focuses on how the nonhuman forms constitute human selves, a layered, multispecies self. When Nick and Olivia are up in the tree, they survive because the tree supports much of their needs. While the danger of being pushed off the tree during storms and rain is very much a possibility, as they both discover, the tree is itself seen as one that reconfigures them: they become *with* the tree rather than remain a distinct species, as human. In *The Overstory*, then, the landscape of fear is indeed one made up by humans as apex predators but, as the individuals experience it, the forest has been mythicized by humans for their own purposes.

Shared Vulnerabilities

A different form of the landscape of fear also emerges in contemporary literature. This is a landscape where humans and the nonhuman share vulnerabilities.

Their embodiment is embedded in a specific context where certain species of humans and nonhumans are both disposable lives.

Take, for instance, Tania James' *The Tusk That Did the Damage* (2015). The Kavanar Wildlife Park where the novel is set is a space where the people who have dwelt in the area for generations, have lived with the plant and animal life, have now become *persona non grata* through a combination of a new legal machinery and corporate greed. In the very first account of the place, the protagonist, Manu, says:

> Humble as it was, our *palli* commanded a five-star view. To the north a phone tower climbed the sky. To the east an owl glared from its bamboo perch, swiveling its head for rodents among the stalks. To the west we watched the sunset pour over the teak-rimmed forest aka Kavanar Wildlife Park.
>
> Our people had been walking the forest long before it took that fussy name. The new laws forbid us from doing anything in the park, not walking, not even picking up a finger length of firewood without being fined for trespass and stealing. Stealing from trees that had dropped us fruit and firewood for centuries! Meanwhile, the laws looked kindly on the greenbacks and timber companies, their rows of rosewood, eucalyptus, teak. (9)

This ecosystem has been previously represented as a space unsafe for elephants because Manu speaks of the killing of elephants even before the above account.

First, James' protagonist – who will be killed by forest guards when they mistake him for a poacher – provides a picture-postcard account of the place, a picturesque setting. Then, he speaks in terms of the indigenous lineage that marks the place as theirs. In the account, Manu presents the place as an idyll, but also casts it in terms of ownership: the ownership of the park has changed hands. The new laws prevent the locals from living as they used to (by depending on the forest for their needs). The elephants and the trees are at risk, as are the human dwellers (who are fined and accused of stealing for doing what they have practised as a community for generations). The fact that the indigenous tribes are forced to take to poaching, as Manu's brother Jayan does, has a clear economic angle to it. Manu looks at his and his family's future:

> So would Jayan and I divvy our plots for the generation to come, on and on, all of us living elbow to elbow, head to toe. I felt my future dragging me deep underground. I thought of my brother and my uncle and the greenbacks

and the farmers. I thought of the elephants and the forest creatures, all their vengeful yellow eyes. (149)

Elsewhere James describes the changes in the entire biome, which affects the elephant population:

Even the forests had changed over the years of his absence, blighted by dying bamboo, patched with green and gold farm.

No sight was stranger than the treeless swaths through which he and his clan used to cross, taking shady refuge beneath the ribs of the trees. Little remained of the rosewood and *aanjili*, only stumps like rivets in the earth. (191)

Taken together, the account complicates the picture of the wildlife park where humans and nonhumans shared an embodied but differential vulnerability – a vulnerable transcorporeality – born of what Ben De Bruyn has described as 'a clash between incompatible claims for social and environmental justice' (143).[9]

The lives of both, the elephant and the locals, are disposable because of the lens through which they are perceived by the machinery of the state and the corporations that claim ownership of the land. Jason Sandhar has persuasively argued that 'the elephant's perpetually shifting roles as a mass murderer, a mascot for animal rights, a deity, and a commodity is refracted through the structural, class, and race inequities that destabilize the species boundary', 'complicat[ing] the apparently stable figure of the animal as Other' (2020: 149). The humans, the redwood trees and the elephants are subject to the same 'necessarily fluid assortment of species boundaries predicated on a network of power that cuts across the global and the local, the human and the nonhuman' (149; see also Walther 2021: 147–148). The transformation and re-classification of the elephant into a 'rogue' is accompanied by the state–corporate combine's efforts at altering the lifestyle of the poverty-stricken indigenous residents of the area. Even among the residents, Jayan is an outcast because he is a poacher: 'Most everyone, Christian and Muslim and Hindu alike, believed killing elephants for money was a sinful pursuit, and worse that he should profit from it' (T. James 2015: 66). Here James implies a social cohesion around the elephants: everyone believes that the pachyderms should not be subject to the same profiteering impulse that humans possess vis-à-vis the earth. The statement, occurring a quarter of the way into the novel, becomes a strike against the specific biopolitical regime that, as Sandhar's quote above indicates, embeds both humans and nonhumans. (The statement of course belies the mixture of care and coercion, two other crucial dimensions of the biopolitical paradigm in the novel, through which the elephants are controlled by the mahouts and caregivers.)[10]

In the human–nonhuman encounter in the landscape of fear, contemporary literature instantiates the predator–prey relationship (see, for example, Julie Leigh's *The Hunter*, 2000) but very often presents the interaction as one in which the relationship is determined by the 'language' each species reads off the other and the language of the biome itself. Amitav Ghosh embeds this interaction in the very nature of the land, whose 'signs' are meant for humans and nonhumans to read in *The Hungry Tide*:

> The freshly laid silt that bordered the water glistened in the sun like dunes of melted chocolate. From time to time, bubbles of air rose from the depths and burst through to the top, leaving rings upon the burnished surface. The sounds seemed almost to form articulate patterns, as if to suggest they were giving voice to the depths of the earth itself. (2004: 24)

The land and the water make their own soundscapes, into and from which, in Ghosh's masterly depiction, human language both feeds and emerges:

> The rivers' channels are spread across the land like a fine-mesh net, creating a terrain where the boundaries between land and water are always mutating, always unpredictable.... When these channels meet ... at these confluences, the water stretches back to the far edges of the landscape and the forest dwindles into a distant rumour of land, echoing back from the horizon. In the language of the place, such a confluence is spoken of as a *mohona* – a strangely seductive word, wrapped in many layers of beguilement. (6)

The entire tide country is a space that obfuscates and confuses human, particularly non-native, perception, as both Kanai and Piya, the outsiders to the region, discover: 'It was the disorientation caused by the peculiar condition of light in the silted water that made her panic ... [the mud] entered her eyes – it had become a shroud closing in on her' (54–55).

It is, as I have argued elsewhere, a landscape that produces uncanny fears and perceptual imbalance in the humans (Nayar 2010). The landscape, which possesses an 'epic mutability', undergoes 'another transformation' in the moonlight, when it becomes 'a silvery negative of its daytime image'. The effect is startling: 'It was the darkened islands that looked like a lake of liquid, while the water lay spread across the earth like a vast slick of solid metal' (Ghosh 2004: 154), an image that is prefigured in an earlier one ('the wood ... like a skin of mirrored metal', 39). Later the sky too serves as a reflecting surface, 'a dark-tinted mirror for the waters of the tide country' (379). After the near-disaster with the crocodile, Piya is in a state of shock: 'The water bubbled again as the reptile sank out of sight: for a moment after its submersion a ghostly outline of its shape remained imprinted on the surface and Piya saw that it was almost as large as the boat' (175). The crocodile appears to linger on, the atmosphere (water) seems to take its shape long after it has disappeared – the uncanny is the continued perception of something ghostly. More importantly, this encounter reveals something else: the animal is almost the same size of the refuge – the boat – and is its dangerous double. The double engendered by the tide country confounds mapping, geological accuracy and even vision. Later, Kanai, trapped in silt and in the mangrove finds it difficult to see clearly (328–329), but believes that he saw a tiger (330–331). Colonization by humans of the land, Ghosh seems to suggest, is the consequence of a mirage where man (it is of course a gendered process) assumes he can control any land (Nayar 2010: 96–97).

In all cases the landscape of fear is constructed, whether in actuality or in myth, for human needs, in which profits are central. The unnamed hunter of the thylacine in Julia Leigh's novel, *The Hunter*, we are told, was one of many who worked for a 'biotech multinational' and expects to be sent to 'Indonesia, Hawaii, Galapagos' for bioprospecting indicating the power of global biocapital to control the present and the future of different lifeforms anywhere in the world (2000: 25, 94). Even progressive companies such as Humboldt Timber, as Mother N says in *The Overstory*, finally fall prey to the profit motive:

Humboldt Timber. For those who don't, they were a family business for almost a century. They ran the last progressive company town in the state and paid incredible benefits.... Best of all, they cut selectively, for a yield they might have sustained forever.

Because they cut the old stuff slowly, they still had several billion board feet of the best softwood on the planet, long after their competitors all along the coast shot their bolts.... But HT's stock price lagged compared to those companies out there maximizing profits.... Right now they're in that second-to-the-last stage: cashing out every salable scrap of timber in the inventory. Which in this case means lots of seven- and eight-hundred-year-old trees.

Trees wider than your dreams are going into Mill B and coming out as planks. Humboldt is cutting at four times the industry rate. (Powers 2018: 214)

America, described earlier in the novel as 'a country that takes even its scraps right from God's table' (5), and the global economy force even such companies as Humboldt to overexploit the land, endangering the trees and the humans alike because, as Powers' Westerford insists throughout the novel, *all* lifeforms are dependent on the forests.

This linkage between the erosion and collapse of the nonhuman and the human because they share an embodied vulnerability, as these texts indicate, eventually undermines the very structure humans have developed to organize the populations – the nation. In Maya Montero's *In the Palm of Darkness*, an analogy is drawn between different extinctions, and the crisis besetting the nation (Haiti):

Where did our fish go? Almost all of them left the sea, and in the forest the wild pigs disappeared, and the migratory ducks, and even the iguanas for eating, they went too. Just take a look at what's left for humans, just take a careful look: You can see the bones pushing out under our skins as if they wanted to escape … to leave behind that weak flesh where they are so battered, to go into hiding someplace else. At times I think, but keep it to myself, I think that one day a man like you will come here, someone who crosses the oceans to look for a couple of frogs, and when I say frogs, I mean any creature, and he will find only a great hill of bones on the shore, a hill higher than the peak of Tête Boeuf. Then he will say to himself, Haiti is finished, God Almighty, those bones are all that remains. (1997: 11)

And later, most explicitly:

How could I explain that Haiti wasn't simply a place, a name, a mountain with a frog that had survived? … What would I say about the way they threw live animals onto their bonfires, about the dust and the stink, that unbearable, unspeakable, unfathomable stench? How would I describe the streets, the open sewers, the human shit in the middle of the sidewalk, the corpses at dawn, the woman whose hands were missing, the man whose face was missing? … God Almighty, how would I make him see that Haiti was disappearing, that the great hill of bones growing before our very eyes . . . was all that would remain? (170–171)

The 'great hill of bones' is a symbol of human mass murder and genocides, and along with the mutilated men and women constitute the political roots of the landscape of fear. As Ursula Heise observes of the novel, Montero 'associates the direct violence perpetrated on humans and the indirect violence that puts nonhuman species at risk.... The endangerment of a particular species, in this narrative ordering, comes to stand as a synecdoche for the dangers that threaten Haiti as a whole' (2016: 166–171).[11]

Farmlands disappear in *The Overstory* as modernization and capitalism proceed at an incredible rate:

> Extinction sneaks up on the Hoel farm – on all the family farms in western Iowa. The tractors grow too monstrous, the railroad cars full of nitrogen fertilizer too expensive, the competition too large and efficient, the margins too marginal, and the soil too worn by repeated row-cropping to make a profit. Each year, another neighbor is swallowed up into the massive, managed, relentlessly productive monocrop factories. (Powers 2018: 17)

The 'monocrop' reference indicts farming methods for the loss of biodiversity, and Westerford sees such farmlands – one of the potent symbols of American modernization – as culpable in the erosion of the forest covert: '[K]inds of life vanish a thousand times faster than the baseline extinction rate. Forest larger than most countries turns to farmland' (374).

The alignment of human and nonhuman on a continuum of shared vulnerability is the focus of Barbara Kingsolver's *Flight Behavior* as well. In the novel, millions of orange monarch butterflies have migrated from Mexico to North America due to climate change. Dellarobia Turnbow, who is seeking to similarly escape from her domesticity, begins to understand the dangers of global climate change when explanations are offered by scientists for the butterflies. Eventually, she understands that climate change had altered flight behaviour of both humans and nonhumans:

> Dellarobia was floored to think of these fragile creatures owning the span of a continent, from Canada to Mexico, moving back and forth across the wide face of a land. Each one was so little and sure to die, yet they constituted a force, like an ocean tide. She was relieved Bonnie hadn't suggested the butterflies had come straight here from Mexico. The thought of them running up here after the landslide and flood, displaced along with Josefina's family, was a worrisome possibility she did not want to entertain. It would give her family's mountain an air of doom. If these butterflies were refugees

of a horrible misfortune, there could be no beauty in them. (Kingsolver 2012, unpaginated)

The butterflies are refugees that have flown up north. There are, Dellarobia discovers, refugees everywhere. The landscape of fear – Mexico with its landslides, the weather that changed so drastically – is now global in scope and effect. The novel also documents other such interconnected disasters and climate shifts, which indicate a world in crisis: Michoacán in Mexico heats up and destroys the monarchs' overwintering habitat as oyamel fir trees, their habitat, are destroyed due to the high temperatures (349). The migration and flowering patterns of milkweed plants have changed (351). The numbers of pests such as fire ants and *Ophryocystis elektroscirrha* parasite are rising as well, thereby causing harm to the other species (147, 243, 349–350). As Markku Lehtimäki citing the work of Antonia Mehnert notes: '[W]e may also think that Kingsolver utilizes the idea of the "butterfly effect" in her novel; therefore, as a butterfly blinks its wings in Mexico, that causes hard rain and floods to happen in North America' (62–63).

And yet for many such as Bear Turnbow, Dellarobia's father-in-law, the butterflies should leave so that the logging company can cut the trees on their mountain and thereby help him clear his debts (once again exemplifying the tension identified by Ramachandra Guha and others between environmental and social [human] justice). This is a landscape of fear, where anthropogenic climate change affects humans and nonhumans differentially, and the poorly adaptable among both are forced to leave their homes. In short, the changes in habitat, life patterns (reproduction, migration) and even the nature of life forms (who survives, who does not) are visible across species and lands, producing a global, national and regional landscape of fear because all parts of the world have been subject to the predations – I use the term in the widest possible sense – of the human.

Multispecies solidarities emerge in odd and sometimes ironic ways in contemporary texts. Many characters wonder, given species loss speeding up in our time, what the extinction timeline for humans looks like. This takes the form of seeing beyond species differences and discerning something else. In these texts characters like Dellarobia correctly see the butterflies as signs of something bigger: 'It's like the butterflies came here, and we might be next. Like they're a sign of something' (unpaginated). More than a sign, the butterflies in the novel are 'sentinel devices'. Vasu, the forest officer in *The Tusk That Did the Damage*, says the same thing about elephants who were entering villages to search for bamboo: 'People can cry and fight all they want, but there will come a time when the bamboo will disappear, then the elephants, then us, and all will be as it was before we arrived' (T. James 2015: 100).

A brilliant moment in *The Hunter* has M pondering over his own fate when he watches the thylacine who is hunting:

> [She] shovel[s] her pointed wolf-like face into the bloody remains of a wallaby…. [M watches] with the same rapt attention he would devote to a film which told the story of his own life, past and future … he holds the animal in his sights, knowing that he is a killer, and that he, too, will be killed. (Leigh 2000: 162)

For David Herman, in this passage 'M's self-narrative begins to converge with the story line(s) he has built up around the tiger' (Herman 2018b: 14; also see Ursula Heise on M 'identif[ying] with the animal he is hunting', 2016: 46). But more than that, the passage gestures at nonhumans as sentinels, presentiments, of the human condition at some moment in the undefinable future. Alyssa Paredes, whose work resonates with the fictional representations above, argues that numerous species – mice, lichen, guinea pigs, birds – have served as '"early warning systems" for the assessment and management of environmental pollution and risk' (2022). Paredes writes: 'In serving as a warning signal of impending threat, they claim, sentinels also signal the existence and transcorporeality of a more-than-human collective, one that is marked as much by solidarity as by vulnerability' (85). What Byron and then Dellarobia after her education at Byron's hands in *Flight Behavior* and Patricia Westerford the disgraced plant scientist in *The Overstory* try to communicate to the world concerned solely with the economics of trees and plantations is, in Paredes' words, 'the uncertainty about whether human and animal bodies were *different enough* to ward off the same bodily effects wrought by a shared toxic environment' (2022: 86, emphasis in original). What M experiences in a moment of predictive reflection is the anticipation of his life and death resembling that of the creature he plans to kill, thus bringing together the human and nonhuman in a state of shared but differential vulnerability.

In both *The Overstory* and *Flight Behavior*, it is species such as Douglas firs and monarch butterflies respectively that draw people from all parts of the continent to the specific sites of protest and action. That is, the sites of protest, centred around specific species, in these texts, are themselves synecdochic of multispecies alliances, however temporary (Otjen 2022: 182). While in *The*

Overstory there are no indigenous voices speaking for the ancient trees – as has been noted by critics (Nichols 2022) – we see a form of interspecies and multiracial solidarities in *Flight Behavior*, with the African American researcher and lepidopterist Ovid Byron making common cause with Dellarobia and becoming instrumental in inspiring her son, Pete, into becoming a scientist. If, as Anastasia Yarbrough argues, 'environmental justice is built on real-life practices of diversity and solidarity while advancing theoretical developments into interconnected patterns of oppression often rendered invisible' (2015: 122), then such alignments in contemporary fiction gesture at a very real possibility. While no character believes or implies that humans are as vulnerable as the trees or animal species they are trying to protect, or seek identification *with* these species, they uniformly see the loss of species and altered behaviour – such as migration – of humans and animals as stemming from a trans-species vulnerability. This effectively makes the landscape of fear a trans-species zone of precarity.[12] Such a zone comes into being with acts of cross-species communication.

Talking (across) Species

Shannon Lambert in her pithy summary of *The Overstory*'s theme of multispecies identity gestures at a collective agency foregrounded in the novel: '[W]e have the impression of a multispecies "we" prior to enunciation – a "we" which does not assert itself in "human" terms through collective vocalisation … but instead through shared chemical – or, as I will frame it, affective – patterns' (2021: 190). These patterns of exchanges form the core of multispecies and cross-species identities and identification, even if humanity did not for a long time accord these exchanges the status of 'communication'. Moving from trees to animals, and their forms of communication, orcas, David Neiwert reminds us, have a very advanced sense of hearing, and this is what they employ to understand the world. However, since humans have defined intelligence in terms of human language, we do not see orcas as particularly intelligent: ·

> Even as we determinedly avoid anthropomorphizing these creatures, we almost reflexively apply a patently anthropocentric definition of intelligence, one involving language and its use. This is a definition that almost automatically places humans atop the heap, since our wired-in instinct for language is arguably one of our greatest evolutionary advantages. (Powers 2018, unpaginated)

It is this hierarchy that creaturely texts interrogate and in some cases subvert. Nonhuman forms of communication and cross-species communication therefore are a key theme in contemporary texts.

Animal studies, posthumanists and others, building on studies of animal behaviour but also anticipating them, have long argued that animals communicate, provided we abandon our modes of perception and practices of power, and listen (Wolfe 2013). In literature, cross-species communication is presented as: the exchange of corporeal-material information, which includes the biochemical, across bodies; acts of sensory perception notably seeing, smelling and listening to the radically Other or nonhuman; movement, shape, texture and pressure (Rigby 2016: 46). Both humans and nonhumans communicate below the level of consciousness (48). Such a listening by humans demands, in Ben De Bruyn's words, paying attention to 'the cultural meanings that various communities of humans have built on top of this nonhuman acoustics' (2020: 10), meanings that occur in literary texts even if in the form of symbols. In creaturely stories and accounts of multispecies relationality, we discern a co-becoming that is the result of exchange and emergence of meanings, immersion in webs of signification that might be linguistic, gestural, biochemical, and so on (van Dooren 2014: 2). In Ursula Heise's words, '"the human" has been formed and transformed amid encounters with multiple species of plants, animals, fungi, and microbes' (2016: 195).

This means, the nonhuman lifeforms around us coproduce our worlds, both real and symbolic: 'People's lifeworlds', write Diogo De Carvalho Cabral and André Vasques Vital, 'are animated by a panoply of vital choreographies, the meanings of which are negotiated both through in-person, real-time encounters and through the reporting of such encounters in writing' (2023: 716). When humans 'read' the landscape for signs of the animal, the animal too does the same, implying a semiotic network based on mutual perception and deriving a certain set of meanings (720). Bio- and ecosemioticians along with ethologists have consistently argued for information exchange in both intra- and interspecies encounters where the exchange can be of a wide variety, from organisms responding to the behaviour of the Other (semethic interactions) and the transfer of material resources between organisms (trophic interactions) to the physical flow of sensory information, as sensed by the organism (Wheeler 2006; Maran 2014a, 2014b; Maran-Kull 2014; Cobley 2016; Rigby 2016; Farina and James 2021).[13] There are other forms of information exchange and communication in landscapes of co-becoming. For instance, the human hunter tracks the animal through its spoor (scent, territorial marks, excrement), and vice versa. Further, animals mark their territory in various ways. Taken together, these marks are a form of communication and, according to some commentators in semiology, are among the oldest signs read by humans (Perrin 2011). For ecosemioticians, the landscape is constituted by and constitutive of a web of signification, of communication exchanges across species.

Acts of cross-species communication are a subcategory of what McKenzie Wark has termed 'xenocommunication', and is integral to the creaturely poetics of contemporary fiction (2014). For Wark, xenocommunication arises in situations of impossible regular communication: 'if regular communication sometimes seems impossible, then it doesn't seem all that ridiculous to imagine it possible to communicate with the impossible, with the infinite, with the great outdoors – the totality' (161). Such a communication, writes Wark,

> can be the irruption within a mundane communication of some-thing inhuman. Or, it can take the form of an alien mode of communication itself, which nevertheless seems legible, at least to someone within the sphere of communication … what is excommunicated to make communication possible are forms of xenocommunication that point to something other than communication as ordered by the powers of the day. (161)

Wark's emphasis on those left out of the ambit of what humans understand as communication – the nonhumans, for our purposes here – inscribes the entire system of communications within a structure of unequal power relations across species. It brings species in alignment, at least temporarily, and contemporary literature (which, of course, repeats these forms of communication in canonical writings that are now being revisited by animal studies and posthumanist scholars) suggests that such exchanges point to a multispecies co-becoming, mutual influence and identity-making. That is, human subjectivity in these texts is constructed through its engagement with the nonhuman, by its very embeddedness in a biome made up of different species with whom humans communicate, and which responds to human presences *in* the biome (keeping in mind the proviso that, as Panos Kompatsiaris [2022] argued, structures of domination and control determine the nature of all cross-species communication).

Xenocommunication and Predation

There is a particular aspect of xenocommunication that emerges in the human–nonhuman relationship in contemporary texts, and that is of humans employing their skills of reading marks and signs for an entirely different purpose: predation. Humans as apex predators read naturally occurring signs – pug marks for example – as a route to the nonhuman. Humans read the marks of the nonhuman, but also leave marks of their own, and the latter in texts like *The Hunter*, serve as reminders of the limitless potential for harm across species.

In James' *The Tusk That Did the Damage*, Manu describes how his elder brother, Jayan, has learnt to read the land and its inhabitants, but for entirely different purposes:

> He learned to read the crop, and I learned to read him. The day before a hunt, he was always glancing at the trees, listening for his omen, the woodpecker. If the woodpecker called from the east, I would glimpse my brother the next morning slipping past the house in his hunting uniform – green half pant and black T-shirt…. (2015: 56)

To hunt, thinks Manu, 'is to read a hidden language' (211). While seeking to get out of the forest, this is what he does: 'I minded the signals: the heaped hill of scat, the sever of a green-hearted branch' (211).

In Julia Leigh's *The Hunter*, the protagonist, the hunter of the title, is an efficient tracker, reading on the mountain slopes, in the soil and on plants signs of the animal he is pursuing:

> At muddy bare patches of soil directly enroute he pauses to inspect for prints: mostly the deep two-toed wallaby spoor, slammed into the mud, or scurrying devil spoor, or the occasional shuffling wombat. No tiger, nowhere a forefoot separated some prominent distance from its toe-pads; no four toes arranged symmetrically around the irregular, almost heart-shaped footpad with two deep grooves extending forwards from the rear border. (2000: 34)

When he finally sees a thylacine print, his first thoughts are: 'it is on this day that he sees the tiger has left him a print: the tiger, or maybe the plateau' (79). The hunter, after a detailed exploration of the area, finds another print. The print becomes the occasion for the apex predator chasing the endling to ponder over its reasons for going this way:

> So, he thinks, what were you doing around here, my tiger? Passing through, yes, for there's nothing here to stop for, but headed where? Back down to the lake by the looks of it, but which way? Not by the route I've taken. A secret way perhaps, but only for initiates. Again his spine grows strong,

and imagines for an instant that beneath the swelling his eye has narrowed, yellowed, deepened. (80)

Here the hunter moves from the language of the marks left behind by the prey into the mind of the prey, trying to ascertain the causes and principles of its movement. He

> wonders if she has a map in mind. Perhaps, he thinks, the lonely years have soured in her, soured her sense of smell so that now she madly wanders through the scrub, pulled one way by one scent, one way by another. (80)

Leigh here explicitly signals the erosion of cognitive abilities in an animal that has been the last of her species. Unable to 'read' scents, speculates the hunter, she is a confused specimen. Leigh is referencing extinction, and the slow erosion of the distinctive features – that have helped the species survive – in the endling. Leigh does not explicitly attribute the blame to human presence and activities. But the fact that the landscape which is supposedly wild and ought to have animal 'marks' is in fact dotted with human footprints, literal and metaphorical, implies an altered topos in which the thylacine is a bit lost or unsettled. For instance, the hunter discovers a 'collapsed trapper's hut' (87), the footprints of bushwalkers (58), the remnants of a human, perhaps killed by the thylacine (97) and cameras set up by the National Parks authority (123–124). These marks of human intervention and presence are marks for the thylacine as well, and constitute a semethic interaction where the 'habit of an organism is interpreted and reacted upon by other organisms, releasing yet other regular behaviours or habits' (Maran and Kull 2014: 44). The animal life on the plateau, in other words, would respond to the human devices, which have been placed on the basis of knowledge of animal behaviour, by modifying *their* (animal self's) routes and behaviour. The hunter speculates on the effect of the cameras and devices on the thylacine: 'If I were a thylacine, he thinks, it would read like a neon billboard' (Leigh 2000: 129). The nonhuman has learnt to 'read' signs of the human.

Devices designed to capture one animal or a specific specimen becomes in *The Hunter* a multispecies trap in a tragic ironic twist that implies the infinite capacity of humans to target more than one species, intentionally or otherwise. The traps set for the thylacine captures other animals: 'wallaby, pademelon, native cat' (58), 'two wallabies, a currawong, a brush-tailed possum, a pademelon' (143), a 'frozen menagerie' consisting of 'pademelons, wallabies (again, more wallabies), devils, native cats, two barred bandicoots, a feral cat, a shiny black currawong and, in one trap, a squat young wombat' (69). Such a description, according to Ben De Bruyn,

> remind[s] us of the other presences in this ecosystem.... Instead of asking us to listen, simply, to one individual animal that will incite sonic awe, the novel plays these rare sounds off against the more mundane noises of larger populations of animals, which create an effect that is closer to curiosity. (2020: 79)

The marks by humans – the traps, set based on animal behaviour, on their routes, dwelling places and places frequented by them – are marks indicative of large-scale and indiscriminate (multispecies) violence.

These marks transform *all* lifeforms into targets of opportunity. Samuel Weber makes the distinction between *skopos* and *telos*, where the former is the target and the latter the fulfilment of an action or set of processes (2005: 5–6). Weber writes: '*Skopos* is already, tendentially, the *tele-scope*, since "the one who aims" is also "the one who surveys." To survey, in this sense, is to command at a distance' (7). *Skopos* 'designates not just the act but also the object of such watching: the mark or target' (7). In Leigh's novel, any animal that accidentally walks into the scene or trap – like the victims of random shootouts or kidnappings, in which no *specific* individual is targeted – means that the 'scope' of the trap or camera was already trained on the particular spot where whoever or whatever turned up would *become* the victim. In other words, the unforeseen or unplanned target is prepared for – scoped – with the trap readied for it. Marks of human violence are spread everywhere, transforming any nonhuman into a target of opportunity and fungible: aiming for the tiger, the trap kills a variety of other species.

Signs, Affect and the Collective

In *The Overstory*, researching trees, Patricia Westerford establishes the fact of vegetal communication:

> The trees under attack pump out insecticides to save their lives. That much is uncontroversial. But something else in the data makes her flesh pucker: trees a little way off, untouched by the invading swarms, ramp up their own defenses when their neighbor is attacked. Something alerts them. They get wind of the disaster, and they prepare. She controls for everything she can,

and the results are always the same. Only one conclusion makes any sense: The wounded trees send out alarms that other trees smell. Her maples are *signaling*. They're linked together in an airborne network, sharing an immune system across acres of woodland. (Powers 2018: 125, emphasis added)

From this she concludes:

The biochemical behavior of individual trees may make sense only when we see them as members of a community. (126, emphasis in original)

Powers is establishing here a case for trees as communicating organisms. Indeed, the entire landscape is a semiotic world, which includes human and nonhuman and even the non-living as communicating entities. Trees communicating through biochemical secretions that are picked up across the woodland by large numbers of trees indicate a trophic exchange of *material* resources, chemicals, through the connected roots but also through the air – what Powers calls 'signaling' in the novel. In the process, Powers argues, a collective agency of the entire woodland comes into being, a community of trees that develop resistance strategies to face the invasion, a state that could be described as 'biosentience', the subjectivity of all living forms (MacCormack 2020: 52).

Later, Powers amplifies this theme of trophic exchange when, in Westerford's researches and work, she finds that other species collaborate in the exchange in an act of communication:

Fungi mine stone to supply their trees with minerals. They hunt springtails, which they feed to their hosts. Trees, for their part, store extra sugar in their fungi's synapses, to dole out to the sick and shaded and wounded. A forest takes care of itself, even as it builds the local climate it needs to survive.

Before it dies, a Douglas-fir, half a millennium old, will send its storehouse of chemicals back down into its roots and out through its fungal partners, donating its riches to the community pool in a last will and testament. We might well call these ancient benefactors *giving trees*. (Powers 2018: 221, emphasis in original)

These are 'giving trees' because they have a conduit, an anastomosing and rhizomatic network of fungi and host trees – Douglas firs – so that categories such as the original and the derivative, primary and secondary are blurred, as the above passage indicates. Exemplifying a symbiotic relationship, the trees and the fungi survive through material exchanges, warning, supporting, feeding and defending each other, a system of communications that covers the entire woodland. There are no guests and hosts here, strangers and natives, except for humans, for all are linked and inseparable. Indeed, Powers imagines the vegetal network as encompassing the planet in an extraordinary multispecies connectivity:

> Messages hum from out of the bark she leans against. Chemical semaphores home in over the air. Currents rise from the soil-gripping roots, relayed over great distances through fungal synapses linked up in a network the size of the planet. (499)

Amitav Ghosh in *The Hungry Tide* integrates three kinds of languages in an ecosemiotic aesthetic not often seen in recent Indian fiction in English. First, the land is a language-scape, possessing signs (visual and aural) that humans need to interpret, just as the nonhuman denizens of the region do.

> The freshly laid silt that bordered the water glistened in the sun like dunes of melted chocolate. From time to time, bubbles of air rose from the depths and burst through to the top, leaving rings upon the burnished surface. The sounds seemed almost to form articulate patterns, as if to suggest they were giving voice to the depths of the earth itself. (2004: 24)

Ghosh represents the storm that is the epicentre of the novel as possessing its own material language.

> [The storm's noise] sounded no longer like the wind but like some other element – the usual blowing, sighing and rustling had turned into a deep, ear-splitting rumble, as if the earth itself had begun to move.... It was as though the sky had become a dark-tinted mirror for the waters of the tide country. (378–379)

While such an account of 'the agency of the storm reworks standard tropes of nature' (Trexler 2014: 218), it still remains a necessary trope, one that communicates the fact that elements of Nature interact to produce soundscapes and lightscapes (thunder and lightning) that then transform the relationships of the humans and nonhumans with the land and each other.

Then, Ghosh depicts the land and its human languages and cultural practices as shaping each other:

> The mudbanks of the tide country are shaped not only by rivers of silt, but also by rivers of language: Bengali, English, Arabic, Hindi, Arakanese and who knows what else ... the tide country's faith is something like one of its great *mohonas*, a meeting not just of many rivers, but a circular roundabout people can use to pass in many directions. (2004: 247)

This cultural context is a linguistic double of the land itself, in Ghosh's mixture of realism and irrealism.

Finally, there is the language of the nonhuman itself, which Ghosh's Piya seeks to not just understand, but also to speculate on how it integrates into Fokir's cognitive frame:

> She imagined the animals circling drowsily, listening to echoes pinging through the water, painting pictures in three dimensions – images that only they could decode. The thought of experiencing your surroundings in that way never failed to fascinate her: the idea that to 'see' was also to 'speak' to others of your kind, where simply to exist was to communicate. In contrast, there was the immeasurable distance that separated her from Fokir. What was he thinking about as he stared at the moonlit river? ... [T]hat was how it was with human beings, who came equipped, as a species, with the means of shutting each other out.... [I]f you compared it to the ways in which dolphins' echoes mirrored the world, speech was only a bag of tricks that fooled you into believing that you could see through the eyes of another being. (159)

When the novel ends, the human technology of the GPS and the nonhuman languages of the river and the dolphins come together, although it had been anticipated earlier in the novel:

> At the start, she had thought they might end up disrupting each other's work – that her soundings would get in the way of his fishing or the other way around. But, to her surprise, no such difficulties arose: the stops required for the laying of the line seemed to be ideally timed for the taking of soundings. In other circumstances, Piya would have had to use the Global Positioning System to be sure ... but here the line served the same purpose.... It was surprising ... that their jobs had not proved to be utterly incompatible – especially considering that one of the tasks required the input of geostationary satellites while the other depended on bits of sharkbone and broken tile. (141)

'All the routes Fokir showed me', says Piya at the end, 'are stored here … that was the route we took on the day before the storm…. That one map represents decades of work and volumes of knowledge' (398).

De Bruyn is accurate when he argues that, in addition to the 'juxtaposition of low-tech and high-tech tools', 'at least in certain sections, this narrative sketches not so much a fish-eye or a dolphin-ear episteme but a GPS-based way of understanding riverine reality' (2020: 37). The novel instantiates xenocommunications as a way of generating a different understanding of reality: riverine, terrestrial and nonhuman.

In similar fashion, *The Tusk That Did the Damage* brings the boy, Manu, face to face with the Gravedigger in a pivotal scene in the novel worth citing in some detail:

> The Gravedigger stood a few yards away, its body obscured by bamboo, its tusks reaching white through the vines, its head looming and vast as a cliff.
>
> Sweat stung my eyes yet I would not blink. I stared at one of the tusks, the tip that had long ago gored a man's galloping heart.
>
> Running seemed pointless and beyond my power. My legs were limp, my hands empty, aside from a fistful of sanitary leaves. I prayed to the tusker as had every numbstruck luckless clod to face a rogue thusly unarmed. Finish me quick.
>
> Aside from an ear twitch, the tusker did not move. Its legs were granite columns, supporting such a spectacular bulk. It regarded me with its honey-hued eyes as if to take my measure, my potential for harm. As I stood there, I felt an odd calm settle over me. Fathoms deep, those eyes, small inside the cliff sides, close to the color of my own. Remote and ancient. Eyes that had seen the wild and not-wild, eyes that knew things.
>
> The whole forest seemed to hold its breath. All at once the Gravedigger came to a conclusion that caused it to turn and saunter off, thrashing aside a tree as if it were of no more consequence than a weed. Thus the Gravedigger departed, quiet as it came, a cool gray moon. It had let me live. (T. James 2015: 197–198)

What does the elephant see when he meets the boy? What is this 'conclusion' the creature comes to? James does not help us answer these questions, but the boy seems to read into the elephant's eyes, wisdom, a calculation about the degree of danger the boy posed to it. Later, his brother Jayan probes Manu about the elephant, but Manu refuses to elaborate.

He [Jayan] would have guessed the Gravedigger, being weak-eyed, had not seen me, that the smeared scat on my arms had kept him from sniffing me out. Or that I had merely faced a dim-witted elephant, not the Gravedigger itself.

But I had looked into the creature's eyes. Dim it was not. (208)

But at one point he admits to the poacher party: 'I cannot face it again' (209). In *The Hunter*, after M has shot the thylacine, he approaches the dying animal to finish her off. The scene is described thus:

he finds himself unable to do the right thing now and finish her off. Ancient words which might once have helped him, words big enough for the beautiful terribleness of the deed, are long lost and out of reach, so he says, whispers, the best he can think of, which is – simply – you won't die alone.

He circles tight, until he can look into her eyes. They are a deep yellowy-brown and when he does look into them he realises that she in turn does not seem to see him – her eyes are blank and vacant and say nothing. (Leigh 2000: 136)

The endling refuses to communicate, or the apex predator sees only a 'blank'. There is, indeed, nothing to be said by either the predator or the prey. The mystifying 'you won't die alone' is intended as a line of comfort, since he cannot think of anything else to 'say' to the last of the species. In *The Tusk That Did the Damage*, the Gravedigger has just killed two humans. When he returns to his herd, he is shunned. James describes the scene in terms of an olfactory language that the beasts understand:

In the forest, wild elephants wanted nothing to do with the Gravedigger, not with the death stench of man tattooed into his skin. He would pad quietly to the watering hole, where a clan was taking rest, but as soon as they caught the tidal stink of his coming, they shrieked and clamored away. (2015: 191)

Nonhuman forms, then, are responding to chemical secretions – language of a kind, a trophic exchange – from neighbours. The collective shunning of the Gravedigger stems from a shared reading of the 'tidal stink', a sign of his acts of violence, a violence that soured the relationship between humans and nonhumans. The response of the 'clan' is, one speculates, born of a sense of self-preservation: the Gravedigger has jeopardized the lives of all elephants.

Isolating him, the rest of the clan assert a collective agency directed at such a self-preservation. This process of communication defines the landscape itself. A landscape infused with signs that may contribute to or alleviate the sense of fear is presented invariably in affective terms in the literature.

Animals respond – as contemporary novels seized with the theme of climate change and resultant crises of the nonhuman imply – to human chemicals and odours. *The Tusk That Did the Damage* tries to give the elephant its own voice and capture how the animal responds to negative and threatening changes in its biome, changes indexed in the language of odours, sounds and chemicals. The Gravedigger is being portrayed here:

> The sky above him wild with stars, and still the Gravedigger could not sleep. He felt a smoldering under his skin, an ache in his tusks, until the breeze brought him the scent of Old Man…. In time, Old Man's smell receded, his footsteps rasping away.
>
> Moments later, another smell spilled through the darkness. The Gravedigger caught the chemical smog, the liquored stink that filled the mouth like bad fruit. (162)

This is a mixture of the trophic – there is the chemical scent the Gravedigger picks up from the human presence –subdermal sensing ('felt a smoldering') and aural inputs (footsteps).

The synaesthesia in the last line – the smell fills the mouth with bad taste – is a clever mode of suggesting the sensory environment in which sight, smell, texture, taste are not separable. It is at once a cause and consequence of his distress. The synaesthesia functions here to indicate the elephant's distress – unable to find succour in the signals he is used to (that from the Old Man), he is instead bombarded with signals that confuse him. The relationship between humans and nonhumans had been, until this point, restricted to the more humane handler, the Old Man, and the elephant. The arrival of new persons, such as Romeo, alters the biome, and the elephant's confusion and distress are palpable.

The important thing is that whether the human intends to or not, xenocommunication is in progress, but the content of this communication appears to be determined by the *intention* of the human sender (*The Overstory* suggested that the trees communicate with the whole woodland because they *intend* to warn, save and support). The elephant *accepts* the sensory information from the Old Man but is distressed by such 'information' from Romeo.

In a situation where the elephant is a captive species and specimen for the human, and at a disadvantage, James treats the acts of xenocommunication as at once enabling and disabling the human–nonhuman relationship, and even determining it. The Gravedigger's response to the new smells and the synaesthesia they induce are to do with *memories* of such smells, and what they were symptomatic of in the past. Very early in the novel, describing how the Gravedigger witnessed the killing of his mother, James describes how he had been himself hurt.

> One man strode toward the Gravedigger, his hair smelling of a sticky odor, some chemical scent mixed with pineapple rot. With the man's every step, the world seemed to tighten. He was holding a knife.

> The Gravedigger smelled urine streaming down his leg. He pressed himself against his mother's still warm belly and waited to die.

> The man walked past the Gravedigger, around his mother's flank. The Gravedigger could not see what the man was doing. All he heard was the soft squeal of the knife. All he smelled was the pineapple rot. (2015: 6)

Later, his caretakers discover that he 'cower[s] from the smell of pineapple' (29). Years later, the smell haunts him: '[I]t was the pomade coming off the pappan's hair, the sticky pineapple rot that slid through the air and up his trunk, shocking his head with a memory from a day long ago, the day his mother roared and sank' (189)

The Gravedigger remembers the Old Man, his 'musk, fresh upon the air, the stepping-stones of his spine' (192). The olfactory memory triggers trauma, repeats a day from the past, but it also signals for the elephant when humans had killed his mother and maimed him. When this same Gravedigger passes domesticated elephants, James writes speculating on his view of them, he sees 'an alarming absence in their eyes', suggesting they had lost their fundamental identity (26). Emma the film-maker's aim is to make a film 'that would exhume the traumas sealed deep inside animal minds' (39). James also achieves something else when she attempts to probe and depict how an elephant thinks. Eschewing the instrumental – how to secure food or safety – the elephant is depicted as considering something else altogether: the human source of his suffering. She also tries to visualize how elephants grieve, with a 'deep-sea murmur' of the older elephants with the skulls of the dead ones, again a sensory memory he carries with him (190). When Amy Donovan speaks of the whale's encounter with fishing, she underscores trauma as the wellspring from which the whale's memories emerge, even as she grows up. Donovan writes: 'Perhaps, the four-year old whale even now bears a memory of ropes, a fear that is generations deep' (2022: 238). Donovan, like James and others, tries to visualize and sense the world *as* the nonhuman perceives it and also speculates that the whales are increasingly troubled by the louder noises that permeate the oceans: 'the ocean is too loud, louder than she remembers, constant interference now, the sea floor throbbing' (239). Mourning for both her mother and her species, Donovan's whale dies.[14] In Louis Nowra's *Into That Forest*, Hannah and Becky, feral children with Tasmanian tigers, recognize that 'tigers don't cry, but they know sadness, and both Dave and Corinna were empty except for sadness' (2012: 66). Like James' Gravedigger, Nowra's Tasmanian tigers and Donovan's whale, grief serves as a unifying affect when Ukhayyad and the camel meet after a break in *Gold Dust*:

> When Ukhayyad returned from his journey, he found the Mahri anxious. He stroked the animal's body and massaged the mended skin. The piebald's eyes were swollen with sadness. He led the camel into the southern pastures where they could be alone. Ukhayyad took some barley out of his sack and held the grain in his hands. The camel turned away. Ukhayyad followed after him with the food, but the animal stubbornly refused his advances. 'I know why you're so rough with me,' Ukhayyad said, returning the grain to his knapsack.
>
> 'You're angry because I left you and went off. I did not abandon you. We had agreed to it together. We've guaranteed the return of your color. Now, you'll return to being a piebald like before. Aren't you looking forward to seeing yourself dappled, beautiful, and rare?'
>
> The piebald's eyes welled up with tears and Ukhayyad hugged him. (al-Koni 2008: 60)

Later too there are references to the camel's eyes smiling and laughing at Ukhayyad (82, 117ff.).

Grief, pain and suffering rather than functionality and instrumental reason could be the foundations for affective multispecies solidarities, suggests much contemporary fiction and theory. Anat Pick, reading J. M. Coetzee's *The Lives of Animals* (1999), argues that even Temple Grandin, celebrated for her attempts to get into the minds of the animals, is 'propelled toward the less interesting thought when otherness becomes a functional rather than an ethical issue' (Pick 2011: 67–68). Instead, argues Pick, we should perhaps speculate on a different category of the nonhuman's thought beyond the instrumental-functional. Pick cites Coetzee's Costello:

> 'How does one use the crates to reach the bananas?' is the least interesting. Sultan [the chimpanzee] could have thought: 'Why is he starving me?' or 'What have I done?' or 'Why has he stopped liking me?' … At every turn … Sultan is driven to think the less interesting thought. From the purity of speculation (Why do men behave like this?) he is relentlessly propelled toward lower, practical, instrumental reason (How does one use this to get that?) and thus toward acceptance of himself as primarily an organism with an appetite that needs to be satisfied. (Cited in Pick 2011: 67)

For Pick, for multispecies belonging and justice, we need a different category of question that we *imagine* the creature to be asking itself: 'this sort of speculation is not Cartesian, but reminds one of Weil's creaturely cry of the heart against injustice: "Why am I being hurt?"' (67).

We see Pick's point instantiated in *The Hungry Tide* too when Piya, horrified at the killing of the tiger by the villagers, speculates on the tiger's pain, 'as if she could see the animal cowering inside the pen, recoiling from the bamboo spears, licking the wounds that had been gouged into its flesh' (Ghosh 2004: 294). James' representation of the elephant's memory of pain triggered by an olfactory signal that communicates across the human–nonhuman border and Ghosh's depiction of Piya trying to visualize and imagine the tiger's pain are literary embodiments of the type of speculation – ethical rather than instrumental – Pick calls for creaturely texts to undertake.[15] In Ibrahim al-Koni's *Gold Dust*, Ukhayyad's purebred camel is injured, with little hope of recovery, according to the elders. Ukhayyad prays to God:

> Lord, divide his share of pain. Let me be the one to lighten his burden. He has already suffered so much. It is not fair that he should suffer by himself all these months – he is mute and unable to express his complaint. But he comprehends. And he feels pain, excruciating pain – otherwise he would not be howling. Purebred creatures do not cry out unless the pain is unbearable. (al-Koni 2008: 36)

Ukhayyad is responding to the nonhuman's pain, interpreting the signs as indicative of a shared vulnerability: the susceptibility to pain. His prayer conflates the human and the nonhuman in this condition of shared vulnerability even as, or maybe because, he reads the signs of pain in the nonhuman.

Admittedly, in xenocommunications there is no exact match between the languages of plants, animals and humans, and no easy translatability. While the problematic anthropocentrism informs even an imagining of the meanings of animal sounds, plant communication and cross-species exchanges, whether in terms of their semethic or trophic interactions, contemporary literature does see such interactions as effecting an empathetic connection across species. When, for example, Ibrahim al-Koni concludes *Gold Dust*, he shows how both the camel and Ukhayyad are killed through mutilation – Ukhayyad is torn apart, in a tragic irony, by camels, and his camel is tortured to death – by the tribesmen. Merging the fate of the human and his nonhuman companion species, al-Koni demonstrates their shared vulnerability to human cruelty: that those who hurt animals will hurt humans too (as Cary Wolfe speaking about the genocides of animals and humans has argued, 2013, and Coetzee's Elizabeth Costello observes when she links the holocaust to animal genocides, 1999).

Animals, as Sundhya Walter argues, disrupt the discourses and myths of modernity which hinge on a separation of the human from the nonhuman. Walther writing of the successes of postcolonial multispecies and ecological fiction says:

> By their very closeness, these human and nonhuman animals living together disturb the imaginative construct of the modern. Even the texts of postcolonial humanism that appear here depend for their force on the interpenetration of species 'zones' in ways that are surprising, disturbing, and transgressive. This disorder is integral to the postcoloniality of these texts in that it pushes back against colonial taxonomies and against ideas of modernity that continue to and construct the postcolonial world as other by pathologizing or exoticizing its multispecies spaces. (2021: 13)

The Biomutation Narrative

Human–animal hybrids and humans turning into animals have long been the stuff of fables in most cultures, from the *Panchatantra* and *Jataka Tales* in India to Ovid in ancient Rome (Sinha 2023; Doniger 2005). Children's and young adult literature and superhero comics in particular have made much of shape shifters and species-defying life forms (Baker 1993). For historians, anthropomorphized animals and zoomorphized humans represent cultural anxieties about human identity (for a collection on such representation in early modern Europe, see Melion et al. 2015).

A wide variety of the humanimal may be found in literature: 'animalized animals', 'humanized animals', 'animalized humans' and 'humanized humans' (Wolfe 2003: 101). Franz Kafka's *The Metamorphosis* (2016 [1915]), of course, made the humanimal a household imaginary. These are species-blurring categories. Species border-crossing themes in contemporary writing are of two kinds, as identified by David Herman:

> The duality of the hybrid (the self in dialogue with an other) and the transmuted one-ness of the metamorphized subject (the self becoming other): these two possibilities define boundary conditions for narratives that resituate the human self by questioning or reconfiguring the human-nonhuman distinction as such. (2018b: 51–52)

These could be 'hypothesized or fictional crossings-over from the realm of the human to the domain of the nonhuman, or vice versa, whereby the human (or nonhuman) self undergoes a temporary or permanent transformation of species identities' (51). In texts where the human is 'in dialogue with an other', the attempt is to think and feel like an animal, to identify as closely with it as possible. In the second, the human metamorphs into the Other, in what Herman terms 'the biomutation narrative' (51).[16] Both are modes where the human self-narrative is decentred and instead the self is distributed across species (2018b). That said, the biomutation narrative suggests that the non-living is also a component of human lifeforms. The inanimate, as David Wills argues, animates human life itself (2016). Human DNA is itself a chemical. To take another, slightly different, instance of multispecies belonging and identity formation, in texts like Margaret Atwood's *Life Before Man* (1979), Sarah Bezan notes the insistence on bone and fossil record of other forms of life, often of extinct animals. This 'ossiferous fiction', as Bezan calls it, shows the deep time of humanity *as* calcium in the form of bone, egg shells and other materials from dead animals that sediment into the earth returns in the form of chemicals that provide nutrients for and shape subsequent lifeforms. In Bezan's words, 'ossiferous fictions teach us to pay attention to the animal forms of life that form the very blueprint of our being' (2021: 483). Ossiferous fiction does not quite fit the definition of 'biomutation' narrative, but signals the inanimate at the heart of all life. (A variant of such fiction would be A. S. Byatt's 'A Stone Woman' [2003], where, as the title indicates, a woman transforms into stone, to which I shall turn later in this chapter.) It embodies 'the human subject's passage into the nonhuman that allows for an affective, cognitive, and temporal shift and rescaling: a fiction of the geologic turn' (Ivanchikova 2021: 15).

Zoomorphism is the opposite of anthropomorphism, and refers to the attribution of animal mental states to humans. Zoomorphism also seeks to understand the animal mind, and to explain the source of human mental states: 'Zoomorphism ... is a general theoretical assumption about how we can explain the human mind and its building blocks. It asserts that we should only posit mental state types that we know from the study of animal cognition' (Nanay 2021: 173). But the thorny question, stemming from Tom Nagel's 'What Is It Like to Be a Bat?' (1974), remains: what mental states do we attribute to and imagine in animals?[17] As in, the question is, since mental states form worlds, what worlds do animals form? To return to Nanay:

> The philosophical explanatory paradigm of zoomorphism tells us to attribute mental states of animals to humans. But of what kinds of animals? There is huge variation in animal cognition from jellyfish to bonobo – what animal mental states should we use in our zoomorphic explanations? (2021: 177)[18]

Stories of feral children are variants of the zoomorphic tale, wherein the children lose their humanity and increasingly resemble and nearly become the animals with whom they live for extended periods of time, and therefore the borders between species and between Nature and culture are blurred, and the feral functions 'as a biopolitical figure of transspecies border/crossing' (Yoon 2017: 137; see Nayar 2019). In other cases, the speaker or narrator functions in the same manner as Elizabeth Costello in Coetzee's eponymous novel, positing herself as an animal whose animality has to stay concealed in polite, human gatherings such as the Tanner Lectures at which she is speaking:

> Now that I am here ... in my tuxedo and bow tie and my black pants with a hole cut in the seat for my tail to poke through (I keep it turned away from you, you do not see it), now that I am here, what is there for me to do? Do I in fact have a choice? If I do not subject my discourse to reason, whatever that is, what is left for me but to gibber and emote and knock over my water glass and generally make a monkey of myself? ... I am not a philosopher of mind but an animal exhibiting, yet not exhibiting, to a gathering of scholars, a wound, which I cover up under my clothes but touch on in every word I speak. (Coetzee 1999: 23–26)

Zoomorphism, Kinship, Passing

In Louis Nowra's *Into That Forest*, when Hannah and Becky are marooned on the shores after their parents are swept away in the floods, they come face to face with the Tasmanian tiger. Hannah, through whose perspective the story comes to us, records their first reactions to the tiger: '[W]e were both wondering if we were going to be its breakfast. We were hungry too' (Nowra 2012: 17). In the space of two sentences, Nowra aligns the human and the nonhuman: what unites them is a physiological state, hunger. Hannah reads the tiger's expression and says, '*It wants to take us home*, I said. Becky said I were loony. But the more I looked at its black eyes, the more I seen kindness' (17, emphasis in original).

From here begins the extended stay of the two girls with the tigers in their den, and their slide towards ferality. The tigress hunts and fetches birds she has killed for them to eat. Hannah adapts faster and Becky – who does not wish to abandon her shoes because 'she were afeared she would become like an animal and stop being a human' (36) – accuses her: '[*Y*]*ou sleep with them. You make noises like them!*' (26, emphasis in original). They learn, however, from the tigers, from things like never touching their tails to hunting like them. As she sees Becky transform, Hannah comments, '[S]he were always a tame girl. I never seen her act like that; it were with such wildness' (35). As the novel proceeds, a deep affection springs up between the girls and the tigers: 'It sounds foolish, but when you are so close to some creature like a tiger you get to really know them and that's what Corinna were saying to me – *We are a pack* … the tigers stopped being animals to me' (36–37, emphasis in original).

It could be argued that the transformation into feral creatures in Nowra is a conscious and *studied* transformation. Nowra's pedagogic plot, I suggest, forces us to read the text for the inversion of the traditional *bildungsroman*. And here the human and the nonhuman study each other:

> It were something that I were learning. I might be studying them, but they studied us as well. When they looked deep at you, you knew they were peering right into your soul and they knew if you were lying or not. You couldn't pretend to them that you were happy when you were not. They knew when we were down in the dumps and would nuzzle and comfort us. (37)

Hannah is fed by the tigress, as if the human were her cub:

> Corinna curled herself next to me and I found meself sucking her nipples, like it were the most natural thing in the world. I filled meself up to brimful

with her warm milk and it made me less sad and less feeling misery for meself. (32)

And slowly the adaptation is complete:

> Becky and I hardly said a word to each other. We were beyond words. When we moved round we did it on all fours, like we had become tigers too. I took off me dress and threw it away. I had no use for that, no use for words. Becky and me were in a heaven made of clouds of perfume. The tigers too. We all had the same expressions of bliss and happiness and we all had eyes that were glassy. We were full as a goog with joy. (55)

And the adaptation begins to affect the material body:

> [S]ometimes in a hunt we found ourselves running on all fours. As our hands and wrists became stronger we didn't even notice we were doing it. Corinna and Dave were our parents now and we copied them. (61)

Hannah begins to be 'excited', like the tigers, by the smell of blood (51). And elsewhere: 'When Dave caught an animal or bird, we'd eat our fill, and then fill our gobs and crawl into the lair with our heads bowed, like kids with really strict parents, and vomit up our food for her' (62).

Nowra's text reads like a pedagogic narrative about what animals, in the role of parents or teachers, can teach us. Hannah and Becky are tutored by the tigers, and in the process forget the skills, mannerisms, language and gait of the *Homo sapiens* as taught by their human family. Becky's initial anxieties about giving up her shoes, clothes and mannerisms convey the anxiety at the shift in tutelage and the identity such a tutelage bestows upon the pupils – of being human. Years after they return from the wilds, Becky has to be reschooled, and Nowra spends a considerable amount of narrative space describing this initiative. Becky never fits in, but the school gardener's dog 'recognised a kindred spirit' in her (129). Playacting does not work, and at a school play, playing Red Riding Hood, Becky inverts the script:

> The boy who were dressed up as a wolf came towards her. She tensed, placed all her attention on him, and lost any sense that she were on stage in front of an audience. It were like she were really in the woods and she were not afeared of the big bad wolf…. Her blood were now hot and pulsating and

forgetting where she were, she moved in on the boy like he were the prey rather than the other way round. (132)

Eventually Becky, who has abandoned humanity and returned to the forest, dies protecting Corinna.

Exposing the fragile nature of human education and culturation, Nowra alters the conventional *bildungsroman*: the girls grow up integrated into the nonhuman world rather than the human one. Later efforts at integrating them *back* into the human social structure fail because, Nowra suggests, the pedagogic practices of the nonhuman takes a stronger hold on the girls. These practices even change the perceptual structures of the girls, accentuating their smell and hearing over the visual.

Although Nowra comes close to proposing an alternative family structure, with tiger-parents, and their progeny consisting of human-pups and tiger pups, he is anticipating what Donna Haraway and subsequent theorists of multispecies belonging speak of as *kinship*. The tigers, to adapt a phrasing from Abby Schroering, are 'like-human but not human, as available for connection but not for identification, and as kin but not family' (2022: 141). Multispecies belonging is not about the replacement of human parents or children with nonhumans but seeking the nonhumans as kin rather than family. Nowra suggests that the kinship changes the girls in irrevocable ways. Years later, after she is taken back to human civilization and becomes a mate on a ship, Hannah continues to see the world through a perspective left over from her feral days: 'Other times I felt as if I were no longer attached to the ship, but like a sea eagle drifting in an air current, unattached to the earth and sea, carefree and happy' (Nowra 2012: 109). Her treatment of and response to other humans has altered too:

> People still say that 'bout me. When I go to the local store the shopkeeper, Mr Dixon, says I stare at him as if he were food. But it's not that. It's not even that I'm listening to his words. What I am doing is closely watching his body and his eyes to see what he's thinking of doing next or what he's actually thinking. It's what me and Becky learned when we were with the tigers. It's the body and eyes that tell what a person is thinking or going to do. (129)

And her perceptions are framed (maybe 'mediated' is a better term) within what she *gained* in the forest:

> An animal afeared is a dreadful thing cos their whole body is scared, even their blood is afeared. Even now, I can't help it, but the squeals of an animal

being killed is something that makes me blood run hot on hearing the sounds and me flesh shiver with anticipation. Me flesh wins over me heart. (144)

When Hannah accompanies Ernie and others in their search for Becky, the forest revives the older senses, perceptual frames and attitudes:

Something were happening to me that I only gradually noticed – I stayed awake most of the night, me hearing becoming real keen, me eyes sharper too.... I heard the slightest rustle of animals looking for prey. I heard the squeal of animals being killed. The sounds of their struggle for life made me tingle with fear and excitement. I felt meself one with the night. (143)

From hunger to perception, Hannah finds kinship with the tigers, a kinship that unfits her for the human race. In this, Nowra looks forward presciently to what Donna Haraway says about kinship:

the stretch and recomposition of kin are allowed by the fact that all earthlings are kin in the deepest sense, and it is past time to practice better care of kinds-as-assemblages (not species one at a time). Kin is an assembling sort of word. All critters share a common 'flesh,' laterally, semiotically, and genealogically. (2016: 103)

In another kind of narrative too we find the human seeking to learn about and with the nonhuman. This is the kind of narrative that David Herman identifies in his account of the biomutation narrative: a narrative in which the self is in dialogue with the Other. Texts like Charles Foster's *Being a Beast* (2016) demonstrate (*a*) a conscious mitigation of the contexts and basis of being human, (*b*) an extension, again consciously done, into the lifeworld of the nonhuman Other and (*c*) a conscious attempt to assimilate and *learn* from the nonhuman Other. This is an attempted kinship (of sorts) across species boundaries and, rather than a species-crossing, it is what I think of as a species-passing.

Foster begins with the aim of the book:

to see the world from the height of naked Welsh badgers, London foxes, Exmoor otters, Oxford swifts and Scottish and West Country red deer; to learn what it is like to shuffle or swoop through a landscape that is mainly olfactory or auditory than visual. (Unpaginated)

Foster claims that he has 'immerse[d] himself in the relevant physiological literature and discover[ed] what is known from the laboratory about the way these animals function' and 'immerse[d] myself in their world' (unpaginated). To this end, he lived in a hole like a badger and ate earthworms like badgers did. When he lived as an otter, he tried to catch fish with his teeth. He speaks of the experience as a 'shamanic transformation' (6), which involves first 'acknowledging the porosity of the boundary between species' (2). It requires an 'epiphanic labour' to move across species (3). He underscores that the human cannot seek 'self-dissolution' and admits that 'there will always be a boundary between me and my animals' (6). He also notes the parallels between the physiology of humans and that of some animals, arising, as he says, from 'our close evolutionary cousinhood.... [T]here are many neurological sequences which it is possible meaningfully to say I share with an animal' (7). But Foster also is certain that

> [i]f you can think your way into the mind of another species, you can think your way into its skin, and ultimately you'll see feathers sprouting from your arms or claws springing from your fingers. (12)

Foster's is an attempt to modify at least temporarily the evolutionary processes that have created human anatomy and physiology in the present form. The book is therefore replete with references to ancestry, human and animal. He does not mutate, let us be clear, into a badger or an otter. He transforms natural settings – creeks, tunnels, woods – into a laboratory and inserts himself into it as both specimen and observer. He attempts to replicate, insofar as his physiology and anatomy allow him, the life of an animal by behaving like them.

Throughout his narrative he speaks of learning – from animals and their behaviour – about the human self and its nonhuman Other. He hopes to 'learn slowly the mythological language in which the land speaks both to me and the badger' (19). He also learns that 'all humans ... know the absurdity of human pretension' (40). He learns that 'real, lasting change is possible – to our appetites, our fears and our views' (40). He learns to 'pay more attention to scent' (44); he learns the 'feel of overgrown hoofs' by not cutting his toenails for months (168). After all these experiments and experiences, he concludes:

> Our anatomy and physiology impose some limits on us.... But our capacity for vicariousness is infinite. Empathise enough with a swift and you'll either

become one or (which may be the same thing), you'll be able to rejoice so
much with the screeching race round the church tower that you'll not mind
being one yourself. (208)

The 'exhilarating inaccessibility of all creatures' he had hoped for (5) remains
beyond the reach of the human except perhaps in the imagination.

In T. Coraghessan Boyle's 'Dogology' (a story which is interspersed with
a fictionalized account of the feral children of Mayurbhanj, Odisha, India),
Julian finds his neighbour, a young woman, Cynthia, spending all her time
with the local dogs, crawling about on all fours, scrounging in garbage bins,
unwashed and dishevelled. (The act of crawling, as Elizabeth Boa has argued
in her innovative reading of Charlotte Perkins Gilman's *The Yellow Wallpaper*
and Kafka's *The Metamorphosis*, serves as a metaphor for dehumanization and
'intractably an image of powerlessness', 1990: 26). In a section of the tale
titled 'Cyanomorph', Boyle describes the woman, who is researching the world
of dogs:

> She'd made a point of sticking it in anything the dogs did, breathing deep
> of it, rebooting the olfactory receptors of a brain that had been deadened
> by perfume and underarm deodorant and all the other stifling odors of
> civilization. Every smell was a discovery, and every dog discovered more of
> the world in ten minutes running loose than a human being would discover
> in ten years of sitting behind the wheel of a car or standing at the lunch
> counter in a deli or even hiking the Alps. What she was doing, or attempting
> to do, was nothing short of reordering her senses so that she could think like
> a dog and interpret the whole world – not just the human world – as dogs
> did. (2006: 34)

Like Foster, Cynthia wishes to *understand* and assimilate herself into the canine
world.

Located between states of conscious, willed empathy and a vivid imagination,
Foster's account of living (almost) like an animal and Boyle's story of the 'dog
lady' (as Cynthia is described) instantiates less a biomutation than a project in
species-passing.

'Passing', as studies of African American literature and culture define it,

> is a deception that enables a person to adopt certain roles or identifies from
> which he would be barred by prevailing social standards in the absence of
> his misleading conduct.... A passer is distinguishable from the person who

is merely mistaken – the person who, having been told that he is white, thinks of himself as white, and holds himself out to be white (though he and everyone else in the locale would deem him to be 'black' were the facts of his ancestry known). (Kennedy 2001: 1145)

It was a means of escaping their racial identity and all that it entailed (Hobbs 2014).[19] But passing in human contexts marked by racism and race-based identification has another aspect to it. Adrian Piper defined racial identification as the shared experience of being visually or cognitively identified as African-American by white society which 'joins me to other blacks' (1992: 30–31). Ron Mallon writing about passing makes the following observation:

Passing in a social category is possible because there is a distinction between those properties that are indicative of category membership (such as easily perceptible racial markers), and those that are central. A property is indicative of category membership if having the property increases the likelihood that one is a member of the category ... having a certain color of skin or a certain way of speaking may be indicative of one's being a member of a particular race, even though skin color and manner of speaking are neither necessary nor sufficient for racial membership. Other properties, however, are more central. (2004: 652–653)

If species markers readily identify humans as distinct from badgers, swifts or deer of Foster's narrative – bipedalism would be a 'central' property, in Mallon's terms – then Foster's attempts to acquire new central traits, as he himself admits, fail because these properties are not solely social or individual constructions but evolution-determined biological traits. Assuming badgers and the rest visually and cognitively identify Foster as an interloper even when he immerses himself in the burrow with their scents, the category membership does not change for the nonhuman even if, temporarily and driven mainly by the twin principles of empathy and imagination, Foster perceives himself to be *like* an animal and is possibly imagining himself as one. When Cynthia abandons her clothing and human habits, she seeks to immerse herself into the feral setting of the dogs. But when the story ends, Boyle hints that Julian is drawn to her and they have sex. The account does appear less as animal fornication than human. Boyle implies that Julian is attracted to her for her human qualities *and* her attempts to abandon them, thus not only blurring the human–nonhuman borders but also indicating that pheromones and chemical-based attractions mark both human and the nonhuman. The pups he encounters when he goes to meet

Cynthia remind him of other (nonhuman) facets of life: he 'smelled them too, an authentic smell compounded of dirt, urine, saliva and something else also: the unalloyed sweetness of life' (Boyle 2006: 55).

Treating Foster's and Boyle's Cynthia's experiments as exercises in species passing, it is possible to see it as a reflection on the biological and social processes that have defined species boundaries (as critical animal studies insists), the changing dynamics of species relations – Foster himself speaks of hunting and now his own experiments born of empathy – on earth. It is a biomutation narrative only in the sense that Foster self-fashions himself in a species- and category-defying way for a limited period of time, recalling Henry David Thoreau's attempts to live in the lap of Nature. In a multispecies world, Foster and Cynthia are attempting, through an immersive experience, a species fluidity, even though Foster finds himself coming up against the wall of species characteristics and biological limitations that can be transcended only through the imagination. That said, the recording of anxieties and fears Foster claims he shares with the nonhuman – for instance, the way both the badger colony and he take shelter from the storm out of a sense of self-preservation – imply an extensionism of the human into the nonhuman world (an extensionism that could be construed, as Foster is well aware, as another form of species colonialism).

Passing, notes Allyson Hobbs, has two sides: 'the delight of "fooling white folks" and prevailing over an unjust racial regime was often accompanied by the agony of losing one's sense of self and one's family' (2014: 60). In species passing, Foster does revel in passing off as a badger and a red deer, but this is accompanied by the irrefutable recognition and agony that he cannot *lose* his humanness entirely even if, briefly and through rigorous training, his sensory capacities increase when in the burrow or crawling along the ground or, like the characters in *The Hungry Tide*, *The Tusk That Did the Damage* and other literary texts, *imagines* that such a change in his capacities has been effected.

The next problem that Foster himself recognizes in the species-passing project is that the biome itself has been reconstructed to mark species. As in the racialized social order with specific stations in life for different races, and their indelible boundaries, in the biome, a species like red deer are 'victims'. Foster writes:

> Their [the red deer's] landscape is the landscape of victims, and invisible except through victim's eyes.... I couldn't be a victim. Imagination and

ingenuity could help me hunt down and see reflected in myself everything except perpetual, defining vulnerability. (2016: 176)

In racial passing, slaves 'bought, traded, and stole clothing; they feigned grief, illness, and injury; and they borrowed, reused, and forged passes and certificates of freedom. With one's liberty hanging in the balance, all sorts of disguises were imaginable' (Hobbs 2014: 30). Foster attempts something similar, eating, sleeping and behaving as close to the animal world as he could, despite the corporeal limitations of being human and not deer or badger or otter. But despite all this, and with all attempts to fit into the skin of the nonhuman, Foster finds that he cannot pass as nonhuman for one reason: on earth, the animals are victims and humans are not. Although Foster does not term the human the 'apex predator', this is precisely what he gestures at. Humanity has transformed the world so that the nonhuman remains a victim, and this is not a role any human can assay. The human, with the best of motives and efforts, cannot *be* an animal because the animal is always already a victim. Disguising as an animal is playing at being victim, although in the unequal nature of the biome, the animal and the human-playing-at-being-animal are two apparently *incommensurable* categories. While this leads to the obvious essentializing of each species – that there is something unique about and exclusive to the human or the animal – Foster discovers that some of the essence of the Other can be sensed: for example, the victimhood of the animals.

Passing was an attempt to experience the life and identity of the Other in the case of the slaves, to experience the freedom of being white. I suggest that Foster's learning at the end of the exercise is not the freedom of being an animal but of the vulnerability of being the Other of the human species.

The Humanimal

In texts like Greg Bear's *Darwin's Children* (2003), Jeff Lemire's *Sweet Tooth* (2021), Marie Darrieussecq's *Pig Tales* (1996) and, among earlier texts, David Garnett's *Lady into Fox* (1922), Alan Moore, Stephen Bissette and John Totleben's *The Swamp Thing* (which is distinctive in that it is a tale of a human-to-plant metamorphosis, 1972–2016), A. S. Byatt's 'A Stone Woman' (2003) and Ursula Le Guin's 'The Wife's Story', the human *becomes* an Other. In Pola Oloixarac's *Dark Constellations*, we are told of plant–insect hybrid/trans-species forms that existed as 'dark patches distributed en masse among humans and nonhumans alike, on a spatiotemporal scale invisible to the eyes of men' (2019: 12).

The metamorphosis of the human into animal, for the purposes of this chapter, has a long history. In the case of contemporary literature, the metamorphosis narrative is an 'opening to what lies beyond and outside the sphere of humanity', as Elana Gomel (2014), following the work of Bernard Waldenfels, says of science fiction (27). In the process, the fiction suggests that humans need to be open to the idea of a different evolutionary trajectory.[20]

There are two significant features of the biomutation narratives that require attention. First, these propose that sentience is not a human privilege alone and make a case for a biosentience that is distributed across all lifeforms, and draws on more than one. Second, biomutation narratives are exercises in prosopopeia, or face-making. Prosopopeia is a vacillation between the self and the Other, giving (a) face to a voiceless entity (Mikkonen 1996). It is also simultaneously a de-facement and a dis-figure. It implies, for J. Hillis Miller, 'a "disfiguring" of the face and figure of the other, or the ascription of a consciousness like my own or different from my own to an appearance in the perceptual field' (cited in Mikkonen 1996: 322).

In the biomutation stories, the transformation is not usually complete. As commentators have observed about Kafka's famous text, *The Metamorphosis* (2016 [1915]), the transformation is indeterminate and incomplete.[21] Kai Mikkonen writes:

> For the cleaning woman who visits Gregor's room, as [Stanley] Corngold explains, the transformation is complete: for her there actually is no metamorphosis, but only the factual presence of a large bug. Gregor's family's treatment of their transformed son, in turn, appears to be ambiguous and shifting, partly because they cannot communicate with him. We readers know, however, that Gregor is somehow 'there' because we can read his narrating consciousness. (1996: 315)

Therefore, human consciousness *coexists* with that of the nonhuman in the texts.

In Byatt's text, as the transformation proceeds, the sensory apparatus also changes, and thereby her engagement with the (human) world.

> She noticed that her sense of smell had grown sharper. She could smell the rain in the thick cloud blanket. She could smell the sulfur dioxide in the car exhausts and the rainbow-colored minerals in puddles of petrol. These scents were pleasurable … skywater, mineral and delicious. The lightning came in

sheets of metal sheen. The thunder crashed in the sky, and the surface of the woman crackled and creaked in sympathy. (2003, unpaginated)

Humans had opted for and prioritized the organic, she realizes, and as she 'became mineral, and looked into the idea of minerals, she saw that there were reciprocities, both physical and figurative'.

The minds of stone-lovers had colonized stones with organic metaphors, like lichens clinging to them with golden or gray-green florid stains. Words came from flesh and hair and plants. Reniform, mammillated, botryoidal, dendrite, hematite. Carnelian is from 'carnal.' Serpentine and lizardite are stone reptiles; phyllite is leafy green. The earth itself is made in part of bones, shells, and diatoms. (Unpaginated)

The inanimate, as David Wills argues, is a part of the human's conscious, subjective experience of the world.

Biomutation texts re-make faces, figuring and dis-figuring in a simultaneous move. Ontologically different creatures appear in the same form, or figure, although the mental continuity of human and nonhuman rarely, if ever, occurs. Thus, the children with furs and antlers in *Sweet Tooth* are morphologically different, but their thought processes, as Lemire (2021) depicts them, remain human, suggesting that the merging of the mental worlds of the human and nonhuman has not occurred within the bodies of these humanimal hybrids.

Biomutation changes habits and behaviour, as the animalized human behaves more and more like the animal. In David Garnett's early *Lady into Fox*, Mrs Tebrick turns into a fox (we are told that her maiden name was, in fact, Fox). Immediately after this transformation, Tebrick 'saw at once that his wife was looking at him from the animal's eyes' (Garnett 1922, unpaginated). He discovers that under or inside the fox, it is still his wife:

So that with his gazing on her and knowing her well, even in such a shape, yet asking himself at every moment: 'Can it be she? Am I not dreaming?' and her beseeching and lastly fawning on him and seeming to tell him that it was she indeed, they came at last together and he took her in his arms. (Unpaginated)

She retains, in Tebrick's perspective, her human cognitive abilities and consciousness:

What helped most to make living with her bearable for him was that she understood him perfectly – yes, every word he said, and though she was dumb she expressed herself very fluently by looks and signs though never by the voice. (Unpaginated)

(He even begins to like her fox-iness: 'Every one of her foxey ways was now so absolutely precious to him'.) But it should be noted that it is Tebrick who believes that his wife-the-fox has altered perceptual and cognitive frames.

Despite these remnants of the human, Mrs Tebrick does become a fox in the full sense, eating raw meat and eventually bearing fox pups, at which Tebrick is outraged and ponders on the issue of her human or vixen morality:

He asked himself: Was not his wife unfaithful to him, had she not prostituted herself to a beast? Could he still love her after that? But this did not trouble him so much as it might have done. For now he was convinced inwardly that she could no longer in fairness be judged as a woman, but as a fox only. And as a fox she had done no more than other foxes, indeed in having cubs and tending them with love, she had done well. (Unpaginated)

Despite these misgivings, Tebrick, like Charles Foster, wishes to live closer to the foxes, and so begins to spend a lot of time at their lair, sleeping on the ground and playing with the pups. Like Foster, he begins to acquire some of the habits of the foxes:

Mr. Tebrick now could follow after them anywhere and keep up with them too, and could go through a wood as silently as a deer. He learnt to conceal himself if ever a labourer passed by so that he was rarely seen, and never but once in their company. But what was most strange of all, he had got a way of going doubled up, often almost on all fours with his hands touching the ground every now and then, particularly when he went uphill. (Garnett 1922, unpaginated)

Garnett's tale, published a hundred years ago, in 1922, brings together the two models of the biomutation narrative: one in which the human seeks to mimic the nonhuman and another in which the human becomes the nonhuman. In both cases, as Garnett suggests, the human storyteller is bestowing a face on both parties: Mr Tebrick undergoes voluntary changes in his person, and thereby mimics the habits of the nonhuman, while Mrs Tebrick retains the personality of a woman or wife even though morphologically she has become a fox. Like Byatt's stone woman, whose emotions at seeing other stone figures are that of a human (not just akin, but of) overjoyed at seeing something it desires, the human-turned-fox behaves like a human would. In Jeff Lemire's *Sweet Tooth*, the humanimal retains a measure of humanity, but also possesses habits and mannerisms of the animal component in her or his body. Thus, the human–rabbit hybrid needs to hibernate (2021, unpaginated) or others with wings can fly (unpaginated). Their eating habits, as in Marie Darrieussecq's *Pig Tales* or Garnett's *Lady into Fox*, are those of the animal part of their bodies. The biomutation tale imposes one figure, the nonhuman, over that of another. the human, and vice versa, so that it becomes difficult to separate the two faces, so to speak. If metamorphosis is the oscillation between the self and the Other, these tales demonstrate just that.

Stories like *Pig Tales* use animalization, especially of the woman, as a symbol of something larger: 'the protagonist's metamorphosis seems like mere accompaniment to her everyday experiences in which she is subjected to physical violations by the male management and clientele, violations that specifically "animalize" her' (Pick 2011: 82). That said, Pick herself rejects what she terms 'an unduly narrow feminist conundrum' in such an interpretation, and instead argues:

> [*Pig Tales*] invites a different reading of species indeterminacy, not as a metaphor for the degeneration of the human – even if this degeneration ultimately signals the always already degenerate state of the so-called human – but as a probing of the permanent interval of species, the trembling space between the human and the animal – *as* the space of the human. (85, emphasis in original)

The narrator's transformation is not complete, as in the case of Kafka's Gregor Samsa and others, since the human consciousness remains firmly in place even when physiological, anatomical and behavioural changes have been effected in her. As Pick notes, she 'oscillates between regarding her bodily transformations as hideous and as alluring, in full recognition of her incomplete humanity' (89). The human, in Pick's argument, is the 'imperfect, terrestrial, and fleshy reflection of an animal' (89). We see this 'reflection' in the optical tropes and themes in the novel:

> I did have some trouble recognizing myself, but there could be no mistake about the look in her eyes.... What I thought I saw at first was a pig wearing that beautiful red dress, a kind of female pig – a sow, if you like – and in

her eyes was that hangdog look I get when I'm tired. You can understand, though, that it was hard for me to see myself in her. Then I decided that it was only an optical illusion, that the intense red colour of the dress was giving me that deep pink complexion in the photo ... and I thought I could see how the impression of a snout, slightly protuberant ears, teeny eyes, and so on was simply caused by the rustic atmosphere of the poster, and especially by those extra pounds I'd put on. Take a perfectly healthy girl, put her in a red dress, have her gain a smidgen of weight, tire her out, and you'll see what I mean. (Darrieussecq 1996: 61–62)

Darrieussecq's narrator sees, and does not quite believe what she sees (since she thinks it is 'an optical illusion'), the animal in the human image, and vice versa. She sees the animal in, or emerging from, herself and vice versa in an uncanny doubling of the human and the animal. Elsewhere too, the narrator speaks of seeing the transformed human in terms that are visually blurred and unclear. For example, describing her lover, Yvan, who takes on a wolf form, she writes:

Something strange came over me when I saw Yvan almost dissolve in the sunshine that streaked his muzzle with fuzzy lines, tamed his wild eyes, shaved off his fur. Yvan glittered – you could hardly see him the halo that surrounded and obliterated him. (107–108)

This 'optical illusion' is the production and sensation of the uncanny that occurs at the borders of the human, or in the course of human becoming. If, as Nicholas Royle has defined it, the uncanny is 'a crisis of the natural, touching upon everything that one might have thought was "part of nature:" one's own nature, human nature, the nature of reality and the world' (2003: 1), then in the biomutation tale it is no longer possible, as Darrieussecq's narrator admits, to grasp the nature of human *or* nonhuman reality. When *Pig Tales* concludes, it is again with a sense of such a surreal, an uncanny, sense of the crisis of the natural:

I write whenever my animal spirits subside a little. The mood comes over me when the Moon rises, and I reread my notebook in its cold light. I try to do what Yvan taught me, but for the opposite reason: when I crane my neck towards the Moon, it's to show, once again, a human face. (Darrieussecq 1996: 135)

Other kinds of posthuman narratives indicate that human evolution, its very future, may be in terms of the humanimal rather than as 'just' human.

In Greg Bear's *Darwin's Children* (2003), the progeny appearing after the SHEVA virus has devastated the world are hybrids, endowed with special abilities, although their outward appearance is human. As human survivors seek to control, even exterminate, these 'mutants' out of the fear that they harbour the virus that will finish off the reminder of humanity, the enhanced children fight back. In Lemire's *Sweet Tooth*, likewise, the humanimals born after the 'accident', as the plague that wiped out most of humanity is described (2021, unpaginated), are hunted by human survivors in order to perform experiments upon them to ascertain how the hybrids are immune to the plague. Resonating with the arguments of Elizabeth Costello in Coetzee's novel and Cary Wolfe's arguments about animal holocausts, Abbott in *Sweet Tooth* makes his intentions towards the humanimals clear. When asked why he would not leave the hybrids alone, he responds: 'Why? There is no "why" anymore. It's just what I have to do. I *will* kill Jepperd. And I *will* rip the cure off those freaks' (Lemire 2021, unpaginated). Lemire's careful juxtaposition of the notorious lines from Auschwitz ('here there is no "why"', as cited by Primo Levi, 2014) with the history of experimentation on animals for medical (but also military) purposes in the name of a cure for humanity suggests that for humanity to survive, a secret must be unlocked from within the hybrid, from an ontologically uncertain species. Later, other soldiers would echo Abbott: 'We got a few [hybrids] and we're gonna cut the little fuckers apart until we find the cure for the fucking sick' (Lemire 2021, unpaginated).[22]

The weaponizing of the hybrids aligns the humanimal theme with the capitalist–military one in Bear (2023). The hybrids are described and attacked for their potential: '[A]rtificial monsters designed to help corporations take over the world. GM Kids, they called them, or Lab Brats, or Monsanto's Future Toadies' (unpaginated). Both Bear and Lemire are making a prognosis of human and earthly futures. The posthuman in these texts, hybrids of humans and animals, are, to adapt the words of Anja Höing, 'set at this very brink between a breakdown of "known" humanism and the unknown posthuman future to face after the collapse' (2019: 71). In Lemire's text, the hybrids start all over again, setting up colonies, starting breeding and replicating (ironically) the very structures of family and lineage, to suggest that the future is irrevocably posthuman and human at the same time. This of course induces fear, as one character indicates in *Darwin's Children*: 'There are always those who fear the future…. They fear change, fear being replaced; one thing they do in their fear is kill children' (Bear 2023, unpaginated). Bear and Lemire imply that the hybrids have a better chance of continuing humanity, albeit in new multispecies forms. Lemire's Gus – the 'deer boy', now a man – puts it thus towards the end of *Sweet Tooth*:

> Man's time was done. They had their chance to live in harmony with the land and they failed.

> Then we were born. The hybrid. We are one with the land. One with the animals that walk it. But we also carry mankind's legacy in our blood and bones so that we are no better than they. We too can fall. We too can fail. We must never forget the face of the gods as man did … for their faces are our faces. And for that we leave this hide to feed the wolves. An offering back to the land that sustains us. (2021, unpaginated)

The mix of paganism and Biblical reference animates the conclusion of Lemire's tale which envisages the future as multispecies, but as multispecies *families*. That is, as commentators have noted, the integration of the nonhuman into the human family becomes an index of their subjecthood, as defined by the humans (Fudge 2000). The nonhuman, writes Jeffrey Karnicky, about bird biographies,

> become companions to humans as they enter into human conceptions of the world. This relationship between birds and humans bears comparison to other human-animal pairings, such as the more common relationship of humans and dogs. (2011: 39)

*

Critics have argued that drawing and describing the worlds of the nonhuman in literature is, at best, a form of anthropocentrism. Brian McCormack summarizes the problem thus:

> Narrative is also at risk of drawing attention away from more precise modes of accounting for divergent forms of lived experience. The tension between attempting to make room for nonhuman meaningful experience (which is an ethical necessity) and the impossibility of doing so with full confidence is not resolved in literary practices that incorporate and dramatize these tensions. Employing a concept of narrative beyond the human is an ethical act, but one that must be undertaken with care…. Just as there is no neutral language for describing nonhuman animal behaviors and minds, there are very few neutral ways of forming relationships with them. (2019: 83–84)

But writers, as we have seen, speculate on the multispecies possibilities. Throughout her *Dark Constellations* Pola Oloixarac speaks of the 'strange rapport between plants and insects', the 'secret pacts between species' (2019: 12). The rest of the novel draws up a series of metaphors that are species-fluid: women are like spiders (19), palms are like octopuses (35), lakes are like sluggish blue animals (135), greenhouses are like insects (144), spoons are like butterflies (188), branches are like coral reefs (190), clouds are like swans (196), voices are like crocodile's eyes (211), and rivers like serpents (219). Bieke Willem sees these metaphors as embodying a 'post-natural' theme for the Anthropocene and its transspecies thinking (2020: 138–139).

Works such as J. M. Coetzee's *The Lives of Animals, Disgrace, Elizabeth Costello* and the texts studied in this chapter textualize the ethics of human–nonhuman relations, even as they ponder over the modes of (re)presenting these in an appropriate textual form. Critics like Marjorie Garber (1999) have noted that when Coetzee speaks of animals, he may well be speaking about literature and its *value* itself. This 'use' of the animal trope, however, could also serve as a means to talk about the 'complex relation of dependency and struggle between the animal and literary studies', in Julietta Singh's phrase (2018: 136). Singh therefore proposes the following approach:

> Rather than to subjugate the ethical question of animal liberation to literary studies, we might instead consider how the text relationally frames and negotiates animals and/as texts. To do so necessitates a willingness toward vulnerable reading, toward a reading practice by which we do not foreclose dependency and struggle among 'subjects' but rather concede to the porousness of our disciplined ways of knowing. (136)

This 'struggle' towards representation, empathy and understanding of differentiated, unequal and yet shared vulnerabilities across species and individual borders is really the task of multispecies texts and modes of reading them. Narratives can and do construct, maybe even instantiate, other-subjectivities. This is why, perhaps, in fiction and nature-writing such as Charles Foster's the absence of a non-neutral language to describe animal behaviour does not deter them from trying to depict a world, a future, in which humans recognize that their identity, their very ontology, has always already been multispecies.

Notes

1. The recent emphasis in plant communications and critical plant studies (Marder, etc.) have provided the groundwork for Powers, McConaghy and others.
2. Dolphins, in particular, have been mythologized as possessing a special affection for humans, being able to read human minds, and of self-recognition in a mirror. For a quick summary, see David Neiwert's *Of Orcas and Men* (2015).
3. James Erin proposes an 'econarratology', which

    > maintains an interest in studying the relationship between literature and the physical environment, but does so with sensitivity to the literary structures and devices that we use to communicate representations of the physical environment to each other via narratives. It also highlights the potential that narratives stand to make to readers' understandings of what it is like for people in different spaces and times to live in their ecological homes by foregrounding the comparative nature of narrative immersion. (2015: 22)

    Despite these attempts, I recognize the condition of uncertainty and limits that marks any human attempts to (*a*) give voice to the subaltern nonhuman and (*b*) understand what we claim is animal language.
4. Wendy Doniger makes a similar point about *Elizabeth Costello*, arguing that animals do speak but we refuse to hear it. See Doniger (1999).
5. I find Petitt's study significant in that while it does not downplay multispecies belonging, it pays attention to how human social relations and power structures determine the organization of nonhuman species and the intraspecies relations, and therefore of any intersectionality between or across species. She writes as one example:

    > [I]ndividuals and intraspecies social groups lead different lives and have vastly varied experiences depending on their positionality in relation to other animals and humans. On the cattle ranches of Colorado, cows, bulls, heifers, and steer calves had different opportunities and faced particular challenges as a result of humans sorting them into these categories. Taking into account both the subjectivity of the mares and cows as well as the way they are organized by local humans, nuancing the categories of mares and cows becomes important. (Petitt 2023: 31)

    Petitt's is, in my view, a necessary corrective to the valorization of inter- and intraspecies connections seen in contemporary human–animal studies.

See also Govindrajan (2018) for a similar approach to interspecies relationships and Narayanan (2023) on the politics of the dairy in India.

6. The question of how to depict nonhuman perspectives, nonhuman voices remains a thorny one, where these cannot be easily placed into *human* storytelling. Broadly, however, one could argue that attempts to do so are indicative of empathetic connections (or efforts at such). On nonhuman focalization of narratives and nonhuman consciousness, see Nelles (2001).

7. Kompatsiaris also finds the idealism of multispecies coexistence troubling:

> Even causes of multispecies flourishing, including animal liberation or the ending of animal torture, are first and foremost brought forward by organisations and groups that fight instrumentally so as to accomplish these aims. The idea of distributed agency as a means to challenge human exceptionalism overlooks the exclusiveness of human agency that both creates miserable conditions for nonhuman others as well as has the capacity to protest in solidarity for abolishing these conditions. And to refer once more to the puffer-invasive, its labelling as a total 'enemy' showcases the dividing lines that humans themselves have to negotiate and cross in relating with radical others. (2022: 11)

Timothy Mitchell has made a case for 'hybrid agency' where nonhuman collectives have played a key role in how human agency itself has developed. Building on Mitchell, Andrew Rose proposes a 'distributed agency'

> to draw attention to my particular understanding of the implications of a postanthropocentric conception of agency.... That is, the phrase hybrid-agency, as Mitchell uses it, lends itself to a conceptualization of agency in which multiple agents (human and nonhuman) convene to create historical change. (2019: 130)

8. Kingsolver writes:

> Now the sun blinked open on a long impossible time, and here was the exodus. They would gather on other fields and risk other odds, probably no better or worse than hers.
>
> The sky was too bright and the ground so unreliable, she couldn't look up for very long. Instead her eyes held steady on the fire bursts of wings reflected across water, a merging of flame and flood. Above the lake of the world, flanked by white mountains, they flew out to a new earth. (2012, unpaginated)

The new flight of the monarch butterflies becomes symbolic of Dellarobia's own 'escape', having decided to enrol in college and thus get away from her domesticity, as critics have noted (Lehtimäki 2022: 66).

9. Stacy Alaimo in *Bodily Natures* (2010) coins the term 'trans-corporeality', which she in a later interview elaborated:

> [T]ranscorporeality does the opposite of distancing or dividing the human from external nature. It implies that we're literally enmeshed in the physical material world, so environmentalism cannot be an externalized and optional kind of pursuit, but is always present, always at hand. (Kuznetski 2020: 139)

10. In a powerful passage describing the training of the young elephant who would go on to become the notorious Gravedigger, Tania James writes:

> A sharp tug to the Gravedigger's right ear. He squealed, swerved right.
>
> !!
>
> !!!
>
> !
>
> !!!!
>
> On and on until the Gravedigger could extract a meaning from each ugly note. *Left! Right! Stand Still! Kneel!* – the last learned by the whack of the stick across his flanks. Pain pulled his mind to a taut and terrible line, its only goal: to do whatever would prevent the pain. (2015: 149, emphasis in original)

In an ironic spin on the care–coercion dialectic, Emma, the American documentary filmmaker, herself experiences the kind of biopolitical power asserted by the local experts, in this case the veterinarian Ravi. When she is ill from food poisoning, Ravi escorts her to the clinic where she has a panic attack:

> Ravi stepped forward. He cupped my head with a hand practiced in the art of calming the frantic and the feral. It occurred to me then that he had the jawline of a film star, or at least a prime-time anchorman. (46)

The same power, the same process is employed to calm the human and the feral or nonhuman, aligning them on a continuum of shared vulnerability.

11. Critics have pointed out that Montero's 'explanations [about the disappearance of frogs] in a supernatural realm [are] squarely beyond the grasp of ecology. Even more strikingly, it also seems to exonerate humans

from any responsibility in the ongoing extinctions and to place the blame on cosmological processes of decline instead' (Heise 2016: 172).

12. Jan Baetens correctly argues that 'animal studies are more and more becoming interspecies studies'. This stems, Baetens proposes, from

> a deepening and broadening of what it means to be human. Instead of being separated from all kind of 'others,' such as nature, woman, nonwhite, animal, but also the unconscious or the machine, man (the gendering of humankind as *man* is of course part of the problem) is now part of a wider environment where these frontiers are blurred and where hard dichotomies are replaced by varying positions on a continuum with no real center. (2018: 184, emphasis in original)

13. Timo Maran defines the scope of biosemiotics to ecocriticism and the humanities in some detail:

> The issues that biosemiotics can bring to the attention of the humanities would include: (1) communicative and sign relations between human cultural activities and other semiotic subjects and their representations in literature and other cultural texts; (2) interrelations between environmental information and literary texts or other human cultural representations and the question of whether the latter may be motivated by the former; (3) the presence and traces of human bodily perception, sensations, and bio- logical organization in literary texts and other human cultural representations; and (4) resemblances and analogies between literary texts or other cultural representations and elements of nature as such and the use of biosemiotic research models in the study of human culture in this aspect. (2014a: 262)

14. I am grateful to Scott Slovic for pointing me in the direction of Donovan's work. Scott's own comments on the Donovan piece and its affective mode when speaking of human–nonhuman relationships and attempting to see, think or feel like the Other can be found in his talk 'Environmental Vulnerability and the Literary Imagination' (2023).

15. Piya's environmental sense and attitudes are clearly at odds with that of the natives of the tide country. While Piya is horrorstruck at the sight of the killing, and wishes to save the tiger, the natives are depicted as embodying nothing less than a certain (in)human bloodlust: '[T]heir faces … in the grip of both extreme fear and uncontrollable rage … screaming in a maddened bloodlust "Maar! Maar!"' (Ghosh 2004: 295). Erin James has argued that while a 'cultural dissonance … leads each to tell strikingly different stories about the tiger',

reading narratives can help bridge imaginative gaps such as the one between Piya and Fokir. A narrative of the events surrounding the tiger's capture from Fokir's perspective, after all, would allow Piya to model and transport herself imaginatively to a world that better corresponds to a local desire for safety and fear of mauling. Alternatively, a narrative of the same set of events narrated by Piya would allow Fokir to imagine the tiger according to a different set of values and proscribed courses of action. (2015: 3)

Others like Graham Huggan and Helen Tiffin have argued that Ghosh has opted out of the more thorny issue of the human–tiger conflict in favour of the comparatively simpler human–dolphin one (2010; also see Mukherjee 2010 for a reading). From other contexts, studies of multispecies co-existence and climate refugees have drawn attention to similar conflicts. For example, exploring the polar bear–Inuit tensions in northern Canada, Julian Reid writes:

The climate migration of human poor, for example, is mostly constructed as a threat to the security of the global liberal order, while the climate migration of non-human animal species is more often constructed as a cause of concern for the wellbeing of the animals themselves … the state argues that the climate migration of the bears indicates their threatened status, while the Inuit argues it to be an expression of polar bear resilience. What does this clash of rationalities and analytics tell us about the different ways in which human and non-human climate migration, security and resilience is constructed today, both in western regimes of climate migration governance, and in indigenous knowledge? (2020: 1)

16. Therianthropy is a condition in which humans identify themselves as 'otherkin', nonhuman kin. It is a controversial subject, and opinion is divided as to whether it is a mental condition or a subculture. Herman in *Narratology Beyond the Human* examines texts from this canon (see 2018b: ch. 2). Zoomorphism, which is the broad category in which therians may be located, is a species-defying theme in literature.

17. Nagel's argument is that humans may *imagine* what it is to be a bat, but humans cannot know what it is to be *like* a bat. Nagel's influential thesis has received much criticism. See, among others, Daniel Dennett, *Consciousness Explained* (1991).

18. Racialized stereotypes in literature have represented particular races in zoomorphic terms: blacks as animals, for example.

19. Hobbs notes that passing was not a happy condition:

> Racial passing is an exile, sometimes chosen, sometimes not…. Between
> the late eighteenth and the mid-twentieth centuries, countless African
> Americans passed as white, leaving behind families, friends, and
> communities without any available avenue for return. Lives were lost
> only to be remembered in family stories. (2014: 4)

20. There is another category of species-blurring in tales dealing with
    terraforming: pantropy. Chris Pak (2016), who has the definitive account of
    terraforming in his book of the same title, describes pantropy as the physical
    modification of bodies. Pak writes:

    > [P]antropy has been expanded to include body modifications other than
    > genetic adaptations, including cyborgization. Colonialism underlies
    > humanity's approach to space colonization in many terraforming
    > narratives, while pantropy opens up the possibility of a less hierarchical
    > relation. (2017: 122–123)

21. As Hans Rainer Sepp notes, 'Gregor's displacement is a result of his alienation
    from the network of normal worldly circumstances without the possibility of
    gaining access to a new world that grants a true sense of security' (2014: 97).
    Sepp also argues that,

    > since his bodily experiences conflict with his worldly imaginations,
    > Gregor's new mode of existence no longer attains a place within a
    > constituted world. But thrown out of worldly constitution and reduced
    > to his corporeal-bodily existence, he wins the right command of his new
    > existence by trial and error of his bodily movements. (104)

22. In Lemire there is also a mix of modern science and myth, where the plague is
    attributed to the human disturbing of Inuit tombs of the gods. Laboratories
    that make use of the remains in the tombs undertake cloning experiments
    under the Project Moreau – undoubtedly a hark-back to Wells' (2005
    [1896]) classic tale – to weaponize the virus found in the tombs (Lemire
    2021, unpaginated).

5

Justice Matters
Human and Nonhuman Toxiconomies

When Catherine Flowers in her memoir, *Waste* (2020), records how Lowndes County, Alabama, 'inhabited largely by poor Black people who, like me, are descendants of slaves', has a serious problem of waste accumulation in people's homes, she points to not just the present and future defined by sewage but to a certain past, a racialized *history* of land- and people-use. Flowers writes:

> You can't understand how rural Alabama wound up with raw sewage in people's yards without first learning about how African Americans were brought here as slaves to work the soil. (4)[1]

Flowers's advocacy-text-cum-memoir documents the acute distress of environmental injustice in areas populated mainly by coloured people and highlights the links between histories of transnational slavery, race, capitalism and contemporary American culture, especially government funding, policies and welfare measures. Environmental harm stems from a history of other kinds of harm suffered by the African Americans, argues Flowers.

The events in Lowndes originate elsewhere, and Flowers' memoir is not merely an exercise in toxichorography – a portmanteau term for chorographic accounts that have toxified ecosystems and communities as their key theme – but presents us with planetary histories of environmental and social injustices, with the two forms of injustice being interlinked.

From a different context, Chen Qiufan in his novel *Waste Tide* (2019) giving us the backstory of Scott Brandle, a researcher for TerraGreen Recycling Co., Ltd., writes of the research group that wished to study 'the impact of illegal logging on the environment and native tribes [in Papua New Guinea] with the goal of forcing the local government to crack down on illegal logging' (unpaginated). This study was not, Brandle recognizes, for either environmental (the forests) or social or civic (the tribes) reasons, but to ensure that the 'Rimbunan Hijau Group could be given a monopoly on the lumber supplies of Papua New Guinea'. Qiufan, through the thoughts of Brandle, calls the bluff when he writes: '[T]he so-called sustainable development was ... just another name for legalized looting' (unpaginated). Qiufan's toxichorography of Papua New Guinea reveals the toxic economy that inflects even the environmentalisms in our time where the environmental harm for the natives emerges from the calculation of environmental benefits that will accrue for the Rimbunan Hijau Group.

Studying the toxichorography presented in personal memoirs and fiction means examining the material and symbolic (meaning-making) forms, the socio-economic processes and the material effects of these processes in the lives of humans, nonhumans and the ecosystem. Such a study assumes that material forms – all matter, whether oil, soil or toxins – are embedded in social systems, and adapts the 'new materialist' approach whose focus is the 'generativity and resilience of the material forms with which social actors interact, forms which circumscribe, encourage, and test their discourses' (Coole and Frost 2010: 27, 26). Reading Flowers' toxichorography through this analytic, we see how Lowndes' ecosystem of toxic waste matter today has emerged from the socio-economic practices of slavery in the USA and its material effects. Qiufan in his novel unmasks discourses and practices of 'sustainable development' and environmental protection or conservation actions as another form of neocolonial exploitation of material resources like lumber. Thus, these texts trace the origins of dumping and environmental racism – the two principal axes of the environmental justice campaigns in the USA (Schlosberg 2007) – and even environmentalism, to settler colonialism, plantation cultures, slavery and contemporary global capitalism. Today's anthropogenic injustices towards people of different races, the nonhuman and the planet, then, are coextensive with the historical rise and spread of what is being called the 'racial' Anthropocene (Vergès 2017).

Environmental justice in fiction, memoirs, advocacy texts and prosopographies – collective or community biographies – is thematized through depictions of different kinds of injustices and their histories in which the material and the symbolic have always merged to define, inform and impact practices and discourses, ideologies and policies. 'Environmental justice' is a lens through which science, colonialism, globalization and development paradigms and their textual manifestations in fiction or memoir may be viewed, and has specific attitudes, ideologies and approaches of its own. An 'environmental justice perspective', writes Byron Caminero-Santangelo in his study of South African fiction, is often associated with 'the environmentalism of the poor'. He lists 'interdependence among precolonial agro-ecosystems, indigenous biodiversity, and the well-being of human communities' as components of this environmental justice perspective (2014: 45).[2]

Environmental injustices and social injustices are entangled, as Stacy Alaimo observes:

[E]nvironmental justice insists upon the material interconnections between specific bodies and specific places, especially the peoples and areas that have been literally dumped upon. Environmental justice social movements and modes of analysis target the unequal distribution of environmental benefits and environmental harms, tracing how race and class (and sometimes gender and sexuality) profoundly influence material, often place-based inequities. (2010: 28–29)

Alaimo's observation can be expanded and scaled differently, as we shall see in the case of many environmental injustice texts: when toxins are dumped into the river or when plastic chokes the oceans, the question of injustice must be extended to include the nonhuman and the planet as a whole.

This chapter addresses the broad theme of environmental justice through a reading of a variety of literary texts and memoirs that interlink environmental and social injustices (what I term 'toxiconomies', to gesture at the toxic *oikos*, meaning both 'dwelling' and the 'economy' of slavery or colonialism). The chapter moves, in terms of its focus, from material matter in and toxified bodies through houses or communities to the level of the planetary, as represented in these texts. Such an analytic of scale, so central to ecological thought (Morton 2012; Chakraborty 2021), enables us to see, first, the individual stories in memoirs, fiction and autobiographies as metonymic of planetary crises and their histories and, second, the relations between the individual, the community or region, and the planet.

The Toxicorpus

Sandra Steingraber opens her memoir, *Living Downstream*, with a linking of her life with the life of a chemical toxin: 'I was born in 1959, and so share a birthdate with atrazine, which was first registered for market that year. In the same year DDT … reached its peak usage in the United States' (2010: 6).

She continues: 'DDT was outlawed the year I turned thirteen' (6). Resonant with T. S. Eliot's image of measuring life out in coffee spoons, Steingraber measures her life in terms of a chemical history of the United States. But she is not alone, she hastens to add, 'for those of us born in the 1940s, 1950s, and 1960s … we were certainly the first generation to eat synthetic pesticides in our pureed vegetables' (10). An entire generation, Steingraber suggests, was toxified.

Having informed us of her bladder cancer and signalled its chemical origins in the toxins from the environment of her growing up – 'all of these substances have an ongoing biological presence in my life' (7) – Steingraber expands the remit of her narrative of toxified bodies. She speaks of toxic matter in more-than-human bodies:

> Aquarium studies in the laboratory show that the same carcinogens known to cause cancer in humans and rodents also cause cancer in fish and mollusks – and they are often metabolized in the same way.… I have developed an idea for a pilgrimage that involves people with cancer traveling to various bodies of water known to be inhabited by animals with cancer – from Cobscook Bay in Maine to the mouth of the Duwarmish River in the Puget Sound. It involves an assembly on the banks and shores of these waters and a collective consideration of our intertwined lives. (140)

And elsewhere:

> In Italy, dogs are more likely to have lymphoma if they live northeast of Naples, where illegal waste disposal is a rampant practice. (People living in this community, known as 'the triangle of death,' also have elevated cancer mortality.) Military dogs in Vietnam exposed to the herbicide Agent Orange suffered from high rates of testicular cancer. Scottish terriers in Indiana have higher rates of bladder cancer if their owners use lawn chemicals. Scotties are particularly prone to bladder cancer and so serve as a sensitive sentinel for bladder carcinogens in the environment, according to veterinarians who are tracking cancer incidence in this breed. (131)

Elsewhere too, Steingraber speaks of animal bodies – such as those of eels – that mediate between toxic matter sites and other animals, like the beluga whales living in distant regions (136). Steingraber also produces documentation about contaminants in food crops like corn (302–303). Steingraber has thereby shown us how all bodies, human, animal and plant, are toxified.

Another memoir, Marie Thérèse Martin's *And Poison Fell from the Sky*, opens with an account of waking up suffocating:

> The air felt so thick in my bedroom that it was hard to breathe. Even though I shut and locked the windows in our drafty old house, pungent odors from the nearby Rumford paper mill always managed to work their way inside. (2022: 12)

Through her growing-up years, this pungent smell had defined everyday life for her and the community as a whole (23). Later Martin records how, in the late 1980s, a dioxin-monitoring programme had to be initiated to track the contamination in fish (159), thus showing us that humans and the nonhuman, the air and the water, have all suffered some form of contamination. Martin lists numerous chemicals exuded from the neighbouring paper mill and asks: '[W]hich of these chemicals was I exposed to just because I lived near the mill?' (113–114). And the answer is: '[A]ll of them, of course' (113). The particulate matter (here Martin cites a local environmentalist) '"easily reach the deepest recesses of the lungs and never come out"' (156). She, like others in the area, comes to be defined by the toxins within her. Matter's dangerous fluidity, especially with toxins, renders the entire world and multiple species unsafe. These are toxic corporii: bodies defined by the poisonous chemicals ingested.

Susanne Antonetta speaks of the 'Roof Dwellers, the People Who Speak in Darkness; we're also the DDT People, the Drink Cadmium People, the Breathing-Isotope People', that is, individuals and communities defined in terms of their levels and types of toxic subjectivity (2001: 137). Dan Fagin documents the cancerous bodies of those working in and living near the aniline dye factories across European cities. Like Qiufan, Steingraber and Antonetta, with their narrative focus on the chemical and molecular foundations of toxicity and their biological effect, Dan Fagin in *Toms River* (2013) explains the properties of the chemical constituents and their combinatorial characteristics, their materiality and intra- and interactive predilections:

> Hydrocarbons proved extremely useful to the new world of chemical fabrication for the same reason that hydrogen and carbon are vital to the chemistry of life. When atoms of hydrogen and carbon form molecules, they tend to arrange themselves into durable structures of rings and long chains in which the atoms bond strongly via shared electrons.

Later, as we shall see, he will locate these relationships and tendencies of the chemicals within industrial processes, which are in turn socially determined in terms of funding, location, product output and, of course, waste disposal.

Charles Moore's disagreement with Ebbesmeyer regarding the biodegradability of the plastics in the ocean in *Plastic Ocean* embodies the chemical and social dimensions of toxic corporii:

> The term non-biodegradable is often applied to plastics, meaning they defy digestion by living organisms. Now research has shown that certain microorganisms very slowly biodegrade plastics in certain conditions.... I had questioned Ebbesmeyer's belief that plastic things break down in the gyre simply from UV exposure. After this trip, we wind up agreeing that a number of scenarios are playing out. Some of the gyre plastics probably began degrading on land, with an assist from pulverizing shoreline waves. But I have another theory. Given the bite marks on many of these plastics, I'm convinced a goodly number of these fragments were nibbled off larger plastic objects by hungry fish and passed as excreta. (Moore with Philips 2011, unpaginated)

Moore forces us to acknowledge the contradictions in human meaning-making (about the term 'biodegradable') but also points to both the assimilation and circulation of matter in resilient ways, the interaction of this matter with non-living processes such as UV exposure *and* living forms such as fish. Bodies, human and nonhuman, are toxified in different but similar ways.

Marla Cone's *Silent Snow*, having provided detailed accounts of the kind of toxins imbibed by polar bears, whales and Inuits in the Arctic Circle, tells us: '[O]nce they [the carcinogenic polychlorinated biphenyls, PCBs] enter our system, some of them never leave – except when they are transferred from mother to child through the womb and in breast milk' (2005: 5). Cone highlights throughout her narrative this resilience of the toxin, whose flows through the biological matter of the human form appears entirely of its own (agential or reactive) making.[3] Cone writes about her discovery of 'high levels of PCBs and other chemicals in the breast milk of Nunavik mothers, chemicals they were passing to their babies' (2). She then gives an account, reported from a scientist of how the PCB molecules work:

> PCBs are not water-soluble, they are lipid-soluble ... sea mammals have an unusual propensity to produce fat ... when they use up their fat reserves in winter, PCBs concentrate and migrate into their vital organs. (21)

In many cases, Inuit bodies, she writes, 'carried such extraordinary loads of chemicals that their bodies and breast milk could be classified as hazardous waste' (32). This is the toxic subject who is the uncanny double – familiar yet different due to the foreign within – of the normative and healthy human. Elsewhere, writing about the effects of mercury, Cone gives us the minutiae of how studies showed the impairment of mental skills among the Faroe Islanders (34). But Cone also expands her focus beyond the human to speak of the polar bears: 'polar bears emerge from their dens with cubs no bigger than preschoolers but already loaded with chemicals' (5). She speaks of the 'minute levels of contamination' that 'seem to suppress the volumes and efficiency of animals' immune cells' (157). The analogy and scaling beyond the human represents a trans-corporeal toxichorography. In a different key, Caroline Flowers speaks of how contaminated water from overflowing and open sewage causes infestations of parasites in the bodies of people in Lowndes: 'of the fifty-five people tested, nineteen had hookworm … an alarming 34.5 percent' (2020: 134). Cone and Flowers both map the specific region through the gathering of information about (*a*) matter (toxins) in the non-living environmental matter – air or water and (*b*) the living matter of human and nonhuman bodies. Toxins circulate through all of them.

Waste permeates the bodies and ecosystems of humans in *Waste Tide* too. Traditionally, people who handle trash and waste 'become trash in our minds' (Morrison 2015: 99). Humans who are rendered redundant or surplus are also rendered into disposable people:

> [D]eclassés individuals, possessing no defined social status, deemed redundant from the point of view of material and intellectual production and regarding themselves as such. 'Organized society' treats them as 'scroungers and intruders', charges them at best with unwarranted pretences or indolence, often with all sorts of wickedness, like scheming, swindling, living a life hovering on the brink of criminality, but in each case with feeding parasitically on the social body. (Bauman 2004: 41)

Trash enters into their very bodies, their dwellings and determines their lives, until their environment (of trash) and their being (corporeal and even emotional) are indistinguishable, even as the economy revolves around the waste industry in *Waste Tide*. Director Lin in the novel summarizes such human lives and the ecosystem in which such lives are lived:

The air, the water, the soil, and the people have been immersed in the trash for too long. Sometimes you can no longer even tell what's trash and what's not in our lives. We rely on waste to feed our families, to grow rich. But the more money we make, the worse the environment gets. (Qiufan 2019, unpaginated)

Questions of justice in toxic memoirs such as *Silent Snow* and certain novels focus on the human and nonhuman equally when speaking of different regions, from the Arctic to the Pacific, from small regions of the USA to larger provinces in China, as seen in this account of the human and animal toxic corporii of Silicon Isle in *Waste Tide*:

There was data showing that the incidence of respiratory diseases, kidney stones, and blood disorders among inhabitants of Silicon Isle was about five to eight times higher than in surrounding areas. In addition, the population produced an abnormally high number of cases of cancer. In one village, every single family had at least one member who suffered from terminal cancer.

Strange fish filled with cancerous tumors had been pulled out of many polluted fishing ponds. The number of stillbirths refused to go down, and rumors spoke of a migrant woman who gave birth to a dead baby whose entire body was dark green and gave off a metallic stink. Elders said that Silicon Isle was already a place of evil. (Qiufan 2019, unpaginated)

Qiufan is speaking of the *flows* of matter, toxic and dangerous to all life forms, from fish to humans. Qiufan's description of the humans goes like this:

Scott observed the men and women living among the trash – the natives called them the waste people. The women did their laundry in the black water with their bare hands, the soap bubbles forming a silver edge around floating mats of duckweed. Children played everywhere, running over the black shores, where fiberglass and the charred remains of circuit boards twinkled; jumping over the abandoned fields, where embers and ashes from burnt plastic smoldered; swimming and splashing in dark green ponds, where polyester film floated over the surface. They seemed to think this was the natural state of the world and nothing disturbed their joy. (Unpaginated)

The waste people are central to the isle's economy and yet are treated as waste and *wasted*. Here, waste is material matter, but is also social: the people who deal in or with waste have been attributed a certain meaning and serve as symbols for the society itself. The waste people in *Waste Tide* lead their lives in a context where 'everything was unfamiliar, strange' (unpaginated), and their inner selves modified and controlled by the 'digital mushrooms' (electronic drugs) that they turn to for entertainment and destressing. The 'digital mushrooms' render them numb and indifferent to the suffering in their lives.[4] These are zombified humans, whose resemblance to healthy humans is minimal. Some form of contaminant has entered all their bodies, writes Qiufan:

> These days, the rich switch body parts as easily as people used to switch phones. The junked prostheses are shipped here. Most have not been decontaminated and still contain blood and bodily fluids, which pose much potential risk for public health. (Unpaginated)

Junked prostheses remain, writhing about on the ground. Waste enters the bodies of the 'waste people' in other ways. Their augmented reality sets were not employed to seek new information or play simulation games because 'they had no need for more junk information – they had plenty of garbage to process on a daily basis already' (unpaginated). The distinction between junk information and the trash they work with breaks down in Qiufan's description. In the process, the information-waste begins to segue into the other waste lying around in Silicon Isle, and into the lives of the waste people, which they experience as uncanny. Their everyday space consists of something foreign *in* their selves and in their settings (the 'revelation of something unhomely at heart of hearth and home', as Nicholas Royle defines the uncanny, 2003: 1) in the form of the materials shipped from all over the world, but whose origins are in China itself. The waste matter they deal with daily, in other words, is native and foreign at the same time – and this is what renders their own bodies, like the bodies of the fish in the water, uncanny in their corporeality.

Other forms of the corporeal uncanny also occur in the novel. Mimi carries within her a genetically modified virus – originally designed to help victims of brain injury or damage and which, Scott Brandle suspects, has enormous economic potential because the strains of the virus could be used to fight brain aging. Mimi, once injected with the virus, experiences an uncanny sense of her own body:

> Right now Mimi was experiencing the hallucination of being a guest in her own body. Since the moment she recovered her consciousness, this sensation had only grown stronger. Even worse, she couldn't control this flesh body as effectively as she had controlled the robot … she'd heard an impossible

conversation being carried on. Inconceivable words drifted out of Mimi's lips and disappeared. She'd seen Mimi grip Kaizong's hand, let go, and then his hands had seized hers. She was certain that she had gone insane…. She had discovered that she felt this world differently. (Qiufan 2019, unpaginated)

She becomes Mimi-mecha, 'no longer a flesh-and-blood human body, but a body made of metal' (unpaginated). In a terrifying scene, Mimi-mecha needs to recharge herself, through the energies in Mimi's comatose body. We are told that 'Mimi's consciousness oscillated rapidly between the robot and the human body, her vision flickering uncertainly'. In this entire exchange, the comatose Mimi revives, even as the charge passes from her flesh-and-blood body to Mimi-mecha (later these are called Mimi 0 and Mimi 1, where Mimi 1 becomes a power-hungry artificial being and has to be killed).[5] When Brandle discovers the potential in *this* Mimi, she is suddenly a valued body even though this body is that of a human 'WASTE GIRL' (as she is called, emphasis in original). Thus, the foreign inside Mimi makes her that contradiction: a valuable waste girl.

> Scott's intuition told him that the secret hidden within this young woman was thousands of times more valuable than the Silicon Isle recycling project. He could even see the paths leading to the goal overlaid on top of the scene in front of him like augmented-reality plans. He would … construct a lie that would bring Mimi away from Silicon Isle and into the international market, where her potential value could be fully exploited. (Unpaginated)

Mimi experiences an uncanny version of herself because of something inside her, which animates her differently. 'The uncanny', writes Kathleen Richardson, 'then, is not triggered by the animation of the inanimate *per se*, but by the animation of the inanimate in a specific type of context' (2018: 118). Mimi's experience of her uncanniness has two contexts: her discovery of herself and the use-value for the others of the foreign within her and of the transformation wrought inside her by the virus. She is valuable as an animated, upgraded, cyborged waste girl. It is when the capitalists discover that there is value (even) in waste and waste people that they are most at risk. The exploitative process and environmental injustices that produced waste people have come full circle: now even the waste people can be exploited.

The working lives of the waste people force us to envision unorthodox forms of social life, the animal, the machine and the human. When certain forms of life – wasted people, the nonhuman – are merely 'vitalized forms of death', in Joshua Bennett's evocative phrase in his study of the animal and black slaves cast as property, they become uncanny bodies and lives (2020: 116–117). The waste people of Silicon Isle are effectively toxic body doubles: they look like healthy humans but, at the level of the molecule, the nerve and the tissue, they carry foreign toxins, lifeforms and particles.

But Qiufan does not presume that 'waste' economics affects only the humans. In an early incident Mimi is horrified that the bioluminiscent jellyfish may be luminous because 'of a reaction between some protein inside them and the high concentration of calcium ions in the wastewater' (Qiufan 2019, unpaginated). Their very biological attributes, Kaizong informs her, stem from toxins. Later, Mimi sees baby jellyfish being sucked into a vortex created by the currents from the waterpipes and the surrounding sea, 'their lives' journey came to an end almost as soon as it had begun' (unpaginated). Kaizong informs her that a vast amount of money is spent every year clearing out the pipes clogged with jellyfish. Mimi asks angrily: 'Why can't people be more compassionate and wait until these beings have left the area before pumping water? Wanting more money doesn't make it okay to kill' (unpaginated). Kaizong retorts: '[T]hey can't even afford to care about human lives, let alone the lives of jellyfish' (unpaginated). All lifeforms, Qiufan suggests, are subject to the toxins.

Toxic corporii haunt these texts: bodies shaped, as it were, by the toxins assimilated since childhood, and producing cancers and other conditions, across species and lifeforms. The toxic coporii are the nodes in the rhizome that encompasses and covers entire neighbourhoods and communities. The memoirs and the fiction embed the toxic bodies in social, economic and cultural contexts so that environmental injustice *and* harm stem from and are linked to social inequalities and devastating economic policies and processes, whether they are racialized economies of slavery or the economies of contemporary techno-capitalism.

Homes, Communities, Neighbourhoods

Sandra Steingraber speaks of the 'darker secrets' of Illinois' soil: it contains '54 million pounds of synthetic pesticides applied each year' (2010: 3–4). She then details the effect of DDT – 'the most common pesticide in fish in North American rivers and streams', and the now-established links to numerous diseases and conditions in humans (5). She writes:

[I]n 2007, 1,102 different industries released more than 114 million pounds of toxic chemicals into air, water, and soil, making Illinois the nation's thirteenth biggest polluter. In the same year, 763 chemical spills occurred – more than two a day – making Illinois ninth among states in number of reported toxic accidents. (6)

The above description *follows* a detailed picture of the region's crops, soil and topography, narrated in visceral (she speaks of the 'tautness in the thighs that comes with ascending a long grade versus the looseness in our feet that indicates descent', 1), chemical (the crops, the water, the soil, and their constituent chemicals) and affective ('it is important to me to maintain a relationship with both Illinoises – the present and familiar one as well as the Illinois that has vanished', 4) terms. That is, the sequence of her narrative moves from a near-idyllic chorography of rolling plains, lush crops, extensive productivity and use-value to a hidden truth: beneath this pastoral landscape lurks poison. Steingraber's toxichorography demythologizes the glories of farmland and rural USA by presenting us an entire region of toxified ecosystems and bodies.

The toxic bodies that populate fiction and memoirs such as Steingraber's are the products not only of the absorption of dangerous chemicals, but also of their being embedded in toxified social and economic systems. Such fiction and memoirs are essentially toxichorographies. Houses, communities and entire neighbourhoods are all toxified in these narratives.

The absence of accurate knowledge, adequate scientific coverage and accurate data about their ecosystem adds to the toxichorographies of Toms River (Fagin), Lowndes Country (Flowers), Maine (Martin), and other such places of patent environmental injustices.

Susanne Antonetta records that her family was asked to stop drinking from their well but not why. Antonetta writes: 'So we all keep ingesting the water and in the nineties it becomes my obsession to find out why our well was declared unsafe' (2001: 115). She makes calls, meets people but no accurate information is available:

Of course my infertility could have happened in my mother's body, the DDT, the swimming in Toms River, by the chemical pipeline leading into the woods. There are facts without anything beneath them, and even if you could tie them to the rock of a real event, no one would know what that might mean. (115)

Elsewhere she documents:

The children of Woburn, Massachusetts, where two wells had been tainted with trichloroethylene (also in the ground at Ocean County, at Denzer and Schafer, Ciba-Geigy and Reich Farms), developed high rates of seizure disorders. So have the children of the Ukraine and other parts of Russia after Chernobyl. (200)

Caroline Flowers informs us that Allensworth wells 'are contaminated with arsenic at levels too high for human consumption' (2020: 186). She adds:

> Arsenic can be removed from water with the proper treatment, but little communities like Allensworth can't afford that solution. So unless a more affordable treatment process is developed or a government agency steps in to help with the money, residents will continue to buy water by the jug, bottle, or tank with their already meager incomes. (186)

Here a community's income levels and the level of chemical contaminant come together, thus demonstrating that chemical effects operate in bodies embedded in social contexts, and chemical effects are mitigated or amplified depending on social policies such as state funding for research, water treatment or welfare measures. In the case of parasitic infections, Flowers notes, the Alabama Health Department had initially been supportive, 'but when the hookworm results came back, they did an about-face'. The state-run organization, observes Flowers, 'denied the possibility'. She concludes that the state had been negligent, and though with 'adequate sanitation' hookworm could have been 'prevented', the state chose to do nothing (134–135).

In the first Odiya Dalit novel, Akhila Naik's *Bheda* (2008, English translation 2017), the nexus between Sachikant Tripathy, the 'forester', and Lochan Haiti operates effectively to steal the timber from the forests of the Sahajkhol jungle. The local 'lower-castes' led by Laltu defend their forests and cause a crisis when they issue, on behalf of the Sahajkhol Jungle Suraksha Committee, an order that 'except for fuel no one will be allowed to cut trees from the Sahajkhol jungle' (unpaginated). They seize the trucks carrying stolen timber, putting the forest officials in an awkward spot. In Naik's text, the caste hierarchies of the social order are instrumental in both human and environmental exploitation, demonstrating that the 'meaning' affixed to people and the environment – as useful, 'lower' castes – determines the fate and future of trees in the area.

Qiufan, as we have seen, makes an inventory of medical anomalies and conditions, then quantifies it, like in any scientific study. The use of terms like 'times higher' and 'high number of cases' is remarkably like the ones to be found in a report or study. Such a quantificatory account of the risky biological matter is then supplemented, in the Derridean sense of both completion and excess, by the affective and the mythic. There are 'rumors' and talk of the isle as 'a place of evil'. Qiufan seems to suggest that it is not enough to inventory the place's many material problems; one needs to pay attention to the meanings the humans bestow upon these states of matter and being. When Kaizong thinks about Mimi's life – 'she and others like her had left their homes to come here under the euphemism of "economic development" so that they could eke out a living in pollution and poison, suffer the prejudice and exploitation of the natives' (2019, unpaginated) – he merges environmental and social injustices that inform and determine 'development' in waste economies like Silicon Isle. The toxic memoirs demonstrate how matter possesses recalcitrance, reactive properties and resilience beyond the purview of the human: which causes them, especially when these are toxins, to interact with other matter to produce disaster.

Toxic economies of the kind Qiufan fictionalizes and the memoirs document, where effluence, waste and toxification are woven into the processes of 'development' and eventually waste disposal, represent the modern industrial economy. As Flowers, Cone, Qiufan and others show, social inequalities are entangled with and embed environmental injustices. In other genres, notably neo-slave narratives and postcolonial fiction, this linkage of the *oikos* of individual and community dwelling(s) is explored in terms of the operations of the slave economy, plantations and the postcolony's agenda of 'development'.

A word about the memoir here. Thomas Couser, adapting Lorraine Adams, speaks of the 'nobody memoir', 'according to whether the author is known before its publication or becomes known only through its publication' (2009: 1). Couser modifies this definition and category to make a case for the 'some body memoir':

> [N]ew nobody memoir is also often the memoir of some body. Far more than the somebody memoir, the nobody memoir is often about what it's like to have or to be, to live in or as, a particular body – indeed, a body that is usually odd or anomalous. Less often, it's about living with, loving, or knowing intimately someone with such a body. (2)

While Couser's classification is accurate when it comes to the disease memoir, it may be useful to think of toxic memoirs of the type Stacy Alaimo (2010) and others examine as 'everybody memoirs'. None of the memoirs I am aware of restricts the account to their individual bodies. Rather, they make the case that while an individual may have a specific kind of cancer from the contaminants, the entire community suffers from some ailment or the other related to, although this is often unverifiable, the toxic matter in the air, soil and water of the locale they live in. An individual's toxified body is a part of a community with other such bodies. The everybody memoir is a prosopography, even when it speaks of the deterioration of an individual body.

Dan Fagin, Caroline Flowers, Sandra Steingraber, Marie Thérèse Martin and others start off with individual examples, but eventually expand their narrative ambit to speak of the community. Note Thérèse Martin's emphasis on the ordinary folk, having a quiet time relaxing on their porches: 'Many of the tenements had outside porches where families could sit on good days, when the wind blew particulate matter downriver.... Their kids played in the streets with balls and tin cans' (2022: 25). There is the universalizing image of the every-human, highlighted in the 'we' in the above passage. The every-body is also captured in terms of the statistics supplied about cancer and other medical conditions prevalent in their communities in the memoirs of Antonetta, Martin and Steingraber. These texts are instances of the 'everybody memoir': toxins affect everyone in the area, and they all become toxic-subjects, a subjectivity defined by the toxins in their bodies that are breaking down under the assault.

There is another feature of the everybody memoir. As Stacy Alaimo has argued in the case of 'material memoirs', 'the pursuit of self-knowledge, which has been a personal, philosophical, psychological, or discursive matter, now extends into a rather "scientific" investigation into the constitution of our coextensive environments' (2010: 20). A community is kept in the dark about the true nature of the toxins poisoning their bodies. The community speculates that they are being poisoned, but accurate information is not forthcoming. The memoirists spend a considerable amount of time researching and documenting these offensive substances. Marie Thérèse Martin records how the local paper mill bosses issued 'intentional lie[s]', claiming that 'dioxin from the mill does not pose a health risk' (2022: 160). 'Wilful ignorance', she admits, carried the day, 'permeating every aspect of our community' (116). The toxicity of the chemicals in the ecosystem, it appears, is directly proportionate to the quantum of misinformation spread by polluting companies and to the levels of ignorance prevalent in the sacrifice zone around it. The population, writes Martin, is 'trapped' by the mill (115). Steingraber documents how Rachel Carson was constantly stymied in her effort to obtain information about polluting chemicals (2010: 18–21). In her own memoir, Steingraber explores biomedical and environmental databases, published work, cancer registries to check on the prevalence of cancer, merging it with her own narrative of being afflicted with cancer, so that her memoir is at once personal and prosopographic. The quantum of information, or, more accurately, the search for appropriate and verifiable information, about the chemicals in the environment and within their bodies is a key feature of the material memoir. Toxichorography is also, therefore, an epistemic project, just like traditional chorographies (Barbara Shapiro 1983).

Everybody memoirs are waste prosopographies, collective biographies of wasted bodies infused with, defined and ruined by toxins in the biome they live in. If individual personhood is now defined in terms of blood pressure, sugar and cholesterol levels, the prosopography of the community is defined by the quantum of DDT or PCB it inhales. Where population genetics at one point recalled an earlier version of humanism that, instead of a hierarchy of races, spoke of the 'united family of man', the everyday memoir's discourse of toxic trans-corporeal connections functions as a unifying discourse. Inheritances, as Susanne Antonetta emphasizes, are not only about genetic material and traits being passed down, but also about toxins and serious flaws being transmitted – and this is the case with most families in places like Maine Valley (Thérèse Martin), Central Illinois (Steingraber) and Toms River (Fagin).

Another form of the waste prosopography may be found in China Miévelle's *Un Lun Dun* (2007). The abcity[6] that is UnLondon is made of the objects that are 'Mildly Obsolete in London', or 'moil'. Moil thrives in UnLondon, and some are friendly (like the empty milk carton that follows and cuddles up with Deeba and Zanna) and some predatory ('they heard the manic wet rustle of the predatory rubbish … the paper fluttered for them as madly as agitated butterflies. The plastic bags reached out of their handles and scrambled towards the girls', writes Miévelle, unpaginated). Buildings, indeed the very architecture of UnLondon, are built from the trash discarded by London:

> The entire three-floor building was mortared-together rubbish. There were fridges, a dishwasher or two, and hundreds of record players, old-fashioned cameras, telephones, and typewriters, with thick cement between them. (Unpaginated)

The inhabitants – the everybody of UnLondon – in UnLondon are at war with the smog – which enters the abcity from the factories of London as one UnLondoner explains to Deeba and Zanna:

Back in your old queen's time … London filled up with factories, and all
of them had chimneys, in houses they burnt coal. And the factories were
burning everything, and letting off smoke from chemicals and poisons.

The chemicals, as a book tells Zanna and Deeba, 'reacted together and made an
enormous, diffuse, cloud-brain … the smog started to think. And that's when
it became the Smog' (unpaginated). Miévelle's fantasy makes a larger point
about toxic or waste prosopography by showing us how waste matter from
one city, culture, region could determine the lives of everybody in another city,
culture and region. Waste circulates and *makes* waste people in other parts of
the city or country, thus distributing conditions of waste. This distribution is
uneven, and offers unequal life chances to, say, working classes and the racial
Other. Here the material distribution of garbage or toxic waste hinges on the
value – meaning – placed on Others' spaces or Other races, and thus merges
environmental and civic or social racisms.

Miévelle's theme resonates with the universalizing of toxic flows that
produces the interconnectedness of places and people that memoirists
Steingraber, Antonetta and others emphasize in their work. In Miévelle's
novel the residents of UnLondon have been resourceful enough to utilize the
materials – waste – coming into their city from London. As an instantiation
of the waste recycling industry, UnLondon appropriates garbage. But Miévelle
also asks: do the 'people' of UnLondon have a choice, given the unregulated
and constant infusion of toxins and urban detritus into their lives? Miévelle
suggests that London's urbanism survives precisely because there is a nether
world – the world of waste recycling – that manages, controls and, where
necessary, assimilates the toxic detritus so that London can live on. The waste
people are essential to keep the city secure: the UnLondoners in Miévelle or
the armies of waste people in the *Waste Tide*. All urban accounts, then, are
also simultaneously accounts of the shadow city, the abcity, of the waste(d)
Others. We could also see Miévelle's novel as allegorizing the transformation
in the neocolonial era of nations or regions in the Global South into dumping
grounds for the wastes from and of the Global North.

Entire communities are made up of toxic corporii, as the everybody memoirs
and fiction show. Such representations of the contemporary wastelanding of
specific regions and cities peopled by such wasted and toxified bodies have their
antecedents in an earlier era where racialized economies enabled the European
races to not only demarcate zones of cultivation but also produce conditions
where certain bodies were rendered disposable.

The slave's body as well as that of the animal were subject to similar exploitative processes in the plantation.[7] The opening paragraph of Edward Jones' *The Known World* brings the two lifeforms together:

> When he, Moses, finally freed himself of the ancient and brittle harness that connected him to the oldest mule his master owned, all that was left of the sun was a five-inch-long memory of red orange laid out in still waves across the horizon between two mountains on the left and one on the right. He had been in the fields for all of fourteen hours. He paused before leaving the fields as the evening quiet wrapped itself about him. The mule quivered, wanting home and rest. (2003: 1)

Man and beast are both exhausted, their bodies beaten. There comes a point when the beast is no longer able to carry on working:

> They [Beau and Morris] saw a young white woman trying to get a white mule to stand up from the muddy road. The mule had been pulling a wagon in the rain, and it wasn't clear to Beau or Morris whether the animal had sat down because it was tired of working or because it just liked sitting down in the rain. (342)

Even the threats issued to the slave are cast in animal terms: as the patroller Counsel says to Moses in the novel: 'If you ever say a word, I will shoot you down like a dog' (371). Animalizing the slave was, then, an established convention, as numerous commentators have noted (Bennett 2020; Pergadia 2018). Animals can be killed without a second thought, as in this scene from Jones:

> The horse began pulling him back. Counsel stopped, sweating, head full of thunder, chest heaving, and he looked the horse in the eyes. 'Come,' he said in as calm a voice as he could manage. 'Come.' He pulled out his pistol. 'When I tell you to come, don't you think I mean it?' The horse did not move. 'Come,' he said, again calmly. He raised the pistol and shot the horse between the eyes. The horse sank on two knees and moaned and Counsel fired once more and the horse collapsed. Its breathing was heavy and he prepared to fire again but soon the breathing stopped. 'Why is coming so hard?' he said to the horse. (E. P. Jones 2003: 242)

Jones elsewhere also implies that the entire land had been transformed into something unrecognizable: even the woods adjacent to the plantation had 'many trees that no one could identify' (3), perhaps suggesting a bioinvasion, which was a characteristic of the plantation landscape (Barua 2023: 13–14).

When a plague affects the plantations in Edward Jones' novel, many of the slaves and the white landowners die.

> [M]ore than half of the slaves on Counsel's plantation had died, some twenty-one human beings.... Ten more slaves died, and that same day the first of Counsel's children died ... in the three days that followed her death the disease swept up nearly all the rest of them, down to the youngest slave, ten-week-old Paula, whose mother had died in childbirth. (2003: 224)

The effect is disastrous on the land *and* the nonhumans:

> The animals would live, too, managing somehow to get by even with all their caregivers dead. The creditors, weeks and weeks later, would not get much for livestock from a place God had turned his back on. A buyer's place might be next if he bought a cow or a horse.... In the end, after Counsel had tried to drive the animals away.... (225)

When death is measured, the slave's dead body and that of the animal occupy the same space. In Jones, describing the flooding of Lynchburg, a (fictional) historian writes:

> The rain led to great flooding, and the Lynchburg historian noted, without hyperbole, that it may well have been the worst any county had suffered since Virginia became a state. Twenty-one human beings lost their lives, including eight adult slaves, five men and three women. All the children, whether white or black or Indian, free or in bondage, were spared. No one counted the livestock and the dogs and the cats that were killed because there were so many. The land was covered with animal bodies for weeks and weeks.(206)

Extreme weather conditions affect the slaves and the animals alike, suggests Jones.

In Cynthia McLeod's novel, when the Europeans seek to avenge the slaves' rebellion, they follow a scorched-earth policy. The captain who heads the expedition finds two villages and

> [d]estroyed the village completely. Everything was set on fire; they burnt the crops and the food stores once they had taken what they themselves needed.

In this case they had first eaten one hundred and eighty chickens before setting the rest on fire. (2010, unpaginated)

This destruction of fields and *food* crops – cassava, ripe corn, bananas – on which the natives depend for survival is repeated at other villages. Elsewhere, McLeod makes the usual analogy of slaves and animal life:

> All the work was done by negro slaves: stupid ignorant creates who had been transported and sold to the plantation owners. Those people were then set to work in the same way as horses or mules. (Unpaginated)

The injustices visited upon the humans in the racialized toxiconomy of the plantation were also visited upon the nonhuman and the land. The human and the nonhuman in the plantation are both disposable bodies. These bodies emerge in the context of extractive colonialism practised by the settlers.

In McLeod's novel Suriname *is* gold:

> There was gold in South America. Not the yellow gold that they had first sought after, but the fertile ground that could produce goods for which there was so much demand: sugar, and now coffee, cocoa, tobacco and cotton. A golden era for the plantation owners and for the bankers in the Netherlands. (Unpaginated)

Another character, Rutger, even thinks of these as 'Suriname gold' (unpaginated), where the land itself is likened to the precious metal because of the sheer quantum of profits it would bring. This induces every Dutchman, 'people who could hardly distinguish a cocoa plant from a coffee plant … everyone had to become a planter', writes McLeod. All plantations begin to expand, says McLeod, showing the unstoppable progress of the extractive colonial economy.

In *Island Beneath the Sea*, Allende sketches the character of the plantation overseer, Cambray. She does so by depicting his attitude towards the slaves on his plantation and the consequence of his approach:

> He boasted that under his command few slaves had fled from Saint-Lazare; his method consisted of breaking their souls and wills. Only fear and exhaustion could conquer the seduction of freedom. Work, work, work to the last breath, which was not long in coming, because no one's bones grew old there; three or four years, never more than six or seven…. In Cambray's view, it was more profitable to replace slaves than to treat them with consideration. Once their

cost was amortized, it was profitable to work them to their death and then buy others younger and stronger. (2010, unpaginated)

Slaves that 'age or illness rendered useless' were 'abandoned ... in the street' (unpaginated). Their average lifespan, as the newly arrived plantation owner, Valmorain, discovers, 'lasted an average of eighteen months before they dropped dead of fatigue or escape' (unpaginated). The slave body wastes away in the toxiconomy of the plantation and is entirely fungible. The slave economy, as Allende shows, hinged on the fungibility of the slave as a commodity, on par with, or even perhaps less valuable than, the cane or sugar she or he helped produce or the animal life that was integral to the process. Black fungibility, writes Tiffany Lethabo King, is the 'capacity for Blackness for unfettered exchangeability and transformation within and beyond the form of the commodity' (2016: 1023). Allende's portrait of the Haitian plantations paints the picture of replaceable slaves, their value calculated in terms of labour output, costs incurred in purchasing them and tenure of their labour before they died or escaped. One slave was the same as the other, since both were valued as labouring hands. But over the centuries, different races (all non-white) were also rendered fungible: 'With the intent to erase the racism that had been the island's curse, all citizens, no matter the color of their skin, were designated negs, and all those who weren't were called blancs', writes Allende (2010, unpaginated). The 'portability of race', which Felicity Nussbaum notes of eighteenth-century racisms, ensured that degrees and kinds of 'blackness' were erased in the flattening body-economies of the plantations. In Gyasi's *Homegoing*, we are shown another kind of fungibility: Africans captured from any part of the country could serve as slaves, interchangeable with other Africans: 'Trade had increased so much, and the methods of gathering slaves had become so reckless, that many of the tribes had taken to marking their children's faces so that they would be distinguishable', 2016: 64.[8]

In a significant symbol for the reduction of the slave to the slave- or labouring-body, Octavia Butler's Dana in *Kindred* (1979) loses an arm in her final time travel back from the plantation era to the present. The first line of the novel says, 'I lost an arm on my last trip home' (9). The actual incident is described in some detail later:

Something ... paint, plaster, wood – a wall. The wall of my living room. I was back at home – in my own house, in my own time. But I was still caught somehow, joined to the wall as though my arm were growing out of

it – or growing into it. From the elbow to the ends of the fingers, my left arm
had become a part of the wall. I looked at the spot where flesh joined with
plaster, stared at it uncomprehending. It was the exact spot Rufus's fingers
had grasped. (261)

Forrest Yerman's neat reading of this incident states:

[T]he past and present in America regarding slavery are not separate ends
on a linear narrative, and that such a relationship [of past and present] has a
profound and disabling effect on everyone, white and black, but especially
for black women who bore, and bare, the brunt of a violent patriarchal white
supremacist society. (2020: 261)

Yerman is right to point to the 'disabling', literal and metaphoric, effects of
slavery. But the symbolism has an additional layer too. The fact that it is a part
of her arm that is, presumably, left behind in the plantation-time is indicative
of the conditions in which the slave was reduced to a pair of working *hands*.
Throughout *Kindred* and the other slave narratives, we are given portraits
of overworked slaves: their hands never at rest. They are indeed only their
labouring hands. Dana, when she returns to the plantation-time, is also
rendered into a slave, and remains connected to her ancestor, Alice, by genealogy
but also literally through the labouring status she shares with Alice. Hence
Butler's symbolism is about more than familial lines: it is about the fungible
slave *body*, where the present-day blacks are tethered to the past in terms of a
corporeal sign such as Dana's phantom arm, of which some part is stuck in the
(slave) past. This is a brilliant metaphorization of the toxiconomies of social
and environmental racisms that Butler undertakes, and echoes the Caroline
Flowers comment that opened this chapter: one cannot really understand
contemporary environmental racism without turning to its racial history
embodied in plantations and slavery that Dana witnesses and experiences, even
though she comes from 1970s New York.

Body-economies and their fungibility takes another form in neo-slave
narratives. These narratives embody what Rebekah Sheldon identifies as a
'somatic capitalism' which 'operates above and below the level of the individual
subject to amplify or diminish specific bodily capacities' (2016: 118). In this
case, somatic capitalism is the investment the plantation owner makes in the
slave body, speculating upon its reproducibility. Sheldon's argument enables
us to see that the plantation's toxiconomies (which is really a bioeconomy),
the maternal (black mother), the filial (white father) and the communal

(the slave community) are embedded in a triad of landownership-capital-biology. Somatic capitalism works, in the case of the plantation narratives, at two levels: the reproduction of a slave body and the role of surrogate (labouring) mothers assigned to slave women in white families.

The woman slave is embedded in what Lin Hua terms a 'patriarchal speculative economy' (2011: 392). The profligacy of the white man in the patriarchal speculative economy – they 'consoled themselves with the stream of young girls of every shade and tone the island offered' (Allende 2010, unpaginated) – transformed the black woman into a sexual object. The black women on the plantations in these novels are subject to the 'modalities of the flesh they do not express: whiteness and maleness ... [they] suffer for being both female and black' (Robertson 2010: 370). The black women served as sexual objects, bearing children who were often sold into slavery or becoming slaves on the same plantation as their parent(s). As Sarah the slave tells Dana Franklin in Octavia Butler's *Kindred*:

> My fourth baby. The only one Marse Tom let me keep ... Marse Tom took all my children, all but Carrie ... Carrie ain't worth much as the others 'cause she can't talk. People think she ain't got good sense. (1979: 76)

In Cynthia McLeod's *The Cost of Sugar*, set in eighteenth century Suriname, she writes of the sexual economy of the plantation:

> Almost all whites had a mulatto woman as mistress or concubine. This satisfied the needs of the man and carried absolutely no responsibility. For of course, no white man would ever be so stupid as to consider marrying one of these women. If such a woman had children by him, then a few guilders sufficed for their care and upbringing. (2010, unpaginated)

In the case of the slave woman, then, fungibility was 'the expansive, inexhaustible use value of Blackness beyond labor: as source of enjoyment, violent domination, and imaginary projection' (Day 2021: 4). Even one's own daughter could be transformed into a sex object, if the white father or master so desired.[9] No one, Allende, McLeod and Jones suggest in the reprising of the era in their neo-slave narratives, was spared.[10]

In Allende's novel, the pregnant slave Seraphine has her hand caught in a machine, and the hand has to be cut off to save her. As she bleeds, the native physician, Tante Rose, recognizes that the loss of blood may kill her, or cause her to have a miscarriage. The overseer Cambray arrives on the scene:

'"[I]f Tante Rose saves her, we will at least have her offspring," he decided, touching Seraphine's bloody belly with the handle of his whip' (Allende 2010, unpaginated). The slave, even in the very act of dying, provides the next generation of slaves in the toxiconomy of the plantation. Seraphine's value is this *next* generation, which is already earmarked as a slave, in her womb. Cambray assumes, in Anita Allen's reading of the plantation narratives, that 'all black mothers were de facto surrogates.... Slave women gave birth to children with the understanding that those children would be owned by others' (1990: 144). Indeed, the grip of somatic capitalism is so strong that the slaves opt to kill their babies because the only future the babies have is of slavery (as Allende describes it in her novel, the mothers induce tetanus in their infants by 'sticking a fine needle into a soft part of the baby's head before the cranial bones hardened', 2010, unpaginated). Tete in Allende's novel has only one question: did Valmorain sell her son? (unpaginated). Sarah in *Kindred* has three of her babies sold by the white master, Weylin. In a different key, a trade in women, Yaa Gyasi's *Homegoing* tells us, cements the friendship between the whites and the tribes (2016: 15).

In almost every text, the white children survive because the black nanny ensures their safety, from the moment of birth to adulthood. Isabel Allende writes of a childbirth in the white master's house, to Dona Eugenia:

> In the corridor a slave with swollen breasts was waiting, recently bathed, her head shaved for lice; she would give her milk to the son of the masters in the big house, while her baby was given rice water in the Negro quarters. (2010, unpaginated)

Allende sketches the power somatic capitalism wields over the bodies and reproductive futures of the black women: the care of the white child is at the cost of the black child. The slave woman is forced to ignore the nourishment of her own child so that she can ensure the feeding of the white progeny in the master's house. In McLeod's novel, Afanaisa the slave woman, the 'mammy', guards the child as her own. Eventually, Sarith's son, Jethro, craves only Mini-mini's presence. Within the somatic capitalism of the plantation economy, the white woman is freed of the responsibility – labour – of mothering after childbirth, while the black women are entrusted with the care of the infants. The infantilizing of the white woman in the plantation is accompanied by the mammy role for the black slave who is disposable and fungible. Cast in the language of the sentimental novel the neo-slave narrative underscores the impossibility of anything but injustice, exploitation and violence in the case of all slaves, whether they are house slaves or farm ones.

Somatic capitalism in the neo-slave narrative becomes the context of a multiracial intergenerational saga in slave and slaveowner families in some of the neo-slave narratives. In other words, the somatic capitalism of the plantation's toxiconomies complicates black history, white history, black families, white families and of course racial identities. The body of the slave on the plantation is the site where the history of racism and its concomitant toxiconomies are inscribed, as Benjamin Robertson has argued about *Kindred* (2010). The slave is a commodity, a victim, a reproduction-machine or a sex-object. The history of the plantation is the history of the reproductive futures of the slave economy, their bodies and their offspring, already earmarked as the property of the plantation owner. (In intergenerational texts such as *Homegoing*, the plantation finds its resonant structure, or double, in the coal mines of nineteenth-century America, where the latter are as exploitative as the former, and in addition, cause 'black lung disease' in the miners.)

To prove this point of the intersection of the flesh and the history it is embedded in, Octavia Butler makes Dana a witness. Dana says of her experience of seeing the slaves:

> I had seen people beaten on television and in the movies. I had seen that too-red blood substitute streaked across their backs and heard their well rehearsed screams. But I hadn't lain nearby and smelled their sweat or heard them pleading and praying, shamed before their families and themselves. (O. Butler 1979: 36)

The stark contrast between staged violence and witnessed violence is the contrast between the toxiconomies of the entertainment industry (which profits from depicting scenes of violence) and the plantation (with its beatings, rapes and killings that characterize the experience of the black slaves). Dana's response to the act of witnessing is also given to us in visceral, fleshy terms:

> I could literally smell his sweat, hear every ragged breath, every cry, every cut of the whip. I could see his body jerking, convulsing, straining against the rope as his screaming went on and on. My stomach heaved, and I had to force myself to stay where I was and keep quiet. (36)

The black or slave witness who kept 'quiet' is the witness to plantation history.

In the contemporary era, the plantation that dehumanized the black peoples is reconfigured as a prison that most often incarcerates black persons. In Jesmyn Ward's *Sing, Unburied, Sing*, the Parchman prison is an uncanny iteration of the plantation that used to be Parchman.

> Damn near fifty thousand acres. Parchman the kind of place that fool you into thinking it ain't no prison, ain't going to be so bad when you first see it, because ain't no walls. Back in the day, it was just fifteen camps, each one surrounded by a barbed-wire fence. Wasn't no brick; wasn't no stone. Us inmates was called gunmen because we worked under the trusty shooters, who was inmates theyselves, but who the warden gave guns to oversee the rest of us. (2017, unpaginated)

Ward uses the term 'oversee' rather than, say, 'supervise', in an explicit nod to the plantation eras where all slaves were under an overseer. Then she adds:

> You don't know the sergeant. You don't know the sergeant come from a long line of men bred to treat you like a plowing horse, like a hunting dog – and bred to think he can make you like it. That the sergeant come from a long line of overseers. (Unpaginated)

Ward makes it clear that there is a continuity of slavery and the plantation cultures into the present (twentieth-century America). The prisoners work exactly as their ancestors did on the plantations:

> From sunup to sundown we was out there in them fields, hoeing and picking and planting and pulling. A man get to a point like that, he can't think. Just feel. Feel like he want to stop moving. Feel his stomach burn and know he want to eat. Feel his head packed full of cotton and know he want to sleep. Feel his throat close and fire run up his arms and legs, his heart beat out his chest, and know he want to run. But wasn't no running. We was gunmen, under the gun of them damn trusty shooters. That was our whole world: the long line. Men strung out across the fields, the trusty shooters stalking the edge, the driver on his mule, the caller yelling to the sun, throwing his working song out. (Unpaginated)[11]

They work at the land and are animalized just as their ancestors were, as Ward shows.

In the cities, the racisms that extend into everyday life take the form of the shooting of black men and boys so that 'in America the worst thing you

could be was a black man. Worse than dead, you were a dead man walking'
(Gyasi 2016: 259–260). Contemporary culture is also a toxiconomy for the
black man. Plantations and mining from the seventeenth century, with their
extractivism and overuse of (slave) bodies and the land, prepare the grounds for
contemporary environmental racisms. Now Africans work in prisons built on
what were once the sites of their ancestors' labour, and Africans still get shot in
the streets.

Plantation toxiconomies also informed and influenced the home, dwelling
and families of the slave-as-property. Even insurance policies for slaves were a
part of the toxiconomies, as Edward Jones shows in *The Known World*:

> Topps told her that for 15 cents a head every two months, her property,
> each working slave over five years old, would be protected from just about
> everything God could think up…. Slave death by mad dogs in fall, winter or
> spring was compensable; canine madness in the summer was an 'ordinary act
> of God,' to be expected, so the policy was mute about that season. Nothing
> came from the loss of an arm or of one or both eyes, because such losses
> were not the best indicia of how much work a slave could still perform….
> No money for a slave hurt or killed by someone while said slave was visiting
> his family on another plantation. Being accidentally shot while assisting the
> master/mistress/their issue while hunting or while traveling with said people
> as long as travel was of three days duration or longer. Being struck by lightning
> while working in the field as long as recuperation was less than three days and
> as long as the slave had not been given sufficient warning…. (2003: 355)

Planters, therefore, had to account for such insurance policies and of forms of
injury to the slave body.

In her pioneering work on the 'plot' – the small patch of land assigned to the
slaves to grow their own vegetables – Sylvia Wynter argued that 'the plot was
also a site of minimal agency and resistance' (cited in McKittrick 2013: 10; also
Wolford 2021: 1623). McKittrick's gloss on Wynter says:

> [T]he plots of land that were given to some slaves so that they could grow
> food to nourish themselves and thus maximize profits – plots of land that
> also became the focus of resistance to the overriding system of the plantation
> economy. (2013: 10)

But oftentimes, the slaves did not acquire even this patch of land. In Natalie
Baszile's *Queen Sugar*, NeNee, pointing to her old grandmother, tells Charley
who hopes to hire their services for her cane farm:

She [the grandmother] worked cane since she was *nine* years old, and this is all she's got. Has she got any money saved? Has she got a pension? Health care? Does she own anything but this trailer and the little speck of sorry-ass ground it sits on? ...Those big cane farmers cut corners with her every chance they got. (2017: 53)

In Jones, Fern Elston the free black woman who could pass for white but is shunned by the white plantation owners, produces a variation of the 'plot': she has a whole wood in her house. Jones writes:

Her parlor dominated by trees, a peach and a magnolia, she and her servants had managed to domesticate.... The trees in Fern's house disoriented most people, those used to the inside always being inside and the outside always being outside ... the trees in Fern's parlor grew to a height of about eight or nine feet, then stopped, as if on command. The peaches born on the tree were very tiny, could fit on a man's thumb, and they were very sweet, too sweet for a pie or cobbler if the cook could manage to collect enough of them. The magnolia blossoms were also small, so beautiful.... (E. P. Jones 2003: 84–85)

The free black woman takes the garden into the house, domesticates it and thereby blurs the distinction between inside and outside. Just as Fern Elston could pass as a white woman, the inside of her house could pass off as the outside.

The slave quarters and homes are depicted as pockets of limited (heterosexual) family life and companionship in the neo-slave narrative. However, the opportunities for such a life in the slave quarters, contemporary novels suggest, were contingent on the white family – its largesse, compassion or cruelty. But houses and homes also serve as powerful symbols of black family life, resistance and agency. They become spaces of interracial alliances and their consequences – which complicate identities and relationships of master and slave – and sources of identity.

A turning point in McLeod's *The Cost of Sugar* is the discovery of Julius' liaison with Mini-mini by Julius's wife, Sarith. In the midst of the uproar, Sarith warns him: '[K]eep your bit of fluff and your concubine somewhere else, then, but not in my house.' Julius announces his intention that Mini-mini will leave their house. It is then that Sarith realizes the enormity of what he has decided:

Sarith now began to think things over. 'She'll leave,' he had said. That meant that he would install her somewhere and then openly acknowledge her as his concubine. He would support her and her child, perhaps buy a house for her, have more children and be with her more and more. (McLeod 2010, unpaginated)

The white woman's fears of a parallel household of the husband or father with his black slave concubine – a different, multiracial *oikos* – gather within Sarith, leading her to sell Mini-mini. When questioned as to her decision, she defends it: "'Am I supposed to accept that my husband's concubine, his truelove, is living in my house? Is that what I'm supposed to do?'" (unpaginated). The recognition and reiteration of the liaison as 'true love' inverts the racial and familial hierarchy that the white house prefers, as Sarith and Esther suggest. Within the space of this house, concubinage and cohabitation, especially if it is 'true love', cannot be permitted. But McLeod does something else too in order to underscore the impossibility of such an *oikos* defined solely by 'true love' between the races.

Although Mini-mini is supposedly the true love of the white man, and she reciprocates his love, her habitation is still the slave quarters. The day after she is sold, Sarith's son, Jethro, whom she, Mini-mini, looks after, goes to look for her: 'Jethro jumped out of bed and ran barefoot downstairs and out to the slave quarters in the grounds. He thrust open the door of the hut where Mini-mini always slept' (unpaginated). 'The hut where Mini-mini *always* slept' captures in a phrase the *segregation* of races and peoples, even when sexual liaisons – or romance – occur across races and within the space of the white house. The sexual economy of the white household does not spill over into the domestic economy of the slave quarters, and thus McLeod subtly calls into question the nature of the interracial sexual relationship.

As for the white slaveowner's house, acculturation has inured the races to their respective roles, suggests Octavia Butler in *Kindred* (1979). Dana, coming into the past from 1976 New York, is unsettled by the fact that she and her white husband find themselves readily fitted into the Weylin household:

'How easily we seemed to acclimatize,' Dana muses. 'Not that I wanted us to have trouble, but it seemed as though we should have had a harder time adjusting to this particular segment of history – adjusting to our places in the household of a slaveholder.' (97)

Butler's critique is savage when she shows Dana actually finding the Weylin household a better fit for her: 'I felt as though I were losing my place here in my own time. Rufus's time was a sharper, stronger reality' (191). And towards the end, on her fourth trip back in time, Butler says, '[Dana was] startled to catch myself wearily saying, "Home at last"' (127). Tim A. Ryan reading the above episodes has proposed:

> Dana does not fully understand that nineteenth-century African Americans are not the only ones to be conditioned in this way. Even as she speaks, Dana too is unwittingly and unconsciously beginning to conform to the system. (2008: 133)

The sense of 'home' that Dana experiences is a critique of the perniciousness of the *oikos* and racialized space the slave was made to inhabit and which *made* the slave, as Dana herself realizes. The space of the white home and the slave quarters define the slave's identity. Even though Dana has the privilege of not sleeping in the slave quarters and shares Kevin's room when in the Weylin house, Butler suggests that this does not alter the fact of her slave identity: within the household, even if not restricted to the slave quarter, the black woman remains a slave. The household is *internally* segregated, and the freedom of movement is the sole prerogative of the white residents.

The slave's household or home comes in for sustained attention in Jones' *The Known World*. Manchester County, in which the novel is set, has black slaveowners like Henry Townsend, who was once a slave but had obtained his freedom and now owned land, and slaves. The principal characters, Henry Townsend and his father, Augustus, William Robbins, Moses are all introduced through a spatialization and locationality. The novel opens with a poignant scene: the slave Moses eating the dirt from the field he has worked in the whole day:

> He had been in the fields for all of fourteen hours. He paused before leaving the fields as the evening quiet wrapped itself about him. The mule quivered, wanting home and rest. Moses closed his eyes and bent down and took a pinch of the soil and ate it with no more thought than if it were a spot of cornbread. He worked the dirt around in his mouth and swallowed, leaning his head back and opening his eyes in time to see the strip of sun fade to dark blue and then to nothing. He was the only man in the realm, slave or free, who ate dirt, but while the bondage women, particularly the pregnant ones, ate it for some incomprehensible need, for that something that ash cakes and

apples and fatback did not give their bodies, he ate it not only to discover the strengths and weaknesses of the field, but because the eating of it tied him to the only thing in his small world that meant almost as much as his own life. (E. P. Jones 2003: 1)

The slave savours the dirt, the land in which he works such extended hours. It becomes the meaning-making process, his dwelling-place, even as he ingests it so that the 'oikos' *becomes* him. There is no other, at least until the point when Moses believes he can build a future with his dead master's wife, Caldonia, maybe within Caldonia's house itself.

Henry Townsend is introduced to the reader as a young boy. The scene is the departure of his parents as free blacks and powerfully invokes the question of home:

At the wagon, Mildred sank to her knees and held on to Henry, who, at last realizing that he was to be separated from her, began crying. Augustus knelt beside his wife and promised Henry that they would be back for him. 'Before you can turn around good,' he said, 'you be comin home with us.' Augustus repeated himself, and the boy tried to make sense of the word home. He knew the word, knew the cabin with him and his mother and Rita that the word represented. He could no longer remember when his father was a part of that home. Augustus kept talking and Henry pulled at Mildred, wanting her to go back onto William Robbins's land, back to the cabin where the fireplace smoked when it was first lit. 'Please,' the boy said, 'please, les go back.' (16)

The boy recognizes a 'cabin' in which he had lived with his mother and Rita as 'home'. This cabin is on William Robbins' land, which is also the familiar and familial territory the boy recognizes as the place he *belongs* to, and to which his parents belong.

Jones here presents the spatial unconscious of the boy as layered between home and home/land. On this home/land, writes Jones, Henry 'knew his master only from a distance' (16). Jones points us to the irony of the slave's situation: the young boy recognizes the white master from a distance but 'could no longer remember when his father was a part of that home'. The white master is more entrenched in his memory than his father at home.

Augustus, Henry's father, 'bought himself out of slavery when he was twenty-two' and 'built a shack – and later a proper house – on land he rented and then bought from a poor white man who needed money more than he needed land' (14). The plot of land is where his identity as a free man is centred, and building first a shack and then a 'proper house' becomes a marker of his freedom, but also of his skill with wood. When his son, Henry, becomes a slaveowner (he owns 'thirty-three slaves and more than fifty acres of land', 5), Augustus and Mildred disapprove and there is no reconciliation between them until Henry is on his death bed. This alienation is also presented in terms of housing:

> His parents as a couple had never slept in the home he and Moses the slave had built, choosing to stay in whatever cabin was available down in the quarters. And they would do it that way when they came to bury their only child. (6)

Since Henry had built the house with his slave – literally, the house that slavery built – and because Augustus and Mildred do not approve of slavery in the first place, they refuse to stay in the Townsend house.

Jones also demonstrates a different kind of continuity between white and black slaveowners with an intertwined image of property and land:

> When Henry, at twenty, bought his first piece of land from Robbins, he told his parents right off. The land was miles from where they lived but a short ride from Robbins's plantation, though it was not connected. By the time he died he would own all the land between him and Robbins so that there was nothing separating what they owned. (122)

'Nothing separating what they owned' in this passage refers to the ownership of land. But in the same paragraph, Jones would tell us:

> But the day he bought from Robbins his first slave, Moses, he did not go to their house and he did not go to them for a long time. He spent that first day of ownership with Robbins, and Moses and he and the white man planned where he would build his house. (122)

Ownership of a slave, like his former white master, causes Henry to believe that he had forfeited the right to his parents' home. The very first plans he makes when he buys the slave, Moses, are of house-building. Jones makes several pertinent points here. Henry introduces the subject of the house to his parents as follows: "'I'm putting up a house. A big house…. It's gonna be a good house, Papa. Even white people will say, "What a nice house that Henry Townsend got"'" (136).

The house serves as an icon of ownership and of freedom for the former slave, Henry. The ownership of a house – or, in this case, building of his house – is coterminous with the owning of another kind of property: the slave. Augustus Townsend, enraged on hearing his son is now a slaveowner, tells him, Henry, of his own act of ownership: 'I promised myself when I got this little bit of land that I would never suffer a slaveowner to set foot on it. Never' (137–138). Augustus here makes a distinction between whites who own both forms of property and blacks who could have one (land, house) without the other (slaves). By speaking of the prohibition of slaveowners setting foot on his land, Augustus Townsend is marking this distinction between white and black landlords as, of course, an economic distinction, but mainly a *moral* one. Whether Henry is a better slave-master than white men is not Augustus' focus at all (in Natalie Baszile's *Queen Sugar*, NeNee, whom Charley was hoping to hire for her inherited cane plantation, says derisively to her, 'I bet you'd be even worse to work for than a white man', 2017: 53, thus implying that black slaveowners are worse than white ones).[12]

Early in the novel we meet the story of William Robbins' 'family' from his black slave, Philomena. This story is also introduced to us by referencing house and home:

> The census noted that the house on Shenandoah Road where the boy lived in Manchester was headed by Philomena, his mother, and that the boy had a sister, Dora, three years his senior. The census did not say that the children were Robbins's flesh and blood and that he traveled into Manchester because he loved their mother far more than anything he could name and that, in his quieter moments, after the storms in his head, he feared that he was losing his mind because of that love. (E. P. Jones 2003: 21)

A separate establishment, this house is not on Robbins' land – he travels to Manchester, which is the county seat – because he loves his black concubine so much, although the state census does not dignify poor Louis with the status of being his son. But what is significant is that this house in which Robbins places Philomena and her children is in a white neighbourhood: 'There was no one else in the county who could have gotten away with putting a Negro and her two children in a house on the same block with white people' (23). Jones is pointing to a subversion of spatial practices that ensured segregation. The white man's temerity in placing his black slave/concubine in a white neighbourhood blurs the question of property and propriety, as the above excerpt suggests. But it also points to something else in a line *preceding* this information about Philomena's house: 'He [William Robbins] did not want her to be on the plantation near a wife who early on had suspected she was losing her husband of ten years' (23). The white man's house is reserved for his white wife. The black concubine cannot even be seen anywhere on the rest of his property, the plantation. A wealthy man, he owns property elsewhere, and is able to place his concubine and their children secluded and distant. Robbins in the process violates the codes of segregation. Taken together, it also demonstrates how the land, the house and the black woman were all, equally, property. The impropriety of (*a*) having his slave lover in the same house as his white wife (a theme we saw above in the case of Sarith's objections to Julius and Mini-mini in *The Cost of Sugar*) and (*b*) placing his slave lover and their children in a white neighbourhood is neutralized by his wealth and expansive property, as the official census testifies: 'on one page of the census report to the federal government in Washington, D.C., the census taker put a check by William Robbins's name and footnoted on page 113 that he was the county's wealthiest man' (23).

The question of a suitable *oikos* or dwelling is, Jones suggests, a question of economics, of ownership of people, homes, families and lands, and very often of injustices to all of them.

Planetary Precarity

In Sandra Steingraber's *Living Downstream*, she provides a spatiotemporal toxichorography that is truly planetary:

> Because of air, we each consume suspected carcinogens released into the environment by people far removed from us in space and time. Some of the chemical contaminants we carry in our bodies are pesticides sprayed by farmers we have never met, whose language we may not speak, in countries whose agricultural practices may be completely unfamiliar to us. Some of the chemical contaminants we carry with us come from long-defunct products of industry – objects manufactured, used, and discarded by people of a previous generation. When we sit down to eat a meal of, for example, freshwater fish, we are linked to all these people through the medium of air.

> Conversely, chemicals dumped and sprayed in our own neighborhoods, fields, and landfills have drifted to distant territories and found their way into the diets of the people who live there. I sometimes think of this multitude of connections while walking through Illinois corn and bean fields.

I wonder where the chemicals sprayed in these fields when I was growing up here now reside. On what mountainside, in what forest or lake bottom, in whose bodies do they lodge now? (2010: 175)

Steingraber's community resembles the 'downwinders' of Utah and the Aboriginals of Marshall Islands who were directly impacted by nuclear tests during the mid-twentieth century. Like the indigenous peoples and the downwinders, Steingraber's community occupies a sacrifice zone.

'Sacrifice zones' are defined by Stephen Lerner as

areas dangerously contaminated as a result of the mining and processing of uranium into nuclear weapons ... [to] be expanded to include a broader array of fenceline communities or hot spots of chemical pollution where residents live immediately adjacent to heavily polluting industries or military bases. (2010: 3)

For Lerner, the term 'dramatizes the fact that low-income and minority populations, living adjacent to heavy industry and military bases, are required to make disproportionate health and economic sacrifices that more affluent people can avoid'. This 'pattern of unequal exposures constitutes a form of environmental racism' (3). But the problem now is that there are no spaces that are not sacrifice zones anywhere in the world, to a greater or lesser degree, and imbuing its denizens with unequal life chances.

When, for instance, Marie Thérèse Martin – who actually uses the term 'sacrifice zone' (2022: 125) – writes of Maine's 'cancer valley', the disease being a product of the toxic output of the paper mills in the area, she notes the distinctions between poor-quality worker housing and that of the 'mill bosses' with their landscaped gardens. Many of the 'hourly workers' who were 'responsible for the actual labor of making paper' 'worked without shoes' and 'lived in tenements ... near the dirtiest stretch of the Androscoggin river' (24–25). The wind 'blew particulate matter downriver' as these workers sat on the outside porches of their houses. They, however, 'seldom complained' (25), and anyway they had been 'taught compliance on Sundays' (25). Martin, having given us details of the 'river [which] was a landfill and toxic waste dump' (41), clearly identifies the town as a sacrifice zone for the working classes, whose everyday lives and long-term illnesses were of no consequence to the corporate bodies that owned and ran the mill. The environmental injustice that afflicts and affects the life chances of the workers is embedded in social inequalities:

low income, low prioritizing of protective equipment (not even shoes to wear within the factory) and welfare systems. Later she notes that paper mills are a 'self-reporting industry' on which 'no state agency runs checks', and as a result the mills could lie with impunity (160).

Matter, especially toxic matter, is embedded in social structures and the political economy of regions and nations, as Martin and Steingraber's excerpts indicate. Science, bureaucracy, the state all contribute to the management of matter and objects as diverse as PVC, fowl and fish, humans and soil. Policies that cause unequal life chances for different species, races and ethnicities within species, regions and nations are key topics in the toxic memoirs. However, the memoirs and the fiction make it a point to document that the circulation and assimilation of toxic matter extend far beyond its place of origin. Toxic matter is centrifugal in its movement, spreading outwards. In other words, toxic memoirs and fiction map a planetary toxichorography – an oxymoron, of course.

In *Waste Tide*, the digital mushrooms (electronic drugs) consumed by the waste people in Silicon Isle are a part of the global hallucinogen empire. Yuanyuan Hua rightly reads this theme of the control of the waste people as 'one of the dirty secrets of monopoly capital schemes to control the inner nature of the laborers' (2020: 676). As Qiufan describes it:

> The electronic drugs were created in every corner of the globe, and those desperate to escape reality or yearning for stimulation, most of them the poor of the third world, sought them out eagerly. (2019, unpaginated)

It is the 'poor of the third world' who most eagerly seek them out. These electronic hallucinogens render the users into waste people too, as the novel suggests: 'The woman, a migrant with no local attachments, had become addicted to digital mushrooms and lost the ability to work' (unpaginated). Closely resembling the zombies of capitalist modernity, the waste people of Silicon Isle are, to adapt a phrase from Susan Signe Morrison, 'uncanny figments to be ignored and shunted aside' (Morrison 2015: 105). They are enmeshed in global networks as waste capitalism spreads its stranglehold over land, human and nonhuman alike.

Waste Tide documents the toxiconomies where the entire region (the eastern Guangdong province) has been wasted, its economy thriving on waste even as the environment and the workers' bodies are irremediably wasted:

Metal chassis, broken displays, circuit boards, plastic components, and wires, some dismantled and some awaiting processing, were scattered everywhere like piles of manure, with laborers, all of them migrants from elsewhere in China, flitting between the piles like flies. The workers sifted through the piles and picked out valuable pieces to be placed into the ovens or acid baths for additional decomposition to extract copper and tin, as well as gold, platinum, and other precious metals. What was left over was either incinerated or scattered on the ground, creating even more trash. No one wore any protective gear.

Everything was shrouded in a leaden miasma, an amalgamation of the white mist generated by the boiling aqua regia in the acid baths and the black smoke from the unceasing burning of PVC, insulation, and circuit boards in the fields and on the shore of the river. The two contrasting colors were mixed by the sea breeze until they could no longer be distinguished, seeping into the pores of every living being. (Qiufan 2019, unpaginated)

It is the globalization – indeed mainly, Americanization – of waste that Silicon Isle is embedded in. Qiufan writes:

The crushed plastic would then be melted down, cooled, formed into pellets to be sold to coastal factories, where they would be turned into cheap plastic products the bulk of which were exported to countries around the world so that people everywhere could benefit from the affordable 'Made in China' merchandise; when those wares broke down or became stale, they turned into trash to be shipped back to China, and the cycle began again. (Unpaginated)

This continuity of the process, the doubling, is at the heart of the toxiconomies. The waste comes from outside China and yet is Chinese in origin, at once foreign and native.

Currently the only clean Nature in Silicon Isle (the setting of the novel) is to be found in a museum:

The museum was too bright, too clean, just like the whitewashed and rewritten history it tried to present, just like the version of Silicon Isle that the natives tried to show outsiders. It was infused with a false, shallow technological optimism. In this building, there was no Basel Convention, no dioxins and furans, no acid fog, no water whose lead content exceeded the safe threshold by 2,400 times, no soil whose chromium concentration exceeded the EPA

limit by 1,338 times, and of course nothing about the men and women who
had to drink this water and sleep on this soil.... (Unpaginated)

The unreal nature of Nature in the museum is at once that of Silicon Isle and
yet not of it, having been sanitized – and of course in adherence to global
conventions and through the employment of advanced technologies.

Ironically, the waste industry of Silicon Isle revolves around the *promise*
of environmental clean-ups and ecojustice. As Scott Brandle, the 'economic
hitman' (as he sees himself, unpaginated) puts it:

> Our plan would create tens of thousands of new, green jobs with full benefits.
> And due to TerraGreen Recycling's superior technology, the processing
> would be far more efficient and reduce the losses currently experienced with
> manual dismantling and processing. Economic output would be increased by
> at least thirty percent. But most importantly, we will allocate special funds
> to help Silicon Isle in a comprehensive plan for environmental remediation.
> We'll return your home to its former glory: blue skies and clear water.
> (Unpaginated)

The stress on efficiency and output is carefully counterpoised with the
'environmental remediation' programme for which, Brandle says, the company
will allocate funds. That is, out of the profits of a waste industry, which has
polluted all resources in the region, will come the ecojustice initiative of
cleaning up the environment. The 'blue skies and clear water' can only be made
possible by the very techno-capitalists who have poisoned them in the first
place. (But this is not really the core of the American offer which conceals
something insidious: to obtain rare earth metals that have military potential.)
And, as Brandle admits, this waste industry, environmental degradation and
American interventions are not new: he has seen it in the Philippines before:
'It was an odor that he had once experienced in a rubber-incineration plant
in the Philippines, after which he had felt like gagging for a whole week'
(unpaginated). But, as Director Lin points out, the entire TerraGreen Recycling's
'plan requires the thousands of workshops across the island to be eliminated,
and future e-waste would be sorted, dismantled, and processed by you. Do you
understand what this means to *them*?' (unpaginated, emphasis in original). Lin
is referring to the three principal clans who '[h]ave monopolized all the e-waste
recycling and processing business on Silicon Isle: a yearly processing capacity
of millions of tons and an economic output measured by billions of dollars'
(unpaginated).

In short, the very act of implementing a plan of ecojustice on the isle would be an act of terrible economic injustice to the native dwellers of the region. Toxiconomies thrive because that is the only form of economy that sustains the people:

> The natives didn't care to earn such low profits – but their big business was what caused most of Silicon Isle's surface water and groundwater to be undrinkable in the first place. *That's the price that must be paid for economic development, everyone said.* (Unpaginated, emphasis in original)

As Chen Kaizog discovers, the residents respond to any solution to their waste problem with 'we'd rather live with trash and waste' (unpaginated). The waste itself is described thus: 'Waste is dirty, inferior, lowly, useless, but omnipresent. They produce waste every day; they can't live without the waste people' (unpaginated). Qiufan's text deals with the inescapability of environmental injustice in contexts where the differential assessment of the 'oikos' – home or dwelling and management – results in weightage being tilted towards only one, management, as we can perceive from the passages above dealing with the economics of waste.[13]

Elsewhere Qiufan shows the global networks of racial capitalism, of which the waste economy is one component:

> Since the FDA strictly regulated clinical trials conducted in the United States, many high-risk drug trials had been moved to developing countries: Iaşi, Romania; New Delhi, India; Mégrine, Tunisia; Santiago del Estero, Argentina – in these corruption-ridden, mismanaged regions of the world, hundreds, even thousands, volunteered to be trial subjects for pennies. Most of the money went to the hospitals, the doctors, and the recruiters of the trial subjects, while the pharmaceutical companies obtained the data they needed to secure FDA approval and then made billions with the new drugs.

> Many of the subjects were underage and had to lie to be in the trials. Poverty meant that they couldn't afford expensive modern medical care, and their bodies were thus highly sensitive to the active ingredients of trial drugs – like pristine laboratory mice. For their troubles, they received a few wrinkled dollar bills, a free breakfast, unknown side effects, the risk of a lengthy incubation period, and a high probability of dying from complications.

> This was the price of progress: winners take all. (Unpaginated)

Qiufan shows us how a neo-slave economy centred on the racially differentiated bodies operates across continents. The poor citizens of the Global South subject themselves willingly – or as much willingness as is possible for the poor – to medical experiments for a 'few wrinkled dollar bills, a free breakfast' and an entire future of uncertain side effects. These too are waste people: their bodies rendered into experimental flesh in place of full personhood.

The sacrifice zones that make up the toxichorographies in these texts are not necessarily the result of toxins spewing from local industries. They are also the effects of a regime where specific sites, occupied by particular racial and ethnic communities, are denied basic infrastructural necessities. Catherine Flowers notes that 'it's not unusual for residents of poor and marginalized communities to be forced to pay for infrastructure that doesn't work' (2020: 20). In Lowndes County, she records, a decision was made to 'build a landfill that would accept garbage from outer counties … a classic example of treating a poor county as a dumping ground' (101). In other words, unfair social structures and unequal systems produce, amplify and transmit the chemical toxins across bodies, regions and the planet itself. The social embeds the chemical, so to speak.

In *Toms River*, Dan Fagin illustrates this embedding (having already explained the chemical processes of the dyes, as cited earlier):

> The river was the obvious place to dump the wastewater, but the Toms was not a wide, fast-flowing river like the Rhine or the Ohio. It was, and still is, a serpentine, languid stream, with a current slow enough to encourage cedar swamps and beaver dams. The stretch beside the factory is less than fifty feet wide, and the river stays narrow until it reaches the heart of town two miles away. There, the Toms finally widens and becomes tidal as it nears Barnegat Bay. In 1952, fishing and small-scale tourism were the cornerstones of the struggling local economy, and the river rolled right past the pillared 1850 courthouse that was the seat of power for State Senator William Steelman 'Steets' Mathis, the county's political boss and, not coincidentally, an avid fisherman. (2013, unpaginated)

Preceding this account, Fagin has traced a genealogy of the dye industry across England and Europe. He notes how William Henry Perkin made the mauve dye, how his success was being monitored by Switzerland's Johann Rudolf Geigy-Merian and 'Alexander Clavel … a Frenchman who resettled in Basel' (unpaginated). Pointing to the intellectual property regimes (IPRs) and the geopolitics of the time, Fagin writes:

To Geigy and Clavel, there seemed to be no reason not to try to out-Perkin Perkin, especially because the young Englishman had failed to secure patents in any countries except his own. Even if he had, it would not have mattered, since Switzerland did not enforce patents and would not recognize any chemical process as protectable intellectual property for another fifty years. (Unpaginated)

If the ecosystem of patenting had been different, the story of dye manufacture would arguably be different, Fagin implies. Then Fagin tells us how these European developments converge in his own backyard:

By the end of 1859, Geigy and Clavel had each established his own thriving aniline dye manufacturing operation in Basel, within a few miles of each other on canals near the Rhine. In doing so, they set their firms on course to become two of the largest chemical manufacturers in the world – and eventual partners in a sprawling manufacturing operation in a small New Jersey town that had its own history of piracy: Toms River. (Unpaginated)

'The growing evidence of harm did nothing to slow the industry's growth,' observes Fagin, implying that scientific and medical evidence was not adequate for business houses, licencing authorities and the state to curb the toxifying factories: this is the toxiconomy of aniline in world history. Fagin is pointing to the meaning of the toxins, which is social and collective, attributed by business houses to 'evidence of harm'.

Thus the story of dye manufacture moves across continents and geopolitics of the previous century, and shows a continuity of toxic matter and its circulation that informs the chorography of, first, Europe and then the USA. Fagin returns to his genealogy and narrates the story of Johann Jakob Müller-Pack 'who in 1860 leased one of Geigy's factory sites and formed his own company to make aniline dyes on a grand scale'. Fagin continues:

[I]n 1862 the Geigy family built a second factory for aniline production and rented this one to him also. The new factory was larger and required even more arsenic acid: 200 kilograms per day, or 441 pounds. That was too much for a lagoon to handle alone (even one that was unlined and leaked like a sieve), so this time Müller-Pack adopted an additional disposal method that would become all too familiar a hundred years later in New Jersey: He discharged his arsenic-laced wastewater into the nearest waterway – in this case, a canal beside the plant that led to the Rhine. On the outskirts of

London, Perkin was doing the same thing in the canal next to his factory, though on a smaller scale and with less arsenic. (Unpaginated)

The method of disposing the wastewater was adopted in Europe and England, and then, of course, it came to the USA:

The story of what happened next is uncannily similar to what would happen in Toms River more than a century later. (Unpaginated)

The chemicals have literally and metaphorically migrated to the USA after their contamination of human bodies, the land and the river waters of Europe in Fagin's genealogy of toxification. And, notes Fagin, 'manufacturers ... paid Toms River Chemical to take their waste and pump it into the Atlantic', transforming the Atlantic into a toxic waterscape that flowed around and in contiguity with multiple continents. The material forms with which different social actors – medical personnel, scientists and business owners – interact to different ends (from interpretation of possible hazards to profits) remain resilient, and in circulation, across countries.

Marla Cone too draws a genealogy of toxification by bringing together geopolitics and political economy. She first observes how 'colonizers brought smallpox and other lethal diseases to the far North, wiping out entire communities of native people' (2005: 43). She thus references the 'ecological imperialism' that was a feature of the 'discovery' of the 'New World', as Alfred Crosby (1995) has persuasively argued. She then makes the connection between the eras – and the politics – more explicit in the next sentence: '[T]oday, the outside world is imposing a more subtle, insidious, and intractable scourge on the Arctic' (43). Earlier and present exploitative, threatening and dangerous colonialisms are mirror images, suggests Cone. She then turns to the Report of the Arctic Monitoring and Assessment Program (AMAP). She first tells us that 'the circumpolar north has been transformed into an immense living laboratory where scientists are gradually unravelling the fate of contaminants on earth and their effect on all its inhabitants, from pole to pole' (40). Thus, Cone underscores the relevance and the connectedness of the North to the entire planet, even as she highlights the role of scientific processes. Cone is also deeply conscious of the social dimensions to scientific reports and discoveries. When the various studies indicate that whale meat is toxic to the Inuits, she cites multiple arguments from the social sciences. She notes that 'pollution is a social injustice' wrought by the wealthier nations on the distant lands (51).

But she also recognizes the social and ethical dilemma in trying to advise the Inuits on a change of traditional diet: 'efforts to alter Inuit diets can unwittingly trigger permanent cultural changes' in a society where hunting defines their way of life and their identity (51). She makes the point about the scientists' and public health officers' dilemma – 'torn between encouraging Inuits to keep eating their traditional foods and advising them to reduce their consumption' (49). Cone cites a Greenlander: '[A]s a culture where you harvest the surplus of nature, people in other parts of the world have to acknowledge this is a sound way of life' (82).[14] A trans-corporeal and transnational toxic subjectivity is visible here because the Inuit's body, land and water, and culture are all subject to the toxins that come from elsewhere. The body of the human and the nonhuman (in Cone the focus is the polar bear but also the seal and the whale) become diseased, infertile and toxic to anyone or anything that consumes their body. Cone's observes that 'it's their [Greenlanders'] greatest irony to discover that their food has been tainted by what they perceive as the excesses and waste and greed of the industrial world' (82). Cone traces the routes and roots of the toxins inhabiting Inuit bodies and polar bears, whales and seals through cultural practices (hunting and using surpluses from nature) and different attitudes (greed, excesses) and biology (the blubber of whales, the dietary habits of polar bears) that generate unequal risks and unequal life chances for the Greenlanders, the nonhuman residents of the Arctic, and the developed nations.

The difference of, say, Cone's work from the localized toxicographies such as Fagin's, Flowers' or Steingraber's is the scale: Cone notes how vastly different regions on the planet, and their residents, are being constantly toxified. But even Catherine Flowers, although interested mainly in Lowndes County, compares the environmental injustices for African Americans to those of the Global South populations when she writes: 'I began to wonder if third-world conditions might be bringing third-world diseases to our region' (2020: 17). Flowers writes elsewhere: '[Environmental injustice is] … the same in places from rural white Kentucky to unincorporated Latinx neighborhoods in California to Native American reservations in the West. It plagues people in Alaska and Hawaii' (20).

Echoing Flowers is Imbolo Mbue's *How Beautiful We Were*, in which Thula, who has gone from Kosawa in Africa to the USA, is reporting on the conditions of shared precarity between the two regions:

Their [Americans'] government is not concerned about the sanctity of their land. In this country, governments and corporations are friends too … there's another place, on the other side of the country, where children are drinking poisoned water. The government knew the water was poisoned and did nothing about it. Listening to this, I thought I was in a bizarre dream in which America had revealed itself to be Kosawa…. Every day land the size of a small village is lost, all because oil corporations have the liberty to do as they please…. (2022: 208)

That even the USA is subject to toxified populations (racially and ethnically marked) from poor sanitation is the crux in both Flowers' memoir and Mbue's novel, and both point to the social structures of environmental injustice that occurs with such alarming frequency everywhere on the planet.

The world, it appears, is united in a toxic geography and genealogy where the toxins are recurrent in different regions and their origins lie in similar industries (such as the paper mills, dyes, nuclear power). We have now, as these instances show, not only a planetary toxichorography full of toxic corporii but a globally connected toxiconomy, the antecedents of which lie in the slave economy of the 'New World' plantations, the industrialization of Europe and also manifest in the continuing, racially inflected exploitation of indigenous people and lands such as Chen Qiufan portrays.

Similar instantiations of this genealogy of toxic planetary connections is visible in the neo-slave narrative of Cynthia McLeod, Yaa Gyasi, Isabelle Allende and in the writings of ecowarriors like Wangari Maathai. Here transnational connections and global networks impact, adversely, the social relations of the indigenes, their sense of belonging and their relationship with their land. Social inequalities are exacerbated even as the land, with the rise and expansion of commercial agriculture for export, erodes in its quality.

Isabelle Allende writes of Haiti's history in *Island Beneath the Sea*:

[T]he original inhabitants of the island, the Arawaks, had called it Haiti before the conquistadors changed the name to La Espanola and killed off the natives. In fewer than fifty years, not a single Arawak remained, nor sign of them; they all perished as victims of slavery, European illnesses, and suicide. (2010, unpaginated)

Allende also alerts us to the environmental costs of the European invasion:

The earth, like the sky and water, had no owner until the foreigners, using the forced labor of the Arawaks, took control of it in order to cultivate never-before-seen plants. It was in that time that the custom of killing people with dogs was begun. When they had annihilated the indigenous peoples, the new masters imported slaves, blacks kidnapped in Africa and whites from Europe: convicts, orphans, prostitutes, and rebels. (Unpaginated)

The land's labour and wealth (for the white plantation owners) was linked to transnational trade and exports, and determined by European consumption and tastes:

At the time Toulouse Valmorain arrived there, a third of the wealth of France, in sugar, coffee, tobacco, cotton, indigo, and cocoa, came from the island. There were no longer white slaves, but the number of blacks had risen to hundreds of thousands. The most intractable crop was sugarcane, the sweet gold of the colony; cutting the cane, crushing it, and reducing it to syrup was labor not for humans, as the planters maintained, but for beasts … the slaves were starving and the plantation had been saved from ruin only because the world was consuming sugar with increasing voraciousness. (Unpaginated)

Elsewhere in the novel, the plantation owner Valmorain is debating the evils of slavery with the doctor, Parmentier. Annoyed by the physician's moral stance on slavery, Valmorain finally declares:

Someone must manage the colonies if you are to put sugar in your coffee and smoke a cigar. In France they avail themselves of our products, but no one wants to know how they are obtained. (Unpaginated)

In *Homegoing* Gyasi underscores another form of plantation culture that altered the African landscape: the cultivation by non-native plants:

Ohene Nyarko came back a week later with the new seeds. The plant was called cocoa, and he said it would change everything. He said the Akuapem people in the Eastern Region were already reaping the benefits of the new plant, selling it to the white men overseas at a rate that was reminiscent of the old trade. (2016: 147–148)

Gyasi elaborates on this bioinvasion theme:

Within months Ohene Nyarko's cocoa trees had sprouted, bearing their gold and green and orange fruit. The villagers had never seen anything like it, and they were so curious, so eager to touch and open the pods before they were ready, that Ohene Nyarko and his sons had taken to sleeping outside so that they could keep watch.

'But will this feed us?' the villagers wondered. (148)

Although the plants flourish, they change the dynamics of the village, as farmers incur debts to procure the plants for their fields. Slowly, the social fabric of the community frays. In *The Heart of Redness* there are plans such as a 'retirement village for millionaires [with] trees imported from England: 'We'll uproot a lot of these native shrubs and wild bushes and plant a beautiful English garden' (Mda 2000, unpaginated). The rhetoric of wild bushes (nature) versus 'English garden' (culture) is a colonial one, as we know, but it has been appropriated by the natives who begin to see the land as a commercial space rather than the space of their ancestors and their cultural identity.

The global demand for and circulation of products like sugar, as Sydney Mintz (1985) has shown, was responsible for the rise of the Plantationocene, and therefore of both slavery and the re-planting of the land with alien crops and species (a form of bioinvasion). Colonialism, as Jason Moore (2017) has demonstrated, resulted in catastrophic environmental changes in South America, Africa and Asia and in the process produced a 'Cheap Nature' (2). This 'Cheap Nature' is itself the lure, as Valmorain discovers when he wishes to leave Europe to make a career elsewhere in Allende's (2010) novel: '[T]he climate was similar to that in the Antilles.' he thinks about Louisiana, 'and the crops were the same, with the advantage that there was much more space and land was cheap.' Investing in a land to extract its resources – what Lisa Tilley terms 'extractive investibility' (2021) – is easier in the colonies settled by violence. He thus hopes to 'acquire a large plantation and exploit it without political problems or rebelling slaves' (Allende 2010, unpaginated). Valmorain here thinks as a member of the European elite that produced the networks of commodities and capital, and in the process constructed a certain kind of racialized labour and Nature or landscape for their exploitation.

In her memoir, Caroline Flowers notes the history of Central Valley, California, where the arrival and spread of white settler cultures altered the ecosystem:

The Tachi tribe of the Yokut people ... had fished its [Tulare Lake] waters and hunted along its shores for centuries. But with the white settlers came the realization that the arid land of the valley, once the floor of a mighty inland sea, was unbelievably fertile.... As more white settlers flocked to

California … rivers were dammed and canals were built to divert water….
Now the great Tulare Lake is no more. (2000: 184–185)

Flowers assesses the impact of dams in terms of a history of settler colonialism,
mapping the ways in which the indigenous tribes lived *with* Nature – arguably
a romanticization – and the settlers sought to *control* Nature. The diminishing
and eventual disappearance of the natural ecosystem, the lake, is coextensive
with the disappearance of the indigene as Flowers links environmental and
social injustices in the aftermath of colonialism. (Elsewhere too Flowers speaks
of her encounters with students from the indigenous population, who educate
her on their tribes' fight for sovereignty and civil rights, thereby again linking
environmental and civil racisms, 90–94.)

Alexis Wright also makes references to the global circuit of capital, slaves and
natural resources in *The Swan Book*. Describing the elite of the area, Warren
tells Oblivia at their wedding:

> *These are all very close friendships….* Red said they were rolling in money. *Most
> of which is the laundered profits of exploiting natural resources which has wound
> every cent of its way around the globe many times before it lands in this multi-
> coloured fashion parade….* (2013, unpaginated, italics in original)

Wright's Oblivia responds viscerally to the opulence, excesses and surplus
consumption in white Australian society:

> It was a banquet, more food than the girl had seen in her entire life, and
> the sight of so much food for one meal made her nauseous, and unable to
> eat. Inside her loneliness, she felt the pangs of hunger the night she had
> raided the fishing nets in the swamp, and had not found a single fish. Then,
> she lost track of the number of cattle, pigs, sheep, and poultry slaughtered,
> and vegetable fields that had been raided, the sea emptied, and all of this –
> deteriorating into the guts of seagulls eating the rubbish. (Unpaginated)

Oblivia, as Temiti Lehartel points out, 'perceives the food processing scheme and
tracks back where the food items come from and how they were obtained' and
the use of verbs like '"slaughtered," "raided," "emptied" and present progressive
"deteriorating" point to the current short-sighted extractive capitalist model
paired with a progressing throw-away culture' (2022: 7–8).

Colonization and global trade transformed the relationship of the indigenes
with their lands, as white settlers introduced new crops, altered the nature of

ownership and patterns of agriculture. Wangari Maathai (2007) captures the transformation of sacred indigenous lands into commercialized sites of extraction best when speaking of the Kenyan landscape, and shows how environmental and social injustices go together in Africa. The changes introduced, she writes, included processes like 'logging, clear-cutting native forests, establishing plantations of imported trees, hunting wildlife, and undertaking expansive commercial agriculture' (6). This meant, she argues, the erosion of the soil, loss of water sources and the loss of biodiversity. And further, the changes in the land drove, she writes, cultural changes: 'Hallowed landscapes lost their sacredness and were exploited as the local people became insensitive to the destruction, accepting it as a sign of progress' (6). Linking the wisdom of the native peoples, their practices and the land's health – all of which have been destroyed by, first, colonialism and then by the postcolony's subservience to global and neocolonial powers – Maathai writes:

> I later learned that there was a connection between the fig tree's root system and the underground water reservoirs.... The reverence the community had for the fig tree helped preserve the stream.... The trees also held the soil together, reducing erosion and landslides. In such ways, without conscious or deliberate effort, these cultural and spiritual practices contributed to the conservation of biodiversity. (46)

Maathai summarizes the effects, and the native residents' complicity:

> [W]hen Kenya was colonized and we encountered Europeans ... we converted our values into a cash economy like theirs. Everything was now perceived as having a monetary value. As we were to learn, if you can sell it, you can forget about protecting it. (175)

In Imbolo Mbue's *How Beautiful We Were*, we are told that the government of the region 'had given us [the Kosawa area] to Pexton [the oil firm]. Handed, on a sheet of paper, our land and waters to them' (2022: 11). Oil is not separable from the socio-political contexts in the postcolony, Mbue suggests, because the premium placed on the natural resource has altered the society and state–civil society relations. From a different but not unrelated context, eco-warrior C. K. Janu in her *Mother Forest*, a memoir of her life and that of her tribe, declares 'in the forests one never knew what hunger was' (2004: 2). Janu's focus is on local forms of environmental injustice that erode cultural values and lands. Describing how the tribals burn the undergrowth, she writes: 'When the virgin earth catches fire it gives out a strange smell. Like it is being roasted alive. It is a scary sight when the hill catches fire. In the night it looks as if a human being is being burnt alive' (1–2). The postcolony is marked by native landlords who did not care for the land or the people on it:

> Since the *jenmi* [local term for landlord] was the only provider of work, our people were quite frightened of him.... When our people worked in the fields there would be a man dressed in a sleeveless shirt standing on the ridge supervising our work. We were quite frightened of him. In those days we were afraid of almost everything. The backs of our people seem to be so bent because they have been terrified of so many things for so many generations. When our people speak they don't raise their eyes and that must be because they are so scared.... In those days just getting a glimpse of the *jenmi* was a terrifying experience for our people. (12–15)

The rhetoric of fear in Janu is captured in the image of the bent backs and lowered eyes of the tribal labourer slaving away on the land (Nayar 2014: 5). More importantly, the attitude of the new landlords – natives too – towards the land is resonant of that of the white colonials who saw land exclusively as revenue-generating and delinked from local cultural values.

C. K. Janu, like Maathai, focuses on the loss of cultural values and identity of the original dwellers, the tribals, of the land:

> The life cycle of our people, their customs and very existence are bound to the earth. This is more so than in any other society. When projects are designed without any link to this bond, our people suffer. This may be wrong if looked at from the point of view of civil society. But it is self-evident when we go to the newly formed colonies. (2004: 47)

The quasi-spiritual element in Janu's assertion, as in the case of Maathai's mention of the indigenes' reverence for the fig tree cited above, is an important aspect of the tribal claim to the land for, as Andrew Gray has demonstrated in the context of the Amazonian Arakmbut peoples, territorial links are legitimized through the spirit world (Gray 1997: 119–121). Janu suggests that her people's bond with the land is partially validated through the presence of ancestral spirits – hence her battle for the community's sacred burial sites.

In other cases, the poverty of the residents of the land is compounded not only by droughts – which are the result of commercial-interest-driven deforestation – but by inflexible revenue systems. In Naik's *Bheda* the already marginalized Dalit communities live in abject poverty:

> Every year during the month of Pausha the dewan appointed by the king of Kalahandi used to camp there to collect revenue. Till the month of Magha the gauntias of the Kalahandi region used to collect revenue from their respective villages and reach the camp to deposit it on the given day.

> That year the news was that the camp would start on the third day of the new moon night in the month of Magha. But since there was drought in Firozpur village Lochan Gauntia was extremely anxious. His tenants had no grain. They hardly managed a meal a day. Where would they get their revenue from? But the revenue had to be deposited. (2017, unpaginated)

In such a context, the upper classes and castes continue to thrive in this postcolony, and Naik implies that this prosperity stems from the link between caste, deforestation and commercialization of the land's products. The Marwari is busy smuggling timber out of the forest, notes a character, Kartik, in the novel:

> In the name of mahua and neem seeds, he is carrying on a business, dealing in timber planks. He keeps sal, dhawnra, mahogany, and teak planks inside the truck and covers them up with sacks full of mahua, neem, and tamarind.... (Unpaginated)

Those tasked with protecting the land are the ones who prey on it: 'Some villagers even complained that it was the forester who had allowed people to cut trees by taking bribes from them' (unpaginated). The battle for natural resources is at the heart of all tensions in these novels. If in *Bheda* the forest turns out to be a curse rather than a blessing for the tribals, in Mbue's novel, it is oil: '[B]y our sixth year of life ... our parents had come to know the fullness of the curse that came from living on land beneath which oil sat' (2022: 28).

In texts like Naik's, Maathai's and Janu's, while colonialism is a backdrop and its legacies ever-present, the critique of postcolonial prospecting and greed is based on a recognition that the postcolonial state and its favoured classes are as indifferent to the question of environmental justice as the white man was. In Zakes Mda's *The Heart of Redness*, the debate around the proposed casino and tourism industry demonstrates that the question of environmental and species justice was more complicated than both the romanticization of the pastoral and the glamour of 'development'. What would a culture prioritize: human commerce or the environment? Human lives or plants and animals? Those objecting to the casino argue:

> [A] project of this magnitude cannot be built without cutting down the forest of indigenous trees, without disturbing the bird life, and without polluting the rivers, the sea, and its great lagoon. (2000, unpaginated)

There is a strong romanticization of the native way of life in Mda – which Byron Caminero-Santangelo likens to a cosmopolitan bioregionalism (2014: 96–97) – that is simultaneous with a critique of this pastoral ideal and the cultural beliefs. One such set of prophecies that causes the natives to kill vast heads of cattle went like this:

> The Strangers said I must tell the nation that all cattle now living must be slaughtered. They have been reared by contaminated hands because there are people who deal in witchcraft. The fields must not be cultivated, but great new grain pits must be dug, new houses must be built, and great strong cattle kraals must be erected. (Mda 2000, unpaginated)

Mesmerized by the prophetess Nongqawuse, the chiefs see and hear visions:

> As the chiefs approached the river they were overwhelmed by a wonderful fear. There was an explosion and great rocks fell from the cliffs overlooking the river. Soon the whole valley was covered with mist. The air was filled with the bellowing of cattle, the neighing of horses, and the bleating of sheep and goats.

> 'Cast your eyes in the direction of the sea,' Nongqawuse commanded.

> And in the sea the chiefs saw hundreds of cattle. Over the horizon a great crowd of people appeared and disappeared again. (Unpaginated)

When they plead with the prophetess to bring the 'new people' closer, she says: 'The new people will come only when you have killed all your cattle.' This vision and prophecy is then echoed by the elders:

> The present animals are contaminated. So are the present crops. The Strangers made it clear that the new ones will not come unless we do as we are told. The new people, our ancestors, will not rise from the dead until we

have cleansed the earth by destroying all our cattle and all our crops both in the fields and in the granaries. (Unpaginated)

Mda is pointing to native cultures and belief systems that are as instrumental in perpetuating species injustice – cattle, crops – as the foreigners who come to their land seeking profits. The glorification of such a pastoral ideal, despite instances of species injustice inherent in them, is an exoticization, Mda suggests. The college-educated Xoliswa Ximiya, for instance, says Mda,

> is not happy that her people are made to act like buffoons for these white tourists. She is miffed that the trails glorify primitive practices. Her people are like monkeys in a zoo, observed with amusement by white foreigners.... (Unpaginated)

As the opinion is divided about the arrival of the foreigner and the casino and the conservation of the native lands, we meet a critique of pastoral idealism in the text:

> It is foolish to talk of conserving indigenous trees. After all, we can always plant civilized trees. Trees that come from across the seas. Trees that have no thorns like some of the ugly ones you want to protect. Trees like the wattle and the bluegum that grow in the forest of Nogqoloza. You know that Nogqoloza is a beautiful forest because the trees there were planted in straight lines many years ago. Although we do not like white people for causing the sufferings of the Middle Generations, we must at least thank them for planting the forest of Nogqoloza. (Unpaginated)

The land of the forefathers will be destroyed, argues Zim, and 'we ... will not gain anything from this'. Development will bring 'things enjoyed only by rich people who will come here and pollute our rivers and our ocean' (unpaginated).

Where the argument concerns cultural identity and cultural beliefs – centred around their land – opinion is divided between those who think it is unconscionable to transform the village and its people into 'a museum that pretends that is how people live' because 'real people in today's South Africa don't lead the life that is seen in cultural villages'. They argue:

> [T]he bulk of what tourists see is the past ... a lot of it an imaginary past. They must be honest and say that they are attempting to show how people used to live. They must not pretend that's how people live now.... In the

real-life situation you don't find abakhwetha hanging around the village, women in their best amahomba costumes grinding millet and decorating walls, while maidens are dancing, and right there in front of the house young men are fighting with sticks. It's too contrived. (Unpaginated)

It simply 'excavate[s] a buried precolonial identity of these people … a precolonial authenticity that is lost' (unpaginated). Mda's is a sustained exploration of the tension between environmental justice movements, development and its concomitant opportunities (a character, Lefa Labello, shouts at Zim when the latter says they will gain nothing, 'you will get jobs') and the romanticization of the old world. There are, Mda shows, no easy answers to the questions of justice. In Mbue's *How Beautiful We Were*, even though the oil corporation Pexton exploits the land and the people ruthlessly, the residents of the area 'couldn't deny the fact that Pexton had offered our grandfathers jobs and a chance to partake in the wealth that would be created from the drilling … it had become clear to everyone that the only way to partake in the oil wealth was to work for Pexton' (2022: 73). The conflict between the inherited sense of a sacred home or land and employment-wealth divides the people in Mbue, exactly as it does in Mda.

The debates in *The Heart of Redness* and *How Beautiful We Were* echo similar ideological and rhetorical battles in the case of the First Nation people in Canada and Australia. In Alexis Wright's fiction, notably *Carpentaria* (2006) and *The Swan Book* (2013), she brings the Aboriginal world view into conflict with capitalism, colonialism and globalization. Environmental injustice in texts like *The Swan Book* is never an isolated state but linked to colonial and patriarchal violence against the land and its women. Set sometime in the future, the Aboriginal's swamp is termed 'Swan Lake'. But Wright gives the swamp a life and voice of its own:

[T]he swamp's natural sounds of protest were often mixed with lamenting ceremonies. Haunting chants rose and fell on the water like a beating drum, and sounds of clap sticks oriented thoughts, while the droning didgeridoos blended all sounds into the surreal experience of a background listening, which had become normal listening. (2013, unpaginated)

Wright, like Janu, Maathai and others, speaks of the attempted transformation of the sacred sites of the Aboriginals into dumpyards. The army had managed a 'large-scale sweep-up of the ocean's salty junk and dumped it in the lake sacred to the Aboriginals. The result is a 'strange panorama of toxic waste swimming on the surface of the water' (unpaginated). Wright continues:

> That could not be allowed to rot into the sacredness of the ground. Their conscience flatly refused to have junk buried among the ancestral spirits. These were really stubborn people sticking to the earth of the ancestors, even though they knew well enough that the contaminated lake caused bellyaches, having to eye each cup of tainted water they drank from the lake, but drinking it anyway. (Unpaginated)

The connection of the people with the land, embodied in Aboriginal culture, a connection under strain and gradually obliterated (the protagonist is, incidentally, named 'Oblivia'), is Wright's subject. When Oblivia finally returns to her home with the hope of rebuilding it, Wright suggests, a nation can rise again. This rebuilding cannot be another version of the colonial era, as Adelle L. Sefton-Rowston (2016) has argued about Wright's utopian vision. Yet, despite Wright's bioregionalist perspective, she does think in terms of planetary and human histories that have altered the earth forever. Sefton-Rowston writes:

> Only heaven knows, there were millions of people throughout the world who either offered pigs as sacrifices to their Gods, or flowers, or the first grain of the new season's crop. There were even others who offered their own people to the Gods. Now the day had come when modern man had become the new face of God, and simply sacrificed the whole Earth. (2016, unpaginated)

From across the world, the Dene people, long-time residents of the Northwest Territories of Canada and the subject of Joe Sacco's graphic text on Canada's settler-colonialism, *Paying the Land* (2020), are, like the characters in Mbue, Mda and others, divided in their views: between the job potential of the mining operations, and the environmental and cultural damage these operations bring.

The first image or drawing, even before the story opens, features a human sitting outside a hut – the gender is not clear, the drawing is focalized from the rear – and two dogs watching a sun rise over the horizon. We see the forest area, the spaces open before the human and animal viewers. The image recurs on page 5, this time with a young man sitting to the side of the other three (the human and the dogs). The accompanying text says:

> You were required to get up early, usually when it's dawn, so you can say hello to the sun when it comes out. (5)

The drawing on the following page, which is the page announcing the chapter title 'You Find Yourself in the Circle', shows a crying infant, just delivered (the umbilical cord is visible), being held up to the distant forests and mountains and the proximate river or lake. The baby is centred in this full-page drawing, but is positioned such that the setting – Nature – seems to encompass the child. Taken together the three images set the tone for the story and the debates that follow. The opening images clearly provide a 'prospect view'.

Writing about the landscape painting tradition in eighteenth-century England and Europe, John Barrell theorized the prospect view: 'landscapes which seek to exhibit substantial, representative forms of nature arranged in a wide extent of land' (1992: 42). Terming this the 'panorama', Barrell argues that

> among the meanings attached to the panoramic view, may be the notion of a wider society, and the notion of the ability to grasp objects in the form of their relations to each other; among the meanings attached to the occluded view, from a low viewpoint, are seclusion, of course, and privacy as something opposed to the social in its more extended sense…. (45)

Barrell continues:

> On the one hand is the ideal, panoramic prospect, the analogue of the social and the universal, which is surveyed, organised, and understood by disinterested public men: men who regard the objects in painted landscapes always as representative ideas, intended to categorise rather than deceptively to imitate their originals in nature; men therefore who study objects not in and for themselves – not for example the individuals in a society, considered *as* individuals – but in terms of their relations. They are enabled to do this by their ability to abstract, and by their ability to comprehend and classify the totality of human experience. (56, emphasis in original)

In contrast with such a view is what Barrell calls the 'occluded view':

> On the other hand is the occluded landscape, which has so far been treated as representing the 'confined views' of the private man, whose experience is too narrow to permit him to abstract. Such landscapes conceal the general view by concealing the distance … a cottage, for example, embosomed in trees which permit the distance to appear only as spots or slices of light – is emblematic of a situation in life from which no wider prospect is visible. (56)

Sacco's prospect views, while not exactly in the form of the landscape paintings that Barrell theorizes, do exhibit some of the same features. They, for example, underscore the human *in* the land, embody a set of relations between the trees, the open vista, the human, the animal and the sun. In the second image, the baby is centred in the lap of Nature, more or less, and the biome shows trees, mountains, water and the human-made object, the boat. Sacco embeds the human and the animal within the biome. He does not idealize Nature as a pure and distant 'thing' because the hut, the boat, the sledge are man-made. When he repeats the image on page 5, he places it in the middle. Above it is a *tableaux vivant*, capturing Dene life. It shows the Denes have cut trees, and used the wood. In the prospect view, the second image on the page, we now have a more crowded foreground: with the young Paul also watching the sunrise. But he is positioned in the image in such a way – behind and off to the right – that it appears he is watching the other man and the dogs watching the sun, almost as though he is a witness to the older Dene taking in the vista.

While Barrell speaks of the viewers of such prospect views as 'public' men (rarely women), Sacco's focus, I suggest, is on the connectedness of forms of life – plant, animal, human – with the non-living – water, land, mountain. The page enables Sacco to literally offer the prospect of living *with* and *off* the land, as the Denes do. Their prospects are connected to the land, its seasons, its fauna and flora, its topography, as captured in the three images. The infant is being offered to the land, as a ritual perhaps, so that the land recognizes the arrival of the new human within the biome. As the text's narrators tell us repeatedly, their lives were entirely defined by the landscape and its features, whether this was about their hunting expeditions or the way they lived in their settlements. In short, the human's prospect is intimately connected to the land, which must therefore be represented and seen as a prospect view, connecting various objects within it and their interrelations.

Later, Paul tells the story of the Denes – how they lived, their cultural practices, the hardship and toil, their interactions with and dependence on their dogs and the natural world:

But we knew that it was cold when you had a hard time finding animals.

By the season, by the moon, you can tell where the animals usually are, and sometimes they're not there … when it's really cold … they start hiding. (Sacco 2020: 19)

The above text accompanies a different kind of prospect view: it shows two human silhouettes in the middle of a snow-enveloped setting. The trees cast long shadows, and the trees tower over the humans. Sacco's brilliant use of scale shows the natural world dwarfing the human, reducing the human to just a little more than a figure in the land populated by large trees and expanses of snow. Unlike in Sacco's traditional style of bearing witness and witnessing, these images do not contain Sacco. We encounter the Denes – anonymized in the images – and Nature in the same frame, and come to witness the difference in scale and, perhaps, power between them. The accompanying text suggests the Denes 'read' the signs in Nature – the animals have gone into hibernation, signifying winter. The seasons 'tell' the location of the animals. The entire prospect forces us to 'regard the objects in painted landscapes always as representative ideas, intended to categorise', in Barrell's words already cited: the trees, the humans and the land are objects that represent living *in* nature in mutually dependent ways. The messiness and crowded nature of the scenes involving the Denes set up the theme of colonialism and the consequent alterations to the prospect view.

I extend the idea of the 'prospect' in another direction to read Sacco's second key theme – the colonization of Dene-land. I argue that the prospect *view* changes, both for the Denes and for the companies that arrive there – to prospect for the wealth lying under the land. In later chapters, we see the prospect view with roads and heavy vehicles. Sacco interrupts the prospect view with a giant tanker-truck making its way on the mountain road, almost centring it by cutting through it (2020: 34). The top left of the image shows workers at a turbine. The image immediately below is also what I shall call an interrupted prospect view: it shows giant machinery digging through the land, fallen trees and, in the distance, the tree cover cut into square plots with roads running between and through them, the machine in the midst of all. If the original 'prospect view' was a marker of class – the disinterested upper-class gentleman views the vista – the interrupted prospect view in Sacco foregrounds racial capitalism.

A Dene comments later in the narrative: 'they're [the whites] putting cut lines on our land looking for oil and gas' (65). These marks on the land are in contrast to the worship of the land by the Denes. This text accompanies an image of white men using survey equipment examining the prospect. It is not a prospect view, but *prospecting*. The white man arrives with his heavy machinery, surveys the land and changes the prospect view into a zone of prospecting, of digging through the ground – which, as Janu, Maathai, Mda note, is sacred to the Aboriginal and First Nation people – to the earthy products below: oil and gas. In fact, Sacco prepares us for the view below the prospect view – which invites my interpretation of the 'interrupted prospect view' – with a panel depicting the fracking process (33). Sacco gives us a transverse view so that we see the mountains and trees on the top of the panel, with the land interrupted by the wellhead. Then we see the earth in cross section, with the drilling, the pipelines and the shale that is penetrated by the drilling so that the 'oil and/ or natural gas flows through the fractures, into the well and up to the surface' (33). This panel with the technical narrative and images interrupts the story, but is essential for Sacco to point to the enormity of fracking: the costs to the environment. He notes in the accompanying text that the material pushed into the land is a 'toxic mixture of water, sand, and chemicals at extremely high pressure' (33). He adds that the mixture 'open[s] up fractures in the shale' – that is, it breaks through the subsurface and fractures the integrity of the land below. In other words, oil and gas are the prospects beneath the prospect view, what lies hidden under the surface. The white man arrives and, in place of admiring the prospect view that connects the various objects on the land, proceeds to prospect below it. The machinery and the white man merge here to constitute the racial capitalism that is the equivalent of the upper-class gentleman leisurely admiring the vista. It is not the vista that draws the white man, but what the vista conceals: oil.

Sacco also tells us that contemporary fracking and oil extraction are iterations of older forms of 'exploiting the land' which 'has a long history here'. He refers to the Hudson Bay Company and the trade in pelts (35). Immediately after this panel, he again offers a miniature prospect view. A young Dene watches the vista, while other, presumably older men, work to build huts and sledges (35). This is the Dene prospect view. But the accompanying text tells us that like the fur trade in previous eras, 'the extraction of resources today has left an indelible mark on those people indigenous to the region, the Dene' (35). Slowly the cultural impact of the extraction industry enters the story, with alcoholism, drug use and prostitution ruining the local cultures (106–107), even as fracking divides the people – those who see it as offering jobs and those who see it as destroying the environment and the community even as large humans – and Sacco draws a giant-sized man wielding a saw slicing through a tree here – cut into the environment (39). The interrupted prospect is underscored soon after in an image where the prospect view has in its foreground a tangle of pipes and machinery and the mountains in the distance: one cannot see the prospect except through the machinery (42).

Sacco also provides a history of environmental exploitation and therefore of injustice when he traces the Acts, treaties and policies that enabled the white races to come to Canada and then dominate it. Like Edward Jones, Cynthia McLeod and others who link plantation economies to the European consumer society, Sacco observes that the Canadian Northwest Territories was 'already long established as the chief source of fur for Europe's fashion industry' (60). The transfer of ownership of the land from the Denes to the European settlers, and then the arrival of the companies instantiate environmental and species injustice, the destruction of the Denes' habitat and habits.[15] Finally, Sacco links the history of environmental exploitation with the displacement of the indigenes, the enforced taking-away and schooling of the Dene children in the Indian Residential School System and the continuing aftermath of this originary violence.[16]

These texts present the merger of environmental and social injustices. The lakes, crops and plants were drawn into global production and consumption patterns which in turn determined the nature and extent of land-use. Even the labouring bodies of slaves were enmeshed within these same patterns. Thus, slavery of the Africans in the Americas was not, Yaa Gyasi reminds us in *Homegoing* (2016), a phenomenon dictated and organized only by the whites in Africa. When Effia believes that their tribe would sell 'gold and fabric to the white men', Fiifi corrects this misapprehension:

Abeeku has made an alliance with one of the most powerful Asante villages. We will help them sell their slaves to the British.

And so, the white man came to their village. Fat and skinny, red and tanned. They came in uniform, with swords at their sides, their eyes looking sideways, always and ever cautious. They came to approve of the goods Abeeku had promised them. (12)

And later:

[T]he British had been inciting tribal wars for years, knowing that whatever captives were taken from these wars would be sold to them for trade. His mother always said that the Gold Coast was like a pot of groundnut soup. Her people, the Asantes, were the broth, and his father's people, the Fantes, were the groundnuts, and the many other nations that began at the edge of the Atlantic and moved up through the bushland into the North made up the meat and pepper and vegetables. This pot was already full to the brim before the white men came and added fire. Now it was all the Gold Coast people could do to keep from boiling over again and again and again. (89)

In the course of this trade in slaves, tribes also caught and sold members of other tribes to the British. Africa, Gyasi implies, destroyed itself through this complicity.[17] Gyasi locates slave trade within the global movement of crops, land ownership and profits, like Allende and McLeod in their novels.

*

Marla Cone writes in *Silent Snow*: '[T]oday, about two hundred toxic pesticides and industrial compounds have been detected in the bodies of the Arctic's indigenous people and animals' (2005: 23). This is what Cone calls the 'Arctic Paradox', where the land 'untouched by contemporary ills, so innocent, so primitive, so natural, [is] the home to the most contaminated people on the planet' (3). She declares: 'I had stumbled on what is perhaps the greatest environmental injustice on Earth' (3). The planet is in peril through the global circulation of slaves, commodities like sugar and chemical effluents over the centuries. Social and economic structures and systems like plantations, paper mills or the dye industry have been toxiconomies in the sense they toxified the land, the social fabric and the bodies of humans and nonhumans across the planet.

Other forms of toxiconomies also find their expression in contemporary literature. There are texts that address specific forms of animal vulnerability – for instance, Bryan Christy's *The Lizard King* (2008) about animal trafficking – and specialized forms of human vulnerability, such as organ trade in fiction such as Benyamin's *Body and Blood* (2020), Tess Gerritsen's *Harvest* (1996) or Manjula Padmanabhan's play *Harvest* (1997), that also need to be studied for the 'environmental justice perspective', but which are not included here. In these texts too, bodies that waste away, mutilated and experimented on, become subject to the flows of global capital. Set in regions marked for their 'exotic' fauna and flora, the literature of trafficking (of animals, organs, people) depicts how these biological commodities are displaced from their homes and biomes and inserted into a global circuit.

The planet itself is now one gigantic sacrifice zone, since there is no territory or terrain entirely free of toxic matter, but as Marie Thérèse Martin asks, 'whose sacrifice are we talking about? And who decided a sacrifice had to be made? Were those being sacrificed and those who made the sacrifice experiencing the same thing?' (125). Environmental injustice stems from social inequalities and injustices that construct unequal life chances for humans and nonhumans. The everybody memoir, the prosopographies and chorographies of regions present a toxic genealogy of the present planetary crisis. Underscoring the *interconnectedness* of people, cultures, regions and material forms (living and non-living, human and nonhuman, responsive and reactionary), these genres ensure that we *see* mutual dependence, or mutually assured destruction. Prosopographies and choreographies necessarily expand outward as this chapter has shown, from individual bodies in Maine or Louisiana to the planet itself, where Inuits in the far north suffer the consequences of polluting industries in the USA, where fallout from Chernobyl spreads across Europe, and where beluga whales, seals and fish in the water bodies of the planet imbibe toxins from all over.

What emerges from the texts studied in this chapter is a *planetary toxichorography*, a global sacrifice zone. Each of these texts, then, addresses with varying degree of intensity – ranging from despair to anger, hope to hopelessness – questions of environmental, ecological and species justice.

Notes

1. Things have not changed all that much for Alabama, if news reports are to be believed, for it remains a dumping ground for waste from all over the USA (Milman 2019). I am grateful to Anna Kurian for directing me to this news item.

2. For a comparable parallel, the Romantic literary tradition, see Newman (2019), who calls for attention to 'the environmental significance of literary texts that we have previously understood as being exclusively concerned with social justice' (8).

3. On whether non-living objects have agency, or they are merely reactive and have consequences, see Hornborg (2016) and Kompatsiaris (2022) and their response to Karen Barad and the 'new materialists'.

4. The mushrooms are of various kinds:

    > [S]ome induced insane hallucinations; others could be guided by the user's consciousness to some extent, like taking a journey of inner discovery; one flashed the mysterious smile of a Western woman, but produced no other effects. (Qiufan 2019, unpaginated)

5. Kathleen Richardson, writing about 'technological animism' also argues:

    The making of automata raised questions about what was human or machine, living or dead, animate or inanimate – the very questions that, I argue, technological animism infuses into our ontological milieu. Automata produced 'uncanny' effects in audiences.... (2018: 119)

6. I use the term to convey the sense of a city that is beneath and not quite the same as the city.

7. Maan Barua has argued that three aspects of the Plantationocene need to be examined: 'the violent exploitation of labor power as well as other-than-human work in the quest to produce cheap nature ... the beneficiaries of landscape transformations [and] the proliferation of nonnative plants' (2023: 13–14; see also Chao 2022).

8. Felicity Nussbaum writes:

    [R]epresentations of people of colour in the eighteenth century mutate through the spectrum of tawny, sallow, olive, mulatto, sooty, and ebony of East Indian, West Indian, American Indian, Pacific Islander, and North and sub Saharan African, all of whom are at times designated in British (if not American) parlance as 'black'. In some cases we can assign the muddles to historical accident, and in others to geographical confusion.... In the imaginative geography of the eighteenth century, Ethiopia (often a synonym for Africa) seems to migrate from Africa to Arabia and back again. It is sometimes contiguous to Egypt and sometimes depicted on the western side of the continent, though Ethiopia eventually comes to represent a lost and unrecoverable premodern glory in the later Ethiopianism movement. (2009: 143–149)

9. Butler complicates this desire-for-the-black-woman theme in *Kindred* in interesting ways. Alice, Dana's slave ancestor, summarizes it when she says to Dana:

    He likes me in bed, and you out of bed, and you and I look alike if you can believe what people say.... Anyway, all that means we're two halves of the same woman – at least in his crazy head (O. E. Butler 1979, unpaginated).

    Christine Montgomery and Ellen C. Caldwell write about this transgenerational 'doubling', as they term it, of the two women:

    Rufus loves them both – Alice as his concubine and Dana as his surrogate mother and confidant.... Alice is the Negress; Dana the American.

Alice is the enslaved; Dana the time traveling "free" woman. Alice is the object of Rufus's sexual desire, Dana the object of his emotional desire. (2020: 156)

10. Sheryl Vint defines the neo-slave narrative as 'an African American genre that investigates the history of slavery and reworks the nineteenth century slave narrative tradition' (2007: 241).

11. Ward's Jojo recalls the stories his grandmother told, of being kidnapped from their homes and transported across the ocean, and into 'another world … to be made a animal' (2017, unpaginated). Jojo himself has visions and delusions wherein he sees the slaves working on the plantation:

> I look out at the fields but I don't see birds. I squint and for a second I see men bent at the waist, row after row of them, picking at the ground, looking like a great murder of crows landed and chattering and picking for bugs in the ground. One, shorter than the rest, stands and looks straight at me.... I blink and the men are gone and it is just fog rolling, wisping over the fields that stretch out endlessly.... (Unpaginated)

Later, the animal metaphor when speaking of the slaves or prisoners would shift:

> I landed in a field of endless rows of cotton, saw men bent and scuttling along like hermit crabs, bending and picking. Saw other men walking in circles around them with guns. (Unpaginated)

12. In Natalie Baszile's *Queen Sugar*, NeNee, whom Charley was hoping to hire for her inherited cane plantation, says derisively to her, 'I bet you'd be even worse to work for than a white man' (2017: 53), thus implying that black slaveowners are worse than white ones.

13. In a different assertion of what may be called the techno-animist uncanny in the novel, services for the afterlife and its economies are also now available, as Kaizong discovers:

> [Y]ou can go to the site to do banking for the afterlife. You can open accounts and buy hell money for dead relatives: coins, bullion, and credit cards are all in use over there. Money deposited in the accounts can be used by the dead for any product, housing, or service available in the afterlife – and, of course, to pay all kinds of taxes over there, too... As long as you really believe that the other world exists, believe that your dead loved ones are living there, and that it's possible to do something to let them know that you're thinking of them – then it's all real. (Qiufan 2019, unpaginated)

This closely resembles the kind of technology embodied in Eternime where a human could collect one's thoughts and ideas and make an AI clone that would interact with the loved ones after one's death (https://medium.com/@mariusursache/the-journey-to-digital-immortality-33fcbd79949, accessed on 13 January 2024).

14. This emphasis on sustainable and necessary hunting may be seen in other Aboriginal texts as well. For instance, in Witi Ihimaera's Maori novel, *The Whale Rider*, Koro Apirana says, '[W]e never try to overfish, for to do so would be to take greedy advantage' (1987: 38).

15. In Kate Beaton's *Ducks* (2022), the endpapers carry prospect views of the Cape Breton, Nova Scotia. This framing vista, however, opens to a startling discovery. Cape Breton's 'main export [in the 2000s] is people' (10). Beaton draws a dining room with 'empty chairs around the table' before stating 'the only message we got about a better future was that we had to leave home to have one' (10). Beaton's work moves sharply in, from the breath-taking prospect view of the land to the inside of a home with framed pictures and empty dining rooms, to highlight the lack of *prospects* in the region. On the very next page, drawing isolated buildings in two adjacent panels, she writes of the two 'diametrically opposed experiences [of Cape Breton]': 'a deep love for home, and the knowledge of how frequently we have to leave it to find work somewhere else' (11).

16. Johannes Schmid notes that Sacco presents the Denes' 'intracommunal violence, including domestic abuse, sexual abuse, child neglect, but also rampant cases of suicide and substance abuse … as an aftereffect of the trauma caused by the IRSS, which produced a generation bereft of their social ties' (2022: 112).

17. Saidiya Hartman in *Lose Your Mother* (2011) explores the histories of African tribes selling other Africans to the white slave traders: '[C]ontrary to popular belief Africans did not sell their brothers and sisters into slavery. They sold strangers: those outside the web of kin and clan relationships, non-members of the polity, foreigners and barbarians' (5). Hartman notes how the ruling classes conquered the area and 'subjugated the original inhabitants, who first became their slaves and then their subjects' (189). In such a context, the 'royalists and elites, like their European counterparts, envisioned the stateless and the sovereignless as suited for slavery' (190).

Bibliography

Primary Texts ·

Ackerman, Diane. *The Rarest of the Rare: Vanishing Animals, Timeless Worlds*. New York: Vintage, 1995. Ebook.

Abramson, Neil. *Unsaid*. New York: Hachette, 2011. Ebook.

Adams, Douglas and Mark Carwardine. *Last Chance to See*. New York: Ballantine, 1990.

al-Koni, Ibrahim. *Gold Dust*. Trans. Elliott Colla. Cairo: American University in Cairo Press, 2008. Ebook.

Allende, Isabel. *Island Beneath the Sea*. Trans. Margaret Sayers Peden. HarperCollins, 2010. Ebook.

Ammons, A. R. *Garbage*. New York: W.W. Norton, 1993.

Antonetta, Susanne. *Body Toxic*. Berkeley: Counterpoint, 2001.

Atwood, Margaret. *Oryx and Crake*. London: Virago, 2013 [2003].

———. *The Year of the Flood*. London: Virago, 2010 [2009].

———. *MaddAddam*. London: Virago, 2014 [2013].

Bacigalupi, Paolo. *The Windup Girl*. Hachette Ebook, 2011.

———. *The Water Knife*. London: Orbit, 2015. Ebook.

Banerjee, Sarnath. *All Quiet in Vikaspuri*. New Delhi: HarperCollins, 2015.

Baszile, Natalie. *Queen Sugar*. New York: Viking, 2017. Ebook.

Baxter, Stephen. *Flood*. London: Orion, 2008. Ebook.

Bear, Greg. *Darwin's Children*. New York: Ballantine, 2003.

Beaton, Kate. *Ducks: Two Years in the Oil Sands*. London: Jonathan Cape, 2022.

Benyamin. *Body and Blood*. Trans. B. R. Swarup. New Delhi: HarperCollins, 2020. Ebook.

Boyle, T. Coraghessan. 'Dogology'. In Boyle, *Tooth and Claw*, 32–56. New York: Penguin, 2006.

Bradbury, Ray. 'A Sound of Thunder'. 1952. http://www.astro.sunysb.edu/
    fwalter/AST389/ASoundofThunder.pdf. Accessed on 14 June 2023.

Bradley, James. 'Is It Possible to Write Good Fiction about Climate Change?'
    City of Tongues, 22 March 2010. https://cityoftongues.com/2010/03/22/is-
    it-possible-to-write-good-fiction-about-climate-change/. Accessed on 11 May
    2023.

———. *Clade*. London: Titan, 2017. Ebook.

———. *Ghost Species*. London: Hodder Studio, 2020. Ebook.

Butler, Octavia E. *Kindred*. Boston: Beacon, 1979.

Byatt, A. S. 'A Stone Woman'. *The New Yorker*, 13 October 2003.

Christy, Bryan. *The Lizard King*. New York: Hachette, 2008. Ebook.

Church, George and Ed Regis. *Regenesis: How Synthetic Biology Will Reinvent
    Nature and Ourselves*. New York: Basic Books, 2012. Ebook.

Church, George M. 'Epilogue'. In Ben Mezrich, *Woolly: The True Story of the
    Quest to Revive One of History's Most Iconic Extinct Creatures*. New York: Atria,
    2017. Ebook.

Cocozza, Paula. *How to Be Human*. London: Hutchinson, 2017.

Coetzee, J. M. *The Lives of Animals*. Edited by Amy Gutmann. Princeton,
    NJ: Princeton University Press, 1999. Ebook.

Cokinos, Christopher. *Hope Is the Thing with Feathers: A Personal Chronicle of
    Vanished Birds*. New York: Penguin, 2009. Ebook.

Cone, Marla. *Silent Snow: The Slow Poisoning of the Arctic*. New York: Grove,
    2005. Ebook.

Conrad, Joseph. *Heart of Darkness*. In *Youth, Heart of Darkness, The End of the
    Tether*, 43–162. London: Dent, 1974.

Corwin, Jeff. *100 Heartbeats: The Race to Save Earth's Most Endangered Species*.
    New York: Rodale – Random House, 2009. Ebook.

Crichton, Michael. *Jurassic Park*. New York: Ballantine, 1990.

Darrieussecq, Marie. *Pig Tales: A Tale of Lust and Transformation*. Trans. Linda
    Coverdale. London: Faber and Faber, 1996.

Fagin, Dan. *Toms River: A Story of Science and Salvation*. New York: Bantam,
    2013. Ebook.

Flowers, Catherine Coleman. *Waste: One Woman's Fight Against America's Dirty
    Secret*. New York and London: The New Press, 2020. Ebook.

Forshall, Beatrice. *The Book of Vanishing Species: Illustrated Lives*. London:
    Bloomsbury, 2022.

Foster, Charles. *Being a Beast*. London: Profile, 2016.

Garnett, David. *Lady into Fox*. 1922. https://www.gutenberg.org/ebooks/10337.
    Accessed on 25 March 2023.

Gee, Maggie. *The Flood*. London: Saqi, 2004. Ebook.

Gerritsen, Teri. *Harvest*. London: Headline, 1996. Ebook.

Ghosh, Amitav. *The Hungry Tide*. Delhi: Ravi Dayal, 2004.

————. *The Great Derangement: Climate Change and the Unthinkable*. Chicago: Chicago University Press, 2016.

————. *The Nutmeg's Curse: Parables for a Planet in Crisis*. New York: Penguin, 2021.

Glass, Michael. *Ultimatum*. Phoenix, Arizona: Wright Convention Center, 2012.

Golding, William. *Lord of the Flies*. New York: Penguin, 2009.

Greenberg, Joel. *A Feathered River Across the Sky: The Passenger Pigeon's Flight Into Extinction*. New York: Bloomsbury, 2014. Ebook.

Gyasi, Yaa. *Homegoing*. New York: Penguin, 2016. Ebook.

Habila, Helon. *Oil on Water*. London: Hamish Hamilton, 2011. Ebook.

Hayes, Nick. *The Rime of the Modern Mariner*. London: Jonathan Cape, 2011.

Ihimaera, Witi. *The Whale Rider*. Rosedale, NZ: Penguin, 1987. Ebook.

James, Tania. *The Tusk That Did the Damage*. London: Vintage, 2015.

Janu, C. K. *Mother Forest: The Unfinished Story of C. K. Janu*. Written by Bhaskaran. Trans. N. Ravi Shanker. New Delhi: Kali for Women, 2004.

Jones, Edward P. *The Known World*. New York: HarperCollins, 2003. Ebook.

Jones, Cynan. *Stillicide*. London: Granta, 2019.

Kafka, Franz. 'The Metamorphosis'. In Kafka, *The Metamorphosis and Other Stories*. Trans. Ian Johnston. Peterborough, ON: Broadview Press, 2016 [1915].

Kingsolver, Barbara. *Flight Behaviur*. New York: HarperCollins, 2012. Ebook.

Kolbert, Elizabeth. *The Sixth Extinction: An Unnatural History*. New York: Henry Holt, 2014. Ebook.

Le Guin. 'The Wife's Story'. In Le Guin, *The Compass Rose: Short Stories*. New York: Bantam, 1982.

Leigh, Julia. *The Hunter*. London: Faber and Faber, 2000.

Lemire, Jeff. *Sweet Tooth Compendium*. Brubank, CA: DC Comics, 2021.

Lessing, Doris. *The Fifth Child*. London: Flamingo, 2001 [1988].

————. *Ben, in the World*. London: Flamingo, 2000.

Levi, Primo. *If This Is a Man*. Trans. Stuart Woolf. Boston: Little, Brown, 2014. Ebook.

Maathai, Wangari. *Unbowed: A Memoir*. New York: Anchor, 2007.

Martel, Yann. *Life of Pi*. New York: Harcourt, 2004.

Martin, Marie Thérèse. *And Poison Fell from the Sky: A Memoir of Life, Death, and Survival in Maine's Cancer Valley*. Maine: Islandport, 2022.

Martin, Paul S. *Twilight of the Mammoths: Ice Age Extinctions and the Rewilding of America*. Berkeley and London: University of California Press, 2005.

Mbue, Imbolo. *How Beautiful We Were*. Edinburgh: Canongate, 2022.

McConaghy, Charlotte. *Migrations*. London: Vintage, 2021a.

———. *Once There Were Wolves*. London: Vintage, 2021b.

McLeod, Cynthia. *The Cost of Sugar*. Trans. Gerald R. Mettam. London. HopeRoad, 2010.

Mda, Zakes. *The Heart of Redness*. New York: Picador-Farrar, Straus and Giroux, 2000. Ebook.

Mezrich, Ben. *Woolly: The True Story of the Quest to Revive One of History's Most Iconic Extinct Creatures*. New York: Atria, 2017.

Miévelle, China. *Un Lun Dun*. New York: Ballantine, 2007. Ebook.

Milman, Oliver. '"We're Not a Dump": Poor Alabama Towns Struggle under the Stench of Toxic Landfills'. *The Guardian*, 15 April 2019. https://www. theguardian.com/us-news/2019/apr/15/were-not-a-dump-poor-alabama-towns-struggle-under-the-stench-of-toxic-landfills. Accessed on 23 June 2023.

Montero, Mayra. *In the Palm of Darkness*. New York: HarperCollins, 1997.

Moore, Alan, Stephen Bissette and John Totleben. *Saga of the Swamp Thing*, 6 vols. New York: DC Books, 1972–2016.

Moore, Charles with Cassandra Philips. *Plastic Ocean: How a Sea Captain's Chance Discovery Launched a Determined Quest to Save the Oceans*. New York: Penguin, 2011.

Naik, Akhila. *Bheda*. Trans. Raj Kumar. New Delhi: Oxford University Press, 2017.

Natarajan, Srividya, S. Anand, Durgabai Vyam and Subhash Vyam. *Bhimayana: Experiences of Untouchability*. New Delhi: Navayana, 2011.

Natarajan, Srividya and Aparajita Ninan. *A Gardener in the Wasteland: Jotiba Phule's Fight for Liberty*. New Delhi: Navayana, 2011.

Nowra, Louis. *Into That Forest*. Crows Nest, NSW: Allen and Unwin, 2012.

Neiwert, David. *Of Orcas and Men*. New York: Overlook Hardcover, 2015.

Oliver, Mary. *Dream Work*. New York: Atlantic Monthly, 1986.

———. *Winter Hours: Prose, Prose Poems, and Poems*. Boston: Houghton Mifflin, 2000

———. *Red Bird*. Boston: Beacon, 2008.

Oloixarac, Pola. *Dark Constellations*. Trans. Roy Kesey. New York: Soho Press, 2019.

Owen, David. *Thylacine: The Tragic Tale of the Tasmanian Tiger*. Crows Nest, NSW: Allen and Unwin, 2003.

Patil, Amruta. *Kari*. New Delhi: HarperCollins, 2008.

Powers, Richard. *The Overstory*. London: Vintage, 2018. Ebook.

Qiufan, Chen. *Waste Tide*. Trans. Ken Liu. New York: Tom Doherty, 2019.

Quammen, David. *The Song of the Dodo: Island Biogeography in an Age of Extinctions*. New York: Scribner, 2004.

Rich, Nathaniel. *Odds Against Tomorrow*. New York: Farrar, Straus and Giroux, 2013. Ebook.

Sacco, Joe. *Paying the Land*. London: Jonathan Cape, 2020.

Schulz, Kathryn. 'The Ten Best Weather Events in Fiction'. *New Yorker*, 20 November 2015. https://www.newyorker.com/books/page-turner/the-ten-best-weather-events-in-fiction. Accessed on 11 May 2023.

Sen, Orijit. *River of Stories*. New Delhi: Kalpavriksh, 1994.

Serpell, Namwali. *The Old Drift*. London: Penguin, 2019. eBook.

Shute, Nevil. *On the Beach*. Harmondsworth: Penguin, 2010 [1957].

Shyam, Venkat Raman Singh and S. Anand. *Finding My Way*. New Delhi: Navayana, 2016.

Smith, Alexis M. *Marrow Island*. New York: Houghton Mifflin, 2016.

Snyder, Gary. *Mountains and Rivers without End*. Washington, DC: Counterpoint, 1996.

Steingraber, Sandra. *Living Downstream: An Ecologist's Personal Investigation of Cancer and the Environment*. New York: Da Capo, 2010.

Stone, Richard. *Mammoth: The Resurrection of an Ice Age Giant*. London: Fourth Estate, 2002.

Sudbanthad, Pitchaya. *Bangkok Wakes to Rain*. London: Sceptre, 2019.

Vandermeer, Jeff. *Hummingbird Salamander*. New York: HarperCollins, 2021.

Vaughan, Brian K. and Pia Guerra. *Y: The Last Man. Compendium*. New York: DC, 2020. 2 vols.

Vyam, Subhash with Gita Wolf. *Water*. New Delhi: Tara, 2018.

Ward, Jesmyn. *Sing, Unburied, Sing*. New York: Scribner, 2017.

Wells, H. G. *The Island of Doctor Moreau*. London: Penguin, 2005 [1896].

Wright, Alexis. *The Swan Book*. Artamrmon, NSW: Giramondo, 2013.

Secondary Texts

Abrell, Elan. *Saving Animals: Multispecies Ecologies of Rescue and Care*. Minneapolis and London: University of Minnesota Press, 2021.

Ahuja, Neel. 'Postcolonial Critique in a Multispecies World'. *PMLA* 124, no. 2 (2009): 556–563.

———. *Bioinsecurities: Disease Interventions, Empire, and the Government of Species*. Durham and London: Duke University Press, 2016.

Alaimo, Stacy. *Bodily Natures: Science, Environment and the Material Self.* Bloomington and Indianapolis. Indiana University Press, 2010.

———. *Exposed: Environmental Politics and Pleasures in Posthuman Times*. Minneapolis: University of Minnesota Press, 2016.

Albrecht, Glenn, G. M. Sartore, L. Connor, N. Higginbotham, S. Freeman, B. Kelly and G. Pollard. 'Solastalgia: The Distress Caused by Environmental Change'. *Australasian Psychiatry* 15, Suppl. 1 (2007): S95–S98.

Allen, Anita L. 'Surrogacy, Slavery, and the Ownership of Life'. *Faculty Scholarship at Penn Law* 805 (1999): 139–149.

Andersen, Ross. 'Welcome to the Pleistocene Park'. *The Atlantic*, April 2017.

Aravamudan, Srinivas. 'The Catachronism of Climate Change'. *Diacritics* 41, no. 3 (2013): 6–30.

Archer, David. *The Long Thaw: How Humans Are Changing the Next 100,000 Years of the Earth's Climate*. Princeton, NJ: Princeton University Press, 2009.

Archer, David and Raymond T. Pierrehumbert (eds.). *The Warming Papers: The Scientific Foundation for the Climate Change Forecast*. Marsden, MA: John Wiley, 2011.

Ashton, Emily. *Anthropocene Childhoods: Speculative Fiction, Racialization, and Climate Crisis*. London: Bloomsbury, 2023.

Askland, Hedda Haugen and Matthew Bunn. 'Lived Experiences of Environmental Change: Solastalgia, Power and Place'. *Emotion, Space and Society* 27 (2018): 16–22.

Athanassakis, Yanoula. *Environmental Justice in Contemporary US Narratives*. Abingdon: Routledge, 2017.

Baetens, Jan. 'Interspecies Relationships in Graphic Micronarratives: From Olivier Deprez to Avril-Deprez'. In *Animal Comics: Multispecies Storyworlds in Graphic Narratives*, edited by David Herman, 183–200. London: Bloomsbury, 2018.

Barad, Karen. 'Posthumanist Performativity: Toward an Understanding of How Matter Comes to Matter'. *Signs: Journal of Women in Culture and Society* 28, no. 3 (2003): 801–831.

Barrell, John. *The Birth of Pandora and the Division of Knowledge*. London: Macmillan, 1992.

Barua, Maan. 'Plantationocene: A Vegetal Geography'. *Annals of the American Association of Geographers* 113, no. 1 (2023): 13–29. DOI: 10.1080/24694452.2022.2094326.

Batcho, Krystine Irene. 'Nostalgia: The Paradoxical Bittersweet Emotion'. In *Nostalgia Now: Cross-Disciplinary Perspectives on the Past in the Present*, edited by Michael Hviid Jacobsen, 31–46. Oxford: Routledge, 2020.

Bate, Jonathan. *Romantic Ecology: Wordsworth and the Environmental Tradition.* London: Routledge, 1991.

———. *The Song of the Earth.* Cambridge, MA: Harvard University Press, 2000.

Baucom, Ian and Michael Omelsky. 'Knowledge in the Age of Climate Change'. *The South Atlantic Quarterly* 116, no. 1 (2017): 1–18.

Bauman, Zygmunt. *Wasted Lives: Modernity and its Outcasts.* Cambridge: Polity, 2004.

Bennett, Jane. *Vibrant Matter: A Political Ecology of Things.* Durham, NC: Duke University Press, 2010.

Bennett, Joshua. *Being Property Once Myself: Blackness and the End of Man.* Cambridge, MA: The Belknap Press of Harvard University Press, 2020.

Bennett, Tony. *Pasts beyond Memory: Evolution, Museums, Colonialism.* London and New York: Routledge, 2004.

Bezan, Sarah. 'CanLit's Ossiferous Fictions: Animal Bones and Fossils in Margaret Atwood's *Life Before Man* and Carol Shields's *The Stone Diaries*'. In *The Palgrave Handbook of Animals and Literature*, edited by Susan McHugh, Robert McKay and John Miller, 473–486. Cham: Palgrave-Macmillan, 2021.

Beville, Maria. *Gothic-postmodernism: Voicing the Terrors of Postmodernity.* Amsterdam: Rodopi, 2009.

Boa, Elizabeth. 'Creepy-crawlies: Gilman's "The Yellow Wallpaper" and Kafka's "The Metamorphosis"'. *Paragraph* 13, no. 1 (1990): 19–29.

Bonneuil, Christophe and Jean-Baptiste Fressoz. *The Shock of the Anthropocene: The Earth, History and Us.* Trans. David Fernbach. London: Verso, 2016. Ebook.

Bowker, Geoffrey C. 'Biodiversity Datadiversity'. *Social Studies of Science* 30, no. 5 (2000): 643–683.

Bracke, Astrid. *Climate Crisis and the 21st-Century British Novel.* London: Bloomsbury Academic, 2018.

Buckland, David, Olivia Gray and Lucy Wood. 'The Cultural Challenge of Climate Change'. *The South Atlantic Quarterly* 116, no. 1 (2017): 97–109.

Buell, Lawrence. 'Toxic Discourse'. *Critical Inquiry* 24, no. 3 (1998): 639–665.

———. *Writing for an Endangered World: Literature, Culture, and the Environment in the U.S. and Beyond.* Cambridge, MA and London, England: Belknap Press, 2001.

———. *The Future of Environmental Criticism.* Marsden, MA: Wiley Blackwell, 2005.

Butler, Judith. *Precarious Life: The Powers of Mourning and Violence*. London: Verso, 2004.

Cabral, Diogo De Carvalho and André Vasques Vital. 'Multispecies Emergent Textualities: Writing and Reading in Ecologies of Selves'. *ISLE: Interdisciplinary Studies in Literature and Environment* 30, no. 3 (2023): 705–727. DOI:10.1093/isle/isab024.

Caminero-Santangelo, Byron. *Different Shades of Green: African Literature, Environmental Justice, and Political Ecology*. Charlottesville and London: University of Virginia Press, 2014.

Carnell, Rachel and Chris Mounsey (eds.). *Stewardship and the Future of the Planet: Promise and Paradox*. London and New York: Routledge, 2022.

Carrigan, Anthony. 'Postcolonial Disaster Studies'. In *Global Ecologies and the Environmental Humanities: Postcolonial Approaches*, edited by Elizabeth DeLoughrey, Jill Didur and Anthony Carrigan, 117–139. New York: Routledge, 2015.

Castricano, Jody (ed.). *Animal Subjects: An Ethical Reader in a Posthuman World*. Waterloo, ON: Wilfrid Laurier University Press, 2008.

Chakrabarty, Dipesh. 'The Climate of History: Four Theses'. *Critical Inquiry* 35, no. 2 (2009): 197–222.

———. 'Postcolonial Studies and the Challenge of Climate Change'. *New Literary History* 43, no. 1 (2012): 1–18.

———. 'Afterword: On Scale and Deep History in the Anthropocene'. In *Narratives of Scale in the Anthropocene: Imagining Human Responsibility in an Age of Scalar Complexity*, edited by Gabriele Dürbeck, Philip Hüpkes. London and New York: Routledge, 2021.

Chao, Sophie. '(Un)Worlding the Plantationocene: Extraction, Extinction, Emergence'. *eTropic* 21, no. 1 (2022): 165–191.

Chao, Sophie, Karin Bolender and Eben Kirksey (eds.). *The Promise of Multispecies Justice*. Durham and London: Duke University Press, 2022.

Chrulew, Matthew. 'Reversing Extinction: Restoration and Resurrection in the Pleistocene Rewilding Projects'. *Humanimalia* 2, no. 2 (2011): 4–27.

Chrulew, Matthew and Rick De Vos. 'Extinction'. In *The Edinburgh Companion to Animal Studies*, edited by Lynn Turner, Undine Sellbach and Ron Broglio, 181–197. Edinburgh: Edinburgh University Press, 2018.

Chute, Hillary. *Disaster Drawn: Visual Witness, Comics and Documentary Form*. Harvard University Press, 2016.

Cielemęcka, Olga and Christine Daigle. 'Posthuman Sustainability: An Ethos for Our Anthropocenic Future'. *Theory, Culture and Society* 36, nos. 7–8 (2019): 67–87.

Cixous, Hélène. 'Fiction and Its Phantoms: A Reading of Freud's *Das Unheimliche* (The "Uncanny")'. *New Literary History* 7, no. 3 (1976): 525–548.

Clark, Timothy. *Ecocriticism on the Edge: The Anthropocene as a Threshold Concept.* London: Bloomsbury, 2015.

Cobley, Paul. *Cultural Implications of Biosemiotics.* Cham, Switzerland: Springer, 2016.

Colebrooke, Clarie. *Death of the PostHuman: Essays on Extinction.* Vol. 1. Ann Arbor, MI: Open Humanities Press, 2014.

Collard, Rosemary-Claire and Kathryn Gillespie. 'Introduction'. In *Critical Animal Geographies: Politics, Intersections, and Hierarchies in a Multispecies World*, edited by Kathryn Gillespie and Rosemary-Claire Collard, 1–15. New York: Routledge, 2015.

Compton, Caroline. 'The Temporality of Disaster: Data, the Emergency, and Climate Change'. *Anthropocenes – Human, Inhuman, Posthuman* 1, no. 1 (2020): 1–14. DOI: https://doi.org/10.16997/ahip.24.

Coole, Diana and Samantha Frost (eds.). *New Materialisms: Ontology, Agency, and Politics.* Durham and London: Duke University Press, 2010.

Cooper, Melinda. *Life as Surplus: Biotechnology and Capitalism in the Neoliberal Era.* Seattle, WA: University of Washington Press, 2008.

Couser, G. Thomas. *Signifying Bodies: Disability in Contemporary Life Writing.* Ann Arbor: University of Michigan Press, 2009.

Couzin, Iain D. 'Collective Cognition in Animal Groups'. *Trends in Cognitive Sciences* 13, no. 1 (2009): 36–43.

Crist, Eileen. 'On the Poverty of Our Nomenclature'. *Environmental Humanities* 3, no. 1 (2013): 129–147.

Cronon, William. 'A Place for Stories: Nature, History, and Narrative'. *Journal of American History* 78, no. 4 (1992): 1347–1376.

———. 'The Trouble with Wilderness: Or, Getting Back to the Wrong Nature'. *Environmental History* 1, no. 1 (1996): 7–28.

Crosby, Alfred W. *Ecological Imperialism: The Biological Expansion of Europe, 900–1900.* Cambridge: Cambridge University Press, 1995.

Crump, Thomas. *The Anthropology of Numbers.* Cambridge: Cambridge University Press, 1990.

Dalley, Hamish. *The Postcolonial Historical Novel: Realism, Allegory, and the Representation of Contested Pasts* . Basingstoke: Palgrave Macmillan, 2014.

Davis, Janae, Alex A. Moulton, Levi Van Sant and Brian Williams. 'Anthropocene, Capitalocene, ... Plantationocene? A Manifesto for Ecological Justice in an Age of Global Crises'. *Geography Compass* 13, no. 5 (2019). e12438. DOI: https://doi.org/10.1111/gec3.12438.

Dawson, Ashley. 'Biocapitalism and Extinction'. In *After Extinction*, edited by Richard Grusin, 173–200. Minneapolis and London: University of Minnesota Press, 2018.

Day, Iyko. 'On Immanence and Indeterminacy: Black Feminism and Settler Colonialism'. *EPD: Society and Space* 39, no. 1 (2021): 3–8.

De Bruyn, Ben. *The Novel and the Multispecies Soundscape*. Cham, Switzerland: Palgrave-Macmillan, 2020.

De Vos, Ricardo. 'Extinction Stories: Performing Absence(s)'. In *Knowing Animals*, edited by Laurence Simmons and Philip Armstrong, 183–195. Leiden: Brill, 2007.

Deckard, Sharae. 'Ecogothic'. In *Twenty-First-Century Gothic: An Edinburgh Companion*, edited by Maisha Wester and Xavier Aldana Reyes, 174–178. Edinburgh: Edinburgh University Press, 2019a.

———. 'Water Shocks: Neoliberal Hydrofiction and the Crisis of "Cheap Water"'. *Atlantic Studies* 16, no. 1 (2019b): 101–125.

Deckard, Sharae and Kerstin Oloff. '"The One Who Comes from the Sea": Marine Crisis and the New Oceanic Weird in Rita Indiana's *La mucama de Omicunlé*'. *Humanities* 9, no. 86 (2020): 1–14.

DeLoughrey, Elizabeth. 'Heliotropes: Solar Ecologies and Pacific Radiations'. In *Postcolonial Ecologies: Literatures of the Environment*, edited by deLoughrey and George Handley, 235–253. Oxford: Oxford University Press, 2011.

———. 'Ordinary Futures: Interspecies Worlding in the Anthropocene'. In *Global Ecologies and the Environmental Humanities: Postcolonial Approaches*, edited by Elizabeth DeLoughrey, Jill Didur and Anthony Carrigan, 352–372. New York: Routledge, 2015.

———. 'The Sea Is Rising: Visualising Climate Change in the Pacific Islands'. *Pacific Dynamics* 2, no. 2 (2018). https://english.ucla.edu/people-faculty/ elizabeth-deloughrey/. Accessed on 11 May 2023.

———. *Allegories of the Anthropocene*. Durham and London: Duke University Press, 2019.

———. 'Mining the Seas: Speculative Fictions and Futures'. In *Laws of the Sea: Interdisciplinary Currents*, edited by Irus Braverman, 144–163. New York: Routledge, 2022. https://english.ucla.edu/people-faculty/elizabeth-deloughrey/. Accessed on 11 May 2023.

DeLoughrey, Elizabeth, Jill Didur and Anthony Carrigan. 'Introduction: A Postcolonial Environmental Humanities'. In *Global Ecologies and the Environmental Humanities: Postcolonial Approaches*, edited by Elizabeth DeLoughrey, Jill Didur and Anthony Carrigan, 1–30. New York: Routledge, 2015.

Dennett, Daniel C. *Consciousness Explained*. Boston: Little, Brown and Co, 1991.

Dentith, Simon. *Parody*. London and New York: Routledge, 2000.

Dessler, Andrew E. and Edward A. Parson. *The Science and Politics of Global Climate Change: A Guide to the Debate*. Cambridge: Cambridge University Press, 2019.

Devi, Mahaswetha. 'Pterodactyl, Puran Sahay, and Pirtha'. In Devi, *Imaginary Maps: Three Stories*. Trans. Gayatri Chakravorty Spivak, 95–196. New York: Routledge, 1995.

Diehm, Christian. 'De-extinction and Deep Questions About Species Conservation'. *Ethics, Policy and Environment* 20, no. 1 (2017): 25–28.

Dillon, Sarah. 'Imagining Apocalypse: Maggie Gee's *The Flood*'. *Contemporary Literature* 48, no. 3 (2007): 374–397.

Doniger, Wendy. 'Reflection'. In J. M. Coetzee, *The Lives of Animals*, edited by Amy Gutmann, 93–106. Princeton, NJ: Princeton University Press, 1999.

———. 'Zoomorphism in Ancient India: Humans More Bestial than Beasts'. In *Thinking with Animals: New Perspectives on Anthropomorphism*, edited by Lorraine Daston and Gregg Mitman, 17–36. Columbia University Press, 2005.

Donlan, Josh, Joel Berger, Carl E. Bock, Jane H. Bock, David A. Burney, James A. Estes, Dave Foreman, Paul S. Martin, Gary W. Roemer, Felisa A. Smith, Michael E. Soulé and Harry W. Greene. 'Pleistocene Rewilding: An Optimistic Agenda for Twenty-First Century Conservation'. *The American Naturalist* 168, no. 5 (2006): 660–681.

Donovan, Amy. 'Raw, Dense and Loud: A Whale's Perspective on Cold Water Energy'. In *Cold Water Oil: Offshore Petroleum Cultures*, edited by Fiona Polack and Danine Farquharson, 238–263. London and New York: Routledge, 2022.

Edwards, Justin. *Gothic Passages: Racial Ambiguity and the American Gothic*. Iowa City: University of Iowa Press, 2003.

Edwards, Justin, Rune Graulund and Johan Hoglund (eds.). *Dark Scenes from Damaged Earth: The Gothic Anthropocene*. Minneapolis and London: University of Minnesota Press, 2022.

Elden, Stuart. 'Terrain, Politics, History'. *Dialogues in Human Geography* 11, no. 2 (2021): 170–189.

Endres, Danielle and Samantha Senda-Cook. 'Location Matters: The Rhetoric of Place in Protest'. *Quarterly Journal of Speech* 97, no. 3 (2011): 257–282.

Escobar, Arturo. 'Whose Knowledge, Whose Nature? Biodiversity, Conservation, and the Political Ecology of Social Movements'. *Journal of Political Ecology* 5 (1998): 53–82.

Farbatco, Carol. 'Climate Change and Island Populations'. In *Routledge Handbook of Ethics and International Relations*, edited by B. J. Steele and E. A. Heinze, 405–418. Oxford: Routledge, 2018.

Farina, Almo and Philip James. 'Vivoscapes: an Ecosemiotic Contribution to the Ecological Theory'. *Biosemiotics* 14 (2021): 419–431.

Feldner, Maxmilian. 'Representing the Neocolonial Destruction of the Niger Delta: Helon Habila's *Oil on Water*'. *Journal of Postcolonial Writing* 54, no. 4 (2018): 515–527.

Ferdinand, Malcom. *Decolonial Ecology: Thinking from the Caribbean World*. Trans. Anthony Paul Smith. Cambridge: Polity, 2022.

Finkleman, Leonard. 'De-extinction and the Conception of Species'. *Biology and Philosophy* 33, no. 32 (2018). DOI: https://doi.org/10.1007/s10539-018-9639-x.

Forsyth, Miranda, Brunilda Pali and Felicity Tepper. 'Environmental Restorative Justice: An Introduction and an Invitation'. In *The Palgrave Handbook of Environmental Restorative Justice*, edited by Brunilda Pali, Miranda Forsyth and Felicity Tepper, 1–23. Cham, Switzerland: Palgrave Macmillan, 2022.

Freitas, Joana Gaspar de. 'Making a Case for an Environmental History of Dunes'. *Anthropocenes – Human, Inhuman, Posthuman* 1, no. 1 (2020). DOI: https://doi.org/10.16997/ahip.4.

Fudge, Erica. *Animal*. London: Reaktion, 2002.

Galgiano, Monica, John C. Ryan and Patricia Viera. *The Language of Plants: Science, Philosophy, Literature*. Minneapolis: University of Minnesota Press, 2017.

Ganguly, Debjani. 'Catastrophic Form and Planetary Realism'. *New Literary History* 51, no. 2 (2020): 419–453.

Garber, Marjorie. 'Reflection'. In J. M. Coetzee, *The Lives of Animals*, edited by Amy Gutmann 73–84. Princeton, NJ: Princeton University Press, 1999.

Garrard, Greg. *Ecocriticism*. London: Routledge 2011. Rev. and Expanded. 2nd ed.

———. 'Worlds Without Us: Some Types of Disanthropy'. *SubStance* 41, no. 1 (2012): 40–60.

——— (ed.). *The Oxford Handbook of Ecocriticism*. Oxford: Oxford University Press, 2014.

Gaynor, Kaitlin, Joel S. Brown, Arthur D. Middleton, Mary E. Power and Justin S. Brashares. 'Landscapes of Fear: Spatial Patterns of Risk Perception and Response'. *Trends in Ecology and Evolution* 34, no. 4 (2019): 355–368. DOI: https://doi.org/10.1016/j.tree.2019.01.004.

Goderie, Roland, Wouter Helmer, Henri Kerkdijk-Otten and Staffan Widstrand. *The Aurochs: Born to Be Wild – The Comeback of a European Icon*. Zutphen, The Netherlands: RoodBont, 2022.

Gomel, Elana. *Science Fiction, Alien Encounters, and the Ethics of Posthumanism: Beyond the Golden Rule*. Basingstoke: Palgrave Macmillan, 2014.

Govindrajan, Radhika. *Animal Intimacies: Interspecies Relatedness in India's Central Himalayas*. Chicago: University of Chicago Press, 2018.

Gray, Andrew. *Indigenous Rights and Development: Self-Determination in an Amazonian Community*. Providence, RI: Berghahn, 1997.

Greenough, Paul and Anna Lowenhaupt Tsing (eds.). *Nature in the Global South: Environmental Projects in South and Southeast Asia*. Durham and London: Duke University Press, 2003.

Guha, Ramachandra and Juan Martinez-Alier. *Varieties of Environmentalism: Essays North and South*. New York and London: Routledge, 1997.

Gunn, Joshua and David E. Beard. 'On the Apocalyptic Sublime'. *Southern Journal of Communication* 65, no. 4 (2000): 269–286.

Gustafsson, Karin M. 'Environmental Discourses and Biodiversity: The Construction of a Storyline in Understanding and Managing an Environmental Issue'. *Journal of Integrative Environmental Sciences* 10, no. 1 (2013): 39–54.

Hampton, Gregory Jerome. *Changing Bodies in the Fiction of Octavia Butler: Slaves, Aliens, and Vampires*. Lanham, Maryland: Lexington, 2017.

Haraway, Donna. *When Species Meet*. Minneapolis: University of Minnesota Press, 2008.

———. *Staying with the Trouble: Making Kin in the Chthulucene*. Durham: Duke University Press, 2016.

Hartman, Saidiya. *Lose Your Mother: A Journey Along the Atlantic Slave Route*. New Delhi: Navayana, 2011.

Heatherington, Tracey. 'From Ecocide To Genetic Rescue: Can Technoscience Save the Wild?' In *The Anthropology of Extinction: Essays on Culture and Species Death*, edited by Genese Marie Sodikoff, 39–66. Bloomington and Indianapolis: Indiana University Press, 2012.

Heise, Ursula. *Sense of Place and Sense of Planet: The Environmental Imagination of the Global*. New York: Oxford University Press, 2008.

———. *Imagining Extinction: The Cultural Meanings of Endangered Species*. Chicago and London: University of Chicago Press, 2016.

———. 'Climate Stories. Review of Amitav Ghosh's *The Great Derangement*'. *Boundary 2*, 19 February 2018. https://www.boundary2.org/2018/02/ursula-k-heise-climate-stories-review-of-amitav-ghoshs-the-great-derangement/. Accessed on 24 December 2022.

Helmreich, Stefan. 'Waves: An Anthropology of Scientific Things'. *HAU: Journal of Ethnographic Theory* 4, no. 3 (2014). DOI: https://doi.org/10.14318/hau4.3.016.

Herbrechter, Stefan. *Before Humanity: Posthumanism and Ancestrality.* Leiden: Brill, 2022.

Herman, David. 'Introduction: More-Than-Human Worlds In Graphic Storytelling'. In *Animal Comics: Multispecies Storyworlds in Graphic Narratives*, edited by David Herman, 1–27. London: Bloomsbury, 2018a.

———. *Narratology Beyond the Human: Storytelling and Animal Life.* Oxford: Oxford University Press, 2018b.

Hobbs, Allyson. *A Chosen Exile: A History of Racial Passing in American Life.* Harvard University Press, 2014.

Hofmeyr, Isabel. 'Provisional Notes on Hydrocolonialism'. *English Language Notes* 57, no. 1 (2019): 11–20.

Höing, Anja. 'Uncanny Pets: Posthuman Dimensions of the Depiction of Companion Animals in 21st-Century British Literature'. *Anglistik: International Journal of English Studies* 30, no. 2 (2019): 69–82.

Hornborg, Alf. 'Artifacts Have Consequences, Not Agency: Toward a Critical Theory of Global Environmental History'. *European Journal of Social Theory* 20, no. 1 (2016): 95–110.

Hua, Linh H. 'Reproducing Time, Reproducing History: Love and Black Feminist Sentimentality in Octavia Butler's *Kindred*'. *African American Review* 44, no. 3 (2011): 391–407.

Hua, Yuanyuan. 'The Dual Alienation in *Waste Tide*'. *Comparative Literature Studies* 57, no. 4 (2020): 670–685.

Huggan, Graham and Helen Tiffin. *Postcolonial Ecocriticism: Literature, Animals, Environment.* London: Routledge, 2010.

Hurley, Kelly. *The Gothic Body: Sexuality, Materialism and Degeneration at the fin de siècle.* Cambridge: Cambridge University Press, 1995.

Hutchinson, Ben. *Lateness and Modern European Literature.* Oxford: Oxford University Press, 2016.

Ilott, Sarah. 'Postcolonial Gothic'. In *Twenty-First-Century Gothic: An Edinburgh Companion*, edited by Maisha Wester and Xavier Aldana Reyes, 19–32. Edinburgh: Edinburgh University Press, 2019.

India Water Portal. 2012. https://www.indiawaterportal.org/topics/privatisation. Accessed on 23 July 2022.

Isenberg, Andrew C. *The Destruction of the Bison: An Environmental History, 1750–1920.* New York: Cambridge University Press, 2000.

Ivanchikova, Alla. 'Geomediations in the Anthropocene: Fictions of the Geologic Turn'. *C21 Literature: Journal of 21st-century Writings* 6, no. 1 (2021): 1–24.

Jacobsen, Michael Hviid. 'Introduction: In Times of Nostalgia: The Brave New World of a Grand Old Emotion'. In *Nostalgia Now: Cross-Disciplinary Perspectives on the Past in the Present*, edited by Michael Hviid Jacobsen, 1–28. Oxford: Routledge, 2020.

James, Erin. *The Storyworld Accord: Econarratology and Postcolonial Narratives.* Lincoln and London: University of Nebraska Press, 2015.

Jeyifo, Biodun. *Wole Soyinka: Politics, Poetics and Postcolonialism.* Cambridge: Cambridge University Press, 2004.

Johns-Putra, Adeline. *Climate Change and the Contemporary Novel.* Cambridge: Cambridge University Press, 2019.

Kadonaga, Lisa. 'Who Gets a Second Chance?' In *Jurassic Park and Philosophy*, edited by Nicholas Michaud and Jessica Watkins, 143–166. Chicago: Open Court, 2014.

Kaplan, E. Ann. *Climate Trauma: Foreseeing the Future in Dystopian Film and Fiction.* New Brunswick, NJ: Rutgers University Press, 2016.

Karavitis, John V. 'Raptor Rights'. In *Jurassic Park and Philosophy*, edited by Nicholas Michaud and Jessica Watkins, 121–142. Chicago: Open Court, 2014. Ebook.

Karnicky, Jeffrey. 'Ornithological Biography, Animal Studies, and Starling Subjectivity'. *Humanimalia* 3, no. 1 (2011): 31–59.

Kennedy, Randall. 'Racial Passing'. *Ohio State Law Journal* 62, no. 3 (2001): 1145–1194.

Kermode, Frank. *The Sense of an Ending: Studies in the Theory of Fiction.* Oxford: Oxford University Press, 2000.

Khullar, Anita. 'Water Crisis in India: The World's Largest Groundwater User'. The Energy and Resources Institute. TERI, 24 March 2022. https://www.teriin.org/article/water-crisis-india-worlds-largest-groundwater-user. Accessed on 23 July 2022.

King, Tiffany Lethabo. 'The Labor of (Re)reading Plantation Landscapes Fungible(ly)'. *Antipode* 48, no. 4 (2016): 1022–1039.

Kirksey, Ebin. 'Lively Multispecies Communities, Deadly Racial Assemblages, and the Promise of Justice'. *The South Atlantic Quarterly* 116, no. 1 (2017): 196–206.

Klinkenborg, Verlyn. *Timothy; or, Notes of an Abject Reptile.* New York: Vintage, 2006.

Knell, Simon J. 'Museums, Fossils and the Cultural Revolution of Science: Mapping Change in the Politics of Knowledge in Early Nineteenth-century

Britain'. In *Museum Revolutions: How Museums Change and are Changed*, edited by Simon J. Knell, Suzanne MacLeod and Sheila Watson, 28–47. Oxford: Routledge, 2007.

Kohn, Eduardo. *How Forests Think: Toward an Anthropology Beyond the Human*. Berkeley: University of California Press, 2013.

Kolbert, Elizabeth. *Under a White Sky: The Nature of the Future*. New York: Crown House, 2021.

Kompatsiaris, Panos. 'Companion Species and Comrades: A Critique of "Plural Relating" in Donna Haraway's Theory Manifestos'. *Culture, Theory and Critique* (2022). DOI: 10.1080/14735784.2022.2122527.

Kuznetski, Julia. 'Transcorporeality: An Interview with Stacy Alaimo'. *Ecozone* 11, no. 2 (2020): 137–146.

Ladino, Jennifer K. *Reclaiming Nostalgia: Longing for Nature in American Literature*. Charlottesville and London: University of Virginia Press, 2012.

Laist, Randy (ed.). *Plants in Literature: Essays in Critical Plant Studies*. Amsterdam: Brill-Rodopi, 2013.

Lambert, Shannon. '"Mycorrhizal Multiplicities": Mapping Collective Agency in Richard Powers's *The Overstory*'. In *Nonhuman Agencies in the Twenty-First-Century Anglophone Novel*, edited by Yvonne Liebermann, Judith Rahn and Bettina Burger, 187–210. Cham, Switzerland: Palgrave Macmillan, 2021.

Littmann, Greg. 'Let the Raptors Run'. In *Jurassic Park and Philosophy*, edited by Nicholas Michaud and Jessica Watkins, 11–20. Chicago: Open Court, 2014. Ebook.

Lehartel, Temiti. 'Perception Revitalisation and Resistance in *The Swan Book*'. *Commonwealth Essays and Studies* 44, no. 2 (2022). DOI: https://doi.org/10.4000/ces.11355.

Lehtimäki, Markku. 'Polar Bears and Butterflies: Allegory, Science, and Experientiality in Climate Change Fiction'. In *Literary Animal Studies and the Climate Crisis*, edited by Sune Borkfelt and Matthias Stephan, 49–70. Cham, Switzerland: Palgrave-Macmillan, 2022.

Lerner, Stephen D. *Sacrifice Zones: The Front Lines of Toxic Chemical Exposure in the United States*. Cambridge, MA: MIT, 2010.

Lestel, Dominique. 'The Withering of Shared Life through the Loss of Biodiversity'. *Social Science Information* 52, no. 2 (2013): 307–325.

Liebermann, Yvonne and Birgit Neumann. 'Archives for the Anthropocene: Planetary Memory in Contemporary Global South Literature'. *LIT: Literature Interpretation Theory* 31, no. 2 (2020): 146–164.

Lockwood, Alex. 'Hopping, Crawling, Hiding: Creatural Movements on the Path to Climate Emergency'. In *Literary Animal Studies and the Climate Crisis*, edited by Sune Borkfelt and Matthias Stephan, 31–48. Cham, Switzerland: Palgrave-Macmillan, 2022.

Lorimer, Jamie. *Wildlife in the Anthropocene: Conservation after Nature.* Minneapolis and London: University of Minnesota Press, 2015.

MacCormack, Patricia. *The Ahuman Manifesto: Activism for the End of the Anthropocene.* London: Bloomsbury, 2020.

Macfarlane, Robert. 'The Burning Question'. *The Guardian,* 24 September 2005.

Mallon, Ron. 'Passing, Traveling and Reality: Social Constructionism and the Metaphysics of Race'. *Noûs* 38, no. 4 (2004): 644–673.

Maran, Timo. 'Biosemiotic Criticism'. In *The Oxford Handbook of Ecocriticism,* edited by Greg Garrard, 260–275. Oxford University Press, 2014a.

———. 'Biosemiotic Criticism: Modelling the Environment in Literature'. *Green Letters* 18, no. 3 (2014b): 297–311.

Maran, Timo and Kalevi Kull. 'Ecosemiotics: Main Principles and Current Developments'. *Geografiska Annaler: Series B, Human Geography* 96, no. 1 (2014): 41–50.

Marder, Michael. *Plant-Thinking: A Philosophy of Vegetal Life.* New York: Columbia University Press, 2013.

Martin, James. 'Rhetoric, Death, and the Politics of Memory'. *Critical Discourse Studies* 20, no. 5 (2023): 477–490. DOI: 10.1080/17405904.2022.2090977.

Masco, Joseph. *The Nuclear Borderlands: The Manhattan Project in Post-Cold War New Mexico.* Princeton, NJ: Princeton University Press, 2006.

McCormack, Brian. 'Narrative, Meaning and Multispecies Ethical Ontologies'. *HUMaNIMALIA* 11, no. 1 (2019): 64–88.

McCully, Patrick. *Silenced Rivers: The Ecology and Politics of Large Dams.* London and New York: Zed Books, 1996.

McDougall, Russell, John C. Ryan and Pauline Reynolds (eds.). *Postcolonial Literatures of Climate Change.* Leiden: Brill, 2022.

McFarland, Sarah E. *Ecocollapse Fiction and Cultures of Human Extinction.* London: Bloomsbury, 2021.

McHugh, Susan. *Animal Stories: Narrating across Species Lines.* Minneapolis and London: University of Minnesota University Press, 2011.

McKibben, Bill. 'What the Warming World Needs Now Is Art, Sweet Art'. *Grist,* 22 April 2005. https://grist.org/article/mckibben-imagine/. Accessed on 12 May 2023.

McKittrick, Katherine. 'Plantation Futures'. *Small Axe* 17, nos. 3, 42 (2013): 1–15.

Melion, Walter S., Bret Rothstein and Michel Weemans (eds.). *The Anthropomorphic Lens: Anthropomorphism, Microcosmism and Analogy in Early Modern Thought and Visual Arts*. Leiden and Boston: Brill, 2015.

Menely, Tobias and Jesse Oak Taylor (eds.). *Anthropocene Reading: Literary History in Geologic Times*. University Park: Pennsylvania State University Press, 2017.

Michaud, Marilyn. *Republicanism and the American Gothic*. Cardiff: University of Wales Press, 2009.

Mikkonen, Kai. 'Theories of Metamorphosis: From Metatrope to Textual Revision'. *Style* 30, no. 2 (1996): 309–340.

Miller, Theresa L. *Plant Kin: A Multispecies Ethnography in Indigenous Brazil*. Austin: University of Texas Press, 2019.

Mintz, Sidney. *Sweetness and Power: The Place of Sugar in Modern History*. New York: Vintage, 1985.

Mišík, Matúš and Nada Kujundžić. Eds. *Energy Humanities. Current State and Future Directions*. Cham, Switzerland: Springer, 2021.

Montgomery, Christine and Ellen C. Caldwell. 'Visualizing Dana and Transhistorical Time Travel on the Covers of Octavia E. Butler's *Kindred*'. In *The Bloomsbury Handbook to Octavia E. Butler*, edited by Gregory J. Hampton and Kendra R. Parker, 151–180. London: Bloomsbury, 2020.

Moore, Jason. 'The Capitalocene, Part I: On the Nature and Origins of Our Ecological Crisis'. *The Journal of Peasant Studies* 44, no. 3 (2017): 594–630.

Morton, Timothy. 'Everything We Need: Scarcity, Scale, Hyperobjects'. *Architectural Design* 82, no. 4 (2012): 78–81.

———. *Hyperobjects: Philosophy and Ecology after the End of the World*. Minneapolis and London: University of Minnesota Press, 2013.

Morrison, Susan Signe. *The Literature of Waste: Material Ecopoetics and Ethical Matter*. Basingstoke: Palgrave Macmillan, 2015.

Mukherjee, Upamanyu Pablo. *Postcolonial Environments: Nature, Culture and the Contemporary Indian Novel in English*. Basingstoke: Palgrave Macmillan, 2010.

Nagel, Tom. 'What Is It Like to Be a Bat?' *The Philosophical Review* 83, no. 4 (1974): 435–450.

Nanay, Bence. 'Zoomorphism'. *Erkenntnis* 86 (2021): 171–186.

Narayanan, Yamini. *Mother Cow, Mother India: A Multispecies Politics of Dairy in India*. Palo Alto: Stanford University Press, 2023.

Nayar, Pramod K. 'The Postcolonial Uncanny: Amitav Ghosh's *The Hungry Tide*'. *College Literature* 37, no. 4 (2010): 88–119.

———. 'Indigenous Cultures and the Ecology of Protest: Moral Economy and "Knowing Subalternity" in Dalit and Tribal Writing from India'. *Journal of Postcolonial Writing* 50, no. 3 (2014): 291–303.

————. 'The Forms of History: *This Side, That Side*, Graphic Narrative and the Partitions of the Indian Subcontinent'. *Journal of Postcolonial Writing* 52, no. 4 (2016a): 481–493.

————. *The Indian Graphic Novel: Nation, History and Critique*. Oxford: Routledge, 2016b.

————. *Ecoprecarity: Vulnerable Lives in Literature and Culture*. New York: Routledge, 2019a.

————. 'The Climate of Change: Graphic Adaptation, *The Rime of the Modern Mariner* and the Ecological Uncanny'. In *The Routledge Handbook of Ecocriticism and Environmental Communications*, edited by Scott Slovic, Swarnalatha Rangarajan and Vidya Sarveswaran, 26–35. Oxford and New York: Routledge, 2019b.

————. *The Human Rights Graphic Novel: Drawing It* Just *Right*. Oxford and New York: Routledge, 2021.

————. 'Human Stewardship and "Reproductive Futurism" in Dystopian Fiction'. In *Stewardship and the Future of the Planet: Promise and Paradox*, edited by Rachel Carnell and Chris Mounsey, 86–103. Routledge, 2022.

Nealon, Jeffrey T. *Plant Theory: Biopower and Vegetable Life*. Stanford, CA: Stanford University Press, 2015.

Neimanis, Astrida. *Bodies of Water: Posthuman Feminist Phenomenology*. Bloomsbury, 2017.

Nelles, William. 'Beyond the 'Bird's Eye: Animal Focalization'. *Narrative* 9, no. 2 (2001): 188–194.

Newman, Lance. *The Literary Heritage of the Environmental Justice Movement : Landscapes of Revolution in Transatlantic Romanticism*. Cham, Switzerland: Palgrave Macmillan, 2019.

Niblett, Michael. 'Oil on Sugar: Commodity Frontiers and Peripheral Aesthetics'. In *Global Ecologies and the Environmental Humanities: Postcolonial Approaches*, edited by Elizabeth DeLoughrey, Jill Didur and Anthony Carrigan, 268–285. New York: Routledge, 2015.

Nicholls, Lizzy. 'Becoming Indigenous Again: The Native Informant and Settler Logic in Richard Powers's *Overstory*'. *Environmental Humanities* 14, no. 2 (2022). DOI: 10.1215/22011919-9712390.

Nixon, Rob. *Slow Violence and the Environmentalism of the Poor*. Cambridge, MA: Harvard University Press, 2011.

Norman, Jana. *Posthuman Legal Subjectivity: Reimagining the Human in the Anthropocene* Routledge, 2022.

Nussbaum, Felicity A. 'Between "Oriental" and "Blacks So Called", 1688–1788'. In *The Postcolonial Enlightenment: Eighteenth-Century Colonialism and Postcolonial Theory*, edited by Daniel Carey and Lynn Festa, 137–166. Oxford: Oxford University Press, 2009.

Nuttall, Sarah. 'Pluvial Time/Wet Form'. *New Literary History* 51, no. 2 (2020): 455–472.

———. 'On Pluviality: Reading for Rain in Namwali Serpell's *The Old Drift*'. *Interventions* 24, no. 3 (2022): 323–339.

O'Connor, M. R. *Resurrection Science: Conservation, De-Extinction and the Precarious Future of Wild Things.* New York: St. Martin's, 2015. Ebook.

O'Key, Dominic. '"Entering Life:" Literary De-Extinction and the Archives of Life in Mahasweta Devi's *Pterodactyl, Puran Sahay, and Pirtha*'. *LIT: Literature Interpretation Theory* 31, no. 1 (2020): 75–93.

Oksanen, Markku and Helena Siipi. 'Introduction: Towards a Philosophy of Resurrection Science'. In *The Ethics of Animal Re-creation and Modification: Reviving, Rewilding, Restoring*, edited by Markku Oksanen and Helena Siipi, 1–21. Basingstoke: Palgrave Macmillan, 2014.

Olaoluwa, Senayon. 'Dislocating Anthropocene: The City and Oil in Helon Habila's Oil on Water'. *ISLE: Interdisciplinary Studies in Literature and Environment* 27, no. 2 (2020): 243–267.

Ostovich, Steven T. 'Dangerous Memories: Nostalgia and the Historical Sublime'. In *Nostalgia Now: Cross-Disciplinary Perspectives on the Past in the Present*, edited Michael Hviid Jacobsen, 101–115. Oxford: Routledge, 2020.

Otjen, Nathaniel. 'The Climate of Extinction: Resistant Multispecies Communities in Barbara Kingsolver's *Flight Behavior* and Richard Powers's *The Overstory*'. In *Literary Animal Studies and the Climate Crisis*, edited by Sune Borkfelt and Matthias Stephan, 179–200. Cham, Switzerland: Palgrave-Macmillan, 2022.

Pak, Chris. *Terraforming: Ecopolitical Transformations and Environmentalism in Science Fiction.* Liverpool: Liverpool University Press; 2016.

———. '"Then Came Pantropy": Grotesque Bodies, Multispecies Flourishing, and Human-Animal Relationships in Joan Slonczewski's *A Door Into Ocean*'. *Science Fiction Studies* 44, no. 1 (2017): 122–136.

Paredes, Alyssa. '"We Are Not Pests"'. In *The Promise of Multispecies Justice*, edited by Sophie Chao, Karin Bolender and Eben Kirksey, 77–102. Durham and London: Duke University Press, 2022.

Parsons, Laurie. *Carbon Colonialism: How Rich Countries Export Climate Change Breakdown.* Manchester University Press, 2023.

Peet, Richard, Paul Robbins and Michael Watts. 'Global Nature'. In *Global Political Ecology*, edited by Richard Peet, Paul Robbins and Michael Watts, 1–47. Oxford: Routledge, 2011.

Pergadia, Samantha. 'Like an Animal'. *African American Review* 51, no. 4 (2018): 289–304.

Perrin, Oliver Timken. 'Marks: A Distinct Subcategory within Writing as Integrationally Defined'. *Language Sciences* 33, no. 4 (2011): 623–633.

Petitt, Andrea. 'Conceptualizing the multispecies triad: Toward a multispecies intersectionality'. *Feminist Anthropology* 4, no. 1 (2023): 23–37.DOI: 10.1002/fea2.12099.

Pick, Anat. *Creaturely Poetics: Animality and Vulnerability in Literature and Film.* New York: Columbia University Press, 2011.

Piper, Adrian. 'Passing for White, Passing for Black'. *Transition* 58 (1992): 4–32.

Propen, Amy D. *Visualizing Posthuman Conservation in the Age of the Anthropocene.* Columbus: Ohio State University Press, 2018.

Puchner, Martin. *Literature for a Changing Planet.* Princeton: Princeton University Press, 2022.

Punter, David and Glennis Byron. *The Gothic.* Oxford: Blackwell, 2004.

Pyne, Lydia. *Endlings: Fables for the Anthropocene.* Minneapolis and London: Minnesota University Press, 2022.

Rajbhandari, Kritish. 'Postcolonial Fiction, Oceans, and Seas'. *Oxford Research Encyclopedias, Literature.* DOI: Doi.org/10.1093/acrefore/9780190 201098.013.1376. https://oxfordre.com/literature/display/10.1093/acrefore/ 9780190201098.001.0001/acrefore-9780190201098-e-1376;jsessionid= C14A6DD0275C5628ACF26064F316537E?rskey=o6hH3Q&result=20. Accessed on 12 May 2023.

Reid, Julian. 'Constructing Human Versus Non-Human Climate Migration in the Anthropocene: The Case of Migrating Polar Bears in Nunavut, Canada'. *Anthropocenes – Human, Inhuman, Posthuman* 1, no. 1 (2020): 1–12. DOI: https://doi.org/10.16997/ahip.3.

Richardson, Kathleen. 'Technological Animism: The Uncanny Personhood of Humanoid Machines'. In *Animism beyond the Soul: Ontology, Reflexivity, and the Making of Anthropological Knowledge*, edited by Katherine Swancutt and Mirielle Mazard, 110–128. Berghahn, 2018.

Rigby, Kate. *Dancing with Disaster: Environmental Histories, Narratives, and Ethics for Perilous Times.* Charlottesville: University of Virginia Press, 2015.

———. 'Earth's Poesy: Romantic Poetics, Natural Philosophy, and Biosemiotics'. In *Handbook of Ecocriticism and Cultural Ecology*, edited by Hubert Zapf, 45–64. Berlin and Boston: Walter de Gruyter, 2016.

———. 'Ecopoetics'. In *Keywords for Environmental Studies*, edited by Joni Adamson, William A. Gleason and David Pellow, 79–81. New York, USA: New York University Press, 2016.

Robertson, Benjamin. '"Some Matching Strangeness": Biology, Politics, and the Embrace of History in Octavia Butler's "Kindred"'. *Science Fiction Studies* 37, no. 3 (2010): 362–381.

Rose, Andrew. 'Insurgency and Distributed Agency in Karen Tei Yamashita's *Through the Arc of the Rainforest*'. *ISLE: Interdisciplinary Studies in Literature and Environment* 26, no. 1 (2019): 125–144. DOI:10.1093/isle/isy076.

Rose, Deborah Bird. *Wild Dog Dreaming*. Charlottesville: University of Virginia Press, 2011.

———. 'Multispecies Knots of Ethical Time'. *Environmental Philosophy* 9, no. 1 (2012): 127–140.

Rose, Deborah Bird and Thom van Doreen. 'Encountering a More-than-human World: Ethos and the Arts of Witness'. In *The Routledge Companion to the Environmental Humanities*, edited by Ursula K. Heise, Jon Christensen and Michelle Niemann, 120–128. Oxford: Routledge, 2017.

Rose, Deborah Bird, Thom van Doreen and Matthew Chrulew (eds.). *Extinction Studies: Stories of Time, Death and Generations*. New York: Columbia University Press, 2017.

Royle, Nicholas. *The Uncanny*. Manchester: Manchester University Press, 2003.

Rushdy, Ashraf H. A. *Neo-slave Narratives: Studies in the Social Logic of a Literary Form*. New York: Oxford University Press, 1999.

Ryan, Tim A. *Calls and Responses: The American Novel of Slavery since 'Gone with the Wind'*. Louisiana State University Press, 2008.

Sandhar, Jason. 'Plotting the Elephant Graveyard: Anthropomorphism and Interspecies Conflict in Tania James's The Tusk That Did the Damage'. In *Postcolonial Animalities*, edited by Suvadip Sinha and Amit R Baishya, 147–162. New York: Routledge, 2020.

Schama, Simon. *Landscape and Memory*. London: Vintage, 1995.

Schlosberg, David. *Defining Environmental Justice: Theories, Movements, and Nature*. Oxford: Oxford University Press, 2007.

Schmid, Johannes C. P. 'Cultural Genocide in Joe Sacco's *Paying the Land*'. *Journal of Perpetrator Research* 4, no. 2 (2022): 111–144.

Schroering, Abby. 'Playing Against Extinction: "The Dreaded Comparison" and the Distribution of the Human in *Mlima's Tale*'. In *Literary Animal Studies and the Climate Crisis*, edited by Sune Borkfelt and Matthias Stephan, 133–152. Cham, Switzerland: Palgrave-Macmillan, 2022.

Sefton-Rowston, Adelle L. 'Hope at the End of the World: Creation Stories and Apocalypse in Alexis Wright's *Carpentaria* and *The Swan Book*'. *Antipodes* 30, no. 2 (2016): 355–368.

Segal, Michael. 'The Missing Climate Change Narrative'. *South Atlantic Quarterly* 116, no. 1 (2017): 121–128.

Seitzinger, Sybil P. et al. 'Planetary Stewardship in an Urbanizing World: Beyond City Limits'. *Ambio* 41 (2012): 787–794.

Sepp, Hans Rainer. 'Worldly-Being Out of World'. *Environmental Philosophy* 11, no. 1 (2014): 93–108.

Shapiro, Barbara. *A Culture of Fact: England, 1550–1720*. Chicago and London: University of Chicago Press, 1983.

Shapiro, Beth. *How to Clone a Mammoth: The Science of De-extinction*. Princeton, NJ: Princeton University Press, 2015.

Sheldon, Rebekah. *The Child to Come: Life after the Human Catastrophe*. Minneapolis: University of Minnesota Press, 2016.

Shelton, Allison Nowak. 'Learning from Rivers: Toward a Relational View of the Anthropocene'. *English Language Notes* 57, no. 1 (2019): 152–159.

Shiva, Vandana. *Water Wars: Privatization, Pollution, and Profit*. London: Pluto, 2002.

Shukin, Nicole. *Animal Capital: Rendering Life in Biopolitical Times*. Minneapolis and London: University of Minnesota Press, 2009.

Siipi, Helena. 'The Authenticity of Animals'. In *The Ethics of Animal Re-creation and Modification: Reviving, Rewilding, Restoring*, edited by Markku Oksanen and Helena Siipi, 77–96. Basingstoke: Palgrave Macmillan, 2014.

Singh, Julietta. *Unthinking Mastery: Dehumanism and Decolonial Entanglements*. Durham and London: Duke University Press, 2018.

Sinha, Suvadip. *Entangled Fictions: Nonhuman Animals in an Indian World*. New York: Routledge, 2023.

Sinha, Suvadip and Amit R. Baishya (eds.). *Postcolonial Animalities*. New York: Routledge, 2020.

Siperstein, Stephen, Shane Hall and Stephanie LeMenager (eds.). *Teaching Climate Change in the Humanities*. London and New York: Routledge, 2017.

Slovic, Scott. *Going Away to Think: Engagement, Retreat, and Ecocritical Responsibility*. Reno: University of Nevada Press, 2008.

———. 'Environmental Vulnerability and the Literary Imagination'. Lecture. UNESCO Chair in Vulnerability Studies, 'Conceptualizing Vulnerability: A Roundtable'. 10 March 2023. https://ucvulnerabilitystudies.uohyd.ac.in/conceptualizing-vulnerability-a-roundtable/. Accessed on 13 January 2024.

Smith, Felisa. 'After the Mammoths: The Ecological Legacy of Late Pleistocene Megafauna Extinctions'. *Cambridge Prisms: Extinction* (2023): 1–55. DOI:10.1017/ext.2023.6.

Sodikoff, Genese Marie. 'Introduction. Accumulating Absence: Cultural Productions of the Sixth Extinction'. In *The Anthropology of Extinction: Essays on Culture and Species Death*, edited by Genese Marie Sodikoff, 1–17. Bloomington and Indianapolis: Indiana University Press, 2012.

Spicer, Christopher J. *Cyclone Country: The Language of Place and Disaster in Australian Literature*. Jefferson: McFarland, 2020.

Squire, Rachael. 'Where Theories of Terrain Might Land: Towards "Pluriversal" Engagements with Terrain'. *Dialogues in Human Geography* 11, no. 2 (2021): 208–212.

Srinivasan, Vasanthi. *Virtue and Human Ends: Political Ideas from Indian Classics*. Hyderabad: Orient BlackSwan, 2021.

Stoler, Ann Laura. 'Imperial Debris: Reflections on Ruins and Ruination'. *Cultural Anthropology* 23, no. 2 (2008): 191–219.

Stolzenburg, William. *Where the Wild Things Were: Life, Death, and Ecological Wreckage in a Land of Vanishing Predators*. London: Bloomsbury, 2008.

Straß, Hanna. '"A Living Death, Life Inside-out": The Postcolonial Toxic Gothic in Robert Barclay's *Melal: A Novel of the Pacific*'. In *Globalizing Literary Genres: Literature, History, Modernity*, edited by Jernej Habjan and Fabienne Imlinger, 228–240. New York: Routledge, 2016.

Suliman, Samid, et al. 'Indigenous (Im)mobilities in the Anthropocene'. *Mobilities* 14, no. 3 (2019): 298–318.

Sunder Rajan, Kaushik. 'Introduction: The Capitalization of Life and the Liveliness of Capital'. In *Lively Capital: Biotechnologies, Ethics, and Governance in Global Markets*, edited by Sunder Rajan, 1–41. Durham, NC and London: Duke University Press, 2012.

Szeman, Imre and Dominic Boyer (eds.). *Energy Humanities: An Anthology*. Johns Hopkins University Press, 2017.

Thaker, Jagadish. 'Environmentalism of the Poor: Global South Perspectives on Environmental Communication'. In *The Handbook of International Trends in Environmental Communication*, edited by Bruno Takahashi et al., 193–205. London and New York: Routledge, 2021.

The Global Charter for Rewilding the Earth: Advancing Nature-based Solutions to the Extinction and Climate Crises. 2020. https://www.rewildingeurope.com/wp-content/uploads/publications/global-charter-for-rewilding-the-earth/index.html. Accessed on 13 February 2023.

Thomashow, Mitchell. 'Toward a Cosmopolitan Bioregionalism'. In *Bioregionalism*, edited by Michael Vincent McGinnis, 121–131. London: Routledge, 1999.

Tilley, Lisa. 'Extractive Investibility in Historical Colonial Perspective: The Emerging Market and Its Antecedents in Indonesia'. *Review of International Political Economy* 28, no. 5 (2021): 1099–1118.

Trexler, Adam. 'Mediating Climate Change: Ecocriticism, Science Studies, and *The Hungry Tide*'. In *The Oxford Handbook of Ecocriticism*, edited by Greg Garrard, 205–224. Oxford University Press, 2014.

———. *Anthropocene Fictions: The Novel in a Time of Climate Change*. University of Virginia Press, 2015.

Tsing, Anna. *The Mushroom at the End of the World: On the Possibility of Life in Capitalist Ruins*. Princeton and Oxford: Princeton University Press, 2017.

———. 'Invasion Blowback and Other Tales of the Anthropocene: An Afterword'. *Anthropocenes – Human, Inhuman, Posthuman* 4, no. 1 (2023). DOI: https://doi.org/10.16997/ahip.1438.

Turnhout, Esther. 'The Politics of Environmental Knowledge'. *Conservation and Society* 16, no. 3 (2018): 363–371.

Turner, Stephanie S. 'Open-Ended Stories: Extinction Narratives in Genome Time'. *Literature and Medicine* 26, no. 1 (2007): 55–82.

Ulloa, Astrid. *The Ecological Native: Indigenous Movements and Eco-governmentality in Columbia*. New York: Routledge, 2005.

———. 'The Geopolitics of Carbonized Nature and the Zero Carbon Citizen'. *The South Atlantic Quarterly* 116, no. 1 (2017): 111–120.

Väliverronen, Esa. 'Biodiversity and the Power of Metaphor in Environmental Discourse'. *Science Studies* 11, no. 1 (1998): 19–34.

van Dooren, Thom. *Flight Ways: Life and Loss at the Edge of Extinction*. New York: Columbia University Press, 2014.

van Dooren, Thom, Ebin Kirksey and Ursula Münster. 'Multispecies Studies: Cultivating Arts of Attentiveness'. In *Special Issue: Multispecies Studies. Environmental Humanities* 8, no. 1 (2016): 1–23.

Vergès, Françoise. 'Racial Capitalocene: Is the Anthropocene Racial?'. 2017. https://www.versobooks.com/en-gb/blogs/news/3376-racial-capitalocene. Accessed on 30 April 2023.

Vint, Sheryl. '"Only by Experience:" Embodiment and the Limitations of Realism in Neo- Slave Narratives'. *Science-Fiction Studies*, 34 pt2 J1 (2007): 241–261.

Vint, Sherryl and Sümeyra Buran (eds.). *Technologies of Feminist Speculative Fiction: Gender, Artificial Life, and the Politics of Reproduction*. Cham, Switzerland: Palgrave-Macmillan, 2022

Wallace, Molly. *Risk Criticism: Precautionary Reading in an Age of Environmental Uncertainty*. Ann Arbor: University of Michigan Press, 2016.

Walther, Sundhya. *Multispecies Modernity: Disorderly Life in Postcolonial Literature* . Waterloo, ON, Canada: Wilfrid Laurier University Press, 2021.

Wark, McKenzie. 'Furious Media: A Queer History of Heresy'. In *Excommunication: Three Inquiries in Media and Mediation*, edited by Alexander R. *Galloway*,

Eugene Thacker and McKenzie Wark, 151–210. Chicago and London: University of Chicago Press, 2014.

Weaver, Harlan. *Bad Dog: Pit Bull Politics and Multispecies Justice*. Seattle: University of Washington Press, 2021.

Weber, Samuel. *Targets of Opportunity: On the Militarization of Thinking*. New York: Fordham University Press, 2005.

Weststeijn, Thijs. 'Heritage at Sea'. *Aeon*, 28 October 2021. https://aeon.co/essays/must-we-accept-the-loss-of-beloved-heritage-to-the-climate-crisis. Accessed on 14 February 2023.

Wheeler, Wendy. *The Whole Creature: Complexity, Biosemiotics and the Evolution of Culture*. London: Lawrence & Wishart, 2006.

White, Deborah Gray. *Ar'n't I a Woman? Female Slaves in the Plantation South*. New York: W.W. Norton, 1985. Rev. Ed. Ebook.

White, Richard J. 'Animal Geographies, Anarchist Praxis, and Critical Animal Studies'. In *Critical Animal Geographies: Politics, Intersections, and Hierarchies in a Multispecies World*, edited by Kathryn Gillespie and Rosemary-Claire Collard, 19–35. New York: Routledge, 2015.

White, Rob. 'Restorative Justice, Repairing the Harm and Environmental Outcomes'. In *The Palgrave Handbook of Environmental Restorative Justice*, edited by Brunilda Pali, Miranda Forsyth and Felicity Tepper, 27–50. Cham, Switzerland: Palgrave Macmillan, 2022.

Wiggs, Kimber L. 'The Trouble: Family, Genre, and Hybridity in Octavia Butler's *Kindred*'. *Mosaic* 54, no. 1 (2021): 129–145.

Willem, Bieke. 'A "New Continent of Data": Pola Oloixarac's *Dark Constellations* and the Latin American Jungle Novel'. *LIT: Literature Interpretation Theory* 31, no. 2 (2020): 129–145.

Wills, David. *Inanimation: Theories of Inorganic Life*. Minneapolis: University of Minnesota Press, 2016.

Wilson, Edward. *In Search of Nature*. Washington, DC: Island, 1996.

Witzany, Günther. 'Plant Communication from a Biosemiotic Perspective: Differences in Abiotic and Biotic Signal Perception Determinate Conent Arrangement of Response Behavior. Context Determines Meaning of Meta-, Inter- and Intra-Organismic Plant Signaling'. *Plant Signaling and Behavior* 1, no. 4 (2006): 169–178.

Wolfe, Cary. *Animal Rites: American Culture, the Discourses of Species, and Posthumanist Theory*. University of Chicago Press, 2003.

———. *Before the Law: Humans and Other Animals in a Biopolitical Frame*. Chicago and London: University of Chicago Press, 2013.

————. *What Is Posthumanism?* Minneapolis and London: University of Minnesota Press, 2010.

Wolford, Wendy. 'The Plantationocene: A Lusotropical Contribution to the Theory'. *Annals of the American Association of Geographers* 111, no. 6 (2021): 1622–1639. DOI: 10.1080/24694452.2020.1850231.

Yarbrough, Anastasia. 'Species, Race, and Culture in the Space of Wildlife Management'. In *Critical Animal Geographies: Politics, Intersections, and Hierarchies in a Multispecies World*, edited by Kathryn Gillespie and Rosemary-Claire Collard, 108–126. New York: Routledge, 2015.

Yerman, Forrest. 'Finding the Superhero in Damian Duffy's and John Jennings's Graphic Novel Adaptation of Octavia Butler's Science-Fiction-Postmodern-Slave-Narrative, *Kindred*'. In *The Bloomsbury Handbook to Octavia E. Butler*, edited by Gregory J. Hampton and Kendra R. Parker, 259–272. London: Bloomsbury, 2020.

Yoon, Hyaesin. 'Feral Biopolitics: Animal Bodies and/as Border Technologies'. *Angelaki* 22, no. 2 (2017): 135–150.

Yusoff, Kathryn. 'Geologic Life: Prehistory, Climate, Futures in the Anthropocene'. *Environment and Planning D: Society and Space* 31, no. 5 (2013): 779–795.

Index